From Passions to Emotions
The Creation of a Secular Psychological Category

Today there is a thriving 'emotions industry' to which philosophers, psychologists and neuroscientists are contributing. Yet until two centuries ago 'the emotions' did not exist. In this path-breaking study Thomas Dixon shows how, during the nineteenth century, the emotions came into being as a distinct psychological category, replacing existing categories such as appetites, passions, sentiments and affections. By examining medieval and eighteenth-century theological psychologies and placing Charles Darwin and William James within a broader and more complex nineteenth-century setting, Thomas Dixon argues that this domination by one single descriptive category is not healthy. The over-inclusivity of 'the emotions' has hampered attempts to argue with any subtlety about the enormous range of mental states and stances of which humans are capable. This book is an important contribution to the debate about emotion and rationality which has preoccupied Western thinkers throughout the eighteenth and nineteenth centuries and which continues to have implications for contemporary debates.

Dr Thomas Dixon is a British Academy Postdoctoral Fellow at the Faculty of Divinity and a Fellow of Churchill College, University of Cambridge.

From Passions to Emotions
The Creation of a Secular Psychological Category

Thomas Dixon
Faculty of Divinity and Churchill College, Cambridge

CAMBRIDGE UNIVERSITY PRESS
Cambridge, New York, Melbourne, Madrid, Cape Town, Singapore, São Paulo

Cambridge University Press
The Edinburgh Building, Cambridge CB2 2RU, UK

Published in the United States of America by Cambridge University Press, New York

www.cambridge.org
Information on this title: www.cambridge.org/9780521827294

© Thomas Dixon 2003

This publication is in copyright. Subject to statutory exception
and to the provisions of relevant collective licensing agreements,
no reproduction of any part may take place without
the written permission of Cambridge University Press.

First published 2003
Reprinted 2005
This digitally printed first paperback version 2006

A catalogue record for this publication is available from the British Library

ISBN-13 978-0-521-82729-4 hardback
ISBN-10 0-521-82729-9 hardback

ISBN-13 978-0-521-02669-7 paperback
ISBN-10 0-521-02669-5 paperback

To my parents, Kay and Gordon Dixon

A difference of words is, in this case, more than a mere verbal difference. Though it be not the expression of a difference of doctrine, it very speedily becomes so.

The first great subdivision, then, which I would form, of the internal class, is into our intellectual states of mind, and our emotions.
                Thomas Brown, *Lectures on the Philosophy of the Human Mind*, 100–2

Contents

	Acknowledgments	*page* viii
	Note on quotations	x
1	Introduction: from passions and affections to emotions	1
2	Passions and affections in Augustine and Aquinas	26
3	From movements to mechanisms: passions, sentiments and affections in the Age of Reason	62
4	The Scottish creation of 'the emotions': David Hume, Thomas Brown, Thomas Chalmers	98
5	The physicalist appropriation of Brownian emotions: Alexander Bain, Herbert Spencer, Charles Darwin	135
6	Christian and theistic responses to the new physicalist emotions paradigm	180
7	What was an emotion in 1884? William James and his critics	204
8	Conclusions: how history can help us think about 'the emotions'	231
	Bibliography	252
	Index	279

Acknowledgments

This book started life as a PhD dissertation, written at the Faculty of Divinity, Cambridge University, under the supervision of Fraser Watts, whose encouragement and advice over many years have been absolutely invaluable. I also received, at the early stages of this project, very helpful guidance from Nicholas Adams, Brian Hebblethwaite, Douglas Hedley, Nicholas Lash, John Milbank, George Pattison and Janet Soskice. My involvement with the Cambridge University Department of History and Philosophy of Science's Evolution Reading Group, then run by Greg Radick, was extremely rewarding; and I benefited greatly from the criticisms and advice offered by my PhD examiners, German Berrios and John Hedley Brooke.

Sebsequent research has been supported and facilitated by a British Academy Postdoctoral Fellowship, a Junior Research Fellowship at Churchill College, Cambridge and the continued support of the Cambridge Faculty of Divinity. I am very grateful to all these institutions. I have also derived a great deal of benefit and pleasure from my ongoing association with the Cambridge University Department of History and Philosophy of Science, especially through the Science and Literature Reading Group run by Jim Endersby. At Cambridge University Press, Kevin Taylor was very encouraging in the initial stages of the project. Subsequently, Richard Fisher and Alison Powell have both been extremely supportive and efficient. I am also grateful to several anonymous readers who offered comments on the typescript at various stages, and to Audrey Cotterell for her meticulous copy-editing.

I have presented parts of this study to several groups, including the Cambridge University Faculty of Divinity's 'D' Society and its Interdisciplinary Group, the University of Leeds Science and Religion Seminar and the Kings College, London, Emotions Group. I am grateful to all of these for their invitations to speak, and for the many ideas and criticisms that were offered. Many colleagues and friends were kind enough to read some or all of draft versions of the book, and to suggest improvements. James Harris, Russell Manning, Greg Radick, Léon Turner and

Fraser Watts all took particular time and trouble to help me improve the text. I am very grateful to them. I am also indebted to many others for advice and ideas at various stages of this project, including John Hedley Brooke, Janet Browne, Geoffrey Cantor, Hasok Chang, David Clifford, Emma Dixon, Jim Endersby, Dylan Evans, Louise Hickman, James Humphreys, Tristram Hunt, Susan James, Jim Moore, Edward Morgan, Lewis Owens, Jim Secord, Giles Shilson, Robert Solomon, Rebecca Stott, John van Wyhe and Camille Wingo.

For their boundless support and encouragement I am deeply grateful to my parents, Kay and Gordon Dixon, to whom this book is dedicated. Finally, I wish to thank Emily-Claire Hutchinson for her enduring patience and affection, and for preventing me from taking myself too seriously.

Several chapters in this book incorporate material that has appeared in different contexts in other publications, and which is re-used here with permission. I am grateful to:

Blackwell's for permission to re-use material from my article 'Theology, anti-theology and atheology: from Christian passions to secular emotions', published in *Modern Theology* 15 (1999), 297–330.

The University of Chicago Press for permission to re-use material from my article 'The psychology of the "emotions" in Britain and America in the nineteenth century: the role of religious and anti-religious commitments', *Osiris* 16 (2001), 288–320.

Thoemmes Press for permission to re-use material from my introduction to T. Dixon (ed.), *The Life and Collected Works of Thomas Brown, 1778–1820* (8 vols., Bristol: Thoemmes Press, 2003).

Note on quotations

In several cases, when quoting from seventeenth- and eighteenth-century texts (such as those by Thomas Hobbes, John Locke, Samuel Clarke and Francis Hutcheson), I have rendered the quotation in modern form, removing archaic spellings, capitalisations and italicisations.

1 Introduction: from passions and affections to emotions

> The use of the word emotion in English psychology is comparatively modern. It is found in Hume, but even he speaks generally rather of passions or affections. When the word emotion did become current its application was very wide, covering all possible varieties of feeling, except those that are purely sensational in their origin.
>
> James Mark Baldwin, *Dictionary of Philosophy and Psychology* (1905), I, 316

How history can help us think about 'the emotions'

Emotions are everywhere today. Increasing numbers of books and articles about the emotions are being produced; for both academic and broader audiences; by neuroscientists, psychologists and philosophers. As the author of one recent book on the science of the emotions puts it: 'Emotion is now a hot topic.'[1] According to another, the last three decades have witnessed an explosion in emotion studies, in the fields of cognitive psychology, anthropology and literary history, which constitutes a veritable 'revolution'.[2] Recent academic work in a range of fields has celebrated the body and the emotions, in a reaction against the alleged preoccupation with intellect and reason to be found in earlier studies. There is now even such a thing as 'Emotional Intelligence', or 'EQ', analogous to IQ.[3] Being in touch with one's emotions is, for many, an unquestioned good. The existence and the great value of the emotions is obvious to academics and non-academics alike. It is surprising, then, to discover that the emotions did not exist until just under two hundred years ago.

In this book I investigate the creation of 'the emotions' as a psychological category. By seeing how this category was conceived, and by looking at the different psychological categories it replaced during the eighteenth and nineteenth centuries, I aim to provide readers with resources that will help them to step back from the contemporary obviousness of the existence and importance of 'the emotions' and to ask fundamental questions

---

[1] Evans (2001), xiii. [2] Reddy (2001), ix–x. [3] Goleman (1995, 1996).

about this category's meaning and value. In other words, I hope my historical account will stimulate philosophical and psychological reflection. Of particular importance to this story is the displacement, in the history of systematic psychological theorising, of more differentiated typologies (which included appetites, passions, affections and sentiments) by a single over-arching category of emotions during the nineteenth century. Perhaps these past typologies will give readers pause for thought, and encourage them to ask whether the emotions, as we think of them today in psychology and philosophy, really form a coherent category.[4] I will suggest that a more differentiated typology would be a useful tool, and would help us to avoid making sweeping claims about all 'emotions' being good or bad things, rational or irrational, virtuous or vicious. The over-inclusivity of our modern-day category of emotions has hampered attempts to argue with any subtlety about the nature and value of the enormous range of passionate, affectionate, sentimental, felt and committed mental states and stances of which we are capable.

My argument about the historical provenance of modern theories of the emotions is revisionist, especially with respect to Robert Solomon's thesis in his influential book *The Passions: Emotions and the Meaning of Life* (1976, 1993).[5] Solomon's thesis is, in short, that Western thinkers have been prone, right up to the late twentieth century, to take a negative view of the emotions and to think of them as inherently bodily, involuntary and irrational. Solomon blames this negative view of emotions on the influence of rationalist views (in which reason and the emotions are antagonists) that have been dominant among Western philosophers in general and certain Christian theologians in particular.

Solomon's was the first in a spate of books in recent decades that all seek, in one way or another, to rehabilitate the emotions. Philosophers including Ronald de Sousa, Michael Stocker, Dylan Evans and Peter Goldie, the brain scientist Antonio Damasio, and the psychologists Keith Oatley and Robert Lazarus have all contributed to this literature.[6] Many of these writers also echo Solomon's thesis that from antiquity up until the late twentieth century philosophers and psychologists have generally, and misguidedly, thought of reason and the emotions as antagonists. Solomon calls this supposedly prevailing view the 'Myth of the Passions'; Damasio calls it 'Descartes' Error'. One of my aims in this book is to show

---

[4] For a very helpful article summarising recent debates about the natural kind status of 'emotion', and arguing that 'emotion' is indeed a natural kind term, see Charland (2002).

[5] Solomon (1993a).

[6] De Sousa (1987); Stocker (1996); Evans (2001); Goldie (2000); Damasio (1994); Oatley (1992); Lazarus (1991).

how these views on the history of ideas about passions and emotions are themselves, in certain respects, mythical and erroneous.

The historical story I tell here turns Solomon's view on its head. I argue that it was in fact the recent departure from traditional views about the passions (not the influence of those views) that led to the creation of a category of 'emotions' that was conceived in opposition to reason, intellect and will. The category of emotions, conceived as a set of morally disengaged, bodily, non-cognitive and involuntary feelings, is a recent invention. Prior to the creation of the emotions as an over-arching category, more subtlety had been possible on these questions. The 'affections', and the 'moral sentiments', for example, could be understood as both rational and voluntary movements of the soul, while still being subjectively warm and lively psychological states. It is not the case that prior to the 1970s no one had realised that thinking, willing and feeling were (and should be) intertwined in one way or another. Almost everybody had realised this. Too many contemporary writers still appeal, nonetheless, to the idea (in order to create a rhetorical counterpoint for their own account of the value and/or rationality of the emotions) that either a particular individual, or school of thought, or period, or even the entire history of philosophy has been characterised by the view that the emotions (or feelings or passions) are entirely insidious and are to be subjected at all times to almighty reason. Anything more than the briefest of glances at the history of thought establishes that this is a thoroughly untenable idea, even when applied to Stoic or Christian philosophers (those most often accused of passion- or emotion-hatred).[7]

Solomon is quite right to draw attention to the difficult existential and moral questions that arise from thinking of passions or emotions as alien powers that act against our rational will. If our emotions are not our own, then how can we identify with them as expressions of our true selves? And how could we be held morally responsible for actions resulting from them?[8] Solomon's historical account of where this view of emotions as involuntary forces came from, however, is off-target. One of the main problems with his thesis (and with some of the other recent books arguing along similar lines), as will emerge below, is that it does not clearly differentiate between 'passions' and 'emotions', nor does it acknowledge that theorists of the passions often also employed the concepts of 'affections' and 'sentiments' to refer to more cognitive and refined feelings. Solomon's history of ideas about passions and emotions is somewhat distorted as a result. He is by no means the only writer to have overlooked

---

[7] On Stoic and early Christian attitudes to passions, will and reason, see Sorabji (2000).
[8] On the moral dimensions of these problems, see also Oakley (1992).

these distinctions, but is representative of a recent school of thought that emphasises the cognitive and rational aspects of emotions, of which he was one of the earliest and most influential exponents.

The basic historical puzzle

It is an immensely striking fact of the history of English-language psychological thought that during the period between c.1800 and c.1850 a wholesale change in established vocabulary occurred such that those engaged in theoretical discussions about phenomena including hope, fear, love, hate, joy, sorrow, anger and the like no longer primarily discussed the passions or affections of the soul, nor the sentiments, but almost invariably referred to 'the emotions'. This transition is as striking as if established conceptual terms such as 'reason' or 'memory' or 'imagination' or 'will' had been quite suddenly replaced by a wholly new category.

The puzzling historical question, then, at the heart of this book (a question that, equally puzzlingly, has rarely been posed before, let alone answered) is: when and why did English-language psychological writers stop using 'passions', 'affections' and 'sentiments' as their primary categories and start referring instead to the 'emotions'?

The secularisation of psychology

One important element of my answer to this central historical question is that it was the secularisation of psychology that gave rise to the creation and adoption of the new category of 'emotions' and influenced the way it was originally and has subsequently been conceived. Since this is an important part of my argument, it may be worth making some comments here to explain and defend my focus on religious and theological dimensions of the history of psychology in this book.

The first consideration is a prima facie observation about the eighteenth- and nineteenth-century texts in question. At first glance, the shift from the language of passions and affections to the language of emotions seems to provide strong evidence of the way that religious and psychological ideas have been connected in the past. To speak of 'passions and affections of the soul' was to embed one's thought in a network of more distinctively Christian concepts and categories. In contrast, the category of 'emotions' was alien to traditional Christian thought and was part of a newer and more secular network of words and ideas. No one (to my knowledge) ever wrote books called *The Psychology of the Passions* or *The Emotions of the Soul*. 'Emotions', unlike 'affections', 'passions', 'desires' and 'lusts' did not appear in any English translation of the Bible. These simple observations highlight an important fact about the way that these terms derived their meanings from networks of related concepts. The words 'passions' and 'affections' belonged to a network of words such as 'of the soul', 'conscience', 'fall', 'sin', 'grace', 'Spirit', 'Satan', 'will', 'lower appetite', 'self-love' and so on. The word 'emotions' was, from the outset, part of a different network of terms such as 'psychology', 'law', 'observation', 'evolution', 'organism', 'brain', 'nerves', 'expression', 'behaviour' and 'viscera'.

While anti-religious and merely non-religious psychologists were not the only ones to use the word 'emotions', they did so sooner and integrated the category into their psychologies more readily than did their Christian contemporaries. Influential figures in secular science and psychology in the mid-nineteenth century, such as Charles Darwin, Alexander Bain and Herbert Spencer, were among these early 'emotions' theorists (see chapter 5). Christian writers, especially in more conservative environments such as Oxford and Cambridge (and some American colleges) continued to use the terms 'will', 'passions', 'affections' and 'sentiments' much more than the term 'emotions' (see chapter 6). There was, then, a correlation between the adoption of the new 'emotions' discourse on the one hand, and lack of traditional Christian belief on the other. There was also a correlation, later in the century, when the transition to 'emotions' talk had become a fait accompli, between Christian faith and the adoption of cognitive and anti-reductionist theories of emotions.

These prima facie correlations provide the primary reason for taking an interest in religious and theological dimensions of psychology in my historical account of the creation of the category of 'emotions'. It is important to add at the outset, however, that, prior to the emergence of the category of 'emotions', the language of 'passions' and 'affections' was used by both religious and non-religious writers on human mental life, and both terms had a variety of different meanings. 'Passions' for example could be used to refer in a vague way to a broad range of impulses and feelings, or to refer to a smaller set of particularly troubling disturbances of the mind, such as anger and sexual desire. Secular moralists and literary writers, as well as more explicitly theological and religious writers on the faculties of the soul, used the terms 'passions' and 'affections'. So there is no simple identification to be made, for example, between theorists who spoke of 'passions' and 'affections' and Christian thinkers. Nevertheless, the distinction between passions and affections, and the categories themselves, did derive historically from theological psychologies and were well suited to a Christian understanding of the human person in which a free and active will was a particularly important faculty. The will was central to the story of the fall of Adam and Eve, and to Christian concepts of moral responsibility, sin and salvation. Additionally, after the emergence of the category of 'emotions', and an alternative psychological vocabulary, use of the language of 'soul', 'will', 'passions' and 'affections' served, where it had not before, as a mark of allegiance to older ways of thinking about human mental life. It is then a difficult task to distinguish between writings that should be interpreted simply as examples of 'traditional' or 'old-fashioned' thought about mental life, and those that should be described as distinctively 'religious' or 'Christian'. This is where it will be important to look for evidence external to the psychological theories themselves of the religious or anti-religious commitments of the authors under consideration.

Methodological questions: some problems with presentism

In addition to evidence of important links between particular areas of religious and psychological language in the eighteenth and nineteenth centuries, there are some more general methodological considerations relevant to the decision to think about theological and religious dimensions of the history of psychology. I will examine these briefly here before returning to provide an overview of my answer to the historical puzzle of how 'the emotions' came to be created.

Presentism and the omission of a theological dimension

The reasons it is worthwhile trying to understand the theological dimensions of the history of psychology are both historical and psychological. First, historically, understanding these dimensions throws light on where secular psychology came from – what it was building upon and what it was reacting against. Secondly, such an enterprise can help stimulate contemporary psychological theorising. Christian and theistic psychologies of the past (as well as secular ones) provide interesting alternative voices that can give a different angle on contemporary psychological debates about, for instance, theories of emotions. Trying to understand psychological models that are based on metaphysical assumptions that are quite different from those of contemporary academic psychologies helps to bring home the fact that there are many different possible ways of understanding and carving up human mental life. A history that looks especially at religious and theological assumptions in past psychologies might, perhaps even more than a history of secular psychological thought, be able to provide a healthy antidote to the tendency to swallow too uncritically the assumptions, theories and terminologies of contemporary academic psychology.

Histories of philosophy and, especially, of psychology, often display a lack of familiarity with or a lack of interest in these dimensions. So, in the case of histories of theories of passions and emotions, the views of Aristotle, Descartes, Hume, Spinoza, Darwin, James and Wundt on passions and emotions are relatively well-known and have received considerable and repeated attention, to the extent that they have begun to make up a rather one-dimensional and stale canon of historical theorists of passions and emotions.[9] The views of psychological thinkers with religious concerns, such as Augustine and Aquinas, Jonathan Edwards and Joseph Butler, Thomas Reid and Thomas Brown, Thomas Chalmers and William Lyall, James McCosh and George T. Ladd, are much more rarely mentioned.[10]

The omission of a theological dimension from the history of psychology sometimes seems to have been the result of the adoption of 'presentist' methodological assumptions. It is sometimes assumed, for example, that writing a history of psychology involves finding 'precursors' of contemporary psychological thinkers and thoughts. The result, when the contemporary field is largely autonomous and secular, is a rather distortedly secular history, in which past thinkers are of interest only insofar as they 'foreshadow' the 'scientific' psychology of the last century or so. This is the approach taken by Gardiner *et al.* in their general history of past theories of passions, affections, feelings and emotions. These theories are interpreted as a gradual approach towards a satisfactory twentieth-century 'scientific psychological theory'.[11] George Mandler provides an explicit statement of this sort of methodology in a chapter on 'The Psychology of Emotion: Past and Present' in his 1984 cognitive psychology book on emotions and stress:

I approach the history of emotion as a movement toward its current state... I have culled the important milestones of the past hundred years with that goal in mind. I look backward to see what has brought us to the current state of the art... In reviewing these trends, I will stress cumulative influences, believing that the history of science is a history of cumulative insights and cumulative knowledge.[12]

It may sometimes be defensible to approach history in this way, but there are certainly some important objections to doing so. First, such an approach trades on the implicit assumption that the truth of current theory

---

[9] For more on this, see ch. 8, Conclusions.
[10] Susan James is again an exception, at least in the cases of Augustine and Aquinas. James (1997), chs. 1, 3 and 5.
[11] Gardiner *et al.* (1970), 386.   [12] Mandler (1984), 15.

brought us here – it is tacitly teleological. Secondly, in looking only to very similar precursors, it a priori excludes all sorts of influences that do not resemble present-day psychology of emotion and so produces a radically internalist and problematically narrow and naïve account. A particularly stark example of such an exclusion of theology from psychology's authentic past is to be found in Brett's *History of Psychology* (1921) in his treatment of Spencer: 'Spencer produced a change in the attitude toward psychology; he made clearer the sense in which psychology is a *natural* science. The movement aroused great opposition from the advocates of the supernatural quality of the soul, but this was a passing phase that belongs only to the history of culture.'[13] The idea that religion and theology, but not psychology, are parts of 'culture' and the assumption that religiously motivated views about mental life and the soul were not part of a psychological enterprise are both views that are rejected in the present work.

More recent historians of psychology have displayed some similar tendencies. William Woodward, in his 1982 introduction to *The Problematic Science: Psychology in Nineteenth-Century Thought*, mentions several important vehicles for psychological thought in the nineteenth century, including Kantian philosophy, psychobiology, psychophysics, child psychology and social psychology, but does not mention theology. Graham Richards in his equivalent summary of nineteenth-century intellectual enterprises that contributed to psychological thought, in his 1992 study, *Mental Machinery: The Origins and Consequences of Psychological Ideas*, lists philosophers, scientists, psychiatrists, physicians, economists, criminologists and educationalists, but, again, not theologians.[14] It is of interest to debate which of theology, philosophy, medicine, psychiatry or biological science had more influence and in what areas of psychological thought in the nineteenth century; but to omit theology from the picture altogether – especially while including, for example, economics and criminology – is misleading. During the nineteenth century, theologians, preachers and Christian philosophers were amongst the most widely read and influential figures contributing to thought about the soul and mind.

I am certainly not alone amongst recent historians of psychology in seeing a need to broaden the canon of the history of psychology. This broadening has started to happen to some extent, most notably through the efforts of authors seeking to include literary figures in psychology's past.[15] Rick Rylance's book, *Victorian Psychology and British*

---

[13] Brett (1921), III, 215.
[14] Woodward, 'Introduction' to Woodward and Ash (eds.) (1982); Richards (1992), ch. 8.
[15] E.g. Shuttleworth (1996); Reed (1997), Preface; Rylance (2000); Wood (2001).

Culture 1850–1880, is one of the works responsible for this shift, and is also one of the only histories of psychology to have properly recognised *theological* discourse as a form of psychological discourse. Rylance divides nineteenth-century British psychological discourse into four categories – the discourse of the soul, the discourse of philosophy, the discourse of physiology and the discourse of medicine. Each of these discourses persisted throughout the century (albeit in various forms and with varying measures of success), as both Rylance's work and the present study aim to show. Edward Reed has also argued for the importance of the religious dimensions of psychological thought in the nineteenth century. However, he is rather over-stating the case when he claims that 'psychology succeeded in becoming a science in large part because of its defense of a theological conception of human nature typically associated with liberal Protestant theology'.[16] (I will return to Reed's claims in the context of my own conclusions, in chapter 8.)

Paying attention, then, to some of the theological variables at work, the psychological systems that form the subject of this book are sometimes categorised as 'Christian', and sometimes as 'secular', depending on the authorities, methods, concepts and categories adopted in analysing human mental life. There are many texts, however, which are predicated on theistic belief and purport to privilege God (often the Christian God), but which fail to qualify as 'theological' or 'Christian' psychologies since there is little or no use of traditional Christian authorities, methods, concepts or categories. These texts are variously described as 'unchristian', or 'atheological', or as examples of merely metaphysical theism. 'Unchristian' and 'atheological' are terms, like 'amoral', which I intend to indicate the absence of something rather than its inversion or denial.[17] Generally, when I say that a text is Christian, I will mean that the arguments and teachings of the text are 'full-bloodedly' Christian – that they are embedded in the language and teachings of the Christian tradition. 'Metaphysical theism', in contrast, is a term I use to refer to certain beliefs that include the existence of a God who is perhaps conceived of as 'Deity', 'Architect', 'Author', 'Mind', or as 'the All', but who is not described using the language and symbols of Christianity (or any other religious tradition). Texts produced by some moralists, mental scientists and design theologians in the eighteenth and early nineteenth centuries fall into this 'halfway house' category between Christian psychology and thoroughly secular psychology (including works by the moralist Joseph Butler, the Edinburgh moral

[16] Reed (1997), 7.
[17] For a fuller and broader definition and use of the terms 'atheology' and 'atheological', see Dixon (1999). I am not using the term in the same way as the theologian Mark C. Taylor, who has written about 'a/theology'; Taylor (1984).

philosopher Thomas Brown and the neurologist and natural theologian Sir Charles Bell). The works of several authors considered in chapter 6 also fall into this category of 'metaphysical theism', including those by the philosophical psychologist J. D. Morell, the Scottish-Canadian minister and philosopher William Lyall, and Noah Porter, the President of Yale. Christology, Trinitarian theology and the doctrines of sin, the fall and grace are among the omissions of such thin theisms. In the way I use these terms, then, a Christian author can produce a thinly theistic text (or indeed a thoroughly secular one). In calling a psychological text thinly theistic, unchristian, or atheological, I do not preclude the possibility that the author was a committed Christian (as, in fact, was the case with Butler, Bell, Lyall and Porter).

Presentism and the meanings of 'psychology' and 'science'

In his recent study, *Alchemies of the Mind: Rationality and the Emotions* (1999), Jon Elster includes a chapter on 'Emotions before Psychology', which opens with two sentences that illustrate very well the sort of presentist assumptions about psychology and science that I am seeking to challenge: 'The psychological analysis of the emotions is little more than a hundred years old. Darwin's *Expression of Emotion in Man and Animals* (1872) and William James' "What is an Emotion" (1884) are the first studies of the emotions using scientific methodology.'[18] These claims are arguable, but – according to the definitions of psychology and science preferred here – are mistaken. Elster, like Mandler, David Rapaport and others, considers the psychology of emotions to go back only to the late nineteenth century.[19] In fact, the psychological analysis of emotions goes back nearer two hundred than one hundred years (to the lectures delivered in Edinburgh by Thomas Brown between 1810 and 1820). And the psychological analysis of passions goes back millennia (as Elster's own exposition of Aristotle's views implicitly acknowledges). The claim that the psychological analysis of emotions is only one hundred years old depends on defining 'psychology' in a narrow sense as professional academic, scientific psychology. The definition preferred here is that psychology is the systematic study of (primarily human) mental life. Brown's analysis of emotions only fails to be psychological if psychology is required to refer to nerves, brains, viscera, behaviour and other outward and physically measurable events.

[18] Elster (1999), 48; the actual title of Darwin's work was *The Expression of the Emotions in Man and Animals*.
[19] Rapaport (1971) takes Darwin and James to be the authors of 'early theories' of emotions (22–3).

Elster's second claim – that Darwin and James were the first to apply scientific methodology to emotions – is also debatable. Again, scientific methodology was applied by Brown to the emotions and by others before him to the passions and affections. Empiricist and associationist philosophers such as David Hume, David Hartley, Dugald Stewart and James Mill, as well as Brown, all aspired to apply the inductive scientific method to mental life (see chapter 4). Inspired by Bacon, and by Newton's comment at the end of his *Opticks* (1704), that the inductive methods of natural philosophy could be successfully applied also to 'moral philosophy', Scottish empiricists developed systems of 'mental science' that sought to produce laws of mental life on the basis of inward observations or 'introspection'.[20] The Scottish minister and philosopher Thomas Reid – the central figure of the Scottish 'common sense' school – in his *Essays on the Intellectual Powers of Man* (1785), expressed the hope that mental philosophers would 'produce a system of the power and operations of the human mind no less certain than those of optics or astronomy'.[21] The resulting systems of psychology only fail to be applications of 'scientific methodology' if that phrase is defined to mean the discovery only of physical causes and components, to the exclusion of the study of mind qua mind.

It might be considered something of a methodological anomaly that I am prepared to use the term 'psychology' anachronistically (to refer to authors such as Edwards, Watts, Butler, Reid or Brown, who wrote either before the term psychology had been coined or before it had taken on its modern meaning) while insisting at the same time on a scrupulous avoidance of anachronism in the use of the term 'emotions'. The reason for this decision relates to the current use of the terms in histories of psychology and philosophy. In each case the usage favoured in this book is adopted as a corrective to problematic usage in existing secondary literature.

The word 'emotions' is currently often used carelessly and anachronistically to refer to theories that were in fact about 'passions', 'affections', or 'sentiments'. It should, instead, be restricted to those theories that are explicitly about 'emotions'; there are important differences in nuance to all these terms that should not be effaced. The word 'emotions' is

---

[20] David Hume, David Hartley and James Mill all expressed the desire to be the Newton of the mind; see Mischel (1966), 126, 136. For further references to the importance of Bacon, of Newton's comment in the *Opticks* and of scientific methodology in general to Scottish philosophy, see Payne (1828), 17–20; McCosh (1875), 3, 99, 195; Laurie (1902), 1–9, 124–5, 218; Grave (1960), 7, 147–9; Cantor (1975), esp. 128–31; Olson (1975), chs. 1 and 2; Flynn (1988); Wood (1989 and 1990); Emerson (1990); Graham (2001).
[21] Quoted in Flynn (1988), 264.

currently used too liberally by historians of psychology and its reference needs to be narrowed.

The word 'psychology', in contrast, is used rather too restrictively or chauvinistically, as has been noted above, to refer to modern scientific psychology (physiological, behavioural, neurological and evolutionary psychology and, sometimes, cognitive psychology and psychoanalysis) and its precursors. Thus other contributions to the understanding of mental life are often neglected by historians of psychology. One of the aims of this book is to rectify this situation with particular reference to the contributions of theological thought to the emergence of modern psychological concepts, categories and methods. 'Psychology' is used below to refer to a broader tradition of systematic thought about mental life rather than just to modern or scientific psychology.

The word 'science', like the word 'psychology', is at times used below more liberally than is often the case in contemporary discussions. This is in part a result of adopting the language and categories of the eighteenth- and nineteenth-century figures being discussed. The word 'science' as used in contemporary discussions tends to be used to refer to the 'physical' or 'natural' sciences. In this book it will not always be so restricted. Many of the authors under consideration advocated a 'science of the mind', but we would be mistaken to read such a proposition in the light of current meanings of 'science'. A majority of those thinkers discussed below who advocated 'science of the mind' or 'mental science' meant a systematic investigation into the mental causes and mental components of mental states and not their physical causes, correlates or components.[22]

The use of the word 'science' in the singular is always problematic (as is the use of 'religion' or 'theology' in the singular) insofar as it tends to disguise the plural reality of those enterprises to which it refers. The plurality of the sciences is one of the reasons why an espousal of 'science' of the mind is never completely free from ambiguity. Which science, if any, is to be emulated? Is the mind to be chemically analysed into mental elements, or are its states to be botanically ordered and classified, or is the physiology of the nerves and viscera to be used to understand the mind, or are law-like regularities as precise of those of physics the ultimate goal? Does psychology need a Newton or perhaps a Lavoisier or a Darwin to bring about its elevation to the ranks of 'science'?[23] Is the science of the mind in fact to be a science of the mind or a science of something else, such as the brain or behaviour? Is it to be 'science by analogy' or 'physical science proper'?

[22] See n.20.   [23] See James (1894a), 292–3.

Existing histories of emotions

Approaching existing literature on historical developments in philosophy, psychology and psychiatry reveals that it is not widely acknowledged that our concept of 'emotions' has only emerged during the last two centuries, and that it is not synonymous with other categories such as 'passions', 'agitations', 'sentiments' or 'feelings'. This tendency to equivocate is evident in the titles of four of the most interesting books on the subject: Susan James' study of seventeenth-century thought about the passions, *Passion and Action: The Emotions in Seventeenth-Century Philosophy* (1997), Solomon's *The Passions: Emotions and the Meaning of Life* (1976, 1993), Richard Sorabji's *Emotion and Peace of Mind: From Stoic Agitation to Christian Temptation* (2000) and William Reddy's *The Navigation of Feeling: A Framework for the History of Emotions* (2001).[24] James acknowledges the problem of using 'emotions' to refer to the 'passions' discussed by seventeenth-century thinkers: '[T]heir category of passions does not coincide with modern interpretations of the category of emotion... Some early-modern writers use the terms "passion" and "emotion" synonymously. But in following their practice, we need to remember that their sense of these terms diverges from common contemporary usage.'[25] James gives Descartes as an example of an early-modern writer using the terms interchangeably. Leaving aside for the moment the complicating factor that he was writing in French, it is true that in *Les Passions de l'Ame* (1649), Descartes made use of the term '*émotions*' in two ways, first as a synonym for '*passions*' in the broadest sense, and secondly in the phrase '*émotions intérieures*' to refer to a restricted class of intellectual feelings.[26]

It is suggested in chapter 4 that Descartes' use of '*émotions*' as a broad umbrella term for movements of the soul was quite possibly the source of the term 'emotions' in the writings of Scottish philosophers from Hume onwards.

As has already been mentioned, Solomon's use of the terms 'passions' and 'emotions' is somewhat confusing. At times he idiosyncratically distinguishes between the terms by treating 'emotions' as a subset of 'passions'; at other times he problematically treats them as synonyms, defining them both as cognitive judgments that shape subjective reality.[27] The target of Solomon's criticisms, the 'myth of the passions' as he calls it, has three principal components: it teaches that passions/emotions are primarily physiological, that they are non-cognitive feelings and that they are alien involuntary powers that can overwhelm people against their

---

[24] Solomon (1993a); James (1997); Sorabji (2000); Reddy (2001).
[25] James (1997), 7.   [26] James (1997), 196–207.
[27] Solomon (1993a), viii, xvii–xviii, and throughout.

wills. This position is a combination of views; it contains some elements of traditional Christian views of the passions as well as some elements of nineteenth- and twentieth-century physiological theories of emotions. A better historical understanding of the way that theologians and philosophers differentiated between passions and affections in the past, and of how divergence from this model led to the creation of the category of 'emotions', will make it easier for contemporary theorists to be clear about the meanings of these key terms. It is particularly interesting to realise, I argue below, that the three principal teachings ascribed by Solomon to the 'myth of the passions' – that emotions are physiological, non-cognitive and involuntary feelings – are all ideas that gained currency as a result of divergence from traditional teachings about the 'passions' and 'affections' and the concomitant adoption of the secular category of 'emotions' in the nineteenth century.

Kurt Danziger is one of the few historians of psychology to have acknowledged the methodological problems that arise as a result of terminological differences between past and present psychologies. He gives the example of volumes of historical readings in psychology that organise the material under subject headings such as 'motivation', 'intelligence' and so on.

> Almost invariably, those key terms are taken from the accepted vocabulary of twentieth-century (American) psychology and not from the vocabularies of the authors of the selected pre-twentieth-century texts. The use of contemporary terms strongly suggests that the objects of current psychological discourse are the real, natural objects and that past discourse necessarily referred to the same objects in its own quaint and subscientific way. What this organisation of historical material overlooks is the possibility that the very objects of psychological discourse, and not just opinions about them, have changed radically in the course of history.[28]

Although not specifically directed to the problem of the history of 'passions' and 'emotions', Danziger's diagnosis applies extremely well to it. 'Emotions' have only been objects of psychological discourse for approximately two hundred years; before that time 'passions', 'affections' and 'sentiments' were among the mental phenomena discussed by psychological thinkers.[29] A lack of historical perspective can lead towards the implausible view that current academic psychology has

---

[28] Danziger (1990), 336.
[29] Roger Smith (1997) rightly says that 'Passion cannot simply be equated with the modern category of emotion.' He goes on to say that emotion in its modern sense 'was not in common use until the late eighteenth century' (60). I would suggest that while it was used by a handful of aesthetic and mental philosophers in the late eighteenth century, it was not widely used, certainly not in a clearly understood sense, until almost fifty years after that.

produced a fixed set of categories that are the best or only way to categorise human mental life.

The one general history that exists in this area, Gardiner *et al.*'s *Feeling and Emotion: A History of Theories* (1937), suffers from this problem identified by Danziger, of assuming that historical theories are all, in essence, theories of the objects of twentieth-century psychological discourse. Gardiner *et al.* unreflectively treat past theories of passions, affections, feelings, sentiments etc. as theories about 'affective phenomena' or 'emotions' as they have been conceived by psychologists in the twentieth century.

Other than Gardiner *et al.*'s book (which is very useful as a work of reference despite its presentist historiography) the history of emotions has generally taken the form of histories of specific emotions. Among the principal recent contributors to histories of this sort have been Peter Stearns and Carol Stearns, who have produced individual social historical studies of anger, jealousy and fear.[30] There have also been studies on romantic love, sexual sensibility and family relationships.[31] All these studies concentrate on historical changes in social attitudes and standards with regard to the experience and expression of specific emotions. There is, then, a healthy industry in the social history of specific emotions. There has, until recently, however, been a relative poverty of histories of general theories of emotion (and of passions, affections and sentiments).[32] Some of the most useful existing historical studies of ideas about passions and emotions are to be found outside of general mainstream histories of psychology and philosophy, especially in two areas: the history of psychopathology and psychiatry, and literary studies.[33]

---

[30] Stearns and Stearns (1986); Stearns (1989); Stearns and Haggerty (1991).

[31] For reviews of this literature, see Stearns (1993); Pinch (1995).

[32] Recent works have begun to fill this gap, including Richard Sorabji's study of ancient Greek (especially Stoic) and early Christian thought about what he calls 'emotions' (see chapter 2 below for a discussion of the variety of Greek and Latin terms used); Susan James' book on theories of passion and action in the seventeenth century; William Reddy's discussion of both contemporary theories of emotion and of attitudes to passions and sentiments in the period surrounding the French Revolution; an eclectic book by John Cottingham investigating the roles of passion and reason in the ethics of classical antiquity, Descartes and the psychoanalytic school; and a helpful recent article on nineteenth- and twentieth-century emotion theories by Eric Salzen; Sorabji (2000), James (1997), Reddy (2001), Cottingham (1998), Salzen (2001). James Averill and Kathleen Grange have both written informatively on the use of different metaphors for passions and emotions in the past; Grange (1962); Averill (1990). These works, however, have not focussed, as the current study does, on the significance of differences between theories of passions, affections, sentiments and emotions.

[33] For relevant material relating to the history of psychiatry, see Berrios (1996); Hunter and Macalpine (1963); Skultans (1975); Grange (1961); Luyendijk-Elshout (1990); Weiner (1990). Turning to works in literary fields, see Hilton (1988), 314–19; Shuttleworth (1996); Pinch (1996); Elster (1999); Ellison (1999); Wood (2001).

While none of these works ponders the significance of the historical shifts in usage from 'passions', 'sentiments' and 'affections' to 'emotions' at any length, they all broaden the canon and the scope of the history of affective psychology in valuable ways. Indeed, for their purposes, Julie Ellison may be right that it is not always necessary to try, as I do below, to clarify the differences between these terms; she is one of many writers who are happy to use 'emotion' as a catch-all term covering a wide variety of past and present uses of 'passion', 'sensibility', 'sympathy', 'sentiment' and 'affection'.[34]

Science-and-religion historiography has focussed generally on either physics or evolutionary biology. Psychology has been much less attended to by historians of science and religion. This is partly because of the same assumptions made by many historians of psychology – that 'psychology' only began with the work of early professional academic scientific psychologists at the end of the nineteenth century – and also, perhaps, because some take the view that prior to that time psychology was not a 'science' with which 'religion' could engage. Certainly the status of psychology as a 'science' has always been contested.[35] John Hedley Brooke's definitive work, *Science and Religion: Some Historical Perspectives* (1991), and his Gifford Lectures with Geoffrey Cantor, are representative of the literature in treating psychology sporadically and briefly, while giving more extensive coverage to physics, chemistry and (especially evolutionary) biology.[36] Writing in 1988, Boyd Hilton listed geology, astronomy, magnetism, physics, biology, palaeontology and natural history as areas in which historians had appreciated the influence of theological convictions on the development of science.[37] His own work added political economy and social theory to that list. Although some writers in the field of science and religion have recently started to focus on psychology,[38] it still remains largely neglected by historians of the relationships between theology and science, just as theology is largely neglected by historians of psychology.[39]

This study, then, aims to supplement the existing literature, focussing particularly on the significance of the neglected transition from theories of

---

[34] Ellison (1999), 4–5.   [35] Woodward and Ash (eds.) (1982).
[36] Among those whose views of mind Brooke considers are Descartes, Priestley, James, and Freud. See Brooke (1991), 127–30, 171–80, 319–20, 324–5; Brooke and Cantor (1998).
[37] Hilton (1988), x.
[38] E.g. Jeeves (1997); Brown *et al.* (eds.) (1998); Watts (1997, 1998, 2002).
[39] An exception is Spilka (1987): a short article on science and religion in early American psychology, dealing with Hickok, McCosh, Porter and Upham. Jacyna (1981) and Cashdollar (1989) are also exceptions in that they provide studies of nineteenth-century thinkers, from a philosophical and theological point of view, whose psychological thought was seen as a threat to or a defence of Christian orthodoxy. Neither, however, is explicitly a contribution to the history of 'science and religion', nor to the history of psychology.

passions and affections of the soul to theories of emotions. This transition has been addressed only twice in recent years, once in Amélie Oksenberg Rorty's article 'From passions to emotions and sentiments' (1982), and once in a brief section of Kurt Danziger's *Naming the Mind: How Psychology Found its Language* (1997).[40] Rorty criticises contemporary psychologists and philosophers for their lack of interest in previous theories of passions.[41] Her own analysis, however, extends only to Descartes and Hume, and mistakenly supposes 'passions' talk to have been simply unsatisfactory 'emotions' talk.

Danziger, like Rorty, focusses on Hume and argues that Hume's *Treatise* was a watershed that marked the beginning of the end for the dichotomy between reason and the passions. Danziger's theory is that the emergence of the concept of 'emotions', in which he rightly notes that Brown was an important figure (see chapter 4 in this volume), was indicative of the fading of this reason–passion dichotomy. This view is questionable for two reasons. First, the reason–passion dichotomy was not so stark as Danziger and others sometimes suggest: within many traditional and Christian views there had been a place for 'affections' and 'sentiments', which in effect were potentially rational and virtuous passions. Christian writers such as Edwards conceptualised affections in a way that kept reason and will in tension (see chapter 3). Secondly, the reason–passion dichotomy was replaced in the nineteenth century by an even stronger intellect–emotion dichotomy, exemplified in the works of Brown, Chalmers and James amongst others (see chapters 4–7). In the absence of categories such as 'affections' and 'sentiments' that bridged the gap between thinking and feeling, secular psychologies of emotions were left with a simple and sharp dichotomy between cognition and emotion.

In 1905 James Mark Baldwin and G. F. Stout gave an accurate assessment of the historical transition from passions and affections to emotions in their essay on 'emotion' in Baldwin's *Dictionary of Philosophy and Psychology*: 'The use of the word emotion in English psychology is comparatively modern. It is found in Hume, but even he speaks generally rather of passions or affections. When the word emotion did become current its application was very wide, covering all possible varieties of feeling, except those that are purely sensational in their origin.'[42] Baldwin and Stout were right that in the English language the term 'emotions' took over from 'passions' and 'affections' as the dominant term only around the middle of the nineteenth century (and that it was a very broad category). In general, however, it does not seem to have occurred to many

---

[40] Rorty (1982); Danziger (1997), 39–42.   [41] Rorty (1982), 172.
[42] 'Emotion' in Baldwin (ed.) (1905), I, 316.

philosophers or historians of the subject to ask whether contemporary 'emotions' are, or are not, the same things as 'passions' (or 'affections' or 'sentiments').

It may be helpful, in order to clarify what I mean by saying that 'emotions' are not the same things as 'passions' to make a distinction between the extensions and the intensions of these terms. Modern-day uses of 'emotions' have both different extensions and different intensions from older uses of 'passions'. Of course neither term has ever had a fixed meaning or a fixed extension, but there have been general tendencies, and some degree of consensus. The extension of 'emotions' (the items included in the category), for example, tends to include many feelings that might previously have been categorised not as passions but as appetites (e.g. lust), or affections (e.g. religious feelings), or sentiments (e.g. sympathy).

Although there would clearly be a large amount of overlap, as Annette Baier has pointed out, between the extensions of Descartes', Hobbes' and Hume's category of 'passions', Darwin's and other contemporary theorists' 'emotions', and what Spinoza, Kant and many modern psychologists call 'affects', it is going too far to hope that the lists of the items in these categories' extensions would 'be more or less the same, or inter-translatable'. As Baier herself goes on to point out, to take just one more example, the 'passions', but not the 'emotions' or 'affects', tended to include desires and motives in addition to other feelings.[43] Finally, when it comes to thinking about extensions, it is worth noting that there has never been any consensus about the number of passions or emotions, nor about the number of 'basic' or 'principal' passions or emotions. Descartes lists forty-one passions, Hobbes forty-six, Spinoza forty-eight and Hume about twenty.[44] Nineteenth- and twentieth-century lists of emotions have been much longer – James McCosh's *The Emotions* (1880) lists over a hundred. On the question of basic passions or emotions, some, such as Augustine, have sought to reduce all the passions and affections to forms of a single movement – love; others have suggested a longer list of four, five or more basic passions or emotions (Aquinas suggested both four and eleven as possibilities).

The intension of 'emotion' (the definition of the term) has differed very significantly from the intension of 'passion': the former has tended to be defined in an amoral way as an autonomous physical or mental state characterised by vivid feeling and physical agitation, the latter has been defined in more morally and theologically engaged ways as a disobedient and morally dangerous movement of the soul (as well as often being used in a vague and general way to refer to a variety of lively mental states).

---

[43] Baier (1990), 2.   [44] Baier (1990), 5.

Similar points could also be made (about differing extensions and intensions) when comparing modern-day uses of 'emotions' with older uses of 'sentiments' and 'affections' and even with differing uses of the term 'emotions' itself. The details and nuances of these distinctions form the subject of the rest of this book.

Historians of psychology could perhaps benefit from thinking about similar questions of terminology and anachronism that arise in the histories of the physical sciences. Most historians of chemistry would not be prepared to consider dephlogisticated air and oxygen the same thing, nor would the historian of early-modern science be prepared to consider natural philosophers and scientists the same things. Let us consider the case of Joseph Priestley and his creation, in his experiments on airs, of one particular substance that he called 'dephlogisticated air'.[45] We now might look back and say that what he called 'dephlogisticated air' is what we would call 'oxygen'. However it would not be accurate to say that Priestley had a theory of oxygen. His term 'dephlogisticated air' would, I believe, have included in its extension samples that we would consider to be atmospheric air with an increased proportion of oxygen present, as well as samples we would consider to be pure oxygen. And the intension of the term is not the same at all, being defined as it is in terms of a substance – phlogiston – and a whole theoretical apparatus that are both quite alien to our modern-day chemical conceptions of oxygen and combustion. Just as it would thus be confusing to claim that Priestley had a theory of oxygen, so I think it is often confusing to suggest that writers referring to *pathē* (in Greek), to *passiones, affectiones* or *affectus* (in Latin), or to 'passions', 'affections' or 'sentiments', had a theory of emotions.

An Anglophone history

A final methodological note concerns the relative positions given to English-language and non-English-language texts in this study. This story of the creation of the category of 'emotions' during the eighteenth and nineteenth centuries could have been told in many different ways. The decisions that I made about how to present the story, which aspects and writers to focus upon and, especially, which aspects and writers to omit, led to the study taking the particular form that it did. One omission from my narrative is an account of the development of affective psychologies by continental European writers, to complement the account offered of Anglophone theorists.

---

[45] Priestley (1774b).

There are two main reasons why these writers were largely excluded. First, the particular puzzle that this book tackles is why it was that the words 'passions' and 'affections' were displaced by the word 'emotions' in psychological texts during the nineteenth century. Since this is a puzzle that is so specifically about these English words, it is one that is particular to English-language psychological texts. Terminology in affective psychologies written in other languages (e.g. German terms such as *Affekte*, *Leidenschaft*, *Gefühl* and *Empfindung*; and the way that French writers used *passions*, *émotions* and *sentiments*) would form a rich and interesting subject for additional research but one that lies outside the scope of this book.

Secondly, the primary focus of this book is on the history of psychological language and categories rather than on those mental states themselves that have been variously categorised as 'passions', 'affections', 'emotions' etc. This focus also, of course, leads to discussions about the content and implications of theories that employ various terms, such as 'emotions'. However, since one of the leading claims of my argument is that we should not assume that 'emotions' and 'passions' are the same things, it would have been equally problematic for me to look at theories in other languages, with their own different terms and categories and to treat them also as theories of 'emotions'. The assumption that psychological theories, regardless of their language and categories, pick out theory-independent mental states that we can identify with our own current English-language psychological terms is one of the assumptions that this books challenges.

It is not supposed, however, that English-language psychology existed in a vacuum. There are, of course, very interesting links to be made between English-language and continental psychologies throughout the period under consideration; and where these links are particularly pertinent they are discussed. One example of this is the question of whether eighteenth-century English-language writers who used 'emotions' as a psychological category took the term from Descartes' use of *émotions* in his discourse on the passions of the soul.

From passions and affections to emotions: an overview of the argument

The story that I tell below about how the psychological category of emotions came to be created and adopted during the eighteenth and nineteenth centuries proceeds both chronologically and thematically. I start by examining some eighteenth-century Christian ideas about appetites, passions, affections and moral sentiments; and finish by discussing the theories of emotions of William James and his critics at the end of the nineteenth century. Telling the story in this way may suggest a certain interpretation to the reader – that, over time, affective psychologies became gradually less theological and more philosophical, and ultimately more 'scientific'; that at the beginning of the period in question theologians set the agenda and provided the categories to use in discussing mental life and that that role was usurped first by philosophers and then by professional scientific psychologists. This interpretation, while capturing something of what I want to suggest (that there was indeed a gradual process of secularisation), is, on its own, incomplete and flawed.

Like Rylance, I want to stress that theological and philosophical discourses about the soul and the mind did not disappear – they were not completely erased nor entirely superseded. Writers committed to Christian, theistic and metaphysical traditions have continued to produce texts and theories of psychology (in the broad sense) right up to the present day. The processes of secularisation and professionalisation have been incomplete, but are still real. There are two important respects in which a story of secularisation does capture what has happened. First, the proportion of all theoretical psychological texts (broadly construed) that are theological has decreased and the proportion that are both secular and scientific has increased. Secondly, the creation of an academic discipline called 'psychology', which is purportedly autonomous from philosophy and theology, and which endorses a very particular set of methodological and metaphysical commitments largely derived from the physical sciences, has reinforced the tendency for fewer avowedly philosophical, metaphysical, or theological psychologies to be produced or to be taken seriously in an academic context. This could be summed up by saying that cultural and academic authority on psychological (and other) questions has shifted from ecclesiastical and theological texts and institutions to more secular ones.

The initial backdrop I provide to this story of gradual, complex and incomplete secularisation, takes the form of an analysis of patristic and scholastic Christian theologies of the soul. Classical Christian theologians, especially St Augustine of Hippo and St Thomas Aquinas, whose theologies of the soul, its passions and affections are examined in chapter 2, produced models of the human soul in which the passions and appetites, which were movements of the lower animal soul, were distinguished from the affections, which were acts of the higher rational soul. The appetites were hunger, thirst and sexual desire. The disobedience of the lower soul to the higher, and of the body to the soul, experienced in sexual appetite and in the passions was a sign of, and punishment for, the original sin of Adam and Eve. Often, passions were unruly and disturbed the body; they included love, hate, hope, fear and anger. The higher affections of love, sympathy and joy were signs of relatedness to God and held out the possibility of reunion with God. The affections were also signs of the order or direction of the will. A carnal will was affected by worldly objects and, ultimately, by love of self; a holy will's affections were for goodness, truth and, ultimately, God.

It is important to have an understanding of the importance of the will to Christian morality and Christian psychology in order to appreciate the significance of its gradual disappearance in eighteenth- and nineteenth-century works. The destiny of each person was determined by freely taken voluntary decisions – decisions of the individual will. The will was divided by Aquinas into two 'appetites': the higher intellectual appetite (the will proper), whose movements were the affections; and the lower, non-rational sense appetite, whose movements were the appetites and passions. It is particularly important, then, to realise that – contrary to popular opinion – classical Christian views about reason and the passions were equivalent neither to the view that reason and the 'emotions' are inevitably at war, nor to the idea that 'emotions' overpower us against our will. Appetites, passions and affections, on the classical Christian view, were all movements of different parts of the will, and the affections, at least, were potentially informed by reason.

Chapter 3 examines some of the movements away from classical Christian psychology towards more secular and mechanistic views of passions and affections in the eighteenth century, as well as ways that the traditional Christian picture was maintained and developed. Christian thinkers such as Joseph Butler, Jonathan Edwards and Thomas Reid adapted the traditional models in various ways. The tendencies to see passions and affections as 'mechanisms' designed by God, and as 'perceptions', were both symptomatic of psychologies in which the will had become less important. Passions and affections were conceived increasingly as mini-agents in their own right, or as a faculty of their own, rather than as acts or movements of the individual will. This had significant moral and theological implications. The discourse of 'moral sentiments' specifically and the culture of 'sentiment' and 'sentimentalism' more generally, which were fascinating features of this same period, are also referred to in chapter 3. These serve as further examples of the variety of categories and conceptualisations used during this period, which was an age of passions and sentiments as much as it was an 'Age of Reason'.

The initial baptism of the term 'emotions' is the subject of chapter 4. The earliest uses of the term in its modern sense occurred in the school of Scottish empiricist philosophers and mental scientists from David Hume's *Treatise of Human Nature* (1739–40) onwards. The most important text was Thomas Brown's *Lectures on the Philosophy of the Human Mind* (1820) in which 'emotions' was the term adopted for all those feelings that were neither sensations nor intellectual states. Brown developed a new terminology and classification of mental states, motivated by a desire to break away from traditional faculty psychology, and to create a de-Christianised and scientific alternative. 'Emotions' included a wide variety of states that had previously been differentiated, and many of which had been considered active powers of the soul. The term 'emotions' was baptised in a way that suggested these mental states were passive and non-cognitive. The category was over-inclusive and was embedded in a tradition committed to the application of scientific methodology to the study of the mind. However, the application of scientific method and commitment to Christianity were by no means mutually exclusive: the evangelical theologian Thomas Chalmers adopted and even strengthened the non-cognitive, involuntary and mechanical tenor of Brown's 'feeling' theory of emotions.

In chapters 5 and 6 I look at the appropriation of the Brownian category of emotions by physiological and evolutionary psychologists, in the face of (often Christian or theistic) resistance. Physical science replaced mental science as the dominant methodology in works on emotions by Herbert Spencer, Alexander Bain and Charles Darwin in the 1850s to 1870s. The assumption, still made by Christian philosophers and psychologists at this time, that passions and affections were instances of the soul acting upon or using the body, was replaced with the assumption that emotions were instances of the brain and nerves acting upon other parts of the body. The mind or soul per se was not given an active role. Physiological and evolutionary thinkers were quicker to appropriate the category 'emotions' than thinkers within the Christian tradition, some of whom were still speaking the language of 'will', 'passions' and 'affections' in the 1870s. So use of the term was generally indicative of familiarity and sympathy with Brown's secularised mental science. The relationship between these physicalist thinkers and the moral philosophers and natural theologians whose work they were developing upon, was not always straightforward, however. Darwin's relationship with Scottish moral philosophy and Sir Charles Bell's design theology serves as an illustration of these complex relationships. The theories of emotion and expression produced by this generation of scientific psychologists were shaped both positively and negatively by theological and religious ideas. Some Christian and theistic psychologists (for example, William Lyall or James McCosh) adopted the new category of emotions but opposed the physicalist approach of the new emotions theorists and proposed mentalistic and cognitive alternatives.

Finally, in chapter 7, I describe the stage that could be seen as a culmination of the processes narrated in the preceding chapters, namely the professional psychological endorsement of an epiphenomenal and physicalist emotions theory. More presentist and narrower histories of psychology might begin their account of the history of psychological theories of emotions with William James. In this history, in contrast, James' infamous theory is depicted as the culmination of complex processes of secularisation and innovation in psychological discourse. James' iconic 1884 article 'What is an emotion?' made explicit in a new way the tacit epiphenomenalism of the physiological-evolutionary theory of emotions. His theory of emotions – that they were felt awarenesses of visceral activity – was a flagship theory of the new scientific psychological profession. James inverted the traditional assumption that the outward bodily manifestations of emotions were caused by either the activity of the soul or even – as in the case of the physiological-evolutionary school – by the activity of the brain; the viscera were made primary and the brain and its mind secondary by James.

Along with literary, political, sociological and philosophical discourses about mental life, theological discourse about the soul, the mind and its faculties has often been neglected by historians of psychology until recently. An historian of psychology who approaches the past looking for thinkers and thoughts that closely resemble present-day academic psychologists and their theories (in other words, looking for narrowly defined 'precursors') will tend to overlook the rich variety of psychological discourses that have been produced in past eras, and which have (positively and negatively) shaped subsequent ideas. I hope that this study will, then, complement other works that seek to extend the canon of the history of psychology.[46] 'Psychology' as it is generally conceived, as an academic and possibly scientific discipline and profession, did not appear out of thin air in the nineteenth century; rather, it must be seen as, amongst other things, a response to, adaptation of and departure from various theological traditions, assumptions and commitments.

I hope to draw attention to the real complexity of interactions between religious and scientific commitments and traditions in the development of psychological theories. The secular psychologies produced by nineteenth-century scientific and positivist 'emotions' theorists were more than either Christian theology or its inversion in disguise. Worldview commitments – sets of metaphysical and a priori beliefs and narratives – played many different selective and constitutive roles in the production of psychological theories. This observation holds true for all varieties of

---

[46] E.g. Shuttleworth (1996); Reed (1997); Rylance (2000).

psychology – theological, philosophical, scientific and all the different combinations of these.

Finally, my conclusions with respect to the category of 'emotions' itself take the form of questions and suggestions more than substantive proposals. Neither the fact that the category is a relatively new one, nor the fact that it replaced more differentiated typologies, proves that 'the emotions' is a defective category. Nor do these considerations prove that 'emotions' does not pick out a natural kind, nor that a more differentiated typology is to be preferred. These facts do, however, at least help to sow a seed of doubt in our minds about these issues. The story of the creation of this category provides the reader with some alternative typologies, some alternative theories and some evidence of the serious problems run into by those trying to define 'emotions' in the past. I suggest, in the light of this evidence, that the over-inclusivity of the category may be at the root of the infamous problems of definition that have beset philosophers and psychologists of emotion from the early nineteenth century onwards. This over-inclusivity has also made explanations that invoke emotions problematic, since it is not clear what exactly is being appealed to as the cause of a behaviour – an involuntary feeling or a cognitive act? The moral status of 'emotions' is therefore unclear.

Even those philosophers and psychologists today who remain convinced of the propriety of the concept of 'emotion' may find that they can learn from the experiences of eighteenth- and nineteenth-century theorists who were engaged in comparable projects. The moral, cognitive and 'compound' approaches to passions, affections and emotions that I examine below were largely forgotten during the professionalisation of psychological discourse of the late nineteenth century. These approaches have been reinvented in various guises during the twentieth century in ignorance of their relatively recent past incarnations. The details, strengths and weaknesses of previous such theories, discovered and discussed below, may possibly provide interesting resources for contemporary emotion theorists.

2 Passions and affections in Augustine and Aquinas

> The words 'love', 'desire' and so on are used in two senses. Sometimes they mean passions, with some arousal in the soul. This is what the words are generally taken to mean, and such passions exist solely at the level of sense appetite. But they can be used to denote simple attraction, without passion or perturbation of the soul, and such acts are acts of will. And in this sense the words apply to angels and to God.
>
> St Thomas Aquinas, *Summa Theologiae*, 1a.82, 5 ad 1

Classical Christian psychology

Some familiarity with Christian understandings of the soul will be invaluable when it comes to trying to analyse historical transitions of uses and meanings of different psychological terms (such as 'will', 'passions' and 'emotions') in the eighteenth and nineteenth centuries. It is impossible to pin down exactly what 'Christian psychology' is. There have been many different Christian psychologies ranging from biblical views of human minds and bodies to twentieth-century Christianised counselling psychologies. The phrase 'classical Christian psychology' is intended to refer to a core of Christian teaching about the soul that relatively consistently informed Western Christian culture and thought, at least until the nineteenth century. The decisions I have made about what are to count here as 'core' Christian teachings are, of course, by no means intended to be definitive. However, the virtue of providing at least *some* version of mainstream Western Christian thinking as a starting point offsets some of the unfortunate simplifications and generalisations that doing so will involve.

St Augustine of Hippo and St Thomas Aquinas are two pillars of classical Christian psychology, whose theologies of the soul, and of passions and affections in particular, will be examined in this chapter. I hope that these two might (relatively uncontroversially) be considered especially influential and representative exponents of traditional Western Christian thinking. Gardiner *et al.*, in the only general history of theories of emotion, first published in 1937, isolate Augustine and Aquinas as particularly influential contributors to the 'medieval doctrine of the affections'.[1]

These two are also picked out by Susan James, in her study of seventeenth-century theories of the passions, as particularly important figures in the Christian tradition's teachings on the passions:

> On the one hand, Aquinas' immense and continuing influence is partly due to the fact that he embeds the passions in a familiar and orthodox world-view, and explains them as a function of the position of humanity within this all-encompassing scheme. On the other hand, the figure of Augustine towers over philosophers of various denominations. His conceptions of the passions as modifications of a will that may be rightly or wrongly directed remains central to Catholic doctrine... His impact on Luther ensures that this view is taken up within Protestantism, where it is reflected in the emphasis placed by Puritan writers on the need for self-abasement and the constructive role of passions such as self-hatred and despair.[2]

Indeed, Augustine's teachings had a dual influence on Protestant thought, providing warnings against the dangers of the passions (especially lust and anger) and also exhorting the Christian to proper Godly affections of sympathy, compassion, hatred of sin and so on. While Luther and Calvin might be seen to have focussed on Augustine's negative teaching on the passions, Jonathan Edwards was a good example of a Puritan interested in the proper role of the 'religious affections' (see chapter 3). Turning to Aquinas, one influential seventeenth-century writer who appealed to a Thomist theory of the passions was the French painter and art theorist Charles Le Brun, whose theory of the passions would be drawn upon in the following century by the physiognomist Johann Caspar Lavater.[3] In a lecture on expression to the Paris Academy of Painting in 1668, Le Brun defined a passion as 'a movement of the sensitive part of the soul, which is designed to pursue that which the soul thinks to be for its good, or to avoid that which it believes to be hurtful to itself'.[4] As we will see below, this was a faithful rendering of Aquinas' own definition of the passions as movements of the lower part of the soul towards a sense-good or away from a sense-evil.[5]

Augustine's teachings on the passions and affections are to be found in *The City of God*, especially Books IX and XIV, as well as in connection with the narrative of his own struggle with the passions in his *Confessions*, and in several other texts such as *The Free Choice of the Will*, *The Trinity* and the *Expositions on the Book of Psalms*. The principle location for Aquinas'

---

[1] Gardiner *et al.* (1970), 90.   [2] James (1997), 24f.
[3] Hartley (2001), 31.   [4] Quoted in Hartley (2001), 21.
[5] It was not, as Hartley (2001), 21–2 suggests, the same as Descartes' theory, in which the animal spirits acted on the soul to cause the passions.

teaching on this subject is the *Summa Theologiae*, especially 1a.75–83, on 'Man', and 1a.2ae.22–48, on 'The Emotions' (as the Blackfriars translators render *passiones animae*), 'Pleasure' and 'Fear and Anger'.

Biblical approaches to passions and affections were of course central for both these classical Christian theologians. I discuss these below, as well as the specific terms used for passions, lusts and desires in the Greek of the New Testament, and in Latin and English translations. Each also brought the resources of certain classical philosophies to bear on the Christian tradition. So, in understanding Augustine and Aquinas on the passions, we also need to be aware of, for example, Stoic teachings on the passions, 'pre-passions' and the 'inner word', the Neoplatonic preoccupation with distinctions between invisible and visible, constant and changing, and the Aristotelian metaphysics of activity and passivity. Richard Sorabji's recent book on Stoic and early Christian attitudes to *pathē* (a term he translates as 'emotions') is a particularly valuable resource for understanding some of this background.[6]

Aquinas, of course, relied on Augustine as one of his sources, but tended to accord more importance to the substance of Aristotle's metaphysics, especially teachings from the *De Anima*, than to the details of Augustine's writings on passions and affections. (Such was the centrality of Aristotle in the *Summa*, that Aquinas referred to him there simply as *Philosophus*, 'the philosopher'.) As a result, Augustine's influence survived in two forms – his own teachings, and his teachings as 'Aristotelianised' by Aquinas. Aquinas' methodical scholastic analysis of the concepts of passivity and activity, and his systematic classification of the *passiones animae* lacked the personal engagement of Augustine's *Confessions* as well as the rich variety of theological metaphors of the latter's *The Trinity* and *The City of God*. Nonetheless both men were exceptionally influential in constructing the fundamentals of Christian doctrine in general and of the theology of the soul in particular.

Subsequent chapters in this book will trace transitions from Christian to secular psychologies in the eighteenth and nineteenth centuries. This chapter describes the heart of Christian affective psychology, the gradual cultural displacement of which reached its culmination during the nineteenth century. It is, of course, not assumed that nothing happened to Christian psychology between Aquinas and, say, the eighteenth-century psychology of a figure such as Francis Hutcheson.[7] That was certainly not the case.[8] This chapter is intended as a backdrop to the subsequent chapters rather than a continuous chronological prelude to them. Through examining two of the giants of Western Christian theology it is hoped that the central elements that characterised and underpinned

[6] Sorabji (2000).   [7] Hutcheson (1742).   [8] See e.g. Levi (1964); James (1997).

later Christian (and secular) approaches to passions and affections will be better understood.

This chapter will begin with a description of the classical Christian views of the soul found in Augustine and Aquinas. It will become clear that both Augustine and Aquinas believed that the person was a combination of soul and body, although they differed in how exactly they conceived of the relationship of those two elements. Having established exactly which words were used by Augustine and Aquinas in their analysis of the passions and affections – e.g. passions, movements, affects, affections, appetites, perturbations, desires, libido – and what those words might have meant, some of the central motifs of the classical view of passions and affections will be examined.

First, the passions were described frequently by both writers as unruly forces. In this context the need for order and for the exercise of control by reason, will and virtue was emphasised. Secondly, there was a discussion as to which were the proper passions, or more often affects or affections, for a Christian to experience and to aspire to. In general a clear distinction was made by both Augustine and Aquinas between inappropriate passions of the lower appetite directed towards worldly objects and appropriate affections, or movements of the will, directed towards goodness, truth and, ultimately God. Thirdly, passions were seen as symptoms of the fall. They were a sign both of the rebellion of the body against the mind and of the sickness of the fallen soul, a punishment for Adam and Eve's original disobedience to God. Finally, there was the question of the affective life to be expected in the world to come. It was in the world to come that a unified, ordered self, experiencing no passions but only the pure affections of love and joy, could be hoped for.

The soul

Augustine

Augustine separated human beings into the inner and the outer. The inner was superior to the outer. The inner was the intellectual man, who should direct the outer, sensible, organic creature. However, human beings were living in a fallen state, being punished for Adam's original sin of pride; for his placing the pursuit of worldly knowledge over obedience to God. This disobedience was punished with disobedience within our very selves. So all human beings were, for Augustine, houses divided against themselves, in which the inner had to struggle to control the outer. The intellect had to try to marshal the desires of sense and appetite. The outer was also the lower. The sensory man was the lower part, the incorporeal inner man was the higher. That was the true and proper order of things. But in our fallen state – a state that was at the same time sin, trial and punishment – we humans became dis-ordered people. Our familiarity with the world of sense was not a natural state of affairs but a state of sickness.[9] Man's intellect was plagued not only by the disobedience of the body but also by the degeneration, as a consequence of the fall, of the faculties of memory, knowledge and will. In this state of sickness God and the eternal Truth were only obscurely and dimly present to man. Augustine spoke of the 'dense mantle of darkness which I bear for my punishment' in contrast to the light of the presence of God, which Adam and Eve enjoyed before the fall and which the believer could hope for in the hereafter.[10]

There were different aspects of the soul that corresponded to the inner and the outer man, respectively. The inner man was the rational and moral part of a person, their 'soul' in the restricted sense. This uniquely human soul was the seat of reason, which differentiated man from the animals. But Augustine also used the terms 'animal' or 'sensitive' soul and 'nutritive' or 'vegetative' soul to refer to the lower functions of the person – their life, sense perception and animal appetites (e.g. for sex and food). He inherited these categories of nutritive, sensitive and intellectual soul from Aristotle. In this sense, the 'soul' covered all the functions of the person from the organic to the spiritual. However, Augustine also appealed to a more Neoplatonic model that emphasised duality between soul and body, in which 'soul' had a narrower reference.

Augustine was famously set on the track to his conversion to the Christian religion by reading certain 'books of the Platonists'.[11] 'By reading those books of the Platonists, I had been prompted to look for truth as something incorporeal, and *I caught sight of your invisible nature as it is known through your creatures* [Romans 1.20].'[12] These books, commonly supposed to be Neoplatonic works by writers such as Plotinus or Porphyry, opened Augustine's mind to the idea that God and the soul were incorporeal, and that the unchanging (God) was in all ways to be preferred to that which was subject to change. From these books, read in conjunction with the Christian scriptures, Augustine developed his theology.

The distinctions between the invisible and the visible, the incorporeal and the corporeal, and the unchanging Forms and corruptible particulars were central to the writings of the Neoplatonists. Augustine adopted these wholeheartedly. 'I understood with complete certainty that what is subject to decay is inferior to that which is not, and without hesitation I placed that which cannot be harmed above that which can, and I saw that what remains constant is better than that which is changeable.'[13] Indeed, his

---

[9] *Confessions* x; O'Connell (1987), 260. [10] *Confessions* xi.9.
[11] *Confessions* vii.9. [12] *Confessions* vii.20. [13] *Confessions* vii.1.

only real reservation was that these books did not provide a redemptive role for Jesus Christ. It was to the writings of St Paul that Augustine was to turn to supplement Neoplatonism in that regard. There he found the distinction between the works of the flesh and the works of the spirit (Galatians 5) that could to some extent be mapped on to the Neoplatonic distinctions. All of Augustine's work was permeated with the images of the soul journeying inwards and upwards away from the works of the flesh and the earthly city towards the works of the spirit and the City of God: 'I shall not turn aside until you gather all that I am into that holy place of peace, rescuing me from this world where I am dismembered and deformed.'[14] If the inner man was directed upwards towards the immaterial God and the ideal Forms in the mind of that God then he might be saved and might ultimately, to quote from Plato himself, be able to escape 'from this transient world to reality'.[15] This world and his own worldly self were to Augustine not only transient but painful and often hateful. The rational soul was the part created in the image of God, and the part which could strive towards God and hope for the gift of grace and ultimately to be restored in a redeemed likeness of God. This redeemed rational soul would be reunited with an obedient body.[16] Order would ultimately be restored according to Augustine's theological worldview.

The doctrine that in man's soul we find the *imago Dei* (image of God) was a central part of Augustine's theology (see Table 1). It was particularly central to the Trinitarian Christian psychology that he developed in *The Trinity*.[17] Augustine proceeded from the Christian belief that man was created in the image and likeness of God to an investigation of where and what that likeness might be. In both the *De Genesi ad Litteram* and *The Trinity* Augustine started this investigation with an exegesis of Genesis 1.26, 'Then God said, "Let us make man in our image, after our likeness; and let them have dominion over the fish of the sea, and over the birds of the air, and over the cattle, and over all the earth, and over every creeping thing that creeps upon the earth."' Augustine read the doctrine of the *imago Dei* in the light of the second part of this verse and hence argued that the *imago* was situated in that part of the soul that marked man out as superior to the animals, namely the intellectual part of the soul.[18] 'As we climb up inward then through the parts of the soul by certain steps of reflection, we begin to come upon something that is not common to us and the beasts and that is where reason begins, and where we can now recognise the inner man.'[19] Similarly, in the *Confessions*: 'And finally we

---

[14] *Confessions* XII.16. [15] *Republic* 525b. [16] *The Trinity* XIV.23ff.
[17] See especially *The Trinity* IX–XIV. [18] O'Connell (1987), 249. [19] *The Trinity* XII.13.

Table 1 *Summary of Augustine's psychological* imago Dei

God		Imago Dei	
FATHER	Act, Memory	MEMORIA	Act, memory
SON	*Logos*, Reason, Wisdom	SAPIENTIA	Inner word, understanding, wisdom
SPIRIT	Will, Love, Gift	AMOR	Will, love, affections

see man, made in your image and likeness, ruling over all the irrational animals for the very reason that he was made in your image and resembles you, that is, because he has the power of reason and understanding.'[20]

While our animal nature was symbolised by the serpent, harbinger of sensory temptations that may turn us away from God, and our practical reasoning was symbolised by woman, the highest part was associated with man, and with the Word of God, and that part was reason.[21] To quote again from the *Confessions*: 'You made rational action subject to the rule of the intellect, as woman is subject to man.'[22] The same point was made in *The Trinity* XII.3, that man and woman were made one flesh but that woman was subordinate to man in the same way that practical reason was subordinate to contemplative understanding.

Augustine's God was Father, Son and Holy Spirit, three persons in one Godhead. The true image of the Holy Trinity was the mental trinity of memory, understanding and will. This was also expressed as the soul's remembrance, knowledge and love of itself.[23] Augustine ended *The Trinity* with a reminder of the very radical *un*likeness of this trinity to the Holy Trinity, but not before he had tentatively suggested that memory was the image of the Father, self-knowledge the image of the Son, and self-love the image of the Spirit.[24]

The second person of the Holy Trinity was the Word of God, or *logos*. The Word was begotten of the Father but also co-eternal with Him. The Word became incarnate in Jesus Christ. It was specifically the inner word of man, the *imago* of the Word of God, that was central for Augustine. The power of contemplative reason, or *sapientia* (higher wisdom, contrasted with *scientia* – practical, earthly rationality) was crucial for salvation. It was through this reason, or wisdom, that the soul could attain the vision of God, albeit a dim one while on earth, and thus be saved from the sicknesses of concupiscence and cupidity – from the obsession with earthly desires.[25]

---

[20] *Confessions* XIII.32. [21] *The Trinity* XII.
[22] *Confessions* XIII.34. [23] *The Trinity* IX–X. [24] *The Trinity* XV.43.
[25] See e.g. *The Trinity* VIII.3 and *Confessions* VII.17, IX.10, X.40 and XI.9, for accounts of Augustine's own experience of the flashes of insight into the eternal nature of God that are the reward of intellectual contemplation of truth, goodness and beauty.

Having established the tendency to dualistic imagery in Augustine's theology of the soul, in which the incorporeal and rational were superior to the corporeal and irrational aspects of humanity, a *caveat* must be added. Augustine explicitly rejected the doctrine of the Manichees that the flesh was, of its nature, evil. The origin of evil for Augustine was the turning of the will away from God towards human and worldly things.

[I]t was not the corruptible flesh that made the soul sinful; on the contrary, it was the sinful soul that made the flesh corruptible.[26]

The flesh, in its own kind and order, is good. But what is not good is to abandon the goodness of the Creator in pursuit of some created good.[27]

The Devil had no flesh but was nonetheless ruled by the passions of jealousy, enmity and anger. And when St Paul, in his letter to the Galatians, had contrasted the works of the flesh with the works of the spirit, Augustine contended, he meant to contrast human nature (body *and* soul) with the perfection of God, rather than to contrast body with spirit. The anti-Manichean Augustine pointed to the disordered soul, not animal nature or corrupted flesh, as the root of evil passions such as jealousy, anger, envy and licentiousness.[28] They were 'acts of the will'(*voluntates*).[29]

So the contrast between flesh and spirit in Augustine functioned in two ways. First, it was part of a real distinction between man's corporeal animal nature on the one hand, and his incorporeal angelic rationality on the other. The incorporeal part of man undoubtedly had independent existence: 'Mind and spirit, however, are not said relatively but state being. It is not because it is mind and spirit of some man that it is mind and spirit. Take away its being man, which is said with the addition of the body, *take away body therefore, and mind and spirit remain.*'[30] But secondly, and equally importantly, the flesh–spirit contrast was used as a metaphor for the distinction elsewhere expressed as that between the citizen of the earthly city and the citizen of the City of God – a contrast between a well-ordered soul and a disordered one. In this second sense it was a distinction between two sorts of soul, not between soul and body.

In the *De Quantitate Animae* Augustine proposed a hierarchical model of the soul in terms of seven levels or grades of being. The grades started at the bottom with the vegetative and rose to intellectual contemplation of God. In *The Trinity*, further to the inner–outer division, a distinction was made between the inner, intellectual faculties themselves. The highest form of intellect was the contemplation of eternal truths and ultimately

---

[26] *City of God* xiv.3.   [27] *City of God* xiv.5.   [28] *City of God* xiv.2.
[29] *City of God* xiv.6.   [30] *The Trinity* ix.2, emphasis added.

Table 2 *Augustine's model of the soul*[31]

			GOD		
			Angels		
Human, intellective soul	**RATIONAL** (Inner man)	**INTELLECT** (*sapientia*, Man, Adam)	7 6	Vision of God as the highest truth Desire to know the highest truths	*SUCCESS* *STRUGGLE*
		WILL and **MORALITY** (*scientia*, Woman, Eve)	5 4 3	Purification of the soul Ethical evaluations; turn from the world Discursive reason – aesthetic, social, political judgments	*SUCCESS* *STRUGGLE*
Animal, sensitive soul (serpent) **Vegetative** soul	**IRRATIONAL** (Outer man)		2 1	Restricted to animals and man – sense perception, appetite Life-giving principle	
			WORLD		

[31] Based on *The Trinity* XII; *Confessions* XIII; O'Daly (1987), 13f; Brett (1921), I, ch. 10; E. Hill 'Foreword' to Augustine (1991), IX–XIV.

the vision of God Himself. This was termed *sapientia*.[32] The lower form of reason – practical or action-guiding reason – was called *scientia* (Table 2).

Aquinas

The model of the soul described by Aquinas (Table 3) shared many important features with that developed by Augustine nearly nine hundred years earlier.[33] This was not surprising, of course, given that both relied upon the Bible and upon ancient Greek philosophy to a considerable extent. Furthermore, Augustine was one of the principal Patristic writers to whom Aquinas appealed as an authority. Both placed human beings between animals and angels on the scale of being. Both used Aristotle's distinctions between the vegetative, animal and intellectual aspects of the soul. Both differentiated between rational intellect and will on the one hand and irrational lower appetites on the other, giving priority to the rational over the irrational, and priority ultimately to intellect over will. Aquinas hesitated on this last point, arguing that which is higher of intellect (or understanding) and will (or love) depended on the nature of the objects by which they were exercised:

So love of God is better than knowledge of God. On the other hand, knowledge of physical things is better than love of them. But simply speaking understanding is nobler than willing.[34]
There is no infinite regress, for understanding has an absolute primacy. For an act of knowledge must precede every movement of the will, but there does not have to be an act of will prior to every act of knowledge.[35]

Both also categorised the faculties of the soul in terms of struggle and success, motion and rest, the latter of each pair being the ultimate goal of the self.

In the discussion of motion and rest, Aristotelian metaphysics played a constitutive role for Aquinas. It was Aristotle's description of God as an unmoved mover, the active first cause of all motion but unsusceptible to motion Himself, that determined for Aquinas the ontological priority of rest over motion. In his discussion of the faculties of the soul, Aquinas used this priority to bolster the superiority of cognition over will, the 'higher appetite':[36] 'For the activity of a cognitive power is fulfilled when the things apprehended are in the knower, whereas the activity of an appetitive power is fulfilled when the lover is drawn by what is loved. And so cognitive activity resembles rest, whereas the activity of an appetitive

---

[32] *The Trinity* XII.21–5, XIV.1–5.
[33] For a useful basic introduction to Aquinas' model of the soul, and references to further secondary literature, see Cross (1998).
[34] *Summa Theologiae* Ia.82, 3 (henceforth *ST*).   [35] *ST* Ia.82, 3.   [36] *ST* Ia.81, 3.

power resembles movement.'[37] Both intellect (*intellectus*) and will (*voluntas* or *appetitus intellectivus*) were placed above the lower appetite (*appetitus sensitivus*) in Aquinas' hierarchy. This lower appetite was further divided in terms of motion and rest. The lower appetite could be moved by various passions, some were 'irascible' (*irascibilis*), others 'concupiscible' (*concupiscibilis*). The irascible passions (hope, despair, fear, courage, anger) were movements of the lower appetite towards a sense-good (a desirable object of sense) that was hard to attain or away from a sense-evil (an undesirable object of sense) that was hard to avoid. The concupiscible passions (love, hate, desire, aversion, pleasure, sadness) were less movements and more states of potential movement, or of affinity, towards sense-goods or away from sense-evils.[38] In the same way that an earthly object, in the Aristotelian scheme of elements, could be at rest while still having a natural tendency to fall to earth, so a soul could be in a state of rest but still be subject to the tendency to move towards certain sense-objects. Aquinas' classification of the passions will be returned to below.

Another important and related Aristotelian distinction was between passivity and activity. At either end of the Aristotelian scale of being were the absolutes of each. At the top, God was pure activity and, at the bottom of the hierarchy, 'prime matter' was pure passivity. Prime matter was formless – unlike all other kinds of matter. Aquinas did not accept that prime matter existed but treated it merely as the hypothetical absence of all activity. He did, however, largely agree with Aristotle's identification of pure activity with the divine. Specifically, the Christian God now took on this position at the top of the scale of being, being the goal, or final cause of all creation, as well as being eternal, unchanging, and thus pure activity.[39] Human beings fell between the two extremes of pure passivity and pure activity. Broadly speaking the intellective soul was active, in comparison with the more passive sensitive soul. The former was, of course, the seat of the will, the determinant of human action, while the latter was the seat of the senses – faculties that were passively acted upon by external objects. However, the intellective soul was also passive in the sense that, unlike God, its potential for understanding was not always actualised. This passive or 'potential intellect' could be actualised by the active 'agent intellect', which was capable of deriving knowledge of universals (or forms) from the particular external objects perceived by the sensitive soul.[40] In short, the human being was a complex combination of active and passive powers whose final goal was rest in the eternal unmoved activity of God.

[37] *ST* Ia.81, 1. [38] *ST* Ia.2ae.23.
[39] *ST* Ia.75.6; 79.2; James (1997), 48–52. [40] *ST* Ia.79; James (1997), 60f.

Table 3 *Aquinas' model of the soul*[41]

		GOD		
		Angels		
Human, intellective soul	**REASON** and **HIGHER APPETITE**	Understanding	REST	**Universal Objects** e.g. goodness, virtue, truth
		Will (rational)	MOTION	
Animal, sensitive soul	**LOWER APPETITE**	Desire (irrational) *Concupiscible*	REST	**Particular Objects** in world of sense
		Irascible	MOTION	
Vegetative, nutritive soul	Organic functions			
		Inanimate matter		
		Prime matter		

[41] Based on *ST*, esp. 1a.75–80; Kenny (1993).

A significant philosophical departure in Aquinas from Augustine's teaching on the soul – his new approach to the relationship of soul and body – was also based on an Aristotelian doctrine. Aquinas adopted the Aristotelian terminology of matter and form to articulate Christian notions of the differences between body and soul. The form was that which actualised matter – that which determined what sort of object the matter instantiated. Put another way, the form was the set of properties of a particular body. In the case of the human being the body was the matter and the soul was the form. If this doctrine had been applied strictly it would have meant that the soul, the functions and properties of the body, could not exist without the body any more than the living body could exist without the soul (it would then have been reduced to 'prime matter'). On this strict interpretation the soul was incorporeal in that it was a set of properties (such as temperature, shape, movement) rather than a physical thing. 'But if it is only in this sense that a soul is non-bodily', Kenny rightly observes, 'then Aquinas' psychology need not differ from a thoroughgoing materialism.'[42] Indeed, it was the radical materialist interpretation of Aristotle – that form and matter could never exist independently – that aroused such hostility to Aristotelian philosophy amongst Aquinas' contemporaries in thirteenth-century Paris.[43] So Aquinas had to adapt these ideas in a way that confirmed rather than contradicted Christian doctrine. This he did by distinguishing the form of human beings – the rational soul – from other forms. The rational soul, he said, unlike all other forms, was 'subsistent'. That is to say that it existed in and of itself rather than merely as the set of properties of a particular body or object. And since the intellective soul had its own activity, in which the body took no intrinsic part, then, 'the human soul, which is called an intellect or mind, is something incorporeal and subsisting'.[44] So Aquinas steered a middle path between a Platonic belief in the natural immortality of the soul and a radical Aristotelian commitment to the impossibility of a disembodied form (or soul). The resulting doctrine was that the human soul was granted subsistence and immortality through the grace of the Christian God.[45]

This belief in the subsistence of the intellective soul (the soul in the narrow sense) committed Aquinas to the belief that the soul, while not a full person, could and did exist in a disembodied state in the period between

---

[42] Kenny (1993), 131.
[43] Bishop Etienne Tempier condemned Aristotelian philosophy in the 1270s in response to the Averroist teachings of materialists such as Siger of Brabant and Boethius of Dacia. See Lindberg (1992), 234–40, 282–4.
[44] *ST* Ia.75, 2.
[45] *ST* Ia.75.2; 75.6; *Summa Contra Gentiles* 81.6; Kenny (1993), 131ff.

an individual's death and the general resurrection.[46] Like Augustine he was uncompromising on the independent existence of man's incorporeal part: 'the human soul continues in its act of being when the body is destroyed, whereas other souls do not'.[47] Furthermore, he justified the distinction between the intellective human soul and other forms on the grounds that understanding could take place without the involvement of any physical organ.[48] There were substantial as well as metaphorical divisions between soul and body in both Augustine and Aquinas. These divisions were exploited in various ways in classical Christian views of the passions and affections.

Terminology and classification

One of the most important terms in New Testament discussions of passions, desires and affections (in addition to *pathē* or 'passions') was *epithumiai* (translated as *concupiscentiae* or *desideria* in the Vulgate, as 'lusts' in the King James Version, and as 'sinful desires', 'evil desires' or 'passions' in the Revised Standard Version).[49] *Epithumiai* was a classical term used by Plato to refer to instincts, appetites and passions, which took on a new connotation of sinfulness in New Testament usage. Another important concept in the New Testament was the importance of the things of the heart; these included both clean and unclean thoughts and desires – a man could commit adultery in his heart but should seek a pure heart. It is notable, then, that the New Testament picture lacks a strong contrast between the 'head' and the 'heart'. The Christian idea of the 'affections' (which can be both voluntary and virtuous, unlike the passions) could be summarised as being a recommendation of the cultivation of certain 'thoughts of the heart'.

One word that was *not* used in the classical Christian account of passions and affections was 'emotions'. There was no such term in classical Latin or Greek, nor in the Bible (nor, incidentally, do the words 'emotion' or 'emotions' appear in any of the major English translations of the Bible). The closest classical term to 'emotion' etymologically was the Latin *motus*, which just meant 'movement', but was sometimes used more specifically to refer to movements of the soul (see below). The basic category in early Christian affective psychology, as in classical thought, was denoted by the Latin term *passiones* (or, more fully, *passiones animae*), which in turn was a Latinisation of the Greek *pathē*. Many writers have persisted, nonetheless, in referring to the view of 'emotions' held by

---

[46] *Summa Contra Gentiles* 91.6f. [47] *ST* 1a.76, 1. [48] *ST* 1a.75, 3.
[49] E.g. Mark 4.19; Romans 1.24, 6.12, 13.14; Galatians 5.16–24; Titus 2.12, 3.3.

ancient, medieval or early-modern thinkers who wrote about *pathē*, *passiones animae*, or 'passions'.[50] Walsh and Monahan, at various points in their translation of Augustine's *City of God*, render *motus*, *affectus* and *passiones* all as 'emotions'.[51] Eric D'Arcy also unfortunately chooses to render *passiones animae* as 'emotions' in his translation of Aquinas' *Summa Theologiae* Ia.2ae, 22–30. However, strictly speaking, there were no ancient or medieval theories of 'emotions'. In this section I will briefly survey the terms and classifications used by Augustine and Aquinas and will finally focus especially on the distinction between voluntary movements or affections on the one hand and unruly passions on the other.

For the generality of affective phenomena Augustine relied on two phrases – *motus animae* (or 'movements of the soul') and *passiones animae*. One crucial passage in Augustine in which terminology is discussed is *City of God* IX.4. Here he commented that various Latin phrases had been used for what he called the *motus animae* – the movements of the soul. They were all translations of the Greek word *pathē* – Cicero used *perturbationes animae* (perturbations or disturbances), others used *affectus* (affects) or *affectiones* (affections), and those who wished to stick close to the original Greek expression used *passiones* (passions). Augustine himself opted for *passiones* as the best general term.

He adopted what he called the 'well-known' classification of the passions, that of Cicero, which identified four basic perturbations of the soul – desire (*cupiditas*), fear (*timor*), joy (*laetitia*) and sorrow (*tristitia*).[52] But he went further, uniting all four under the single principle of love (*amor*). A right will (*voluntas recta*) or a good love (*bonus amor*) would issue forth in appropriate affections, but a wrong will (*voluntas perversa*) or a bad love (*malus amor*) would produce sinful affections.[53] Susan James has noted that this Augustinian unification of the passions and affections under the single principle of love would later be revived by several seventeenth-century writers.[54]

The Stoic theory that the philosopher, or wise man, was not subject to passions was rejected by Augustine. He refused to believe that a Stoic on a storm-tossed ship (a rich image, itself often used as a metaphor for the passion-tossed soul) would not fear for his life 'with the same trembling and pallor as a Peripatetic'.[55] Augustine poured scorn on the Stoic aspiration to attain *apatheia*, or complete impassivity, in this life.

---

[50] This is sometimes done knowingly and with some discussion of why alternative translations, such as 'passions', were rejected. See, for instance, Sorabji (2000), 7, 17; Sihvola and Engberg-Pedersen (eds.) (1998), VIII, 71, 198; Annas (1992), 103n.
[51] E.g. *City of God* IX.4, XIV.9.   [52] *City of God* XIV.3.
[53] *City of God* XIV.7.   [54] James (1997), 6.
[55] *City of God* IX.4. For a history of the use of the ship metaphor see Grange (1962).

Even if *apatheia* is merely a state in which one neither trembles from fear nor suffers from sorrow, it is still a state to guard against in this life if we want to live as human beings should, in the sense of living according to God's will... And as for those few who, with a vanity which is even more frightful than it is infrequent, pride themselves on being neither raised nor roused nor bent nor bowed by any emotion (*affectus*) whatsoever – well, they have rather lost all humanity than won true peace.[56]

This forceful rejection of Stoic impassivity should be sufficient to illustrate that Augustine did not wish to exclude passions and affections altogether.[57] It is worth noting, however, that the term he used here for proper affect is *affectus* rather than *passiones*.

However, this provisionally positive stance on the necessity of human affections in this life was combined with a more negative attitude to the passions in Augustine's other works. The passions were seen primarily as disturbances to be quashed by the controlling forces of reason and virtue, as inappropriate desires (*cupiditas, libido, concupiscentia*) and lusts after sex and tangible goods, as diseases (*morbi*) of the soul marked by the rebellion of corruptible flesh, and as, at best, appropriate to this probationary earthly state but ultimately to be shed in the future life.[58] All these ways of treating the affections and passions will be examined further below.

Aquinas provided a more complex classification of the passions than the simple four-fold scheme adopted by Augustine. There were three elements of Aquinas' thought on the passions that will be briefly considered here – its dependence on the Aristotelian notion of passivity, its elaboration of the distinction between the irascible and concupiscible appetites and its extensive use of the model of physical movement.[59] Passion (*passio*) was a well-established philosophical category, and an important one in Aristotelian thought in particular. In fact it was the tenth of Aristotle's *kategoriai*, or 'categories', of types of thing that may be predicated of an object.[60] So Aquinas' passions (*passiones animae*) were conceived, at one level, simply as special cases of the fundamental state of being acted upon (*passio*).[61] This is significant since this category

[56] *City of God* XIV.9.
[57] What the Stoic idealisation of *apatheia* was and was not actually intended to exclude is discussed by Sorabji (2000).
[58] On Augustine's various terms for desires and their significance in his theology of the soul see Innes (1997), 75–9.
[59] On Hobbes' subsequent rejection of this scholastic appeal to 'metaphysical motion', see James (1997), 126ff.
[60] Augustine, in contrast to Aquinas, explicitly rejects these Aristotelian categories as misleadingly simplistic and reductionist; *Confessions* IV.16.
[61] James (1997), chs. 2–3, provides an excellent philosophical exposition of the significance of *actio* and *passio* in Aristotle and Aquinas.

of passion was essentially a negative one. As we have seen above, it was a quality from which the divine was absolutely excluded, and which was characteristic of incompletion and imperfection. Passion, for Aquinas, implied imperfection.

> Now passion or passivity implies by its very nature some sort of deficiency; a thing is passive in so far as it is in potentiality to being actualised and thus improved. Those creatures that come nearest to God, the first and completely perfect being, have little of potentiality and passivity in them; others, of course, have more. Accordingly one will find less of passivity, and so less of passion and the emotions (*passiones*), in the cognitive faculties, since they are the more primary powers of the soul.[62]

So, while taking a different, Aristotelian basis for his definition of the passions, Aquinas came to endorse a theory of the passions that was similar to Augustine's, and equally negative. For both these theologians the passions were signs of deficiency and imperfection, and were contrasted unfavourably with the cognitive powers of the soul.

A second innovation in Aquinas' treatment of the passions was his introduction of the distinction between the concupiscible and irascible appetites to Christian psychology. Aquinas took this distinction from William of Moerbeke's translation of Aristotle's *De Anima*. This was a way of distinguishing between two powers of the lower, sensory appetite.[63] The way that Aquinas made the distinction, as we have outlined above, was that the concupiscible appetite was moved by sense-goods or sense-evils per se, while the irascible was moved by the same objects if and when they were difficult to attain or avoid, when they were 'arduous'. Aquinas used this distinction to differentiate between the passions. He posited a total of eleven passions, six of the concupiscible appetite and five of the irascible appetite. The odd number was as a consequence of his notion that anger (*ira*) was the only passion with no contrary (since not being angry is not a passion). The concupiscible passions displayed elements both of rest and of movement. They were experienced as affinity (love and hate), attraction or repulsion to an object (desire and aversion), and if and when the object was attained or finally lost, fulfilled joy or sorrow. The irascible passions were more restricted, displaying only movement and struggle – hope, despair, courage, fear and anger.[64] This categorisation was a dynamic one in which Aquinas imagined a process that involved potentially six stages, starting with an affinity and then a desire, followed by the irascible process of struggle for or against an object, ending with joy

---

[62] *ST* Ia.2ae.22, 2.
[63] Eric D'Arcy, 'Introduction' to *ST* Ia.2ae.22–30, xxv.   [64] *ST* Ia.2ae.25, 1.

or sorrow, depending upon the outcome of that struggle. The concupiscible passions provided both the origin and the terminus of this affective process.

Aquinas further categorised the passions in a two-fold distinction between present-related passions (love, hatred, courage, anger, joy and sorrow) and future-related passions (desire, aversion, hope, despair and fear). He also adopted the same idea of the four 'principal passions' as used by Cicero and Augustine, although he used different words from Augustine for two of them. Instead of desire (*cupiditas*), fear (*timor*), joy (*laetitia*) and sorrow (*tristitia*), Aquinas called the four principal passions hope (*spes*), fear (*timor*), joy (*gaudium*) and sorrow (*tristitia*). Aquinas argued, however, that desire and hope are interchangeable since they both have some future good as their object.[65] The fact that Aquinas used at least three different methods of classification (see Table 4), which stood in an ambiguous relationship with the traditional philosophical and theological schemes on which he drew, is typical of classifications of passions, affections and emotions throughout history. There has rarely been any consensus on the number of passions or of emotions that exist, nor on which of them are 'basic' or 'principal', nor on the way that they should be classified. This lack of consensus and the confusion that seemingly arbitrary differences between individual competing classifications has engendered is one of the invariant features of the history of theories of passions, affections, sentiments and emotions.

The third aspect of Aquinas' theory of the passions that merits brief comment is his extensive use of models of physical movement. One of the principal ways in which Aquinas defined the passions was as movements (*motus*) of the lower appetite. This metaphor derived from the idea in Aristotelian physics that each sort of object had a natural tendency to move in a certain direction. While we would ascribe the falling of objects to earth to 'gravity', the Aristotelian would have ascribed it to the natural tendency of earthly objects to fall, or their 'natural love'. (It is from this Aristotelian metaphysics that we inherit the expression that it is love – in other words, natural motive tendency – that makes the world go round.) This was extended to the passions, which were seen as expressions of the natural tendency of the lower appetite (or sensory love) to move towards sense-goods and away from sense-evils, and of the higher appetite (or rational love) to move towards or away from intellectual goods or

---

[65] *ST* Ia.2ae.25, 4.

Table 4 *Aquinas' classifications of the passions*[66]

	PASSIONES ANIMAE	
	Concupiscibilis Relate to things as good or evil in themselves	**Irascibilis** Relate to 'arduous' goods or evils – hard to attain or avoid
TIME ↓	1 Love (*amor*) Hatred (*odium*) 2 *Desire (desiderium)* *Aversion (fuga)* 3 4 5 6 **Joy** (*gaudium*) **Sorrow** (*tristitia*)	 **Hope** (*spes*) *Despair (desperatio)* Courage (*audacia*) **Fear** (*timor*) Anger (*ira*)

in bold = one of the 'principal passions'
underlined = present-related
italic = future related

[66] Based on *ST* 1a.2ae.23; see also Cross (1998), 313–15.

evils.⁶⁷ In this way Aquinas was again adapting Augustinian thinking to Aristotelian metaphysics.⁶⁸ Augustine's statement that all forms of passion were ultimately expressions of love was rephrased by Aquinas as the statement that all forms of passion were forms of love, which is in turn a form of motion towards or away from some object: 'There is none of the other emotions (*passiones*) which does not presuppose love of some kind. For every other emotion (*passio*) involves movement (*motus*) towards, or repose in some object. Now all movement (*motus*) or repose arises from a sense of affinity with, or attachment to some object; and it is precisely in this that love consists.'⁶⁹ It is tempting to see in such uses of *motus* by Augustine and Aquinas an etymological precursor of the term 'emotions', which is clearly a cognate term. However, as will emerge in later chapters, the senses of 'emotion' that were most significant in the eighteenth- and nineteenth-century psychological adoption of the term were a general sort of bodily, or mental, or even social, agitation or disturbance, rather than simple motion towards or away from certain objects.⁷⁰

We come finally in this section to the central distinction between affections and passions, a classical Christian distinction that was repeated, in various forms, at least until the eighteenth century. It was still prominent, for example in Francis Hutcheson's *Essay on the Nature and Conduct of the Passions and Affections* (1728) and in Jonathan Edwards' *Treatise Concerning Religious Affections* (1746) (see chapter 3). To return to the crucial passage in Book IX of Augustine's *City of God*, we have seen that he considered various renditions of the Greek *pathē* – it was rendered as *perturbationes* by Cicero, as *affectiones* or *affectus* by other Latin writers, and as *passiones* by others who preferred to stick more closely to the Greek, including Augustine himself.⁷¹ Aquinas picked up on this section at the beginning of his treatment of the *passiones animae* and interpreted it as meaning that *passiones animae* were identical to *perturbationes*, *affectus* and *affectiones*.⁷² That interpretation of synonymy continued to be popular with some for many centuries after Aquinas.⁷³ However, it is not an interpretation that is consistent with a fuller reading of Augustine on the passions and affections, nor is it consistent with Aquinas' own writings. The following passage from the section of the *Summa Theologiae* on the will is particularly important:

---

⁶⁷ *ST* Ia.2ae.26, 1.
⁶⁸ *ST* Ia.2ae.22, 1; 23, 2: Aquinas quotes Aristotle as the source of the statement that passion is a kind of movement.
⁶⁹ *ST* Ia.2ae.27, 4.
⁷⁰ On earlier meanings of 'emotion', see the *Oxford English Dictionary*, and Ruckmick (1929), 254–5.
⁷¹ *City of God* IX.4.   ⁷² *ST* Ia.2ae.22, 2.   ⁷³ James (1997), 11.

The words 'love', 'desire' and so on are used in two senses. Sometimes they mean passions (*passiones*), with some arousal in the soul. This is what the words are generally taken to mean, and such passions exist solely at the level of sense appetite. But they can be used to denote simple attraction (*affectus*), without passion (*passio*) or perturbation (*concitatio*) of the soul, and such acts are acts of will (*actus voluntatis*). And in this sense the words apply to angels and to God.[74]

In this way Aquinas differentiated between involuntary passions of the soul, which were disturbances of the sensory appetite and had objects of sense for their objects, and *affectus*, or 'affect', which was a voluntary act 'without passion'. At the level of the sensory appetite, there were various passions, characterised as movements towards or away from objects of sense. At the level of the intellectual appetite – used as a synonym for 'will' – there was 'simple' affect, which was not differentiated into various passions, but had good per se as its object. Elsewhere Aquinas made the same distinction in terms of the difference, which he criticised the Stoics for failing to make, between movements of the will (*motus voluntatis*), which belonged to the intellectual appetite (*appetitus intellectivus*), and passions of the soul (*passiones animae*), which belonged to the sensory appetite (*appetitus sensitivus*).[75] In the section of the *Summa* on 'Man', Aquinas stated that, 'what intelligence grasps is of a different class from what sense grasps'.[76] It was this difference that underpinned the distinction between affect, which had intellectual objects such as knowledge, virtue and truth,[77] and passions, whose objects were particular things grasped by the senses. Clearly the voluntary and active affect, or movement of the will, was superior in this Aristotelian–Christian scheme to the involuntary and passive passions of the soul. Aristotle was cited by Aquinas to the effect that the intellectual appetite was the higher appetite, controlling the lower sensory appetite.[78] In short, Aquinas' 'affect' was comparable to Augustine's 'affections' – both were, unlike passions, voluntary (movements of the will), active and ascribable to the angels and to God.

It was in Book XIV of the *City of God*, that Augustine developed his idea of the voluntary affections of the soul, which contrasted with his negative view of the involuntary passions:

---

[74] *ST* Ia.82, 5, ad 1. See also *ST* Ia.2ae.22, 3, where the same point is made.
[75] *ST* Ia.2ae.24, 3; see also *ST* Ia.2ae.26, 2, where Aquinas contrasts sensory love (*amor sensitivus*) and intellectual or rational love (*amor intellectivus seu rationalis*), the former relating to objects of sense, e.g. food, the latter to some good felt intellectually, with the will, e.g. love of wisdom or truth. See Kenny (1993), 61–5, for a discussion of the problems connected to the distinction between the intellectual appetite and the sensory appetite.
[76] *ST* Ia.80, 2. [77] *ST* Ia.80, 2. [78] *ST* Ia.80, 2; *ST* Ia.81, 3.

Man's will, then, is all-important. If it is badly directed, the emotions (*motus*) will be perverse; if it is rightly directed, the emotions (*motus*) will be not merely blameless but even praiseworthy. The will is in all of these affections (*motus*); indeed they are nothing else but inclinations of the will (*voluntates*). For what are desire and joy but the will in harmony with things we desire? And what are fear and sadness but the will in disagreement with things we abhor?[79]

Walsh and Monahan's translation is again somewhat misleading. *Motus* is translated both as 'emotions' and as 'affections' in the space of two sentences, where 'movements of the soul' or 'movements of the will' would convey the sense more accurately in both cases. The single word *voluntates*, is rendered as 'inclinations of the will'. However, the rather specific image of 'inclination' is not to be found in the original. *Voluntates* would be better translated, as it is by Phillip Levine, in the *Loeb Classical Library* edition, simply as 'acts of will'.[80] Augustine, like Aquinas, made a basic distinction between movements of the will and passions of the lower part of the soul. The identification of these movements of the will with affections rather than passions is supported by the conclusion of the paragraph just quoted: 'Thus, according as the will of a man is attracted or repelled by the variety of things which he either seeks or shuns, so it is changed or converted into one or other of these different emotions (*affectus*).'[81]

The contrast between rational virtuous affections and vicious passions was made explicitly a few chapters later in the same book XIV of the *City of God*. Here Augustine was criticising the Stoic idea that all passions and affections, no matter what their nature, were to be considered vices.

If these emotions (*motus*) and affections (*affectus*) which spring from a love of what is good and from holy charity are to be called vices, then all I can say is that real vices should be called virtues. However, the fact is that when such affections (*affectiones*) are directed to their proper objects, they follow right reason, and no one should dare to describe them as diseases (*morbos*) or vicious passions (*passiones*).[82]

Aquinas supported the same distinction when attacking the same Stoic view – that all passions were evil.

The Stoics made no distinction between sense and intellect, and hence between the sensory orexis (*appetitus sensitivus*) and the intellectual (*appetitus intellectivus*). Accordingly they made no distinction between the emotions (*passiones animae*) and movements of the will (*motus voluntatis*), since the emotions (*passiones animae*) belong to the sensory orexis (*appetitus sensitivus*), and simple movements of the will (*motus voluntatis*) to the intellectual orexis (*appetitus intellectivus*).[83]

---

[79] *City of God* XIV.6. [80] Augustine (1966), IV, 285. [81] *City of God* XIV.6.
[82] *City of God* XIV.9. [83] *ST* Ia.2ae.24, 2.

Table 5 *Terms used by Augustine and Aquinas to contrast affections with passions*

	AUGUSTINE		AQUINAS	
	TERMS USED	PART OF SOUL AFFECTED	TERMS USED	PART OF SOUL AFFECTED
AFFECTIONS	*Motus* *Affectus* *Affectiones* *Voluntates*	*Voluntas*	*Motus voluntatis* *Actus voluntatis* *Affectus*	*Voluntas* *Appetitus Intellectivus*
PASSIONS	*Passiones* *Perturbationes* *Libidines* *Morbos*	*Appetitus*	*Passiones animae* *Concationes* *Morbos*	*Appetitus sentitivus*

In conclusion, it seems reasonable, on the basis of these texts, to identify *motus* with *affectus* in Augustine and Aquinas (and with *affectiones*, which seems to be a genuine synonym for *affectus*).[84] These terms, which can both be rendered as 'affections', referred to acts of will, both in Augustine and Aquinas, and are to be contrasted with *passiones*, which for both writers were not active movements of the will but passive movements of the lower, sensory appetite (see Table 5). It is worth emphasising that it was *not* the case that all affections were good and all passions bad. A bad will produced sinful affections, just as a will directed towards God produced virtuous ones. Passions, in turn, did not need to have to be sinful, as long as they were under the control of reason (see below). However, there was rarely any reference to a positively virtuous passion.

In summary, the suggestion, in *City of God* IX.4, that *passiones* was synonymous with *motus*, *affectus* and *affectiones* does not do justice to the distinctions between passions and affections that were made by both Augustine and Aquinas. Having outlined these two 'classical Christian' models of the soul, and specifically of the passions and affections of the soul, we can move on to consider some of the theological concepts and images that these basic tools were used to construct.

Hierarchies of control

Reason, sex and violence

The need for one part of the soul to dominate over the others is a major theme in both Augustine and Aquinas. In the case of the former,

[84] *Affectus* and *affectiones* are used interchangeably in e.g. *Confessions* IV.6.

his *Confessions* revealed time and again what a passionate man he was, susceptible to lower desires and sexual passions as well as to deep spiritual affections. He clearly experienced these feelings as troublesome and as occasions for sin. He was troubled, for example, by the theologically incorrect grief he felt for the death of his mother, despite his assurance that she was saved in Christ.

> I blamed myself for my tender feelings (*affectus*). I fought against the wave of sorrow and for a while it receded, but then it swept upon me again with full force. It did not bring me to tears and no sign of it showed in my face, but I knew well enough what I was stifling in my heart. It was misery to feel myself so weak a victim of these human emotions,[85] although we cannot escape them, since they are the natural lot of mankind, and so I had the added sorrow of being grieved by my own feelings, so that I was tormented by a twofold agony.[86]

He had earlier experienced immense personal pain at the death of a close friend. The grief was so great that he was 'sick and tired of living and yet afraid to die'.[87] He also recounted in his *Confessions* tales of passions experienced in his search for sexual pleasure, and the pain that separation from his mistress of eleven years caused him. 'The woman with whom I had been living was torn from my side as an obstacle to my marriage and this was a blow which crushed my heart to bleeding, because I loved her dearly.'[88] The *Confessions* leave us in no doubt that Augustine was a very passionate man, but further that he saw his passions and affections as troubling signs of weakness and of a lack of the order and control to which he aspired. This face of Augustine regretted affect as part of the 'natural lot' of humanity, a consequence of the fall.[89] In *The Free Choice of the Will* he provided a vivid picture of this human lot – the state of sickness in which the rational mind was besieged by evil passions:

> Passion (*libido*) lords it over the mind, dragging it about, poor and needy, in different directions, stripped of its wealth and virtue... And all the while, the cruel tyranny of evil desire holds sway, disrupting the entire soul and life of man by various and conflicting surges of passion (*libido*); here by fear, there by anxiety; here by anxiety, there by empty and spurious delights; here by torment over the loss of a loved object, there by a burning desire to acquire something not possessed... On every possible side the mind is shrivelled up by greed, wasted away by sensuality, a slave to ambition, is inflated by pride, tortured by envy, deadened by sloth, kept in turmoil by obstinacy, and distressed by its condition of subjection. And so with other countless impulses that surround and plague the rule of passion.[90]

---

[85] There is no 'emotions' word in the Latin here, but Pine-Coffin chooses 'emotions' to translate '*quia humana*', 'these human things', which refers to the sorrow and tears of the previous sentence.
[86] *Confessions* IX.12.   [87] *Confessions* IV.6.   [88] *Confessions* VI.15.
[89] *City of God* XIV.3.   [90] *The Free Choice of the Will*, pp. 93f.

If such passions and lusts were the symptoms of a diseased soul, then the cure was a restoration of order through the rule of will and wisdom.

For Augustine passions and affections, like the flesh, were not evil in themselves, but only when they failed to be controlled – when they failed to take their proper place in the order of things. Specifically, *reason* was the human principle that was properly in command of the passions. In the well-ordered soul, reason was the guiding principle. 'Even though passions (*perturbationes*) may disturb the inferior part of the soul, a mind thus firmly convinced never permits passion to prevail over rational resolve. On the contrary, the mind is the master and, by refusing consent and by proper resistance it maintains the sovereignty of virtue.'[91] So passions were experienced as unruly natural forces of the lower appetite – part of man's natural lot – that arose independently of the rational will. It was for the mind (the rational part of the soul comprising will and reason) to 'master' these rebels, overcome these tyrants, to muster 'resistance', and protect the 'sovereignty' of virtue and reason.[92] These political and military metaphors were common in classical Christian views of the passions. Augustine explained that the doctrine contained in sacred Scripture was clear, it was that 'the mind is subject to God, to be ruled and aided, while the passions (*passiones*) are subject to the mind to be tempered, tamed and turned to the uses of righteousness'.[93] Note that in both these quotations it was the passions (*perturbationes*, *passiones*) rather than affections that were in need of control. The metaphors of tempering and taming were now added – the passions, in addition to being conceived as rebels, tyrants or enemies, were also like recalcitrant matter or like wild animals.

Of course Augustine was agreeing with the Stoics to some extent in seeing a need to overcome the passions through sound reasoning. However, in addition to rejecting the idea that complete *apatheia* was a goal to be striven for in this world, Augustine also modified the Stoic account of the relationships between passions, reason and the will.[94] Stoic philosophers including Chrysippus and Seneca, had seen passions (*pathē*) as judgments – principally mistaken value judgments about what goals were desirable. The passions on this view were both cognitive and voluntary – they were the result of voluntarily assenting to certain propositions. For Augustine the most troubling passions, lusts, desires and appetites were involuntary movements of the lower parts of the soul, rather than

---

[91] *City of God* IX.4.
[92] Augustine refers to passions as 'rebelling against good thoughts', *Sermons on the Liturgical Season, Easter Season*, Sermon 254.
[93] *City of God* IX.5.   [94] Sorabji (2000), Introduction, chs. 2, 24 and 26.

voluntary judgments.⁹⁵ The Stoic sage overcame the passions by a process that Sorabji compares to modern 'cognitive therapy', namely by realigning his defective beliefs in such a way that acknowledged that real value was only to be found in the development of rationality and virtuous character.⁹⁶ For Augustine the way to overcome the passions was, as we have seen, for reason and the will to struggle with, temper and tame them. Since Augustine saw the passions as involuntary disobedient uprisings of the lower parts of the soul, rather than as defective judgments, the proposed therapy was coercive rather than persuasive.

Two sorts of passion were particularly concerning to Augustine – lust and anger (sex and violence). Indeed in later use, in the seventeenth to nineteenth centuries, and possibly still today, 'passion' has been especially associated with sex and anger. The *Confessions* reveals that sex was Augustine's own demon, and it seems likely that his own desire to control such passions was a significant factor shaping his affective theology. It was particularly disturbing to him that sexual passion, specifically sexual arousal, was not subject to the control of the will: 'lust is a usurper, defying the power of the will and playing the tyrant with man's sexual organs'.⁹⁷ He imagined that Adam would have enjoyed full voluntary control of his genital organs prior to the fall. Such control was a good devoutly to be longed for, according to Augustine.⁹⁸ Anger, along with sexual passion, was denominated a lust (*libido*). And these passions or lusts (*libidines*), of all the passions, were the most 'defective parts of the soul', the ruling factor in every kind of sin, and thus more than any others were in need of 'the necessary moderation of mental and rational control'. They had to be 'bridled and checked by the restraining force of wisdom' – the more disturbing the passions the more forceful was the imagery of rational restraint. In practice this meant that anger could be used in the prevention of public disorder, and lust could be used in connection with 'parental duty'.⁹⁹ But they were not to be enjoyed for their own sake.¹⁰⁰

In a fascinating study of Augustine's attitude to his body and desires, Margaret Miles notices that Augustine's personal solution to the tyranny of his libidinous passions – the subjection of desire to intellect, the replacement of chaos with order – was mirrored in a change of literary style

---

⁹⁵ Sorabji (2000), 355.   ⁹⁶ Sorabji (2000), 1–8.
⁹⁷ *City of God* XIV.20. On the increased role and more elaborated concept of the will, and the struggle between lust and the will in Augustine, see Sorabji (2000), chs. 21 and 26.
⁹⁸ *City of God* XIV.16–17, 26.   ⁹⁹ *City of God* XIV.19.
¹⁰⁰ This differentiation between use (*uti*) and enjoyment (*frui*) is a central Augustinian distinction. No sensual created objects (including literature, drama and music), desires or passions are to be enjoyed for their own sake, but are always to be used or 'referred' to the higher goal of the enjoyment of God, of 'fruition' in God. See Burnaby (1991), 104–8.

in the final three books of the *Confessions*. The disorderly narration of the first nine books, 'full of asides, contradictions, variable address, disjunction, frustrating gaps and omissions, interjection, ejaculation', was replaced by the sober, didactic, doctrinal reasoning of Books X–XIII.[101]

Aquinas, characteristically, provided a more philosophical and less autobiographical approach to the problem of controlling the passions. The natural opposite of passion was action, and the more active part of man was the intellective soul (reason and will). It was therefore the intellect that should be used to suppress passion. As we have seen, Aquinas rejected Cicero's claim that all passions were diseases: 'For the emotions (*passiones*) are not "diseases" (*morbos*) or "disturbances" (*perturbationes*) of the soul, except precisely when they are not under rational control... Emotion (*passiones animae*) leads one towards sin in so far as it is uncontrolled by reason; but in so far as it is rationally controlled, it is part of the virtuous life.'[102] So Aquinas gave the following interpretation to the distinction between movements of the will and passions of the soul proper: passions proper were diseases or disturbances in so far as they were allowed to run wild. However, once under the control of reason, these passions were tamed to become acts or movements of the will, which were quite proper parts of virtuous living. As an example one could imagine the taming by moral reasoning of sexual lust so that it was channelled only into marital sexual relations. While Augustine had said that the root of all human wrong-doing lay in the passions, especially sexual and violent ones, Aquinas looked at it from the other direction: 'the root of all human goodness lies in the reason'.[103]

Man and other animals

For both Augustine and Aquinas the human being was a mixed creature, a combination of soul and body, angel and animal. And each was committed to a strictly hierarchical ordering of these elements. The *imago Dei* doctrine, based on the statement in Genesis 1.26 that man was made in God's image and set above the animals, provided the focus for the assertion of this hierarchy. Aquinas closely echoed Augustine's reading of Genesis when he wrote: 'the activity peculiar to man is understanding; it is by this that he transcends all animals'.[104] In human beings, although not in animals, the faculties of reason and will intervened between perception and action. A sheep runs as soon as it sees the wolf, without any process of thought or interposition of will. 'But man does not move

[101] Miles (1992), 126–30.   [102] *ST* Ia.2ae.24, 2.
[103] *ST* Ia.2ae.24, 3.   [104] *ST* Ia.76, 1.

immediately because of aggressiveness or desire, he waits for the command of the higher appetite, the will... So a lower appetite is not enough for a human motion unless the higher appetite agrees.'[105]

The implication of this statement is important, namely that the will was implicated in any action, even if it was the result of a passion. Hence the hierarchy between the appetites was descriptive as well as normative. Not only should reason control the passions, but also an act of will (itself the result of rational thought) as a matter of fact was the precursor of every human action. Hence while it might suffer passions it was responsible for making the decision to follow or to frustrate those passions.

Aquinas went on to reaffirm that in the three-fold scale of souls – vegetative, sensitive and intellective – the intellective soul, possessed only by humans, stood at the top. Aquinas stated that the human soul's powers 'so transcend the material world that it has an activity and a permanent power to act to which material force contributes nothing. This is the power we call the understanding (*intellectus*).'[106] The significance of this dominance of intellect over body was that the passions were defined by Aquinas as always involving bodily change.[107] Therefore we are left with a picture in which incorporeal reason and will must and do dominate over the passions (which are actions of the sensitive soul and always involve bodily commotion).

It would not be quite right, however, in interpreting this hierarchical dominance of intellect over animal passion, to read it as a condemnation of all that we call 'emotion'. This, I believe, is what Robert Solomon tends to do in his trenchant defence of the value of emotions, *The Passions: Emotions and the Meaning of Life*. As discussed in the Introduction above, Solomon attacks an attitude that he calls the 'Myth of the Passions', which he, along with Amélie Oksenberg Rorty and James Gilman, ascribes to 'modernist' and 'rationalist' thinkers. Solomon in particular picks out Augustine and Aquinas as representatives of the Christian tradition who perpetuate the 'Myth of the Passions' – the view, according to Solomon, that reason must predominate over the emotions.[108]

Augustine and Aquinas do indeed recommend that the passions be subjected to the rule of reason. However, that it is not the same as saying, as Solomon does, that the Christian tradition recommended the subjection of all 'emotions' to reason. The rational mind had its own 'emotions', namely those movements or acts of the will that were known as affects or affections. In other words, the reason–passion dichotomy was decidedly

---

[105] *ST* Ia.81, 3. [106] *ST* Ia.81, 3. [107] *ST* Ia.2ae.22, 1–3.
[108] Solomon (1993a); Rorty (1982); Gilman (1994). See also the Introduction to this volume.

not a reason–emotion dichotomy. The higher part of the soul was properly moved in its voluntary acts – in the expression of its love. Its position above animal passion (sensory appetite) in the hierarchy did not exclude it from all the aspects of life that we would call 'emotions', only from the wild, violent, unrestrained and unconsidered compulsions of passion that it would still seem reasonable advice to seek to avoid.[109]

Virtuous affections and concupiscent passions

Spiritual and worldly objects of affection

Having established that Augustine and Aquinas recommend the restraint of passions but not necessarily of all affections of the soul, we might ask which are the affections that are appropriate to the virtuous life? The answer to this question was extremely simple for both: movements of the soul towards God were appropriate, whereas movements of the soul towards earthly ephemera and created goods (including oneself and other people) were not acceptable. In a way this was a theologised version of the Stoic argument that *pathē* were to be avoided since they revealed an inappropriate desire for worldly things, such as possessions and status, which were not genuine goods. For the Stoic Chrysippus, for example, the only genuine goods were character and rationality.[110] For Christian writers, the highest goods included contemplation of and movement towards God. Since affections were movements of the higher part of the soul, especially the will – the part nearest to God and crucial to the decision to repent (to turn away from self to God) – it was inevitable that appropriate movements towards God would be affections rather than passions (although it was not true, as noted above, that all affections were good – only that all good movements of the soul were affections). And since the part of the soul that was drawn to unworthy earthly objects was the lower appetite, or animal soul, these inappropriate movements of the soul would inevitably be passions.

Augustine gave clear and unequivocal advice on the appropriate affections of the Christian life: 'So far as Christians are concerned, Holy Scripture and sound doctrine agree that the citizens of the holy City of God, who live according to God during this earthly pilgrimage, fear and desire, grieve and rejoice, and because their love is rightly ordered, they think it right to have such feelings (*affectiones*).'[111] Yet again the proper movements of the Christian soul were called affections rather than passions,

---

[109] See McAleer (1999) for a discussion of flesh, concupiscence and appetite and the way that they are ruled by reason in Aquinas' anthropology.
[110] Sorabji (2000), 7–8.   [111] *City of God* XIV.9.

disturbances or desires. The Christian should rightly fear eternal punishment, long for eternal life and hate sin.[112] Proper Christian affections were all part of a perfect love, a well-ordered love, a love from God for God. A perfect love or perfect will was part of a unified self, a self focussed on godly things (truth, virtue, eternity).[113] This unity was contrasted with a disordered or perverted will with its manifold passions and desires. These were the improper elements of the affective life. 'Truly it is by continence that we are made as one and regain that unity of self which we lost by falling apart in the search of a variety of pleasures.'[114] The term that Augustine used for this sickness of the soul, this immoderate and compulsive attraction to earthly things, was concupiscence (*concupiscentia*). Concupiscence was characterised as a spilling, a dissemination, a prodigal pouring out of the will over an endless array of objects of sensual pleasure. Miles uses the image of sexual continence as the key to understanding this part of Augustine's affective theology: 'In Augustine's physical and spiritual universe, the hoarding of seminal fluid became the practice and paradigm of the integrated life.'[115] The soul was to be unified in its turn towards God, not a drop of affection was to be spilled on barren earthly terrain. Augustine even blamed himself for the affective incontinence of grieving over the deaths of the close friend of his youth and even of his mother. Even this was an improper direction of the will towards temporal objects. '[T]he grief I felt for the loss of my friend had struck so easily into my inmost heart simply because I had poured my soul upon him, like water upon sand, loving a man who was mortal as though he were never to die.'[116] And, again, Augustine even went so far as to describe his grief for his mother as a sin.[117] The key to understanding Augustine on this point is to remember that proper affections were part of a single movement towards God, improper passions signs of a prodigal spilling out of the soul over the earth, of a fragmentation of the self.[118]

Aquinas dissented little from this analysis of the difference between the affections of the citizens of the City of God, and those of earth-bound citizens. He pointed out that love and joy were attributed to God and the angels, as was anger. But in each case these were acts of will rather than passions of the soul. These could be experienced in the same way by man, as movements of his higher appetite.[119] Indeed, it seems that every passion and every affection had two forms, an active and a passive. The former was acceptable, the latter not. The anger of God was a divine act, which was not the same at all as the anger of a man

---

[112] *City of God* XIV.5.   [113] See Innes (1997).   [114] *Confessions* X.29.
[115] Miles (1992), 98.   [116] *Confessions* IV.8.   [117] *Confessions* IX.12.
[118] See also Innes (1997), 81ff.   [119] *ST* Ia.2ae.22, 3.

tormented by his irrational lower appetite. Aquinas also examined the phrase 'a passion for the things of God', wondering whether this implied that love of God was a faculty of the lower appetite. His answer was that it did not: 'The phrase "a passion (*passio*) for the things of God" means here a passionate desire (*affectio*) for the things of God, and union with them through love; but this involves no physiological modification.'[120] Here we have another very useful explication of the difference between a passion and an affection (rather unfortunately translated as 'passionate desire' here). Passions proper involved physiological modification and were ungodly. Affections were acts of will, therefore they involved no bodily disobedience, and were quite godly.

In summary, the question of which are the proper and which the vicious affections and passions of the human soul was answered in classical Christian psychologies with reference to the objects of such states, as well as to the part of the soul that moved towards those objects. There were both appropriate and inappropriate forms of anger, love, desire, hate, jealousy, hope and fear. The proper object for each was an incorporeal ideal (injustice, God, sin, eternal life, damnation) and ultimately all, in their acceptable form, were aspects of a love for and movement towards God. The improper objects of these passions and affections were worldly, physical and ephemeral (people, bodies, sex, money, ambition, pleasure, pain). One could conclude from this that while it would be wrong to ascribe a stark dichotomy between reason and 'emotion' to the Christian tradition (since there is a voluntary and rational form of each affection), it would be fair to find in that tradition a strong distinction between the spiritual and the bodily, the former being consistently valued over the latter.

Passions and the body

Passions were, in Christian psychologies, signs of our fallen state. They were symptoms of the sickness of the soul and of the disordered nature of man. Sinful affects fell into two categories – sinful affections and sinful passions. These two categories corresponded in turn to the fallenness of the soul and the disobedience of the body. Man was fallen in both soul and body, and in his fallen state both elements were deformed. The fallen soul was revealed in sinful affections, the disordered body in sinful passions. It was the combination of these two elements that made the whole fallen man, for both Augustine and Aquinas.

---

[120] *ST* Ia.2ae.22, 3.

A good example of the interrelation of soul and body in sinful passion is to be found in Augustine's commentary on his own nocturnal emissions:

> The power of your hand, O God Almighty, is indeed enough to cure all the diseases of my soul. By granting me more abundant grace you can even quench the fire of sensuality (*lascivos motus*) which provokes me in my sleep. More and more, O Lord, you will increase your gifts in me, so that my soul may follow me to you, freed from the concupiscence that binds it, and rebel no more against itself. By your grace it will no longer commit in sleep these shameful, unclean acts, inspired by sensual images, which lead to the pollution of the body: it will not so much as consent to them.[121]

Again the primary concern was with the soul, even in such a case as this, which would today generally be ascribed to some sort of mechanical physical drive. The unclean act of his body, even when he was asleep, was for Augustine a sign of disorder in his soul – it was a voluntary act. Remember that according to Augustine 'it was not the corruptible flesh that made the soul sinful; on the contrary, it was the sinful soul that made the flesh corruptible'.[122] The bodily aspects of the passions were secondary signs of cognitive and volitional disorder. Time and again Augustine returned with disgust to the sexual body: 'To love and to have my love returned was my heart's desire, and it would be all the sweeter if I could also enjoy the body of the one who loved me. So I muddied the stream of friendship with the filth of lewdness (*concupiscentia*) and clouded its clear waters with hell's black river of lust (*libido*).'[123] But again, lust and lewdness and desire for sexual intimacy were not caused by the body but by the soul. The body in Augustine was corrupted by the disordered will, was the object of inappropriate desires, and was used as a metaphor for spiritual deformity. Another example of this metaphorical usage is found in Book III of the *Confessions*: 'I was dragged away from you by my own weight and in dismay I plunged again into the things of this world. The weight I carried was the habit of the flesh.'[124] Note that the weight he carried was not the flesh per se but the 'habit of the flesh', or the works of the flesh (Galatians 5). The habit of the flesh was a condition of the soul, not of the body.

In short, the role of the body in the passions for Augustine was secondary and metaphorical. The flesh was indeed disobedient, but only because of the corruption of the will. The ideal state from which Adam and Eve had fallen and to which human beings should hope to return in the hereafter was one in which proper order was restored and the soul truly controlled every part of the body. Augustine mentioned some

---

[121] *Confessions* X.30. [122] *City of God* XIV.3.
[123] *Confessions* III.1. [124] *Confessions* III.17.

freakish examples of the control that some could exert over their bodies even in their fallen state:

> There are people who can swallow an enormous number and variety of objects and then, by a slight contraction of the stomach, bring up as from a bag whichever object they want, and in good condition... There are individuals who can, without any smell, make musical notes issue from the rear of their anatomy, so that you would think they were singing.[125]

Such were some of the indications of what would have been possible for Adam and Eve before the fall and the ensuing punishment of disobedient flesh. Augustine did not speculate as to whether either of the first humans indulged these skills prior to their expulsion from the garden. Disobedient flesh was not even a necessary part of sinful passions, since the Devil had no flesh but assuredly harboured vicious passions of pride and envy.[126]

It might be worthwhile here to remark upon an unresolved confusion that runs implicitly through thinking on the passions. That is the question of what they are passions of. For Aquinas, as we have already seen, passion by definition was some sort of defect or deficiency. One of the senses in which he articulated this was that the passion was a passion in the body – that it was a change for the worse in the body.[127] He was quite clear that passions always involved some change in the body.[128] In this respect he differed from both Augustine and from the eighteenth-century writer Jonathan Edwards (see chapter 3), both of whom saw bodily changes as ultimately unnecessary accompaniments of passions and affections. Aquinas stated, for example, that passions always caused an increase or decrease in the rate of the heartbeat.[129] He also warned that the passion of love, when excessive, could cause serious harm to the body.[130] In this sense then, although Aquinas used the term *passiones animae*, or passions of the soul, it was the body that was really the passive element – it was the body that underwent change and was acted upon. Strictly, in both Augustine and Aquinas the passions and affections would be better understood as passions of the body, and actions of the soul. Affections were actions of the rational soul and passions were actions of the irrational soul.

There are, however, two senses in which the passions were passions of the soul in classical Christian psychologies. The first is that they were passions of the soul when conceived in the more narrow sense as the intellective (as opposed to vegetative or sensitive) soul. They were instances of the animal soul (sensory appetite) acting upon the rational soul (intellect and will), the latter being required to react against the former to maintain control. So the passions were passions of the intellectual soul as well

---

[125] *City of God* XIV.24. [126] *City of God* XIV.3. [127] *ST* Ia.2ae.22, 1.
[128] *ST* Ia.2ae.22, 1–3. [129] *ST* Ia.2ae.24, 2. [130] *ST* Ia.2ae.28, 5.

as passions of the body. Secondly, they were passions of the soul in that the lower part of the soul was acted upon by external objects of sense – these objects pulled the animal soul to and fro. It was important for the sake of teaching on sin and free will, however, that vicious passions were primarily disorders of the will, which would imply that they were strictly passions of the body (that the disordered will acted upon the body to make it suffer passion). This contrasts with views later favoured by both Descartes and William James that make the body active and the soul or mind passive.[131]

Classical Christian approaches to passions and affections, however the role of the body was interpreted, showed minimal interest in any details of physiology, whereas such details were to become the obsession of psychologists of emotions in the second half of the nineteenth century. By this time 'emotions', unlike 'passions' and 'affections', had become primarily the constructs of biologists, physiologists, evolutionists and neuroscientists rather than of theological or even philosophical psychologists.

The hope for future apathy?

The final way that Augustine and Aquinas formulated their teachings about the movements, passions and affections of the soul was in terms of the world to come. Often a comparison (although not an identity) was drawn between the original state of Adam and Eve and the final state that the faithful should hope for after the general resurrection. In both instances things were in their proper order – the passions obeyed the mind, woman obeyed man and man obeyed God. Such a state of obedience and order would seem to preclude the life of the affections and passions, which could imply that passions and affections were symptoms only of our current conflicted fallen state, and so would vanish in the hereafter. This view was further suggested by the fact that affect and passion were both forms of movement but heaven is eternity in union with God, the unmoved mover – an eternity of rest, not of motion. John Milbank has gone so far as to suggest that the ultimate priority of peace over conflict (or rest over struggle) was the central theme of Augustine's whole theology.[132]

Early Christian writers disagreed about whether Stoic *apatheia* was desirable.[133] We saw above that Augustine rejected *apatheia* as an appropriate goal for someone living according to God's word in this world. His conclusion was that 'an existence devoid of all emotions (*affectiones*)

---

[131] See James (1997), chs. 2–4, for further explanation of the way that the notions of passivity and activity were applied to the passions in the medieval period. On Descartes, see chapter 4 below. On James, see chapter 7.
[132] Milbank (1990), 390.   [133] Sorabji (2000), ch. 25.

disturbing to the spirit and contrary to reason, is manifestly a good devoutly to be longed for, but it is not one that can be attained in the present life.'[134] The implication was that an apathetic or impassive life, even if it was not appropriate to life on this earth, was one to which believers should aspire and which they could hope to attain in the next life: 'we can certainly hope for such a condition, but it will only come true in that beatitude of eternal life which we have been promised'.[135] Aquinas' teaching that cognitive activity resembled rest whereas the activity of the appetites resembled motion also implied a future life with neither passion nor affection.[136] The body, sown in dishonour, would rise in glory (1 Corinthians 15.43); it shall be incapable of suffering and untroubled by sensory desires (e.g. for food or sex), despite retaining nutritive and sexual organs, Thomas taught.[137] He had also established that the anger, love and joy of the angels and God were acts of will unlike human passions.

The conclusion then was that the future beatitude that Christian people could hope to receive through the grace of God was one in which passions played no part and the activity of the will and intellect was unimpeded by the rebellion of lower appetites and corruptible flesh. However, just as the Stoic desire for *apatheia* did not exclude experiencing certain forms of joy (and other virtuous feelings known as *eupatheiai*),[138] so it was not a state of complete apathy that the Christian faithful should expect: 'It is reasonable enough to say that perfect beatitude will be free from every occasion of fear and from every kind of sorrow, but it would be utterly untrue to say that there will be no love and no joy in heaven.'[139] When God finally dwells in the new Jerusalem with His people, 'He will wipe away every tear from their eyes, and death shall be no more, and neither shall there be mourning nor crying nor pain any more, for the former things have passed away' (Revelation 21.4). A rarefied love and joy, the fruition of the intellect's search for God, would be the destiny of those whose wilful struggle against the passions was successful.

Why Christian theologians needed to distinguish between passions and affections

Medieval Western Christian theology introduced a critical distinction between troubling and potentially sinful movements of the soul, which were in rebellion against the rational will – appetites, lusts, desires and

---

[134] *City of God* XIV.9.   [135] *City of God* XIV.9.
[136] *ST* Ia.81, 1.   [137] *Summa Contra Gentiles* 86–8.
[138] Annas (1992), 114–15. On the different early Christian interpretations of *apatheia*, see Sorabji (2000), ch. 25. Some early Church Fathers, such as Origen and Clement, unlike Augustine and Aquinas, believed that *apatheia* could be attained in this life.
[139] *City of God* XIV.9.

passions – and virtuous and potentially godly ones, which were enlightened acts of the higher will – affections. Thus they made some psychological, moral and theological distinctions that were made neither in the classical discourse of the passions (*pathē*) nor in the subsequent discourse of the 'emotions'. This was the result of the Christian desire to say both – against the Stoics – that some human feeling or affection is proper and necessary to this life, but also that God, the angels and perfected humans are free from the turmoil and perturbations of sin and the passions. This was the heart of Christian affective psychology.

3 From movements to mechanisms: passions, sentiments and affections in the Age of Reason

> Appetite, fear, hope and the rest of the passions are not called voluntary; for they proceed not from, but are the will, and the will is not voluntary: for, a man can no more say that he will will, than he will will will, and so make an infinite repetition of the word will, which is absurd and insignificant.
>
> Thomas Hobbes, *Human Nature*, 69

Age of reason, age of passions

In 1755 Samuel Johnson's dictionary of the English language was first published.[1] The entries for 'affection', 'appetite', 'emotion', 'feeling', 'passion', 'sensibility' and 'sentiment' provide a rough-and-ready guide to usage in the middle of the eighteenth century. They reveal that the predominant terms for describing states such as love, fear, joy and sorrow were still 'passions' and 'affections', each of which was given an extensive entry. Isaac Watts, one of the authors discussed below, was quoted as an authority for the entry on 'passions', to the following effect: 'The word passion signifies the receiving of any action in a large philosophical sense; in a more limited philosophical sense, it signifies any of the affections of human nature; as love, fear, joy, sorrow: but the common people confine it only to anger.'[2] 'Passions', as well as being a very general term, referred to the more violent commotions of the mind. The seventh meaning given for 'passion' was 'The last suffering of the redeemer of the world'. 'Affections' was defined (as well as also being a very general term) as encompassing, amongst other things, goodwill, love, or kindness towards other people. 'Appetite' was given the next longest entry of these affective terms, which defined it as a word for physical appetites, sensual desires and violent longings. Next came the entries for 'feeling', 'sensibility' and 'sentiment'. 'Feeling', when used as an adjective, meant 'expressive of great sensibility'; 'sensibility' in turn was defined as 'quickness of sensation' or 'quickness of perception'. 'Sentiment' had a very

---

[1] Johnson (1967).   [2] Quoted in Johnson (1967).

short entry – only two meanings were suggested: thought, notion or opinion on the one hand; and sense or meaning on the other. 'Emotion' too was given only a very brief definition: 'Disturbance of mind; vehemence of passion, pleasing or painful'. The term 'emotion', and its plural 'emotions', were not in common use at this time other than as words denoting any kind of agitation or disturbance (of the mind, of the body, of a mass of people, or even in the weather).[3] None of the thinkers discussed in this chapter made any significant use of the term 'emotions'; instead they referred to 'appetites', 'passions', 'affections' and 'sentiments'.

The figures who form the main focus of this chapter were Christian clergymen, preachers and philosophers. These were not, of course, the only contributors to thought about passions, affections and sentiments in the eighteenth century. Literary figures from Pope and Defoe to Coleridge also contributed significantly to eighteenth-century ideas about passions and affections. Pope, in his *Essay on Man* (1733), like many of the British moralists considered below, aimed to use Bacon's inductive philosophy to produce a 'science of human nature', an 'anatomy of the mind'.[4] Pope's treatment of the passions was especially well known and influential. The following are amongst the most often-quoted lines of his *Essay*:

> In lazy apathy let Stoics boast
> Their virtue fixed; 'tis fixed as in a frost
> Contracted all, retiring to the breast;
> But strength of mind is exercise, not rest:
> The rising tempest puts in act the soul,
> Parts it may ravage, but preserves the whole.
> On life's vast ocean diversely we sail,
> Reason the card, but Passion is the gale;
> . . .
> Suffice that reason keep to nature's road,
> Subject, compound them, follow her and God.
> Love, hope, and joy, fair pleasure's smiling train,
> Hate, fear, and grief, the family of pain[5]

These few lines contain indications of several of the important characteristics of eighteenth-century treatments of passions and affections of the soul: the desire to find a middle position between frosty Stoicism and overheated enthusiasm; the need to moderate passion with reason; and the appeal both to God and nature as efficient psychological agencies. Also, as Kathleen Grange has noted, Pope's treatment was characteristic of a broader eighteenth-century trend towards a view of the mind in

---

[3] On earlier meanings of 'emotion', see the *Oxford English Dictionary*, and Ruckmick (1929), 254–5.
[4] Pope (1993), 7.   [5] Pope (1993), Epistle II, lines 101–8, 115–18.

which passions were more autonomous and active – agents in their own right rather than movements of the will.[6] Eliza Haywood's *Life's Progress Through the Passions* (1748) provided a similar view: 'the passions, those powerful abettors, I had almost said sole authors of all human actions'.[7]

Recent work on the eighteenth century has done much to reappraise its categorisation as a time of 'Enlightenment' and an 'Age of Reason'. While these older characterisations certainly capture some of the dominant cultural concerns of the period, they tend to obscure the significant roles ascribed to and played by passions, affections and sentiments. Much of the recent revisionary literature has looked either to philosophical theories of moral sentiments – most notably that of Adam Smith – or to broader literary and cultural movements concerned with 'sensibility' and 'sentimentalism', in order to enlighten our understanding of the period in different ways. A richer understanding of eighteenth-century culture has thus been produced.[8] I do not seek to reproduce all the insights of this recent literature in this chapter; instead I hope to supplement it with material that has less frequently been examined in either standard or revisionary accounts. And while I am interested to see how the concepts 'moral sense' and 'moral sentiments' fitted into theoretical frameworks of the period, wider cultural movements of sensibility or sentimentalism are largely outside the scope of this history of psychological categories.

The existence of these discourses of sense, sensation, sentiment and sensibility is important to note, nonetheless, as it helps further to complicate the picture, and to emphasise how inadequate and over-general (as well as anachronistic) are accounts that describe this as a period that had either a positive or a negative view of 'the emotions'. Some authors dealt with the value of sentiment in general, or with sensibility, others specifically with the moral sense – an inner sense of right and wrong analogous to the five external senses – sometimes called the 'conscience', others with 'moral sentiments', which were also thought of as particular 'passions' (or sometimes 'affections'), some self-regarding, others more social and benevolent. As will be brought out below, moral sentiments and affections were potentially rational as well as being warm and lively states of mind. The term 'sentiment' had the connotations then that it still has now, of being both a thought or opinion and a feeling. Affections,

---

[6] See Grange (1962). Grange's article is very illuminating, despite the anachronistic use of 'emotions' throughout, especially in drawing attention to ways in which passions were seen as agents in their own right, rather than actions of the will. Particularly good examples of treatments of the passions by literary writers are Pope (1993) and [Haywood] (1748).
[7] [Haywood] (1748), 5.
[8] On Smith and moral sentiments, see 'Introduction' to Smith (1976); Teichgraeber (1986); Dwyer (1998); Griswold (1999); Rothschild (2001). On sentimentalism and sensibility, see Barker-Benfield (1992); Denby (1994); Ellison (1999); Reddy (2001), esp. ch. 5.

similarly, were both cognitive and subjective; felt preferences; rational desires. Neither term is well expressed by the over-arching contemporary term 'emotion'.

Adam Smith's *Theory of Moral Sentiments* (first published in 1759, revised in 1790) is one of the most interesting works to read to get a flavour of the multifaceted nature of moral–philosophical discourse in the eighteenth century. Smith discussed in an integrated way questions of human motivation and morality that would, today, be carved up into separate issues to be dealt with by economics, politics, philosophy of mind, psychology, ethics and theology. As John Dwyer rightly says, Smith and his contemporaries wrote at a time before the introduction of such disciplinary boundaries, and consequently: 'There is a fundamental sense... in which the eighteenth-century discourse of the passions was political.'[9] Smith's terminology was also indicative of the wide variety of terms that were used with reference to the realms of human feeling, and the subtly different nuances they could have. His over-arching category was the 'passions' of human nature. The same term was also used more narrowly for particularly troubling or violent appetites and desires; those most in need of control and government, such as anger and lust. Smith also (much less frequently) used the term 'emotions', although in a vague and equivocal way – sometimes to mean something like movement or agitation, sometimes as an apparent synonym or stylistic variant for 'passions' or for 'feelings' (on similar early uses of the term in other eighteenth-century Scottish works, especially Hume, see chapter 4). In addition, Smith referred to 'moral sentiments' (felt judgments regarding the propriety of others' actions); to selfish or benevolent 'affections' (feelings tending towards actions designed to benefit self or others); and to 'sensibility' (a general susceptibility to passions, sentiments and affections).[10]

Albert Hirschman, in a study of seventeenth- and eighteenth-century moral and social thought, including the work of Adam Smith, has suggested that in this period an important distinction emerged between troubling 'passions' and more cool and calculated 'interests', such as the interest in acquiring wealth, which could override the wilder human passions and provide more innocuous motivations for action.[11] Butler's discussion of how the cool application of the principle of self-love (discussed below) could override the urgings of the particular passions is a good example of this.[12] Hirschman's analysis also supports the more general

---

[9] Dwyer (1998), 7.
[10] Teichgraeber (1986), ch. 1 brings out very clearly the multifaceted nature of this eighteenth-century moral-philosophical discourse of passions, affections and sentiments.
[11] Hirschman (1997). See also Teichgraeber (1986), 93–6; Dwyer (1998), Postscript.
[12] Hirschman (1997), 35.

point of this chapter, that affective discourses and terminologies in the eighteenth century were too complex for it to be possible to discern in them any *single* attitude to human passions (or to 'emotions' or 'feeling' or 'sentiment').

Dylan Evans, who expresses his approval of Adam Smith's theory of moral sentiments, tends to assume that what we now call 'emotions' corresponds to what eighteenth-century writers called 'sentiments'. The 'sentiments', however, were only a part of the picture. Smith and others did not argue, as Evans has it, that 'emotions' were reason's ally – they argued that 'moral sentiments' could be. Most of the same Scottish Enlightenment writers, such as Smith and Thomas Reid, to whom Evans refers as advocates of the rationality of 'emotions' (i.e. moral sentiments), also wrote of the potentially excessive, irrational and wicked nature of the passions, as John Dwyer has noted.[13] Some literature on French and British 'sentimentalism' of the eighteenth century similarly argues that the valuing of natural sentiment, or 'moral sense', as a route to virtue was evidence that 'emotions' or 'sentiment' were being valued more highly, or were not seen as opposed to reason.[14] Such claims misrepresent eighteenth-century thinkers by trying to force a range of views regarding different faculties and feelings into a single view. Whether the general term used is an eighteenth-century one, such as 'passions' or 'sentiment', or a present-day category such as 'emotions', this can be misleading.[15] Writers of this period could (and usually did) have one attitude to moral sentiments, another to sentiment and sensibility more broadly, another to affections, and another to passions. This was not merely an 'Age of Reason', but nor was it merely an 'Age of Passions'. It was an age of reason, conscience, self-love, interests, passions, sentiments, affections, feeling and sensibility.

Revivalists and moralists

How far did eighteenth-century thinkers and teachers endorse classical Christian views of passions and affections? The priority of reflective reason, the distinction between passions and appetites on the one hand and affections on the other, the significance of whether passions and affections had particular and worldly objects or general and spiritual ones – these were all elements of the classical view that were broadly maintained. On the other hand, the importance of the will, the reduction of all affections

---

[13] See Evans (2001), e.g. xi–xii; Dwyer (1998), 7–8.
[14] Reddy (2001), 216; Denby (1994), 240.
[15] For an interesting overview of recent research see Reddy (2001), 154–61.

and passions to love of God or love of the world, the significance of sin and the fall – these parts of the traditional view were somewhat more often (although by no means universally) neglected.

I have chosen the eighteenth-century texts considered below in order to help illustrate particular tendencies among certain philosophical and religious strains of thought. They are not intended either separately or together to form a corpus that is representative of all of eighteenth-century philosophy, let alone all eighteenth-century culture. I have divided these texts into two groups. The first group consists of texts produced by theologians and preachers who are grouped under the heading of 'Christian revivalists'. In spending some time considering these texts, I hope to illustrate the fact that just as this was an age of passions and sentiments as much as it was an age of reason, so it was also an age of religious revivals as much as it was a secularising age. The group of texts in question includes the *Treatise Concerning Religious Affections* (1746) composed by the central figure of the eighteenth-century religious revival in New England, Jonathan Edwards.[16] It also includes works by the English Congregationalist, Isaac Watts, especially his *Doctrine of the Passions Explained and Improved* (1729) and his *Discourses of the Love of God, and its Influence on all the Passions* (1729).[17] These revivalists were characterised by their zeal for piety and personal experience in religion, but only insofar as it was checked and moderated by right reason. The revivalists were concerned to distinguish the truly religious affections of the state of grace from the worldly affections of the 'natural' man. The distinction between passions and affections was used by some of them to highlight this distinction between the states of nature and grace.

The second group of texts given particular attention are those produced by writers who are here termed 'British moralists'. Particularly important texts contributing to thinking about passions, affections and sentiments within this tradition were Joseph Butler's *Fifteen Sermons* (1726), Francis Hutcheson's *Essay on the Nature and Conduct of the Passions and Affections* (1728) and Thomas Reid's *Essays on the Active Powers of Man* (1788). A recent meticulous study by Isabel Rivers of the languages of religion and ethics, reason and sentiment in eighteenth-century Britain elucidates in great detail the influence that the work of Lord Shaftesbury – especially his arguments for the primacy of natural affection in the moral economy – exerted over contributors to this particular tradition of

---

[16] For studies of Edwards, his theology and his role in the 'Great Awakening', see Miller (1952 and 1959); Cherry (1966); Jenson (1988).

[17] On the date of publication of these two works, see Milner (1834), xix; Davis (1948), 141. On Watts' life and work, see Gibbons (1780); Johnson (1785); Milner (1834); Davis (1948); Hoyles (1971); Stephens (1999).

moral philosophy.[18] Often drawing on Shaftesbury's works, these moral philosophers engaged in a debate about the proper roles of reason, passions, affections and sentiments in both individual motivation and social life.

The moralists' concerns were not those of the revivalists. They were not so preoccupied with the characteristics of true religion, nor with the way to discriminate gracious from natural affections. Their concerns were, in fact, despite their own Christian convictions, rather more secular than that. They were involved in a political debate – largely driven by the desire to respond to controversial works by Thomas Hobbes and Bernard Mandeville – about the proper relationship between the individual and the state. This debate extended to questions about the fundamentals of human nature such as whether concern for the welfare of others was natural or whether it must be contrived artificially by the state. This raised further questions about the public and private appetites of man, his duties and responsibilities and the question of moral authority – did it lie with God, with man's natural conscience, or with the artificial machinery of the state? In this way questions that we might now consider separately, some as the subject matter of politics, others as questions of psychology, others of moral philosophy or theology, were intertwined in a single debate.

The groups here called 'revivalists' and 'moralists' correspond fairly closely to the groups distinguished by Harold Simonson, in his analysis of eighteenth-century revivalism and dissent in Britain and North America, as 'Dissenters' and 'Establishmentarians'. The former (including Edwards, the Wesleys and Watts) might also be termed 'evangelicals'; they insisted on adherence to biblical and traditional theological doctrines of the fall, the sinfulness of humanity in its natural state, the need for grace and redemption through Christ and the crucial importance of personal faith; they also advocated a form of church government that devolved power to individuals or congregations. The latter (including Butler) believed that unaided reason was capable of establishing many of the truths of religion (even though such natural religion was certainly imperfect and needed to be supplemented by the ultimate truths revealed in the scriptures); they also taught high, rationalist, 'Enlightenment' views of human nature and, in practice (though often not in theory), privileged natural religion over revealed religion; they also endorsed an established church governed by elders and courts.[19] Another adjective that has been applied to this latter form of religion, especially in the Anglican church, is

---

[18] Rivers (2000), chs. 1–3, brings out the religious heterodoxy and moral ambiguity of Shaftesbury's philosophy, and discusses the ways his thought was taken up by later moralists.
[19] Simonson (1987), especially 363–5.

'latitudinarian'.[20] Broadly speaking, revivalists were proponents of full-blooded, evangelical Christianity, and were often dissenters; the moralists were moderates, who taught a more rationalistic form of Christianity, with greater emphasis on the merits of natural religion.

All these generalisations are, of course, potentially misleading. It would be wrong to suppose that ecclesiological categories such as 'dissenting' or 'establishmentarian' could ever be straightforwardly mapped on to philosophical-theological ones such as 'revivalist' or 'moralist'. Many individuals would defy such simple categorisations. Francis Hutcheson, for example, spent some ten years as a tutor at a dissenting academy in Dublin before taking up the position of Professor of Moral Philosophy at Glasgow in 1730.[21] So, while he might be thought to have roots in a 'dissenting' tradition, he writes in the idiom of British philosophical moralists more than in the language of revivalism. Joseph Butler too had dissenting roots but eventually would become a senior bishop in the Anglican church – and would write as both an establishmentarian and a moralist.[22] There were also significant differences of doctrine amongst individuals within the same category. While Edwards and Watts could both be called 'revivalists', for instance, they took opposing views about the freedom of the will. In his 1754 treatise on the freedom of the will, Edwards repeatedly criticised Watts for what he considered to be the incoherence and absurdity of the latter's notion of a self-determining power in the will.[23] So, while I hope to bring out some genuine and significant contrasts between the moral discourses, theological idioms and metaphysical assumptions of the groups I am referring to here as 'revivalists' and 'moralists', I do so in full recognition of the fact that such categorisations can only be provisional and can conceal differences at the same time as illuminating commonalities.

Concepts of nature and will

The concept of 'nature' was central to discussions of passions and affections in the eighteenth century. Revivalists and moralists used the term in very different ways. 'Natural' had different meanings depending on whether it was opposed to 'supernatural' or 'gracious' on the one hand

---

[20] On the similarity between Hutcheson's religion (and that of the 'moderates' in the Church of Scotland) and the views of Anglican latitudinarians, see Teichgraeber (1986), ch. 2; Rivers (2000), esp. ch. 3. On similarities and differences between latitudinarian and dissenting traditions in the mid-eighteenth century, see Fitzpatrick (1993).
[21] Rivers (2000), 157. [22] Rivers (2000), 164.
[23] See Edwards (1957), Part II, where Edwards refers to Watts not by name but as 'the author of *An Essay on the Freedom of the Will*'.

or to 'artificial' or 'social' on the other. While the revivalists considered the relationship between nature and grace, the natural and the supernatural, and compared the affections and passions of the natural and the saved man, the moralists contemplated the relationship between nature and art, the natural and the social, the individual and the state.

The question as to whether humans were by nature vicious or virtuous was central to the debates engaged in by the moralists. Discussions about 'human nature' replaced discussions about the human 'soul' in the moralist tradition. Ironically it was those thinkers who were most often accused of atheism, such as Thomas Hobbes and Bernard Mandeville, who took the line closest to the classical Christian doctrine – that human beings in a state of nature were selfish and sensual. A critical difference was that the classical Christian view of man in a state of nature was that he was selfish and sensual because postlapsarian, while the Hobbesian view of human nature was that it was selfish and sensual because pre-social. Christian moralists such as Shaftesbury, Hutcheson and Butler argued, in contrast both to evangelicals and to Hobbesians, that human beings were naturally virtuous.[24] Thus, effectively, they did away not only with an idea of the fallen nature of humanity but also with a role for the will in turning from sin and the world to God. The will, a cornerstone of classical Christian psychology, thus slipped into the background for at least some eighteenth-century moralists. On the classical Christian model, passions and affections were movements of the soul – specifically passions were movements of the lower part of the will (the sense appetite) and affections were movements or acts of the higher or rational will (the intellectual appetite). Aquinas, we saw in chapter 2, had differentiated these parts of the will as the *appetitus sensitivus* and the *appetitus intellectivus*; the latter, he also simply called *voluntas*.[25]

The introduction in Germany in the eighteenth century of a third faculty of the soul in addition to understanding and will – the faculty of feeling – was part of a parallel trend away from classical Christian psychology towards a new psychology in which passions, affections, feelings or, ultimately, emotions, were not movements of the will but constituted an independent faculty with their own causal power. Psychological thinkers such as Christian Wolff, Moses Mendelssohn and Johann Tetens were all important contributors to a new tradition of psychological thought in which a third faculty of feeling (*Gefühl* or *Empfindung*) was added to the traditional two faculties of Christian psychology – knowing and

---

[24] For a detailed analysis of the discourses of ethics, religion and natural affection in this period, with particular reference to Shaftesbury, Hutcheson and Butler, see Rivers (2000), chs. 2 and 3.
[25] See Aquinas (1981), 1a.2ae.24, 3.

willing. This tripartite model was given new authority when endorsed by Immanuel Kant in his *Critique of Judgment* (1790) and his *Anthropology* (1798), and by Schopenhauer in *The World as Will and Representation* (1819).[26] The faculty of feeling (*Gefühl*) for Kant was composed of *Affekte* and *Leidenschaft*.[27] These terms did not map straightforwardly on to corresponding English terms such as 'passions', 'affections' or 'emotions'.[28] This separation of the third faculty from the existing faculties of intellect (or understanding) and will was one of the crucial factors in laying the groundwork for various theories of passions and emotions that saw them as both irrational and involuntary. Roger Smith notes of this development, based primarily on the work of Wolff in the 1730s, that it revealed German writers beginning to conceptualise 'the soul as activity in a manner that gradually became independent of theology'.[29]

Some of the eighteenth-century English-language psychological thinkers considered in the present chapter displayed an increasing willingness to ascribe activity and agency to passions and affections as faculties in their own right (rather than being prepared only to ascribe activity to the will). This revealed a parallel divergence from Christian theological psychology, but with two differences from the German developments. First, many of these English-language thinkers worked with models that gave the soul (specifically the will) anything but an active role in determining behaviour. Activity was ascribed instead to supernatural agents (such as Satan and the Holy Spirit) by the revivalists and, by some of the moralists, to secondary causes (such as nature or human nature or the autonomous passions and affections themselves) and to social systems of reward and punishment. Secondly, English-language thinkers on the whole did not fully adopt a Kantian three-faculty model but rather appealed to something like it implicitly or partially.[30] Even Edwards and Reid, probably the two most orthodox Christian psychologists considered in this chapter, both equivocated at times between teaching that passions and affections were movements of the will and that they comprised faculties of the soul in their own right.[31]

---

[26] Gardiner *et al.* (1970), 263–7, 308–11.
[27] See Gardiner *et al.* (1970), ch. 9; Berrios (1996), 18–19.
[28] For a discussion of Kant's distinction between *Affekte* and *Leidenschaft*, see Sherman (1990).
[29] Smith (1997), 203.
[30] Bain, amongst others, later adopted the tripartite model explicitly, see chapter 5 below.
[31] See Edwards (1959), 102, where he talks of the affections being 'moved', which would make no sense on the classical Christian view that affections are movements of the will, rather than a faculty of their own. Reid saw passions and affections as quasi-autonomous active powers rather than simply as movements of the faculty of will.

Another – much more theologically controversial – tripartite model of the human mind would have been found by eighteenth-century readers in the *Ethica* of the heterodox Jew, Benedict de Spinoza. In the *Ethica* (published posthumously in 1677), Spinoza categorised the various modes of thinking under three headings: intellect (*intellectus*), conation (*conatus*) and the affects (*affectus*).[32] Spinoza's system had been, quite apart from the monistic and pantheistic metaphysics it was based upon, much more radical than the three-faculty psychology developed in Germany in the following century. In denying that will and intellect were special faculties, and in reducing all the operations of the mind to different modes of thinking, or thoughts, of equal status, Spinoza was developing a naturalistic, reductionist and non-realist mental philosophy that would find echoes, in different ways, in the succeeding centuries in Scotland, in works by David Hume, Thomas Brown and Alexander Bain (see chapters 4 and 5 below).[33]

Revivalists: Jonathan Edwards and Isaac Watts

Reason and passion

Both passions and emotions have always been recognised to be 'mixed' phenomena to some degree – mental and physical, angelic and brutish, conscious and unconscious, rational and irrational, innate and learned. Watts described the passions as 'these mingled powers of flesh and spirit'.[34] The debate about the proper relationship of reason with the passions, sentiments and affections was one of the characteristic concerns of eighteenth-century thought. One important part of the classical Christian approach was the recommended dominance of reason over the passions. On this view human beings, unlike the brute creation, were endowed with reason and understanding, and this was the highest part of their soul. Another important part of the tradition, however, centred on the love of God as the highest calling of the will; this part of the tradition saw a positive role for affections of love, compassion and joy in the proper Christian life. Both these elements of the classical Christian view – the importance of reason and understanding and the importance of affections and love – continued to be taught in various ways in the eighteenth century.

---

[32] Spinoza (2000).
[33] On Spinoza's mental philosophy and his theory of affects (*affectus*) see the editor's introduction to Spinoza (2000); James (1997), 136–56; Yovel (ed.) (1999), especially Giancotti (1999).
[34] Watts (n.d.), iv.

There are plenty of examples of those who took a strong line on the importance of subduing the passions through the ministration of reason. The Newtonian divine Samuel Clarke, for example, in his *Discourse of Natural Religion* (first published in 1706, having been delivered as the Boyle lectures the previous year), gave the following stern warning: 'For great intemperance and ungoverned passions, not only incapacitate a man to perform his duty; but also expose him to run headlong into the commission of the greatest enormities:[35] there being no violence or injustice whatsoever, which a man who has deprived himself of his reason by intemperance or passion, is not capable of being tempted to commit.' Clarke went so far as to say that, 'This is indeed the great difficulty of life, to subdue and conquer our unreasonable appetites and passions... it is moreover the bravest and most glorious conquest in the world.'[36] A similar view of the necessity of subjecting passions to the rule of reason was offered by John Tottie, Fellow of Worcester College, Oxford, in a sermon preached in St Paul's Cathedral in 1735: 'The original excellency and rectitude of man's nature has been observed to arise in a great measure from the power of his reason, and the due subjection of his passions; and on the contrary, the degeneracy of it to consist in the influence that the passions have gained to enfeeble and pervert his reason.'[37] If the only views offered by Christians in the eighteenth century about the passions and affections were along the lines of these quotations from Clarke and Tottie then generalisations about the Christian view being a wholly rationalistic one that pilloried the passions as negative aspects of fallen humanity might be justified.

It was common, however, to find a more subtle and balanced view taken by Christian thinkers on the relationship between reason and the passions. Not everyone was either a Rationalist or a Romantic. Isaac Watts was not alone in proposing a more balanced approach to this debate. He was indeed, like many other Christians of the age, alarmed by the rise in the status of unaided reason, especially in religion, as he explained in the Preface to his *Discourse of the Love of God and its Influence on all the Passions* (1746): 'That which inclined me, at last, to draw up these discourses, of the use of the passions in religion, into a more regular form, was the growing deadness and degeneracy of our age in vital religion, though it grow bright in rational and polite learning.' Too many people, he continued, thought that the business of the preacher was to teach 'the necessary doctrines and duties of our holy religion by a mere explication

---

[35] I.e. crimes or transgressions.
[36] Clarke (1706), 102–3. For a discussion of Clarke's *Discourse*, see Rivers (2000), 15–16, 79–81.
[37] Tottie (1738), 15–16.

of the Word of God' without re-enforcing these duties by an appeal to the conscience and 'by a pathetick address to the heart'. Too few preachers attempted to awaken the 'holy sensations' of hope, fear, love, joy and the like, Watts complained.[38] His biographer, Thomas Milner, wrote that Watts had been reacting against a majority of the dissenters, as well as against the established church, who all 'agreed in reducing the elements of religion to a few cold theorems and formal observances'.[39] The Aberdeen moral philosopher David Fordyce, who was influenced by leading English dissenting figures such as Philip Doddridge and Watts himself, discerned a similar lack in the preaching of the age. Fordyce called for a less speculative and abstract style of preaching: 'I want to have my Understanding enlightened, my Heart enflamed, every Affection thrilled, and my whole Life reformed.'[40]

The solution to this perceived crisis that Watts and other revivalists proposed was not the complete overthrow of reason, nor the introduction of a wildly enthusiastic religion. Watts was no more an extreme enthusiast than he was a staid moderate.[41] He was well aware that in advocating the use of passions and affections in religion he was potentially opening the door to 'all the wild temptations of fancy and enthusiasm' that could lead to bigotry and persecution, which was why, he wrote, 'I thought it necessary, therefore, to speak of the *abuses of the passions*, as well as the *use of them*, and to guard against mistakes on both sides.'[42] While cold and dry reasoning may have been an unsatisfactory basis for true religion, unchecked passion was no better: 'Ungoverned passions break all the bonds of human society and peace, and would change the tribes of mankind into brutal herds, or make the world a mere wilderness of savages.'[43] Cold reason and ungoverned passions were equally undesirable. The proper course in these matters, for Watts, was to find a middle way. He believed that religion should be 'both passionate and reasonable'.[44]

> In my pursuit of this subject, I have endeavour'd to avoid all extremes; that is, neither to turn religion into a matter of speculation or cold reasoning, nor to give up the devout Christian to all wandering fooleries of warm and ungoverned passion. I hope I have maintained the middle way, which as it is most agreeable to the holy Scripture and to the genius of Christianity, so it has produced the noblest fruits of righteousness in every age.[45]

---

[38] Watts (1746), vii–viii. [39] Milner (1834), 440.
[40] From Fordyce's *Theodorus: A Dialogue Concerning the Art of Preaching*, 2nd edn (1753), quoted in Rivers (1993), 35.
[41] On the differing emphasis on reason and feelings in religion by moderates and evangelicals, see Hilton (1988), 19–21.
[42] Watts (1746), x. [43] Watts (n.d.), v. [44] Davis (1948), 142. [45] Watts (1746), xi.

Milner paraphrased Watts' view: 'pure and unadulterated Christianity dwells semi-distant from the frigid zone of formality as well as from the tropic climes of fanaticism'.[46] It is one of my contentions in this book that Watts' view, that Christian approaches to reason, passions and affections have traditionally been characterised by balance rather than by simple extremes, is in a large measure justified. The joint goals of rational understanding and voluntary love, which formed the bedrock of classical Christian psychology, as long as they were seen together, provided a framework within which ungoverned rationalism and wild enthusiasm were equally unlikely to take hold.

Jonathan Edwards, in his *Treatise Concerning Religious Affections* (1746), placed himself within this same Christian tradition of balance between reason and passion, light and love:[47] 'Holy affections are not heat without light, but evermore arise from some information of the understanding, some spiritual instruction that the mind receives, some light or actual knowledge.'[48] It was by perpetuating the classical Christian distinction between passions and affections that Edwards was able to reach a view that transcended the simple dichotomy between reason and passion.[49] 'Affections' were, one could say, rational passions; they were neither mere cold logic nor ungoverned desire, rather they were movements of the will informed by the understanding. Gracious affections arose from the mind's understanding of divine things.[50] Rodney Fulcher has shown how earlier sixteenth- and seventeenth-century authors, including Pierre de la Primaudaye, Thomas Shepard and Thomas Hooker, were responsible for the transmission of the scholastic understanding of the affections – as actions and movements of the will, subserved by an enlightened understanding – into the Puritan tradition.[51]

John Wesley, who abridged Edwards' *Treatise* for his Methodist brethren, also endorsed this distinction between passions and affections.[52] It had also been evident in a sermon preached by the poet and Anglican clergyman Edward Young on *A Vindication of Providence* (1728). Young

---

[46] Milner (1834), 441.
[47] For an account of the way that Jonathan Edwards and other seventeenth- and eighteenth-century Puritans maintained a creative tension between the will and the understanding, between feelings and intellect, see Fulcher (1973). For a discussion of the applicability of Harold Bloom's notion of 'the American difference' – the ability of pragmatic American thinkers to overcome dualities more characteristic of modern European thought – to Jonathan Edwards, see Jacobson (1987), 384–5.
[48] Edwards (1959), 266.
[49] For further discussions of the 'new sense of the heart' described by Edwards, see John E. Smith, 'Introduction' to Edwards (1959); Wainwright (1990); Jacobson (1987); Jenson (1988), 65–70.
[50] Edwards (1959), 266.　[51] Fulcher (1973), esp. 128–35.
[52] Clapper (1989), 54–5, 140.

took Colossians 3.2 – 'Set your affections on things above' – as his text. Doing this, he said, involved 'each of these acts: to think, to judge, and to love'; judgment in particular was 'necessary for the fixing our affections'.[53] Passions, in contrast, he defined as the 'pains of life': 'they pain the whole soul, they confound the memory, make wild the imagination, and hurt the understanding'.[54]

In the eighteenth century, however, there was a new sense to the word 'passions', not found in classical Christian teachings, which derived from the influence of René Descartes' views on the body and the soul and on the passions of the soul in particular. His *Traité des Passions de l'Ame* was his last work and was published in 1649; it informed thinking about the passions in Europe for at least the next hundred and fifty years.[55] Watts, who had studied Descartes' *Traité*, generally endorsed the Cartesian view of the passions, while Edwards took a less sympathetic view but allowed that the Cartesian model applied to at least some passions and affections.[56]

Soul and body

Passions of the soul, according to Descartes, were a special sort of perception. On his view, in fact, all perceptions were strictly passions of the soul, since they were instances of the soul being acted upon by the outside world by means of the sensory apparatus of the body. Passions of the soul in the narrower sense normally given to 'the passions' were defined by Descartes as perceptions caused by the agitation of the 'animal spirits' (very fine parts of the blood) in the body; passions were somewhat confused perceptions caused by the action of the body upon the soul. (It is interesting to note that Descartes recommended the use of the term '*émotions*' to refer to passions in this restricted sense but that his theory was initially always rendered as a theory of the 'passions' in both the French- and the English-speaking worlds.)[57]

Descartes' theory of the passions departed from the classical Christian theory in two crucially important ways. First, the model of perception displaced that of movement, and secondly, the distinction between soul and body took on a more thoroughly literal rather than metaphorical meaning;

---

[53] Young (1728), 1–11. [54] Young (1728), 34–49.
[55] Descartes (1984). For an analysis of Descartes' theory of the passions, see Rorty (1982); James (1997), especially chs. 5, 8 and 11.
[56] Milner (1834), 438; Davis (1948), 148–9; Watts (n.d.), 18–19; Edwards (1959), 269.
[57] For a further analysis of the significance of Descartes' *Traité*, see the section on Hume in chapter 4 below.

the difference between the soul–body distinction and the spirit–flesh distinction was dropped.[58]

The displacement of the model of movement by a model of perception in understanding the passions was especially significant because of the implications it had in terms of the relative activity or passivity of the soul and the body. On the classical Christian theory, passions were most properly to be understood as passions of the body. The bodily movements and agitations associated with fear, lust, anger and so on were brought about by the self-initiated activity of the sense appetite, which was the lower part of the will.[59] So, classically, the passions were actions of the sense appetite upon the rational will and upon the body. Affections were also acts of the will but in this case of the higher or rational will. But if this model of passions and affections as self-initiated movements of the will was replaced, as it was by Descartes, by a model of perception, the assignment of activity and passivity was reversed. So passions became actions of the body and passions of the soul.[60] This definition of 'passions of the soul' was to have significant theological and psychological consequences, most notably (not in Descartes himself, but ultimately) the disappearance of the will as the locus of human agency, and its gradual replacement by the passions and affections (and later 'emotions') themselves and, finally, by the body.

Edwards was substantially in tune with the classical Christian approach rather than the Cartesian one in insisting that the affections were inclinations of the soul or exercises of the will, which only secondarily made impressions on the animal spirits:

But yet it is not the body, but the mind only, that is the proper seat of the affections. The body of man is no more capable of being really the subject of love and hatred, joy or sorrow, fear or hope, than the body of a tree, or than the same body of man is capable of thinking and understanding. As 'tis the soul only that has ideas, so 'tis the soul only that is pleased or displeased with its ideas. As 'tis the soul only that thinks, so 'tis the soul only loves or hates, rejoices or is grieved at what it thinks of. Nor are these motions of the animal spirits, and fluids of the body, anything properly belonging to the nature of the affections; though they always accompany them, in the present state; but are only effects or concomitants of the affections, that are entirely distinct from the affections themselves, and no way essential to them; so that an unbodied spirit may be as capable of love and

---

[58] For the classical Christian teaching on the distinction between works of the spirit and works of the flesh (which are predicated of a whole person, body and soul) see Galatians 5 and Augustine (1952), XIV.
[59] See e.g. Augustine (1952), XIV.3; Aquinas (1981), Ia2ae.22, 1–3; Ia2ae.28.
[60] As Susan James puts it, 'The passions of the soul, then, are for the most part passive perceptions of bodily motions.' James (1997), 94.

hatred, joy or sorrow, hope or fear, or other affections, as one that is united to a body.[61]

This avowal of the importance of the soul to the exclusion of the body in understanding passions and affections was more forceful than any comparable classical account. Although it expressed a conclusion that inverted Descartes' view about the relative roles of soul and body in the passions and affections, the strength of dualism may be a result of the influence of Descartes more than of the classical Christian tradition. Edwards also conceded that the Cartesian model of the passions applied to some cases, saying that 'there are some instances of persons, in whom it seems manifest that the first ground of their affection is some bodily sensation':

The animal spirits, by some cause (and probably sometimes by the devil), are suddenly and unaccountably put into a very agreeable motion, causing persons to feel pleasantly in their bodies; the animal spirits are put into such a motion as is wont to be connected with the exhilaration of the mind; and the soul, by the laws of the union of soul and body, hence feels pleasure.[62]

While these cases were only allowed as anomalies – the paradigm affection or passion was still seated squarely in the soul – the influence of Cartesian thinking was evident.

The second major development in Descartes' theory of the passions was the thorough and literal division of the human person into two distinct substances, the thinking substance of the soul and the extended substance of the body. While the classical Christian view was in many ways dualistic, there was always a strongly metaphorical element to such dualism. The distinction between the works of the flesh and the works of the spirit was a metaphor used – by St Paul, St Augustine and Edwards, for example – to distinguish between two different sorts of soul, not between a substantial soul and a substantial body.[63]

Increasingly, during the eighteenth century, the literal and substantial dualism already present as one part of classical Christianity, and which Descartes had popularised, took over from more metaphorical dualisms, such as that between flesh and spirit. Watts, for example, adopted a wholly Cartesian model of the person divided into two parts, the 'soul or mind' and the 'animal body'. He also used the Cartesian model of perceptions with bodily causes (rather than movements of the appetite or will) in understanding the passions: '[W]hen we perceive any object with such properties as are before-mentioned, we find usually some ferments of the

[61] Edwards (1959), 98.   [62] Edwards (1959), 269.
[63] Galatians 5; Augustine (1952), XIV; Edwards (1959), 198; see below.

blood, or natural spirits, or some alterations which affect the body, as well as we feel special impressions on our minds.'[64] Watts showed, nonetheless, an awareness of the difficulty of knowing whether to ascribe activity to the soul and passivity to the body or vice versa in understanding the passions.[65] But before Descartes there would have been little difficulty for a Christian psychologist to know that the will (either rational or appetitive) was the source of all such phenomena.

Spirit and flesh

Having emphasised the extent to which the influence of Descartes' theory led to a stauncher soul–body dualism and a more active role for the body in the passions, it should be noted that this was only half the story. Revivalist thinkers were deeply imbued with traditional Christian thought, especially that of St Paul and of St Augustine. It is from these thinkers that Edwards inherited the strong distinction between nature and grace, between the carnal natural man and the spiritual saved man – a distinction that was integral to classical Christian psychology and which must be clearly differentiated from Cartesian soul–body dualism.

Humanity was divided by Edwards into two groups – the natural and the saved. The natural, or 'carnal', man might be touched by the Holy Spirit in its 'common' but not in its 'saving' operations. The saved, or 'spiritual', or 'sanctified', man was touched by the 'gracious' or 'saving' operations of the Holy Spirit. The natural man might be operated upon by the Holy Spirit but the Holy Spirit dwelt within the saved.[66] So when passions for particular worldly objects were ascribed only to the natural man and affections of peace, love and joy ascribed to the spiritual man the distinction was *not* between body and soul, but between two different sorts of person (fundamentally between two souls). This was how Edwards himself put it:

Now it may be observed that the epithet 'spiritual', in these and other parallel texts in the New Testament, is not used to signify any relation of persons or things to the spirit or soul of man, as the spiritual part of man, in opposition to the body, which is the material part: qualities are not said to be spiritual, because they have their seat in the soul, and not in the body; for there are some properties that the Scriptures call carnal or fleshly, which have their seat as much in the soul, as those that are called spiritual.[67]

So passions such as jealousy, anger or lust, may be called 'carnal' or 'fleshly' but they were still seated in the soul. Thus Edwards continued

---

[64] Watts (n.d.), 18.   [65] Watts (n.d.), 13.
[66] Edwards (1959), 232–4.   [67] Edwards (1959), 198.

the tradition of 'metaphorical' dualism found in, for example, Augustine's reading of Paul on the works of the spirit and the works of the flesh (Galatians 5) as opposed to the Cartesian substance dualism about soul and body which seemed to influence his thinking elsewhere.[68]

This distinction between natural and spiritual men was used by Edwards to distinguish between natural and gracious affections. The spiritual man was enlightened by the indwelling Holy Spirit and thus his affections were transformed.

> From hence it follows, that in those gracious exercises and affections which are wrought in the minds of the saints, through the saving influence of the Spirit of God, there is a new inward perception or sensation of their minds, entirely different in its nature and kind, from anything that ever their minds were the subject of before they were sanctified... And this is what I mean by supernatural, when I say, that gracious affections are from those influences that are supernatural.[69]

This new inward perception, Edwards said, was as different from other, natural perceptions as one external sense (say, sight) was from another (say, taste).[70] There are two final comments to be made on this idea that gracious affections, unlike natural affections, were the perceptions of a new internal, supernatural power of sense.

First, we return to the fact that Edwards' understanding of passions and affections, for all its indebtedness to classical Christianity, still bore the marks of its own era. That even gracious affections were treated by Edwards as a species of inner 'perception' analogous to bodily sensations is a telling sign of the extent to which thought about the mind in terms of sensation and (external and internal) perceptions, through the influence of Descartes and Locke, had come to displace models of acts of the will and movements of the soul.[71]

Secondly, what was strikingly different about Edwards' theory, in contrast to theories on both sides of the debate about 'innate ideas', was that this new sense was neither innate to human nature nor acquired through experience but was the result of the direct work of God's indwelling Spirit – it was a supernatural sense. Thus Edwards' theory of affections was full-bloodedly theological. Affections were categorised according to whether they were 'natural' or 'gracious' and God's Spirit, rather than either human nature or experience, was granted real and immediate psychological agency. This thoroughly theological method contrasts

---

[68] See Augustine (1966), XIV.2–5.
[69] Edwards (1959), 205. [70] Edwards (1959), 206.
[71] On Edwards' particular indebtedness to Locke, see Proudfoot (1989), 153–5; Miller (1959). For the opposite view, that Edwards significantly dissents from Lockean and Cartesian epistemology, see Jacobson (1987); Cherry (1966).

in interesting ways with the often atheological methodology applied to the study of human nature and its passions and affections by the British moralists.[72]

Moralists: Francis Hutcheson, Joseph Butler and Thomas Reid

Hutcheson, Butler and Reid were the contributors to the moralist tradition who had the most interesting and influential things to say about the passions and affections. All three were Christian philosophers who were concerned to rebut the reductionist theories of Hobbes and Mandeville, and, in Reid's case, especially of Hume. The Hobbesian view was that man was by nature vicious and acquisitive, driven by passion from one object of desire to the next. Hence Hutcheson and Butler both focussed on the question of what constituted fundamental 'human nature' or, to use another eighteenth-century phrase, what characterised the 'inward frame' of man. The central plank of their strategy was to point to the 'public affections' of mankind – man's allegedly natural impulse to do good to others – as evidence that man was naturally just as inclined to help others as to help himself.[73]

Thomas Reid is included here as a participant in the British moralist tradition. He was also an important figure in the Scottish philosophical tradition that forms the subject of the next chapter, involved as he was in discussions about the application of inductivism to the mind by his mentor Turnbull, and motivated as he was by dissent from certain aspects of Humean empiricism.[74] On balance, however, it is judged that his contribution to discussions about passions and affections belongs best in this chapter rather than the next; the next chapter centres around the creation of the psychological category of 'emotions' (a category Reid never

---

[72] I.e. Their discussion of human mental life was generally naturalistic and philosophical, and was neglectful of the narratives and doctrines of traditional Christianity. As elsewhere in this book, 'atheological' refers to texts and does not imply that their authors were atheists.

[73] For a detailed discussion of Hobbes', Hutcheson's and Butler's contributions to this debate, see Darwall (1995), chs. 3, 8 and 9.

[74] For a good introduction to Thomas Reid's life and work, see Haakonssen (1999); Gallie (1998), ch. 3, on Reid's views on motivation and moral psychology, is particularly relevant to the present study. On Reid and the Common Sense school, see also Grave (1960), McCosh (1875). For further accounts of Reid and his widespread influence in Britain, Europe (especially on the French school of eclecticism of Royer-Collard and Cousin) and America, see McCosh (1875), 8–10; Brett (1921), III, 14–20; Martin (1961); Roback (1964), esp. ch. 4; Bozeman (1977); Page (1980); Hoeveler (1981), esp. ch. 4; Cashdollar (1989); Corrigan (1993); Smith (1997). On the impact of Common Sense philosophy specifically on Charles Darwin's writings, see Campbell (1986).

used) by writers who were very enthusiastic about the application of natural philosophical methods and results to the study of human nature (a question on which Reid was much more cautious).

Reid, like Butler, was a representative of a *via media*, an advocate of broad churchmanship, a moderate.[75] He, like Butler, displayed a willingness to derive moral law and mental philosophy from the philosophy of human nature as much as from the revealed word of God.[76] The moderates of the Scottish church in this period were described, with some hostility, by the evangelical James McCosh in his *The Scottish Philosophy from Hutcheson to Hamilton* (1875), as having 'no faith in the peculiar Bible doctrines of grace', and as being on a road travelled down by Hume towards 'deism and philosophic indifference'.[77] Roger Emerson has provided an excellent summary of the ways that a theological moralism, centred around Calvinist ideas of the fall and grace, which was taught in Scottish universities in the seventeenth century, gave way in the following century to a more thinly theistic brand of morality.[78] Emerson's diagnosis, that in eighteenth-century Scotland 'Ethics had not been secularized, but it had been de-Christianized', is one that, I think, applies also to psychology. The moralists' philosophy of human nature displayed fewer and fewer distinctively Christian characteristics during this period, while still forming part of a theistic rather than secular system.[79]

It is argued here that Butler in particular was responsible for producing a view of the human mind that was shaped more by the philosophical agenda set by Locke, Hobbes and Descartes than by the Christian tradition; in his account of appetites, passions, sentiments and affections, Butler – in spite of his undoubted Christian convictions – produced, in his *Sermons*, an account of the human mind that owed apparently little to Christian metaphysics or theology. The design theology adopted by moralists such as Butler tended to distance God from humanity. The living triune God who was archetype of the human soul, whose love directed the well-ordered will, whose Word enlightened the understanding and whose Spirit could act and dwell in the soul was replaced by a more distant Deity or Maker or Author of nature who could only be inferred from the psychological constitution of man.[80] Butler himself was no Deist, nor a Unitarian, any more than he was actually a mechanist about human beings. His *Analogy of Religion* (1736), in which the importance of

---

[75] On the evangelical and moderate church parties of the Scottish Enlightenment, see McCosh (1875), 86–9. On Reid's membership of the moderate, Arminian (i.e. non-Calvinist) party, see McCosh (1875), 205; Griffin (1990), 426.
[76] Smith (1997), 244.   [77] McCosh (1875), 130.
[78] Emerson (1990), 11–19.   [79] Emerson (1990), 19.
[80] For some of these titles used in the place of 'God', see e.g. Butler (1970), 16, 34.

the Christian doctrine of the fall was defended, was directed against the Deists.[81] However, in his natural theology of the human mind, he adopted language that was more suggestive of deism than trinitarian theology and more suggestive of mechanism than voluntarism. For this reason it is suggested that his writings form part of a halfway house between Christian and secular psychologies, even though he himself did not intend them to be taken that way.

Rational principles and sensory passions

Hutcheson, in his *Essay on the Nature and Conduct of the Passions and Affections* (1728), reproduced Aquinas' distinction between the *appetitus sensitivus* and the *appetitus rationalis*.[82] This distinction between the lower sense appetite and the higher rational appetite (or 'will') had been central to Aquinas' distinction between passions, which were movements of the sense appetite, and affections, which were acts of the will. The sense appetite had particular objects of sense for its objects; the intellectual appetite, or will, had intellectual goods such as knowledge or virtue for its objects.[83] Hutcheson related this classical Christian distinction between the higher and lower appetites to Joseph Butler's distinction between the calm desire for good on the one hand and the particular appetites and passions on the other. He wrote:

> Thus nothing can be more distinct than the general calm desire of private good of any kind, which alone could incline us to pursue whatever objects were apprehended as the means of good, and the particular selfish passions, such as ambition, covetousness, hunger, lust, revenge, anger, as they arise upon particular occasions. In the like manner our public desires may be distinguished into the general calm desire of the happiness of others, or aversion to their misery upon reflection; and the particular affections or passions of love, congratulation, compassion, natural affection.[84]

Although Hutcheson was, then, aware of Aquinas' distinctions, the distinction between passions and affections was not very systematically followed through in his *Essay* (although the distinction between general calm desires and particular passions was). One of Hutcheson's few explicit comments on the difference between passions and affections was to suggest that passions tended to be more violent and less benevolent than affections: 'When the word passion is imagined to denote anything

---

[81] Hilton (1988), 176, 182–3; Brooke and Cantor (1998), 147.
[82] Hutcheson (1742), 30n. Aquinas' original term was *appetitus intellectivus* rather than *appetitus rationalis*, as Hutcheson renders it; see above.
[83] Aquinas (1981), 1a.81, 1–3; 1a.82, 5, ad 1; 1a2ae.24, 2–3; 1a2ae.26, 2.
[84] Hutcheson (1742), 29–30.

different from the affections, it includes a strong brutal impulse of the will, sometimes without any distinct notion of good, public or private.'[85] As Stephen Darwall has also argued, however, there was a fundamental difference implicit in Hutcheson's moral philosophy between, on the one hand, passions and appetites, which did not necessarily have any genuine goods as their objects, but rather tended to be directed to objects of sensory pleasure or pain, and, on the other hand, 'calm desires' or affections, which did have genuine goods as their objects.[86] This distinction was derived from both early Christian and scholastic thought. Reid also figured at the traditional Christian end of the spectrum of views about reason and the passions, especially in his connection of the authority of reason over the passions with an advocacy of man–animal separatism, and in his distinction between brutish passions and appetites on the one hand and familial and other-regarding affections on the other.[87]

The distinction between 'general' and 'particular' objects of affections and desires corresponded closely to the traditional distinction between reason and the passions. Butler put a lot of weight on the difference between 'general' rational cool desires and what he called, interchangeably, the 'particular passions' or the 'particular affections'.

> Every man hath a general desire of his own happiness; and likewise a variety of particular affections, passions and appetites to particular external objects... The object the former pursues is somewhat internal, our own happiness, enjoyment, satisfaction; whether we have or have not, a distinct particular perception what it is, or wherein it consists: the objects of the latter are this or that particular external thing, which the affections tend towards, and of which it hath always a particular idea or perception.[88]

This was virtually identical to the scholastic view of rational and sensory appetites with the subtle but crucial difference that the 'general' object of the rational appetite was not now goodness, virtue or truth per se, nor even union with God, but, *one's own* happiness, enjoyment and satisfaction. Augustine, for one, would have questioned whether anything ever could or should be enjoyed for its own sake rather than simply being used as a means to approach closer to God.[89] Furthermore, Butler resolved the affections not, as Augustine, or the revivalists, would have done, into love of *God*, but into 'rational' or 'cool' self-love; in other words into the 'interest' that Hirschman's essay picks out as the principle looked

---

[85] Hutcheson (1742), 28.   [86] Darwall (1995), 223–33.
[87] See below, and Gallie (1998), 33–41. For more on man–animal separatism and continuism in the history of affective psychologies, see chapters 5 and 6 below.
[88] Butler (1970), 100.
[89] For a discussion of Augustine's distinction between *uti* (use) and *frui* (enjoyment), see Burnaby (1991), 104–8. See also Augustine (1991), IX.13.

to by several eighteenth-century moralists as the best way to restrict the passions.[90] Edwards and Butler also disagreed on this point as a result of their different approaches to 'nature'. Edwards described self-love as a 'natural' – as opposed to a gracious – affection (i.e. self-love was a bad thing).[91] Butler would have agreed that it was a 'natural' affection, but would have argued from its naturalness to the fact that it was part of a divinely designed mechanism for the production of individual and communal happiness (i.e. self-love or self-interest was a good thing).[92]

Despite his tendency away from theocentric psychology, Butler presented the traditional view that cool rational deliberation was the proper prelude to action. This view was in deliberate contrast to the Hobbesian view that what was normally called 'will' was in fact just the strongest appetite in the moment preceding action. Hobbes had recommended that 'will' be renamed 'last appetite in deliberating'.[93] Butler was concerned to replace pure strength of appetite with the authority of rational deliberation or reflection as the proper determinant of action. As the source of this required authority for action, Butler sometimes appealed to the reflective principle of 'conscience' (or 'moral sense' or 'Divine reason') and sometimes to the principle he called 'reasonable self-love', by which he meant cool and rational self-interest, which, in turn, was coincident with virtue and public interest.[94] On other occasions he appealed to both at once: 'Reasonable self-love and conscience are the chief or superior principles in the nature of man: because an action may be suitable to this nature, though all other principles be violated; but becomes unsuitable, if either of those are.'[95] He argued that 'if passion prevails over self-love, the consequent action is unnatural; but if self-love prevails over passion the action is natural: it is manifest that self-love is in human nature a superior principle to passion'.[96]

---

[90] Augustine (1952), XIV.7; Susan James has noted that the Augustinian unification of the passions and affections under the single principle of love became popular amongst many seventeenth-century writers, answering as it did to a strong synthesising tendency in that period; James (1997), 6; Watts (1746), x; Hirschman (1997).
[91] Edwards (1959), 242–3.   [92] E.g. Butler (1970), 20–1.
[93] Hobbes (1997), 36. For an exposition of Hobbes' views on the meaning of 'will' see James (1997), 134–5.
[94] For a discussion of the different possible interpretations of Butler's teachings on conscience, self-love, benevolence and the particular passions, see Frey (1992). Frey himself adopts the model in which the two principles of reflection are conscience and self-love, and these regulate benevolence and the particular passions. Butler's sermons (especially Sermon XI) sometimes seem to fit with this model but at other times (especially in Sermons I–III) a model in which conscience is superior to the general principles of benevolence and self-love, which in turn should regulate the particular passions and affections, seems to prevail. See also Rivers (2000), ch. 3; Hirschman (1997).
[95] Butler (1970), 39. This is one of the key texts supporting Frey's interpretation.
[96] Butler (1970), 32.

Reid, in rebutting the Humean dictum that reason is and ought to be the slave of the passions (which he called a 'mere abuse of words'), similarly insisted on the distinction between brute strength and authority.[97] Reid said that motives such as passions and appetites should not be seen as agents, as they were in the models proposed by Hobbes and Hume, but rather as advocates. In the views of Hobbes and Hume, as Reid understood them, 'Nothing is left to the agent, but to be acted upon by the motives as the balance is by the weights.' The human agent must have a role, which was compared by Reid to that of a judge who listens to the advocates pleading opposite sides of a case. The advocate (passion) that prevailed did not do so by strength alone but as a result of the deliberations of the judge (reason). This was one of the things that separated man from 'the brutes' – he can make judgments about what course of action to take, rather than simply being driven by whatever appetite or passion happens to be strongest.[98]

Public and private

In his sermons, Butler took the Hobbesian assertion that humans were entirely driven by self-interest, and attacked it from two angles. The first way was connected to his view of the natural superiority of rational reflection over the particular passions and affections. He acknowledged that people were often driven by particular passions but disputed that this meant that they were driven by self-interest.

> Men daily, hourly sacrifice the greatest known interest, to fancy, inquisitiveness, love or hatred, any vagrant inclination. The thing to be lamented is, not that men have so great regard to their own good or interest in the present world, for they have not enough; but that they have so little to the good of others. And this seems plainly owing to their being so much engaged in the gratification of particular passions unfriendly to benevolence, and which happen to be most prevalent in them, much more than to self-love.[99]

Butler did not say that Hobbes was wrong to say that men were acquisitive and selfish and lustful and brutish in their behaviour. Butler quite agreed that men were driven by love, hate and any vagrant passion or appetite into foolish and destructive behaviour. Butler's point was, rather, that it was actually not in their interest to do so. Hobbes was wrong to equate the gratification of passions with the pursuit of self-interest.

---

[97] Reid (1788), 212. On the difference between the Humean and Reidian views of moral decision making (feeling versus judgment) see Graham (2001).
[98] Reid (1788), 291–300; see also Gallie (1998), 33–41.   [99] Butler (1970), 14–15.

At first glance this answer seems to be in tune with the traditional Christian distinction between the virtuous affections of a well-ordered will (conscience and self-love in Butler) and the disobedient passions of the fallen soul with their particular worldly objects (ungoverned passions in Butler). What is curious about Butler's first answer to Hobbes, however, is that it gave no explanation of the existence and power of ungoverned passions. On the classical view, ungoverned passions took their power from the sensory appetite, which was in rebellion against the rational will as a consequence of the fall and which was a symptom, therefore, of original sin.[100] Human beings suffered the internal disobedience of the appetite to the will as a punishment for the disobedience of Adam and Eve to God. On the classical view, the predominance of passions over affections was the sign of a disordered will in which reason was failing to subdue the disobedient lower appetite, and in which love of self and the world was predominating over love of God.

Butler, in contrast, neglected the role of the will in explaining the existence and power of ungoverned passions. He explicitly denied that there was any such thing as 'ill-will in one man towards another' and instead blankly insisted that public and private passions and affections were all designed to lead to right behaviour and that they generally did so. Passions and affections 'only secondarily and accidentally' lead to evil.[101] The omission, in his treatment of the passions and affections, of the concepts of will, love of God, obedience, sin and the fall left Butler's 'ungoverned passions' as unexplained malfunctions of the human machine. This development of a view of passions as autonomous, ontologically basic psychological agencies (rather than as movements of a corrupt will) was one of the most significant developments in the moralist tradition, which could be interpreted as a result of a movement away from Christian soteriological psychology.

Butler's second answer to Hobbes' claim that human beings were exclusively motivated by self-interest was to point out that people had both private and public affections – people were moved to help other people quite as spontaneously and naturally as they were moved to act in their own private interest: 'there is a natural principle of *benevolence* in man; which is in some degree to society, what *self-love* is to the *individual*'.[102] It was not disputed in the eighteenth century any more than it is now that human beings sometimes did things that were in the interests of others. What was disputed then, as it still is now (particularly in the

---

[100] See e.g. Augustine (1952), XIV.3; Augustine (1961), X; Augustine (1991), IX–XII. See also O'Connell (1987), 260; Innes (1997), 73–5.
[101] Butler (1970), 24.   [102] Butler (1970), 19–20.

debates surrounding sociobiology and evolutionary psychology), was why human beings behaved in such a way. The Hobbesian said that it was because society had been cunningly organised in order to induce people to act against their nature but for the common good.[103] Butler, however, said that human beings acted in the interests of others for the same reason that they acted in their own interest – that they were designed to do so:

> The sum is, men have various appetites, passions, and particular affections, quite distinct both from self-love, and from benevolence: all of these have a tendency to promote both public and private good, and may be considered as respecting others and ourselves equally and in common: but some of them seem most immediately to respect others, or tend to public good; others of them most immediately to respect self, or tend to private good: as the former are not benevolence, so the latter are not self-love: neither sort are instances of our love either to ourselves or others; but only instances of our Maker's care and love both of the individual and the species, and proofs that he intended we should be instruments of good to each other, as well as that we should be so to ourselves.[104]

Like the first answer to Hobbes, this second answer also sounds traditional – the passions and affections were to be resolved ultimately into the love of God. But note that the private and public passions and affections of man were not, for Butler, conduits or expressions or movements of the love of God but evidence of the love of God, proofs of 'our Maker's care'. Instead of a living God acting or moving through the passions and affections of the will, an absent Maker was observable in them or signified or evidenced by them. Hutcheson had made the same use of human affections as evidence of the benevolence of the Deity rather than as vestiges or images of God.[105]

Secondly, God had not made people agents of good to each other by his love, which moved their will, which in turn determined their actions; instead God had made people instruments of his love – puppets without agency who could be used to bring about the greater purpose of social happiness. The implication was that passions and affections were determined, not by an individual's will, but exclusively by the Maker's design. As already noted, that left unanswered the questions: why do passions created by the Deity to promote individual and social happiness need to be 'governed'? Why is their ungoverned gratification so often not in anybody's interest? Without an account of a fallen, disordered human will with real agency in the world it was hard to answer such questions.

---

[103] See e.g. Mandeville (1970), 81–92.
[104] Butler (1970), 21.   [105] See Hutcheson (1742), 246.

Voluntary or mechanical?

One model that was widely used for the human mind during the eighteenth century (an age of industrialisation and mechanisation) was the machine. Hobbes had also used this metaphor in *Leviathan*:

> For seeing life is but a motion of limbs, the beginning whereof is in some principal part within; why may we not say, that all *automata* (engines that move themselves by springs and wheels as doth a watch) have an artificial life? For what is the heart, but a spring; and the nerves but so many strings; and the joints but so many wheels, giving motion to the whole body, such as was intended by the artificer?[106]

Hobbes did not believe humans were agents nor did he believe in the reality of sin (morals were artefacts of the legislating state and not ultimately real). Human beings, like machines, were designed, had no real agency and no free will.

Descartes had taught that animals were mechanical automata. Lord Shaftesbury also endorsed this view, linking it to animals' motivation solely by passions and affections rather than by reflection: 'It has been shown before, that no animal can be said properly to act otherwise than through affections or passions, such as are proper to an animal. For in convulsive fits, where a creature strikes either himself or others, it is a simple mechanism, an engine, or piece of clockwork, which acts and not the animal.'[107] The clockwork Hobbesian model could be applied to animals since they were not supposed to be agents, to have a will (at least not a rational will) and therefore they were not considered capable of sin. As long as the traditional Christian division between mankind and brute creation was preserved it was coherent to treat animals as machines and human beings as agents. Reid shared this view.[108] However, thinkers such as Hobbes and, in the eighteenth century, de la Mettrie, sought to erode the distinction exactly by showing that Descartes' view of animals could perfectly well be extended to human beings.[109] In the infamous *L'Homme Machine* of 1747, de la Mettrie simply set aside the Cartesian soul to reduce man to the same status as the animals. The mechanical physiology of the autonomous Cartesian body did not need, he claimed, to be supplemented with the mysterious Cartesian soul, any more than Newton's mechanical universe had needed to be supplemented by a mysterious and

---

[106] Hobbes (1997), 9.
[107] Shaftesbury (1999), 195.   [108] Reid (1788), 205–15, 295–300.
[109] This position was strengthened by advances in physiological psychology in the nineteenth century. For a definitive statement of the way that scientific man–animal continuism demanded the extension of Descartes' analysis to human beings, see Huxley (1894).

unpredictable God. De la Mettrie did for Cartesian anthropology what Pierre Laplace would later do for Newtonian cosmology – neither needed those theological hypotheses.

So, while the application of the machine analogy by thinkers such as Hobbes or de la Mettrie (who did not believe in free human agency and who wanted to erode the Christian distinction between men and animals by describing both as machines driven by passion and appetite) was entirely understandable and coherent, there were cases where it seemed a less appropriate strategy. What was particularly problematic was the application of the machine model to human beings by those who purported to defend a traditional Christian view and to believe that human beings had agency and could sin. Butler was a prime example. This is how he expressed the analogy:

> Let us instance in a watch. – Suppose the several parts of it taken to pieces, and placed apart from each other: let a man have ever so exact a notion of these several parts, unless he considers the respects and relations which they have to each other, he will not have anything like the idea of a watch... But let him view those several parts put together, or consider them as to be put together in the manner of a watch; let him form a notion of the relations which those several parts have to each other – all conducive in their respective ways, to this purpose, showing the hour of the day; and then he has the idea of a watch. Thus it is with regard to the inward frame of man. Appetites, passions, affections, and the principle of reflection, considered merely as the several parts of our inward nature, do not at all give us an idea of the system or constitution of this nature: because the constitution is formed by somewhat not yet taken into consideration, namely by the relations, which these several parts have to each other; the chief of which is the authority of reflection or conscience. It is from considering the relations which the several appetites and passions in the inward frame have to each other, and above all the supremacy of reflection or conscience, that we get the idea of the system or constitution of human nature. And from the idea itself it will as fully appear, that this our nature, i.e. constitution, is adapted to virtue, as from the idea of a watch it appears, that its nature, i.e. constitution or system, is adapted to measure time.[110]

So, in response to the Hobbesian claim that humans were self-preservation machines Butler did not reply that humans were not machines but, rather, that humans were virtue-making machines; machines with conscience and self-love as their regulators. The central idea that humans were like machines had, it seemed, been left unchallenged. A shift in worldview had taken place so that the questions now asked were about what sort of a machine the human mind was, rather than, for example, about why the will was disordered or how the carnal man could be saved.

---

[110] Butler (1970), 5–6.

Despite the fact that Butler gave an answer opposed to Hobbes' answer, he found himself inhabiting a Hobbesian-mechanistic world as a result of asking such questions.

Butler was aware of the very problem being suggested here, that watches were not agents: 'If we go further, there is indeed a difference, nothing to the present purpose, but too important an one ever to be omitted. A machine is inanimate and passive: but we are agents. Our constitution is put in our own power. We are charged with it: and therefore are accountable for any disorder or violation of it.'[111] All of which would seem to be very good reasons not to preach that human beings are like watches. As Shaftesbury's comments about animal automatism quoted above illustrate, a machine model was most appropriate for a being driven by passions and affections with no real rational or moral agency. Although Butler did not believe this to be the proper way to think about human beings, his use of the machine as a model of the human being – especially given the highly influential role his teachings had throughout the eighteenth and nineteenth centuries – marked a shifting of the Christian tradition away from a soteriological anthropology towards a more mechanistic one.[112]

In one particularly striking passage, in the first of the fifteen sermons Butler preached at the Rolls Chapel in 1726, he noted that human beings performed certain tasks automatically and without reflection, such as eating when hungry. He continued as follows:

> It may be added, that as persons without any conviction from reason of the desirableness of life, would yet of course preserve it merely from the appetite of hunger; so by acting merely from regard (suppose) to reputation, without any consideration of the good of others, men often contribute to the public good. In both these instances they are plainly instruments in the hands of another, in the hands of Providence, to carry on ends, the preservation of the individual and good of society, which they themselves have not in their view or intention.[113]

Replace 'Providence' with 'the selfish genes' in this quotation and Richard Dawkins appears.[114] Hobbes, Butler and Dawkins have all, in their different ways, implied that we are blind and lumbering automata being manipulated by something else, which has real agency. For Hobbes it was the state, for Butler it was Providence, for Dawkins, selfish genes. In all three cases the individual will seem to be either an illusion or quite powerless. In the place of an individual will Butler proposed 'Providence'

---

[111] Butler (1970), 6.
[112] Thomas Chalmers was particularly influenced by Butler, and it is no coincidence that his view of emotions was organic, mechanistic and necessitarian, leaving little or no room for the will. See chapter 4.
[113] Butler (1970), 21.   [114] Dawkins (1976).

(or our 'Maker') as the ultimate agent of our passions and affections. The proximate agent was 'human nature', which the individual merely 'follows'.[115] Thus, in his sermons, Butler gave the impression (unintentionally, no doubt) that supernatural and natural (for him, primary and secondary causes) could combine to squeeze out the agency of the individual will. Stephen Darwall alludes to this problem in noting that, on one reading at least, Butler implied that the judgments of conscience were simply given to the individual automatically, 'because of the way God has fashioned our psyche'.[116] In 1776 Samuel Cooper, in a sermon preached before the University of Cambridge, expressed a similar view to Butler's: 'our internal constitution is so formed, that we naturally and necessarily love those who love us, and that we naturally and necessarily dislike those who dislike us'.[117] Mechanical design-theology metaphors, which pictured human nature as a divine artefact, were conducive to a psychology in which agency appeared to be ascribed either to the intelligent foresight of the Maker, or to secondary causes such as 'nature' or 'human nature', rather than to the self-initiated activity of the will.

Theological and atheological methods in the works of eighteenth-century Christians

In this chapter I have tried to show that prior to the emergence of the category of 'emotions', passions and affections were already being conceptualised by several influential Christian writers in a way that owed less and less to the Christian tradition. In the moral philosophical works these individuals produced, Christian concepts, traditions, models and metaphysical assumptions were being edged out by more secular arguments, mechanistic images and secondary natural causes. And even in the cases of Edwards, Tottie and Watts, where a more traditionally Christian and scriptural approach was taken to passions, affections and the soul – as evidenced by the agency attributed to the Holy Spirit and to Satan – the influence of Cartesian dualism and of the idea that passions were a sort of perception, led to significant departures from established Christian views.[118]

---

[115] For two illuminating discussions of the role and significance of Butler's 'Follow Nature' doctrine, see Millar (1988), and Brinton (1991).
[116] Darwall (1995), 283.   [117] Cooper (1776), 3.
[118] Edwards' treatise in particular, unlike the works of the moralists, is packed with scriptural references. For example, in his discussion of the common pattern in religious experiences of despair being superseded by joy, he adduces many scriptural examples such as the Children of Israel suffering humiliation before being delivered from Egypt, and the woman with a haemorrhage who suffered for twelve years before being cured. See Edwards (1959), 152–6.

But it was among some of the eighteenth-century British moralists, more than among the revivalists, that a 'scientific' and naturalistic way of thinking about passions and affections increasingly took hold. Their thin design theology, their neglect of the doctrines of sin and the fall, their departure from a will-centred affective psychology and their tacit introduction of a three-faculty rather than a two-faculty psychology, all took them away from traditional Christianity, to the extent that little distinctively Christian remained. Their teachings on passions and affections can be seen as a halfway house on the road towards the more secular psychologies of the nineteenth century.

The revivalists had retained a theocentric approach; this was increasingly displaced by anthropocentrism in the moralists' psychology. The focus on nature in general – 'the art whereby God hath made and governs the world' – and on human nature in particular, rather than on God Himself as the ground of passions and affections, was another significant move made by some writers in the moralist tradition.[119] Passions and affections were subservient to natural self-love, according to Butler, rather than to the love of God, as was taught by classical Christianity and by Edwards and Watts. The love of God, Watts had taught, 'rules and manages, awakens or suppresses all the other passions of the soul'.[120] God, for the moralists, was now the inferred architect (distant designer of the soul) rather than the living archetype (the God in whose image human beings were made). The locus of authority for these moralists, furthermore, was increasingly natural and moral philosophy as much as it was Scripture or doctrine. This contrasted with revivalists such as Tottie who held that we could only know our own nature and that of God through Revelation.[121] Butler explicitly drew attention to the fact that the superiority of conscience could be demonstrated 'exclusive of revelation'.[122]

There were three ways of thinking about the passions and affections of the soul that were particularly characteristic of these eighteenth-century moral philosophies. All three involved the endorsement of analogies that were later to be taken literally by reductionist and scientific psychologists.

The first analogy, which was used by both moralists and revivalists, was that between inner and outer sensations. As we have seen, passions and affections (including the moral sense and moral sentiments) were described as a sort of inner sensation or perception, by analogy with the

[119] Hobbes (1997), 9. Roger Smith notes that Shaftesbury and Hutcheson showed a new willingness to derive moral law from human nature rather than from God's word. Smith (1997), 244.
[120] Butler (1970), 38–9. Watts (1746), x.
[121] Tottie (1738), 20.   [122] Butler (1970), 36.

external senses of taste, touch, sight and so on. Reid's opposition to the reduction of complex acts of the mind, of which sensation or feeling was only one element, to sensation or feeling alone, displayed awareness of the reductionist tendency of the analogy.[123] Sensationalist and associationist thinkers such as Hartley, Condillac and James Mill would later replace the view that passions and affections were like outward sensations with the view that they just were modes or combinations of sensations – Spencer and Bain also tended towards this latter view in their works on emotions.[124]

The second analogy was that between artificial mechanisms and human beings. We have seen how moralists such as Hobbes, Butler and Shaftesbury took the view that human beings (in mind and in body) were like machines. This analogy was taken literally by more reductionist thinkers such as, in the eighteenth century, de la Mettrie and, in the nineteenth century, Spencer and Huxley, all of whom held that human beings just were machines.[125]

The third analogy found in several eighteenth-century texts of moral philosophy was between the sciences of matter and the science of mind; an analogy that was taken much further by the Scottish mental scientists who form the subject of the next chapter. The 'moral arithmetic' and 'inward anatomy' of the moralists were attempts to apply Baconian inductivism to the mind by methodological analogies.[126] It was again Reid, in his critique of Hume's attempt to construct a causal and law-like science of human nature, who showed most caution about pursuing the analogy between the necessary laws of Newtonian physics and the operations of an active human mind: 'There are many important branches of human knowledge, to which Sir Isaac Newton's rules of Philosophizing have no relation, and to which they can with no propriety be applied. Such are Morals, Jurisprudence, Natural Theology, and the abstract Sciences of Mathematicks and Metaphysicks; because in none of those sciences do we investigate the physical laws of Nature.'[127] Reid would certainly have accepted that the philosophy of mind and morals could be illuminated by inductive observations and generalisations, and in this sense could resemble natural philosophy. The view that Reid resisted was that the science of the mind could, like the natural scientific study of matter,

---

[123] Reid (1788), 471–2.
[124] On sensationalism and associationism, see chapter 4 below. On Spencer and Bain, see chapter 5 below.
[125] On the determinism and epiphenomenalism of Spencer and Huxley, see chapter 5 below.
[126] See e.g. Shaftesbury (1999), 194–5; Clarke (1706), 81–112. For an interesting reference to Hutcheson's proposed mathematicisation of morals, see McCosh (1875), 200.
[127] Quoted in Haakonssen (1999); see also Reid (1788), 291–300.

result in the production of causal laws.[128] The stricter analogy between the sciences of mind and matter was later extended further by those who held that the scientific study of mind just *was* the study of matter; the data of the science of mind, for such thinkers, were anatomical, physiological, neurological, evolutionary and behavioural facts (see chapters 5 and 7).

The presence of an increasingly mechanistic worldview was revealed by the sorts of questions that were asked by some eighteenth-century philosophers, leaving aside the different answers that were given. Butler was asking questions about what sort of machine the human mind was, what its components were and how the divine engineer had fitted them together. This contrasted with questions asked by those, such as Tottie, who considered the crucial questions in relation to human mental life to be: what degree of perfection did the mind of man originally have? Why did man degenerate from this state of mental perfection, and in what ways? How far will God's goodness allow man to recover the loss?[129]

The morally and religiously prescriptive treatments of religious affections produced by Edwards and Watts provide an interesting contrast with later detached, more 'objective' scientific treatments. As the leader of a revivalist community, Edwards sought to prescribe the proper affections that were to be felt by members of his church, the proper objects of such affections, their proper occasion, proper mode of expression and so on. Being affected in the right way was a condition of full membership of Edwards' revivalist community. Edwards constantly reminded his flock of their obligation to be affected: 'The piety which God requires, the only one he will accept, is one which engages the heart and inclines the self as a whole towards the divine glory in a love which is unmixed.'[130] The morally driven categorisations of passions and affections as either instances of private self-love or public benevolence, provided by the moralists, are also examples of morally engaged affective psychologies. Samuel Clarke, for example, spoke not just of man's nature but also of his duty: 'he ought to bridle his appetites, with temperance; to govern his passions, with moderation; and to apply himself to the business of his present station in the world, whatsoever it be, with attention and contentment'.[131]

Reid provides a good example of a forgotten exponent of what today might be called 'cognitive' and 'component' approaches to appetites, passions and affections. Reid believed, in opposition to Hume's reductionism, that reflective cognitive states (such as beliefs and desires) were

---

[128] On the different interpretations of the 'science of mind' given by Hume and Reid, see Graham (2001), which argues that Reid saw science as the process of uncovering providential design, while Hume saw it as simply the accumulation of brute facts about observable regularities.

[129] Tottie (1738), 3–5. [130] Edwards (1959), 15. [131] Clarke (1706), 97–8.

irreducible components of complex mental states that combined with, but were not mere products of, more basic sensations and feelings:

> Thus the appetites of hunger and thirst are compounded of an uneasy sensation, and the desire of food and drink. In our benevolent affections, there is both an agreeable feeling and a desire of happiness to the object of our affection; and malevolent affections have ingredients of a contrary nature. In these instances, sensation or feeling is inseparably conjoined with desire. In other instances, we find sensation inseparably conjoined with judgment or belief, and that in two different ways. In some instances, the judgment or belief seems to be the consequence of the sensations, and to be regulated by it. In other instances, the sensation is the consequence of the judgment.[132]

Reid went on to say that it was normally the belief or judgment that caused the feeling rather than the other way around. Two important points should be made about the above quotation. First, the use of metaphors of 'compounded' appetites and 'ingredients' in mental states was a novel one in this period, and one that revealed indebtedness to analytic models derived from optics and, perhaps, from chemistry. In the century following Reid's *Essays* the use of component models developed in two ways – it was perpetuated in non-reductionist and Christian ways by, for instance, McCosh, as well as being adapted to more reductionist ends in the 'chemical' and 'aggregate' models of Brown, Spencer and Bain.[133] Secondly, it is interesting to note that Reid was here proposing a view with a certain amount in common with twentieth-century 'emotion' theorists who propose a cognitive approach, notably Solomon, Lyons, Thalberg, Marks and Searle, all of whom ascribe a critical role to cognitive beliefs and desires in the production (or constitution) of emotions.[134] The cognitive view was used here by Reid in defence of Christianity and in opposition to Hume's anti-Christian reductionism.[135]

Those thinkers who might be styled the most 'orthodox' of Christians in this period, especially Edwards, generally produced a more balanced system of affective psychology than did those who departed from the Christian tradition. This balance is especially noticeable in the attempts by Watts and Edwards (reminiscent of Augustine's idea of *amata notitia* or 'knowledge with love') to overcome a simple dichotomy between reason

---

[132] Reid (1788), 472.
[133] On Newton, optics and Hume, see chapter 4 below and n.16 to the Introduction. On Brown and chemistry, see chapter 4 below. On images of movement in traditional Christian affective psychology, see especially Aquinas (1981), Ia.2ae.22–7. On reductionist 'aggregate' theories, see chapter 5 below. On later nineteenth-century component approaches, see chapter 6 below.
[134] Solomon (1993a); Lyons (1980); Thalberg (1984); Marks (1982); Searle (1983), 32–6.
[135] Contrast this with the suggestion that Christian attitudes were responsible for promoting a non-cognitive view of passions and emotions; Solomon (1993a), XIX, 9–10.

and passions and instead to find a middle way in which knowledge and love were kept in balance.¹³⁶ This contrasted with the approach of the moralists, who recommended the subjection of the passions to reason but, unlike the revivalists, made little attempt to maintain the voluntary and/or intellectual nature of the passions or affections. Again, the prevalence of Hobbesian concerns may have been the main reason for this development. Hobbes had made a stark division between head and heart, cognitive and motive powers, rational powers of the mind and animal powers of the body.¹³⁷ A similarly strict dichotomy between intellect and emotion would later be proposed by Thomas Brown and by William James, at the beginning and the end, respectively, of the nineteenth century.¹³⁸

The dissemination of psychological models in which passions and affections were conceived as a faculty in their own right meant that they came to be seen as alien powers rather than as movements integral to the self. The replacement of a bipartite psychology by a tripartite one (tacitly or explicitly) led to a view of passions, affections or, later, emotions, that was not only in contrast with intellect or reason, but also distanced from the will and hence from individual desires, goals, agency and moral responsibility.

---

¹³⁶ Augustine (1961), XII.15. On Edwards' version of *amata notitia*, the 'new sense of the heart', see n.49 above.
¹³⁷ E.g. Hobbes (1994), 2–3, 30.   ¹³⁸ See chapters 4 and 7 below.

4 The Scottish creation of 'the emotions': David Hume, Thomas Brown, Thomas Chalmers

> A difference of words is, in this case, more than a mere verbal difference. Though it be not the expression of a difference of doctrine, it very speedily becomes so... The first great subdivision, then, which I would form, of the internal class, is into our intellectual states of mind, and our emotions.
>
> Thomas Brown, *Lectures on the Philosophy of the Human Mind*, 100–2

Philosophy of the mind in the eighteenth and nineteenth centuries

By around 1850 the category of 'emotions' had subsumed 'passions', 'affections' and 'sentiments' in the vocabularies of the majority of English-language psychological theorists. It had become the most popular standard theoretical term for phenomena such as hope, fear, love, anger, jealousy and a wide variety of others. This chapter examines texts reflecting that transition. Having been concerned, so far, predominantly with the works of theologians, preachers and religious thinkers, I now want to examine a more secular philosophical tradition. In this chapter my focus will be on works of 'mental science' produced during the eighteenth and early nineteenth centuries, especially by certain Scottish empiricist philosophers and their followers. Before moving on to that part of the story, a few introductory words about the differences between various eighteenth- and nineteenth-century schools of philosophy of mind will help to set the scene and to introduce some perhaps unfamiliar terminology.[1]

A Priorism, sensationalism and associationism

During the eighteenth and nineteenth centuries, views about the nature of the mind (or soul) were categorised by, amongst other things, their

---

[1] A useful introduction to nineteenth-century philosophical-psychological discourse is Rylance (2000), ch. 2.

position on an axis of which A Priorism and sensationalism were the two extremes. The A Priorist considered mental faculties to be prior to experience – they were innate powers of the mind (or soul). The sensationalist believed the reverse – that mental faculties were the products of experience. A Priorists tended to be associated with Kant's views on mental categories' active role in shaping experience and with Reidian faculty psychology, while sensationalists were seen as the descendants of John Locke, who had taught in his *Essay Concerning Human Understanding* (1690) that there were no innate ideas but that the mind was, at birth, a *tabula rasa* which was shaped by experience. John Stuart Mill in 1859 named the two schools the a priori and a posteriori schools; the former he associated with Plato and Reid, the latter with Aristotle, Locke, Hume and Hartley.[2]

The term 'sensationalism', coined by the philosopher J. D. Morell in his *Speculative Philosophy of Europe* (1846) to refer to the mental philosophy of the Mills, Auguste Comte and G. H. Lewes, became a widely used term for those who believed all mental powers (including the internal sense) to be the products of experience alone.[3] 'Sensationalist', rather like 'materialist', was a term more often used by its opponents than its purported proponents (Morell himself was opposed to the sensationalist approach). The most famous exposition of pure sensationalism had been that of Etienne de Condillac in his *Traité des Sensations* (1754). In the *Traité*, Condillac described a statue gradually coming to life, one sense at a time, and how all the powers of the soul would be produced by those sensations alone. In nineteenth-century debates on the nature of mind the word 'sensationalist' was used where a twentieth- or twenty-first-century writer might use the word 'reductionist'. In the place of the reductionist claim made in our own time that we are 'nothing but a bundle of neurones', the claim was allegedly made by sensationalists that we are 'nothing but a bundle of sensations'; this in turn was a more reductive form of the earlier Hobbesian assertion that we are 'nothing but a bundle of passions and affections' (see chapter 3).

Locke himself, despite being claimed as the intellectual ancestor of thinkers at the reductionist end of the spectrum, had not been an extreme sensationalist. He had, rather, believed the powers of the mind to be derived from two sources – first, sensations, but also the internal reflection of the mind upon its own activity, which he called the 'internal sense' or simply 'reflection'. Belief in these two sources of ideas was characteristic

---

[2] [Mill] (1859), 287–95.
[3] Morell (1846), I, x, 64–72. See also Warren (1921), especially ch. 7, which deals with French thinkers such as Condillac and Bonnet whom Morell would certainly have classified as 'sensationalists'; Cashdollar (1989), 40–1.

of the Lockean philosophy developed by the 'associationists'.⁴ Associationism was connected most frequently with the name of David Hartley, whose *Observations on Man* (1749) was widely considered the source of the doctrine.⁵ The associationists held that all mental states, faculties or powers – from beliefs and desires to moral feelings and complex passions or emotions – were wholly acquired rather than innate. For example, the repeated association of contact with flames with physical pain could produce the fear of fire. Nineteenth-century associationists included Thomas Brown, the Mills, Alexander Bain, Herbert Spencer and G. H. Lewes. The difference between 'sensationalism' and 'associationism' – aside from the often derogatory overtones of the former – was that the former was more crudely reductionist, and explained complex phenomena as mere aggregates of basic bodily sensations, whereas the latter explained them as properties of complex learned associations, and gave a greater role, as Locke had, to the mind's power of reflection.⁶

Common sense

'Common sense' was a label applied to representatives of a predominantly Scottish school of philosophy of the eighteenth and nineteenth centuries. The principal figure and founder of the school was Thomas Reid, whose views on reason and the passions were discussed in chapter 3, alongside those of Hutcheson and Butler. Indeed it was partly from their ideas on the inner moral sense that Reid developed his own theory of common sense. Reid's *Enquiry into the Human Mind on the Principles of Common Sense* (1764) set out to respond to the sceptical arguments of Hume about the existence of the human soul and of Berkeley about the existence of the material world. One distinctive element of the common sense approach was the claim that all rational beliefs were based on certain self-evident truths, which could be seen to be true without the help of philosophical inquiry or religious teaching. It was this appeal to the reliability of human intuition or 'common sense' that earned the school of thought its name. These intuitions included logical and moral axioms as well as belief in the uniformity of nature and in the existence of an external world.⁷

---

⁴ See Warren (1921), 156–7; Russell (1991), 589–95.
⁵ Rylance (2000), 55–62, provides a particularly helpful description of nineteenth-century associationist psychology. For another useful summary, see Warren (1921), ch. 6. Warren considers Hobbes, Locke, Berkeley and Hume to be forerunners of associationism; the associationists proper are considered by him to be Hartley, Brown, James Mill, Bain, Spencer and Lewes. See also McCosh (1861 and 1875); Klein (1970), 82–4, ch. 18; Rapaport (1974); Berrios (1996), 19–20; Fancher (1996), 50–3.
⁶ See [Mill] (1859), 287–95.   ⁷ Haakonssen (1999).

The influence of the common sense school, when applied to mental philosophy, principally derived from its ability to provide a third way, beyond the dichotomies of materialism versus idealism, A Priorism versus empiricism.[8] To borrow a phrase from Charles Cashdollar, the common sense school could be characterised as 'judicious conservatives' who struck a balance between tradition and theology on the one hand and new scientific and philosophical ideas on the other. William Hamilton and James McCosh were influential nineteenth-century advocates of common sense teachings in Britain and America.[9]

Locke, Newton and mental science

Some Scottish writers on aesthetics, especially Lord Kames, in his *Elements of Criticism* (1752) and Archibald Alison, in his *Essays on the Nature and Principles of Taste* (1790), were early users of the category of 'emotions' as a general psychological term referring to vivid feelings, perceptions and sensations.[10] It was the associationist mental scientists, however, who provided the most influential early uses of the term 'emotions'. Hume's early use of the term in his *Treatise of Human Nature* (1739–40) was significant. The chemist, philosopher and theologian Joseph Priestley was another early user of the term within the associationist tradition of mental science, in his essays on Hartley's theory of the mind (1775).[11] For both Hume and Priestley, however, 'emotions' fulfilled an undefined role, while 'passions' and, to a lesser extent, 'affections', remained the established categories that they favoured. Thomas Brown's treatment of the emotions in his Edinburgh *Lectures on the Philosophy of the Human Mind* (1820) was a watershed; he was the first mental philosopher to give the term a coherent, systematic and central role instead of 'passions and affections', or 'active powers'. 'Emotions' was a term baptised by Brown – a follower of Hume's in many respects – within a mechanistic 'science of the mind'.

One of the dominant modes of psychological thought in the decades either side of 1800 was natural theology. The same design-theology

---

[8] Most common sense philosophers were, however, representatives of the a priori rather than the associationist psychological school – i.e. they more readily appealed to innate intuitions and ideas than to experience as the ground of complex psychological abilities. For an illustration of the way that the common sense and associationist approaches to mind contrasted, see Priestley (1774a).
[9] On Reid's life and works and the common sense school see n.74 to chapter 3.
[10] Kames (1765); Alison (1790); for more on Kames' views on emotions, passions and sentiments, see Rauch (1975), 300–1; Craig (1980); Danziger (1997), 41; Pinch (1996), 4–6, 49–50. On Alison, see Francis Jeffrey's review of the second edition of the *Essays*, [Jeffrey] (1811); see also Kallich (1999).
[11] Priestley (1775), xxvii–xxviii.

paradigm could be applied to the inner world of the mind as had already been extensively applied to the world of external nature and the human body. Mind and body could both produce evidence of the intelligence and benevolence of the Creator. As Thomas Chalmers would put it, 'a mental constitution might as effectually bespeak the hand of an intelligent Maker, as does a physical or material constitution'.[12] Henry Brougham, in his *Discourse of Natural Theology* (1835), described the human mind as 'by far the most singular work of divine wisdom and power'.[13] Brougham claimed that natural theologians had, in their enthusiasm for finding evidence of contrivance in the material universe, neglected this source of evidence of divine design.[14] There was some truth in this, but Brougham appears to have overlooked the influential contributions of Butler and Chalmers, to name just two particularly important figures, to the natural theology of the mind. Brougham's assertions, that 'The structure of the mind, in every way in which we can regard it, affords evidence of the most skilful contrivance', and that 'The feelings and the passions with which we are moved are devised for purposes apparent enough, and to effect which their adaptation is undeniable' were both extremely similar to the statements about the mind in general and the passions and affections in particular made by Butler in his sermons a century earlier (see chapter 3).[15]

Boyd Hilton's work has illustrated how eighteenth-century moralists' discussions about the moral sense, private vices, public virtues and the motivation of individuals in society developed, during the nineteenth century, into more specialised debates about political economy.[16] This was partly through the way that Butler's thought was revived, developed and applied by Chalmers and others. Butler's influence was arguably greater in the nineteenth century even than it had been in the eighteenth.[17] This chapter, in a similar way, shows how Hutcheson's, Butler's and Reid's speculations about human passions, affections and sentiments were developed, especially via Brown and Chalmers, into a more specialised psychological discourse about the 'emotions'.

Another figure whose influence was still felt in this period was John Locke, the father of the associationist school of psychology. As well as using the analogy between outward and inner sensations in describing the passions, Locke had adopted another of the analogies characteristic of the halfway house between Christian and secular psychologies – the trope of inward 'observation', derived from the modelling of mental philosophy on

---

[12] Chalmers (1853), 349. Hilton (1988) writes of Chalmers: 'Natural theology was transferred from the physical to the mental and applied to the relations between men' (186).
[13] Brougham (1835), 54.   [14] Brougham (1835), 52.   [15] Brougham (1835), 59, 64.
[16] Hilton (1988).   [17] Hilton (1988), 170–84.

experimental natural philosophy.[18] The empirical approach to the mind replaced the admonition of the Delphic oracle and of St Augustine to 'know thyself' with the rather more prosaic call of the mental scientists to 'observe thyself'. And instead of finding, as Augustine had, vestiges or images of the Triune God in the human mind, the mental scientists, as the moralists had before them, found evidences or proofs of a Deity.[19]

Just as natural theology could equally be based on the physical or the mental, so the scientific methods of observation, experiment and induction could equally be applied to either realm. There has been considerable debate about the extent and nature of the influence of 'science' on figures who are deemed to be actors in the 'Scottish Enlightenment'.[20] P. B. Wood has investigated this question with particular reference to the teaching of moral philosophy at Marischal and King's colleges in Aberdeen in the eighteenth century. He picks out Reid's mentor George Turnbull as having been a particularly important figure. Turnbull's commitment to 'apply myself to the study of the human mind in the same way as to that of the human body' was one shared by many of the Scottish mental and moral philosophers responsible for the introduction of the term 'emotions'.[21] At the turn of the nineteenth century, the recent chemical revolution was a particularly influential source of methodological comparisons for these authors.

Even some conservative Christian philosophers in this period engaged in a sort of thinking about mental reality that was almost entirely secular. The central Christian concepts of original sin, the fall and grace through Christ were absent from the pages of their texts. Even those who in other contexts would have insisted (and indeed did insist) on the centrality of these doctrines accepted the application of an entirely unchristian set of terms and methods when it came to psychology. One writer who fitted this particular bill and is discussed below was Thomas Chalmers, the evangelical preacher who led the 'Disruption' of 1843, which saw the creation of the Free Church in Scotland by ministers disillusioned with the established church.

For the proponents of mental science, the texts of Bacon, Locke and Newton replaced those of St Paul, St Augustine and St Thomas Aquinas

---

[18] Locke (1975), 229–30.
[19] See e.g. Chalmers (1853), 29 and throughout. Also see chapter 3 in this volume on Butler's use of design theology in his psychology.
[20] On the application of the methods of 'science' and natural philosophy to the study of the mind see n.20 to the Introduction of this volume.
[21] Turnbull quoted in Wood (1990), 133. On the debate between Francis Jeffrey and Dugald Stewart on the difference between observation and experiment and which was practised by the inductive mental scientist, see Payne (1828), 2–5; McCosh (1875), 344–5; Chitnis (1986), 68–9; Flynn (1988).

as the most often cited authorities on the realities of human mental life and the proper way to study it. Newton's comment at the end of his *Opticks* (1704), that the methods of natural philosophy could be successfully applied also to 'moral philosophy' became a 'proof text' on a par, in terms of frequency of allusion amongst mental scientists, with many a favourite biblical text of classical and revivalist theologians of earlier generations. A whole new scientific tradition with its own 'Scriptures' (such as Bacon's *Novum Organum*, Locke's *Essay* and Newton's *Opticks*) was emerging during this period. Wood refers, for example, to the 'almost Biblical status of Bacon's writings in eighteenth-century Scotland'.[22] Another recent commentator argues that through the influence of eighteenth- and nineteenth-century Scottish philosophers, Bacon and Newton came to be regarded as 'virtual Protestant saints'.[23]

An early user of the term 'emotions': David Hume

David Hume's liberal use of the term 'emotions' in his *Treatise of Human Nature* (1739–40) was the earliest sustained use of the term in the English language in a way that is similar to present-day usage.[24] For most of the eighteenth century, moral and mental philosophy of a similar genre in both Scotland and England continued to use 'passions' (along with 'desires' and 'appetites'), 'affections' and, sometimes, 'moral sentiments', as the basic categories of affective psychology. Hume also used these categories but in conjunction with a relatively frequent (if ambiguous) use of the term 'emotions'.

Book 2 of Hume's *Treatise* was entitled 'Of the Passions'. He divided all the perceptions of the mind into impressions and ideas. The impressions were further divided by Hume into primary and secondary impressions. Primary impressions were internal or external bodily sensations – of the bodily constitution and its animal spirits or of sight, sound, touch and so on. He continued: 'Secondary, or reflective impressions are such as proceed from some of these original ones, either immediately or by the interposition of its idea. Of the first kind are all the impressions of the senses, and all bodily pains and pleasures: Of the second are the passions and other emotions resembling them.'[25] Unlike Descartes, then, Hume did not think that passions were the direct result of the movement of animal spirits (feelings with bodily causes). Rather he believed that they were secondary impressions of feelings, produced by the combination of a sensation with an idea. So Hume removed passions 'and other emotions resembling them' one degree further from primary bodily movements

[22] Wood (1989), 90–1. [23] Campbell (1986), 354.
[24] Hume (1978). [25] Hume (1978), 275.

than Descartes had done, while adopting the same basic 'perception' model favoured by both Locke and Descartes.

Annette Baier, in her study of Hume's *Treatise*, suggests that Hume used 'emotions' to mean raw, non-cognitive feelings, sensations, or agitations of the spirits. She contrasts this with Hume's understanding of the passions and sentiments as secondary, cognitive impressions with intentional objects.[26] This is an interesting suggestion, and one that would fit well with my overall argument here that the new category of 'emotions', when it did finally emerge as an established category, was a particularly non-cognitive one, unlike the categories of passions, affections and sentiments as they were used in the eighteenth century and before. However, unfortunately, I am not sure that Hume's uses of 'emotions' can all be interpreted, as Baier suggests, as meaning 'sensations' or 'bodily disturbances'. There are many cases of apparent equivocation (both in the *Treatise* and in Hume's *Enquiry Concerning the Principles of Morals*) between 'passions' and 'emotions', although 'passions' was the central and most frequently used category. In most instances Hume seemed to intend 'emotions' to be read as a rather vague and general term to mean something like 'feelings' or 'movements' or 'agitations' of the mind. In this sense an emotion could be said to be something 'which attends a passion'.[27] In other places, however, Hume seemed to use 'emotions' as a synonym or stylistic variant for 'passions',[28] as well as for 'affections';[29] he also used 'emotion' to mean a movement of the bodily 'spirits',[30] as well as an 'immediate feeling' or 'sensation'.[31]

So, sometimes Hume contrasted 'emotions' with cognitive passions, seeing them as mere 'impressions of sensation', as Baier suggests, but sometimes included them along with passions as secondary 'impressions of reflexion'.[32] (In the works of Thomas Brown and others in the nineteenth century it became standard to distinguish quite clearly between mere sensations on the one hand and emotions on the other – on the grounds that the latter had a mental rather than a bodily origin; see below.) Sometimes Hume used 'emotions' as an umbrella term encompassing many mental powers or feelings that had traditionally been differentiated – and continued to be differentiated by more conservative Christian psychologists such as Thomas Reid later in the century.[33] Hume's use of 'emotions' was thus fairly similar to Adam Smith's use

---

[26] Baier (1991), 160–70, 180–1.   [27] Hume (1978), 419.
[28] E.g. Hume (1978), 276, 288, 347, 415–18.   [29] E.g. Hume (1978), 283, 334.
[30] E.g. Hume (1978), 354, 373, 421.   [31] E.g. Hume (1978), 286, 358.
[32] Hume (1978), 8; see Baier (1991), 164.
[33] For further examples of the broad and vague sense of 'emotions' in Hume, see Hume (1978), 365, 369. For further discussion of Hume's theory of the passions see Gardiner et al. (1970); Rorty (1982); Teichgraeber (1986), ch. 3; Lind (1990); Baier (1991), especially chs. 6 and 7; Pinch (1996), ch. 1.

of it in his *Theory of Moral Sentiments* of 1759 (see chapter 3), but more frequent and more various.

Some particular observations about Hume support the contention that 'emotions' was, from its earliest English-language psychological uses, a term associated with a set of assumptions and narratives that were derived from secular and 'scientific' resources. First, Hume stood out from most other moral and mental philosophers of the period by asserting, famously, that 'Reason is, and ought only to be the slave of the passions, and can never pretend to any other office than to serve and obey them.'[34] This claim was an inversion of traditional Christian psychology in two ways. First, it deliberately inverted the hierarchical psychology in which 'reason' governed the passions and appetites. Secondly, the assertion that reason should be the slave of the passions depended on a Hobbesian view of the mind as a stream of passions and desires which were mini-agents in themselves. Hume talked of passions (rather than persons) 'choosing means' to achieve desired ends.[35] In fact will, along with reason, was reduced by Hume to one felt impulse amongst many others. Will, while 'properly speaking not comprehended among the passions', was treated along with them, in the same section of the *Treatise*, as 'nothing but *the internal impression we feel and are conscious of, when we knowingly give rise to any new motion of our body, or new perception of our mind*'.[36] As for reason, that was the 'vulgar' name for what in reality were calm passions.[37] So the two pillars of a classically conceived Christian soul – will and reason – vanished in Humean psychology, to be replaced by a multitude of passions, sentiments, affections, desires or emotions, each the product of the learned association of certain impressions with other impressions of pleasure or pain in past experience.[38]

With the disappearance of the faculties of reason and will and the reduction of all mental life to a stream of 'passions' or 'emotions', a major conceptual difficulty arose – what are passions or emotions passions or emotions *of*? The tacit ontology of Hume's *Treatise* was one where passions or emotions were not of anything (such as a soul or will or even perhaps of a body) but were those mini-agents that comprised the entirety of what was meant by 'I'. 'A passion,' Hume said, 'is an original

---

[34] Hume (1978), 415. Unlike Descartes and the Stoics, Spinoza too had denied that reason could have absolute power over the passions. On Spinoza's theory of the affects (*affectus*) in his *Ethica*, see n.33 to chapter 3 in this volume.

[35] Hume (1978), 415–18; for more on the personification of passions and sentiments in Hume, and in eighteenth-century philosophy and aesthetics, see Pinch (1996), 23, 44–50. For more on Hume's 'ethics of sentiment', see Rivers (2000), ch. 4.

[36] Hume (1978), 399.   [37] Hume (1978), 413–22.

[38] On Hume's position relative to more materialist associationists such as Hartley and Priestley, see Yolton (1983), ch. 3.

existence, or, if you will, modification of existence.'[39] Baier wonders how to make sense of this passage, in the light of Hume's view that passions and sentiments were secondary rather than primary impressions.[40] The answer perhaps is that in this section Hume is emphasising that – whatever the impressions and ideas that brought about a particular passion – the passions were not the movements of a faculty of the soul, such as the will, but were, rather, psychological atoms. Passions were, in this sense, to be seen as ontologically basic – original realities complete in themselves, not movements of a self or will.[41]

In other words, Hume espoused a non-realist view of the will. Like Hobbes before him and Brown after him, Hume rejected faculty psychology (still adopted by most Christian mental philosophers) and saw the mind instead as a single chain of basic impressions and ideas. Will was just one 'impression' – in other words, a feeling – amongst others, including love, hate and the other passions; a passive impression received ultimately from the action of external objects and/or the body. Brown (and later Bain, Spencer and Darwin) also produced systems in which volition was just one of the emotions rather than an autonomous principle or faculty.

Secondly, Hume, along with George Turnbull, who was mentioned above, was one of several writers eager to pursue a study of the human mind using the methods and concepts of natural philosophy. He treated passions and emotions as mental impressions caused by basic impressions and ideas in a necessary and law-like way. His endorsement of a strong analogy between the physics of matter and the science of mind, appealing to Newton's optics as a methodological paradigm, produced a mental science in which there was no spontaneously acting will, but only sensations, impressions (including passions and affections) and actions connected in chains of cause and effect.[42]

Thirdly, the fact that Hume's *Treatise* was composed during a period of three years (1734–7) when he was resident in France might be more than a coincidence. James McCosh, an orthodox representative of the common sense tradition, whose own book on the emotions will be considered in chapter 6, certainly saw a connection between Hume's incipient sensationalism and religious scepticism and his residence

---

[39] Hume (1978), 415.   [40] Baier (1991), 160–4.
[41] See Rorty (1982); Yolton (1983), 49, 148; Pinch (1996), 21–4. For a discussion of how Butler intimated a similar view of the autonomous agency of the passions, see chapter 3 above.
[42] On liberty and necessity see Hume (1978), 399–412; on Hume's science of human nature see also Rivers (2000), ch. 4. On Hume's controversial theory of cause and effect, the interpretation of which has been a subject of considerable debate, see Craig (2000).

in France.⁴³ McCosh also alluded to the many historical connections between Scottish and French learning from the Middle Ages onwards.⁴⁴ Further, it is certain that Hume would have read Descartes' treatise on the passions of the soul before or during his sojourn in France and it is quite possible that it is from that treatise that Hume borrowed the term 'emotions' ('*émotions*' in Descartes). It is at least consistent with this hypothesis, though far from conclusive, that Johnson's dictionary gave the French '*émotions*' as the origin of the English word 'emotions'.⁴⁵

Descartes made two uses of the term '*émotions*'. He divided all our thoughts into actions (volitions) and passions (perceptions). Of the latter there were two kinds: passions caused by the soul and passions caused by the body. The passions 'proper' – those states normally called passions, rather than all passive (perceptual) mental states – fell into this latter category, of passions caused by the body. Specifically they were 'caused, maintained and strengthened by some movements of the spirits', where the 'spirits' were animal spirits – very fine parts of the blood. The passions, Descartes said, could also be called sensations or perceptions. 'But it is even better to call them emotions [*émotions*] of the soul, not only because this term may be applied to all the changes which occur in the soul... but more particularly because, of all the kinds of thought which the soul may have there are none that agitate and disturb it so strongly as the passions.'⁴⁶ So the first sense of '*émotions*' was just as a synonym for passions – a synonym that could cover all the changes in the soul but which particularly drew attention to the agitation caused by the motions of the animal spirits in the passions proper. It is possible that Hume's use of the term 'emotions' was derived from this use of the term in Descartes' *Traité*.⁴⁷ (The second way Descartes used '*émotions*', which Hume showed

---

⁴³ McCosh (1875), 119–29, provides an interesting description of Hume's time in France as well as furnishing the reader with a pastiche of rumours, gossip and personal insults against Hume, all of which were relished by McCosh as weapons with which to discredit Hume's philosophy.

⁴⁴ McCosh (1875), 24–5.   ⁴⁵ Johnson (1967).

⁴⁶ Descartes (1984), 68. For an extremely good analysis of Descartes' theory of the passions, see James (1997), 94–108.

⁴⁷ It is ironic that while the term 'emotions' seems to have found its way into English-language psychology from Descartes via Hume's *Treatise* and other works, French psychologists were still using the categories of '*sentiments*' and of '*passions*' in preference to '*émotions*' as late as the start of the twentieth century. e.g. Thomas Ribot, *La Psychologie des Sentiments* (1896); *Essai sur les Passions* (1907). On French writers' treatments of emotions, sentiments and anxiety in the late nineteenth century, including those of Janet, Ribot, Féré, Brissaud and Hartenberg, see Berrios (1996), 271–3, 296, 337–9. Also see Baldwin (ed.) (1905), III, 1040–50, for more examples of French texts of the late nineteenth and early twentieth centuries that are about *les passions*.

no sign of having adopted, was in the phrase '*émotions intérieures*', which referred to a category of peculiarly intellectual feelings.)[48]

Fourthly and finally, Hume was the most religiously sceptical of all the major figures of the Scottish Enlightenment.[49] It is perhaps of some significance that one of the first significant psychological uses of the term 'emotions' came from the pen of a religious sceptic.

Hume had relatively few supporters in his own lifetime and even fewer in the immediate wake of the Revolution and the 'Terror' in France, when any philosophical tendency towards sensationalism or scepticism was automatically pilloried as 'materialism' and 'atheism'. During this period, before Brown resurrected some of Hume's doctrines in the 1810s, another Scot, Thomas Reid, held sway in the fields of mental and moral philosophy. Some of his doctrines, which were often characterised by opposition to Hume's positions, were discussed in chapter 3. We now move on to consider the way that Hobbesian and Humean psychology was reinvigorated by Brown in his introduction of a mental chemistry of sensations, thoughts and emotions.

The inventor of the emotions: Thomas Brown (1778–1820)

Lectures on the Philosophy of the Human Mind

The question that was initially the driving force of this study was: why, around 1820–1850, were the theoretical terms 'passions' and 'affections' displaced by the psychological category that we now predominantly use to describe love, hate, jealousy, anger, joy, sorrow and so on, namely 'emotions'? Certainly one of the most important factors in effecting this transition was a series of lectures published posthumously in 1820, the year that their author died. The lectures in question were the *Lectures on the Philosophy of the Human Mind* by Thomas Brown, Doctor of Medicine and Professor of Moral Philosophy in the University of Edinburgh.[50]

Brown's *Lectures* was the single most important work in introducing the term 'emotions' as a major psychological category to the academic and literary worlds during the first half of the nineteenth century. His theory of 'emotions' tied together several features of affective psychologies that had become detached from Christian psychology as part of an influential

---

[48] John Yolton has suggested that Malebranche was another important French influence on Hume's thinking about the passions and the animal spirits. Yolton (1983), 175–6; on Malebranche's views on the passions, see also Gardiner *et al.* (1970), 170–82; James (1997), ch. 5.
[49] See Gaskin (1988); Addinall (1991), ch. 2.
[50] On Thomas Brown's life and works see Dixon, 'Introduction' to Brown (2003); Harris (2002); and Welsh (1825).

secular psychological system. For these reasons Brown is the pivotal figure in this history. A further reason for making a particular study of Brown is that, despite his considerable influence during the first half of the nineteenth century, his thought has received little attention from historians of philosophy and psychology since the nineteenth century.[51] Those works that do refer to Brown's mental science have tended to focus on his cognitive 'laws of suggestion' rather than on his treatment of the emotions.[52] Richard Olson has, in addition, provided an analysis of Brown's philosophy of mathematics and science.[53] It is especially surprising that Gardiner at al.'s *Feeling and Emotion: A History of Theories* (1937), does not mention Brown at all.

Some writers have described Brown as, alongside Thomas Reid and Dugald Stewart, a representative of the Scottish common sense school.[54] There were certainly many fundamental doctrines Brown shared with this tradition. However, unlike his intuitionist and realist predecessors, Brown drew heavily on the empiricist associationism of Hume and Hartley (although Brown preferred the term 'suggestion' to 'association').[55] Given the scepticism and empiricism of his philosophy, and the extent to which he presented himself, at least, as an opponent of Reid, the designation 'common sense philosopher' might not quite fit the bill. Sir James Mackintosh and Leslie Stephen were perhaps closer to the mark: Mackintosh described Brown's philosophy as 'an open revolt against the authority of Reid', while Stephen argued that in Brown's hands the philosophy of common sense had been transformed into 'pure empiricism'.[56]

---

[51] An important exception here, and a very useful study of the influence of a Baconian view of science on the mental philosophy produced by Brown and other early-nineteenth-century Scots, is Robertson (1976).

[52] There are, to my knowledge, only two monographs devoted exclusively to Brown: the biography by Welsh (1825), and Réthoré (1863). For studies of Brown's mental science that are included in more general works, see Porter (1874), 408–13; McCosh (1875), ch. 44; Stephen (1900), 267–87; Warren (1921), 74–7; Klein (1970), 674–96; Murphy and Kovach (1972), 57–61; Hoeveler (1981), 118–20; Danziger (1997), 41–2; Richards (1992), 332–9. The most valuable of these are McCosh's, Stephen's and Klein's studies.

[53] Olson (1975), chs. 4 and 5.

[54] E.g. Martin (1961), 3; Hunter and Macalpine (1963), 335; Olson (1975), 26; Murray (1983), 104.

[55] References to Brown's *Lectures* are to the first one-volume edition of 1828 – this version is reprinted as vol. VI of the collected life and works; Brown (2003). Since there are so many different editions of the *Lectures*, I will also put in brackets after the page references to the 1828 edition, the numbers of the lectures. On association and suggestion, see Brown (1828), 213–16, 279–81 (L. 33, 43), and throughout. For an analysis of the middle position that Brown took between the traditional Scottish school and the more radical Associationists such as Hume and Hartley, see Warren (1921), 70–80, 157–63. See also [Mill] (1859), 287–8; McCosh (1875), 328–30.

[56] Mackintosh: quoted in Porter (1874), 410; see also Klein (1970), 676. Stephen (1900), 285.

Brown's frequent criticisms of Reid in his *Lectures* would have been understood by his hearers and readers also to be attacks on his predecessor, Stewart. This, indeed, was precisely how Brown himself intended them. He wrote, in a letter to a friend about the experience of delivering his course of lectures, 'I was very much *constrained*, as you may believe, by the unpleasantness of differing so essentially from Mr Stewart on many of the principal points. But...*Dr Reid's* name fortunately served every purpose, when I had opinions to oppose in which Mr Stewart perhaps coincided.'[57]

Brown's philosophy combined the emphasis on intuitive universal beliefs characteristic of the common sense school with an inherent sympathy for Humean scepticism. Brown could, perhaps, be best described as a 'common sense sceptic'. A quip of Brown's, asserting the similarity of the Reidian and Humean philosophies, suggests that he did indeed think it quite possible to combine the two. 'Reid,' Brown said, 'bawled out that we must believe in an outward world; but added, in a whisper, we can give no reason for our belief. Hume cries out we can give no reason for such a notion; and whispers, I own we cannot get rid of it.'[58] Brown's aim was simply to assert each proposition with equal force.

Brown's *Lectures* was one of the most successful philosophy books of the period, going through twenty editions.[59] The *Lectures* were widely acknowledged to be the most successful and popular work of their kind ever to have appeared. Henry Cockburn's comments in his *Memorials* were representative of many similarly positive appraisals. He spoke of Brown's *Lectures* as one of the most 'delightful books in the English language', which had enjoyed 'unexampled success'.[60] Writing at the end of the century, the British philosopher Robert Adamson wrote of the book, in the *Encyclopaedia Britannica*: 'It is no exaggeration to say that never before or since has a work on metaphysics been so popular.'[61] McCosh, in his *History of the Scottish Philosophy*, painted a vivid picture of the immense success, popularity and influence of Brown's lectures in Edinburgh and beyond:

A course so eminently popular among students had not, I rather think, been delivered in any previous age in the University of Edinburgh, and has not, in a

---

[57] Quoted in Welsh (1825), 195.
[58] Mackintosh (1837), 346; also Brown (1820b), 142–4.
[59] On the extent of Brown's influence on nineteenth-century psychological thought see Stephen (1900), 271–87; Page (1980), 60–1; Richards (1992), 332–9; Reed (1997), 68–76. Stephen, Richards and Page all say that the *Lectures* ran to nineteen editions. However they ran to at least twenty. The Cambridge University Library holds a twentieth edition, to which both Welsh's memoir of Brown and Chalmers' preface to the ethical sections are appended: Brown (1860).
[60] Cockburn (1909), 347. [61] Quoted in Trotter (1901), 431.

later age, been surpassed... His lectures were published shortly after his death, and excited an interest wherever the English language is spoken, quite equal to that awakened by the living lecturer among the students of Edinburgh. They continued for twenty years to have a popularity in the British dominions and in the United States greater than any philosophical work ever enjoyed before. During these years most students were introduced to metaphysics by the perusal of them, and attractive beyond measure did they find them to be. The writer of this article would give much to have revived within him the enthusiasm which he felt when he first read them.[62]

J. D. Morell, a philosophical psychologist responsible for popularising the German Idealisms of Fichte and Schelling in his *Historical and Critical View of the Speculative Philosophy of Europe in the Nineteenth Century* (1846) and in his *Elements of Psychology* (1853), also gave a first-hand account of the great enthusiasm originally aroused in him by Brown's lectures (before he was led via Reid and Hamilton to his later passion for German philosophy). Morell had been impressed by Locke's *Essay* but it had left him hungry for more:

I next betook myself to the Lectures of Dr Thomas Brown, hoping to find there the satisfaction I required. In this hope I was not *for the time* disappointed. The style was so captivating, the views so comprehensive, the arguments so acute, the whole thing so complete, that I was almost insensibly borne along upon the stream of his reasoning and eloquence. Naturally enough I became a zealous disciple; I accepted his mental analysis as almost perfect; I defended his doctrine of causation; with him I stood in astonishment at the alleged obtuseness of Reid.[63]

The effects of the charismatic Dr Brown on the young Morell only began to wane after a period of study in Glasgow convinced him that there was a depth in Thomas Reid's philosophy that he had not previously appreciated.

Most significantly from the current point of view, Brown was the first major mental philosopher systematically to replace 'passions' and 'affections' with 'emotions' in his lectures. Reid, writing in 1788, and his pupil James Beattie, writing in 1790, while making occasional ill-defined references to 'emotion', as a sort of feeling or disturbance, had relied almost exclusively on the traditional categories of 'passions' (desires and aversions connected with bodily commotion) and milder 'affections' as derived particularly from Aquinas via the reformed Scholasticism of figures such as Hutcheson.[64] Dugald Stewart, Brown's predecessor in the Edinburgh Chair of Moral Philosophy and a follower of Butler and Reid,

---

[62] McCosh (1875), 322, 324.   [63] Morell (1846), I, vi–vii.
[64] For an account of the traditional categories in Aquinas, see Aquinas, *Summa Theologiae*, 1a.82, 5 and 1a.2ae.22–7. For Hutcheson's version, see chapter 3. Beattie (1976), 235–55. On Beattie, see McCosh (1875), ch. 29.

divided the active powers into 'appetites', 'desires' and 'affections'; he used 'emotion' as a rough synonym for 'feeling' but not as a significant psychological category.[65]

Brown made the terminological transition from the 'active powers' – 'appetites', 'passions', 'desires' and 'affections' – to the 'emotions'. Indeed, several nineteenth-century writers picked out Brown's treatment of the emotions as the high-point of his work. McCosh, for example, made the following remarks: 'Some place higher than any of his other excellencies his eloquent exposition of the emotions, – an exposition which called forth the laudations both of Stewart and Chalmers, the latter of whom wrote a preface to that part of his lectures which treats of the feelings.'[66] Further evidence of the importance of Thomas Brown's use of 'emotions' is to be found in the fact that several of the earliest writers on 'emotions' from the 1820s onwards made explicit reference to Brown's definition and classification of the emotions at crucial points in their texts.[67] The Edinburgh-educated William Lyall's *Intellect, the Emotions and the Moral Nature* (1855) was one of the first books published in North America to have 'emotions' in its title. Lyall's philosophy was summarised by an obituarist as 'a modification of Brown's'.[68]

Lack of religious commitment

Two further traits place Thomas Brown firmly within the Humean rather than the Reidian tradition: first, he was reputed to be religiously sceptical; secondly, he was a strong advocate of a new 'science of the mind'. He wrote his mental philosophy within the design theology framework that he shared with Butler, Chalmers and others. His use of philosophical-theological language was more thin and formulaic than theirs, however. An additional difference is that although Butler and Chalmers did both adopt a relatively atheological methodology in their treatments of the human mind, they also composed works of Christian theology. This was not true of Brown – he was no theologian. His references to God or the soul were relatively few, and his use of terms such as 'divine Being', 'Preserver

---

[65] Stewart (1828), 15, 22–3, 75, 231–92.
[66] McCosh (1875), 332; the book that McCosh almost certainly had in mind was, in fact, a volume with a preface by Chalmers, of the lectures that relate to ethics: Brown (1846) (although of course feelings and emotions were important features of Brown's ethics). James Douglas, a wealthy landowner and defender of conservative theology, considered Brown's work essentially heretical and unacceptable but made an exception for Brown's writing on the emotions which, he said, displayed 'great acuteness'; Douglas (1839), 378.
[67] E.g. Payne (1828), VI, ch. 6; Ramsay (1848), 1–3; Cooke (1852), chs. 4 and 8; Lyall (1855), 287–9; Bain (1865), 606; McCosh (1880).
[68] Quoted in Page (1980), 59. For more on Lyall, see chapter 6.

of Nature', 'Author of Nature', 'Eternal One' and 'divine Author' were indicative of his preference for natural over revealed religion; his text had no theological depth (in terms of doctrine or imagery) and, unlike the works of Watts, Wesley, Edwards and even Butler, Brown's work relied exclusively on metaphysics in preference to Scripture and tradition. Only six of the hundred *Lectures* were devoted to Brown's natural religion. In these the Deity was described, in an almost deistic tone, as single, good and omniscient, 'the one designing Power', whose existence was known by inference from the natural world.[69] In the *Lectures* there were no references to Scripture, to the fall, to Christ, to the Holy Spirit, to grace, to sin, to salvation; in short there was no Christianity.

We can also seek evidence of Brown's religious commitments in sources other than his own *Lectures*. We know from his biographer, Revd David Welsh, and from other sources, that Brown was an advocate of the separation of academic posts from religious requirements. He was particularly hostile to the practice in Scotland of electing only clergymen to chairs. He even published a pamphlet on the question, in support of the layman John Leslie's candidature for the Chair in Natural Philosophy in opposition to the candidate of the moderate party of the church. The incident serves as a useful reminder of how complicated the relationships between 'science' and 'religion' can be: an unlikely alliance emerged between Brown, a deistic believer accused of atheism himself, and Leslie, the candidate supported by the evangelical wing of the kirk. Brown's pamphlet defended Leslie against the charge that Hume's theory of causation led to atheism; so deist and evangelical were united by their desire to see a Humean, and a layman, elected to the Chair of Natural Philosophy.[70] These intricacies aside, the practice of favouring clergymen in competitions for academic posts, in fact, proved a significant obstacle to Brown's own eventual appointment as the professor of moral philosophy in Edinburgh in 1810, since he was a mere doctor of medicine rather than of divinity and was not a cleric.[71] The only explicit reference Welsh's memoir made to Brown's views on religion was to describe his attitude as 'The most perfect toleration of all religious opinions'.[72] In private, however, the evangelical Welsh was more uneasy about the subject. 'No one lamented more than Dr Welsh,' Welsh's biographer later recalled, 'his distinguished friend's religious views. He, during Dr Brown's life, pressed on him the arguments in favour of the Christian faith', but without success.[73]

[69] Brown (1828), 623 (L. 93).
[70] Welsh (1851), 14–16; McCosh (1875), 284, 320. On the Leslie affair, see also Stephen (1900), 270–1; Morrell (1975); Brown (1982), 24–7; Chitnis (1986), 25, 30, 73, 96; Hilton (1988), 24–5.
[71] Welsh (1851), 14–26.   [72] Welsh (1851), 55.   [73] Dunlop (1846), 24.

Three of the nineteenth-century's leading historians of philosophy, Robert Blakey, Morell and McCosh, all accused Brown of producing a philosophy of mind that was at least allied with, if not identical to, French sensationalism.[74] Brown himself was, in fact, very critical of Condillac and the sensationalists for their 'extreme simplification' of Lockean mental philosophy, but he was much more inclined towards their general approach of reducing complex mental states to more primary sensations than he was to the conservative Reidian doctrines of irreducible powers and faculties.[75] This is how Brown himself put it: 'While I am far from conceiving, therefore, with Condillac and his followers, that all our states of mind are mere sensations modified or transformed, since this belief appears to me to be a mere assumption without even the slightest evidence in our consciousness, I am equally unwilling to admit the variety of powers, of which Dr Reid speaks.'[76] Note that the final authority on all these questions was the 'evidence of consciousness', a point that will be returned to shortly. Brown, in fact differed from Condillac only in that Condillac claimed that sensations somehow were transformed into more complex mental states whereas Brown preferred the statement that certain primary sensations invariantly preceded more complex mental states; he called Condillac's system a form of 'intellectual alchemy', in contrast to his own mental chemistry.[77] Both were nonetheless involved in a reductionist sort of mental science.[78]

Another fact used against Brown by his conservative critics was that phrenologists (often accused of materialism and atheism in this period) claimed his metaphysics as supportive of their own system.[79] The leading British advocate of phrenology, the Scot George Combe, in the introduction to his *Elements of Phrenology* (1828), showered praise on Brown's system, noting that his conclusions in many respects harmonised with those of phrenology, especially his treatment of the 'moral emotion'.[80] All this was enough of an indication for many that Brown's system must itself have been theologically suspect, in spite of Brown's own complete lack of enthusiasm for phrenology.[81] Finally, Brown was condemned for allegedly espousing two Humean views: a non-realist interpretation of causation and a belief in necessitarianism. On the Humean view – or the popular understanding of it at least – the word 'cause' merely referred to an invariable

---

[74] Blakey (1848), IV, 28; McCosh (1857), 404–9; McCosh (1875), 10; Morell (1846), II, 27, 33.
[75] Brown (1828), 208 (L. 33).   [76] Brown (1828), 213 (L. 33).
[77] Brown (1828), 208–13 (L. 33).
[78] On the similarity of Brown's and Condillac's systems, despite Brown's claims to the contary, see Stephen (1900), 282–4.
[79] Cooter (1984), 39–50; Young (1973), 187–8; Bain (1904), 27–8.
[80] Quoted in Welsh (1825), 520.   [81] Welsh (1825), 520–1.

antecedent rather than to anything possessed of a mysterious power or agency.[82] This denial of efficient causality was thought by Blakey and others (including the philosopher Lady Mary Shepherd, and the Irish barrister and philosopher Henry O'Connor) to lead to out and out atheism.[83] In 1851 a critic of Henry Atkinson and Harriet Martineau's controversial *Letters on the Laws of Man's Nature and Development* claimed to detect the influence of Brown's philosophy of cause and effect on Atkinson's atheistic metaphysics.[84] Looking back at the end of the nineteenth century, the agnostic thinker Leslie Stephen even judged that Brown, in his view of the meaning of 'cause' and 'effect', had been an anticipator of Comte, describing him as a man 'clearly on the way to positivism'.[85] John Stuart Mill had earlier described Brown as 'entirely positivist'.[86] Revd John Ballantyne, writing in 1828, had judged the system of his fellow Scot to be one 'of the *most rigid necessity*, as much so as that of any *fatalist* either of ancient or modern times, and is liable to all the objections which every modification of *fatality* must inevitably encounter'.[87]

Natural philosophy and mental chemistry

There was a correlation between Brown's personal and professional alienation from the Christian religion and the Christian establishment in Scotland and his search for alternative authorities and methods in his philosophical work. It was in the language and ideology of the natural sciences that Brown found alternative and potentially inclusive ways of describing human mental life. In 1797 he, along with a handful of like-minded fellow students in Edinburgh such as Henry Brougham, Francis Horner and Francis Jeffrey (all of whom were later involved in founding the *Edinburgh Review*), had formed a philosophical club called the Academy of Physics.[88] Its aim, according to Brougham, was to apply 'the Newtonian philosophy' to 'every subject to which induction and reasoning can be applied'.[89] One of the subjects for investigation laid down in the minutes of the Academy's first meeting was 'The physics of mind, or the philosophy of mind, excluding religious controversies and party

---

[82] On the question of how to interpret Hume's theory of cause and effect see Craig (2000). For Brown's own theory of cause and effect see Brown (1818); also see Dixon, 'Introduction' to Brown (2003).
[83] Blakey (1848), IV, 39–46; [Shepherd] (1824); O'Connor (1837), 85–94.
[84] Bushnan (1851), 36–46; Atkinson and Martineau (1851).
[85] Stephen (1900), 273; see Cashdollar (1989), 54–5.
[86] Cashdollar (1989), 157.   [87] Ballantyne (1828), 27–8.
[88] See Dixon, 'Introduction' to Brown (2003); Welsh (1825), 498–506; Grave (1960), 2–3; Cantor (1975); Chitnis (1986), 62–6. McCosh (1875), 319 erroneously calls the club the 'Academy of Sciences'. For more on Francis Jeffrey's circle and the foundation of the *Edinburgh Review*, see McCosh (1875), 337–45; Cantor (1975), 131–4.
[89] Quoted in Olson (1975), 11–12.

politics'.⁹⁰ It was the ambition of the Academy's members to construct a tolerant and de-Christianised mental science modelled on the physics of matter.

Philip Flynn, in his study of the Scottish mental scientists of the eighteenth and nineteenth centuries, has suggested that both Locke and Descartes had seen the authority of consciousness as a desirable replacement for the Scholastics' slavish obedience to the authorities of the Christian tradition.⁹¹ This suggestion is also applicable to Brown, who, like Reid and Stewart before him, made frequent disparaging comments about the Schoolmen's approach to mental science.⁹² This opposition to Scholastic forms of knowledge (especially dogmatism and faculty psychology), combined with a passion for religious toleration and inclusivity, led to the construction of an atheological psychology in which authority was given to individual consciousness and mental science rather than religion or theology. The balancing of church dogma with individual experience as a source of moral and religious authority was already a central feature of the many varieties of Protestant theology – this same shift was now extended to the realm of psychology.⁹³ In this way, the creation of a secular mental science couched within an only superficially theistic framework could be seen as the product of the application of certain originally Protestant principles, as well as a relatively autonomous natural philosophical inductivism, to the creation of knowledge about human mental life.⁹⁴

Brown termed his mental philosophy variously 'physiology of the mind', 'mental chemistry', 'mental science', 'intellectual physics' and even 'the physical investigation of the mind'.⁹⁵ However, Brown's 'mental science', like that of moderates such as Reid and Stewart as well as that of the Associationists Hume, Hartley and James Mill, was a purely mentalistic and introspective discipline.⁹⁶ It was a science, like chemistry

---

⁹⁰ Quoted in Welsh (1825), 499.   ⁹¹ Flynn (1988), 264–5.
⁹² E.g. Brown (1828), 2–3, 9–10 (L. 1, 2). On the Protestant 'reformed Scholasticism' taught in the Scottish universities of the seventeenth and eighteenth centuries against which Brown was reacting, see Moore (1990), 38–42. On McCosh's later perpetuation of the tradition of Scottish Protestant Scholasticism, see Hoeveler (1981), esp. chs. 4 and 5.
⁹³ On the appeal to subjective faith-experiences as alternative sources of authority to metaphysical theology and scriptures in Protestant thinkers such as Edwards, Schleiermacher, Kierkegaard and James, see Proudfoot (1989). Griffin (1990) makes the same point: 'It is, of course, a very Protestant contention that each man can have access to trustworthy encounters with what passes for reality, and eighteenth-century divines of a latitudinarian stripe, some of whom derived inspiration from Tillotson, often carried the view to the most democratic extremes' (429).
⁹⁴ This may be a case that fits well with Reed's view that psychology was the product of the extended application of Protestant views of human nature; see e.g. Reed (1997), 7.
⁹⁵ Brown (1828), 3, 23–30, 57–67, 97 (L. 1, 5, 10–11, 16); Richards (1992), 336–8.
⁹⁶ Mill (1829). On Hume, Mill and Hartley see Mischel (1966).

or physiology, in that it analysed the whole into parts, classified those parts and described the dynamics of their interaction. But it was not a physical science – it had nothing to say about chemistry or physiology *tout court*, it simply analysed and classified mental phenomena qua mental phenomena. Leslie Stephen provided the following summary, in his 1900 *English Utilitarians*: 'We may then say briefly that Brown carries out in his own fashion the conception of psychology which makes it an inductive science parallel to the physical sciences, and to be pursued by the same methods. We have to do with "feelings" instead of atoms, and with mental instead of "material" chemistry.'[97] Brown's mental science sought to discover the 'natural laws of thought and emotion'.[98] Emotions connected, together with sensations and thoughts, in chains of cause and effect modelled on Newtonian physics and subjected to analysis on the model of the new natural science of chemistry, replaced the passions and affections of a classical Christian soul.

The 'science of mind' methodology and rhetoric was designed to draw on the success and status of the physical sciences. Bacon's *Novum Organum* and Newtonian physics (especially the *Opticks*) were still the most popular sources of authority and methodology.[99] However, as new physical sciences made new advances, the mental scientists chose new sources of methodological analogies. While eighteenth-century moral and mental philosophers such as Shaftesbury, Hutcheson, Hume and Reid had drawn analogies with arithmetic, mathematics, optics, physics, anatomy and natural history, Brown was particularly impressed with chemistry.[100]

In recommending his own 'chemistry of the mind', Brown made a point of boasting of 'the chemical discoveries we have made of late, with a rapidity of progress as brilliant as it is unexampled in the history of any other science'.[101] Horner, another member of the Academy of Physics, had also turned to the new chemistry in his search for the fundamental principles of scientific inquiry that could be applied to mind and society.[102] About a quarter of the subjects discussed by the Academy had

---

[97] Stephen (1900), 284.   [98] Brown (1828), 15 (L. 3).
[99] On the importance of Newton's comments about the application of the inductive method to the 'moral' realm, see n.20 to the Introduction to this volume.
[100] On the analogies with mathematics, physics, optics and anatomy made by earlier thinkers, see chapter 3 in this volume, and the earlier sections of this chapter. For a discussion in particular of the roles of anatomy and natural history as sources of analogies and ideas in mental and moral philosophy in eighteenth-century Scotland, see Wood (1989).
[101] Brown (1828), 28–9 (L. 5). On the rapid advances in chemistry at the end of the eighteenth century, see Crossland (1980); Melhado (1985). For a collection of essays on the development of chemistry, philosophy and other disciplines in the Scottish Enlightenment, see Jones (ed.) (1988).
[102] Cantor (1975), 119.

pertained to chemistry.[103] Brown returned to the theme at the outset of Lecture 16, 'On the Classification of the Phenomena of Mind':

The science of mind, as it is a science of analysis, I have more than once compared to chemistry, and pointed out to you and illustrated its various circumstances of resemblance. In this, too, we may hope the analogy will hold, – that, as the innumerable aggregates, in the one science, have been reduced and simplified, the innumerable complex feelings in the other will admit of a corresponding reduction and simplification.[104]

Something like this 'chemistry' model had also been used by Joseph Priestley. Priestley was a significant figure both in the 'chemical revolution' and in the dissemination of associationist psychology, itself a form of mental chemistry.[105] It was partly through his influence that chemistry had become associated with reductionism, materialism and political radicalism.[106]

In 1775, Priestley had produced an edition of Hartley's *Observations on Man* to which were appended his own reflections on the mind. Hartley had written that 'our passions or affections can be no more than aggregates of simple ideas united by association'.[107] Priestley also used an implicitly 'chemical' model to explain the generation of 'complex emotion' from simple elements: 'If a variety of painful emotions, and disagreeable feelings, have been associated with the idea of the same circumstance, they will be excited by it, in one general *complex emotion*, the component parts of which will not be easily distinguishable; and by their mutual associations they will, at length, entirely coalesce, so as never to be separately perceived.'[108] George Payne, both the Mills, George Ramsay, Thomas Laycock and G. H. Lewes all later borrowed from Brown the analogy between psychology and chemistry – both were sciences of analysis and arrangement.[109] John Stuart Mill observed that 'the laws of the phenomena of mind are sometimes analogous to mechanical, but sometimes also to chemical laws'.[110] In his *System of Logic* (1843), Mill would later quote Priestley's view that the sensations were the mental 'elements' from whose combination compound mental states could be generated.[111] Mill himself

---

[103] Cantor (1975), 123.   [104] Brown (1828), 97 (L. 16).
[105] Priestley was responsible to a significant degree for the dissemination of Hartley's associationist *Observations on Man*; Priestley's gloss emphasised the materialistic and necessitarian aspects of Hartley's psychology. For Priestley's materialism, see Priestley (1775); Yolton (1983), ch. 6. For an account of Reid's opposition to Priestley's materialistic psychology, see Sutton (1998), ch. 14.
[106] Brooke and Cantor (1998), ch. 10, esp. 326–9.
[107] Hartley in Priestley (1775), 202.   [108] Priestley (1775), xxviii.
[109] Payne (1828), 67; Mill (1843), II, 500–6; [Mill] (1859), 294–5; Ramsay (1853), 79, 89–91; Laycock (1861), 4; Klein (1970), 696, 705–9; Richards (1992), 336; on Brown's influence on the Mills more generally, see Stephen (1900), 271–87. On Lewes' use of the analogy: Rylance (2000), 308.
[110] Mill (1843), II, 502.   [111] Mill (1843), II, 500–6, 508–9.

used the comparison with chemistry to endorse a non-reductionist form of associationism; in psychology, as in chemistry, for Mill, effects often had properties that were not reducible to the properties of causes.[112] Later, Bain and Spencer would revive the more reductionist 'aggregate' view, which had been favoured by Hartley, Bentham, Brown and James Mill (see chapter 5).

The borrowing of methods, concepts, status and authority from physical sciences such as chemistry was a hallmark of the a posteriori or associationist school of psychology of which Brown was a representative. Combined with a thin and unintrusive theism, this adoption of the methods and concepts of science made Brown's highly popular *Lectures* a powerful and influential exemplar for later nineteenth-century psychologists.[113]

Non-realism and opposition to common sense philosophy

Brown's system of the mind was shaped by opposition to Reid's a priori faculty psychology just as much as Reid's own system had been shaped by opposition to Hume. The three most important ways in which Brown disagreed with Reid were also ways in which he tended to agree with Hume. First, he endorsed a quasi-Humean view of cause and effect: 'To express, shortly, what appears to me to be the only intelligible meaning of the three most important words in physics, immediate invariable antecedence is power; the immediate invariable antecedent, in any sequence, is a cause; the immediate invariable consequent is the correlative effect.'[114] I call this only quasi-Humean, since it is much more stark and simple than Hume's own theory, which was not simply a 'mere uniformity' view like Brown's.[115] Secondly, Brown – as we have seen – took a strong view of the analogy between the physics and chemistry of matter and the physics and chemistry of mind. Thirdly, as a corollary of the first two points, power, cause and effect were construed in an equally non-realist way when applied to mental states. Brown's position was one of radical nescience, which he took further than the standard confessions of ignorance about the connection between mind and matter also made by Reid and Stewart. Not only could we not know what ultimately underlay the phenomena that were ascribed to mind and matter, Brown argued, but also there were no real faculties and powers of the mind; there were

---

[112] On Mill's non-reductionist view of mental chemistry and its difference from James Mill's and Bentham's aggregate view, see Wilson (1998), 215–18, 240–5.
[113] See the quotation from Porter (1874) at the head of chapter 5 in this volume.
[114] Brown (1828), 38 (L. 7); see 30–7 (L. 6) for a full defence of this view.
[115] See n.82 below.

only 'simple sequences of the Phenomena of the Mind'.[116] To infer the existence of permanent subjects of mental states was an accident of our constitution that should not lead us to believe in them:

> One very important circumstance of agreement, in the physical investigation of mind and matter, we found to be that, of both matter and mind, the successive phenomena are all which we truly know, though, by the very constitution of our nature, it is impossible for us not to ascribe these to some permanent subject... What matter is, independent of our perception, – what mind is, independent of its temporary varieties of feeling, it is impossible for us to discover; since, whatever new knowledge of matter we can suppose ourselves to acquire, must be acquired by our perception, and must, therefore, be relative to it; and whatever new knowledge we can suppose ourselves to acquire of mind, must be itself a state or affection of the mind, and, therefore, only a new mental phenomenon to be added to those with which we were before acquainted, as one of the many states in which the permanent substance mind is capable of existing.[117]

Where the common sense school had taught that the mind had a certain number of fundamental powers or faculties, including reason, will and consciousness, Brown said that there was only a succession of different 'states' or 'affections' of the mind.

While Brown taught that the mind existed and was unified and single, this was more of a methodological assumption than an ontological commitment. The same could be said of his assertion of the existence and unity of the Deity. In an early meeting of the Academy of Physics in 1797 certain principles had been laid down to which all the members consented. One of the principles represented the view still taken by Brown in his *Lectures*: 'Mind exists, – a something, of the essence of which we know nothing, but the existence of which we must suppose, on account of the effect which it produces; that is, the modification of which we are conscious.'[118] We 'must suppose' the existence of something that causes conscious feelings but it was an epistemological horizon or boundary rather than an ontological item for Brown.

> All which we know, or can be supposed to know, of the mind, indeed, is a certain series of these states or feelings that have succeeded each other, more or less rapidly, since life began; the sensation, thought, emotion, of the moment, being one of those states, and the supposed consciousness of the state being only the state itself, whatever it may be, in which the mind exists at that particular moment.[119]

Brown's positivist epistemology, derived from his view of the physics of matter, created a mental ontology in which the only solid features were

---

[116] Brown (1820b), x.   [117] Brown (1828), 57 (L. 10).
[118] Quoted in Welsh (1825), 502.   [119] Brown (1828), 71 (L. 12).

states or feelings of the mind.[120] The mind disappeared from the picture and the reader was left with free-standing thoughts and emotions. We will see in the following chapters that observational epistemology, again derived from the physical sciences, led to the definition of emotions ultimately as only observable and physical phenomena.

New psychological categories

This brings us to Brown's classification of mental states. For the reasons just elaborated it is significant that it was a classification of mental states (or 'feelings' or 'affections' of the mind as he also called them) rather than of mental powers or of faculties of the soul. Brown was iconoclastic in his approach to previous classificatory schemes. He gave short shrift to the classical division endorsed by Christian theologians between the understanding and the will – 'a division which is very ancient, but though sanctioned by the approbation of many ages, very illogical' – and argued that Reid's division between the intellectual powers and the active powers of the mind was really just the same system 'under a change of name'.[121] Brown was a self-confessed and enthusiastic innovator: 'There is always some advantage gained, by viewing objects according to new circumstances of agreement or analogy... I am convinced that no one has ever read over the mere terms of a new division in a science, however familiar the science may have been to him, without learning more than this new division itself.'[122] He went on to warn that a new terminology in mental science could have a powerful effect on one's view of mental reality but that it should *not*, however, be read as an invention of new powers, faculties or substances but merely as a new way of classifying the modifications of the mind. He continued: 'A difference of words is, in this case, more than a mere verbal difference. Though it be not the expression of a difference of doctrine, it very speedily becomes so.'[123] This quotation serves very well as a summary of my argument about the effects of the adoption by Brown and others of 'emotions' as a new psychological term. It speedily became, as a result of its association with Hume's and Brown's commitments to nescience and mental science, not just a verbal difference but a difference of doctrine. Immediately after having given this analysis of the possible effects of introducing new terminology, in Lecture 16, Brown introduced his new classification of mental phenomena into sensations, thoughts and emotions (summarised in Table 1).

---

[120] On Thomas Reid's opposition to the use of hypotheses in science, and his own consequent tendency towards an apparently 'positivist' philosophy of science, see Campbell (1986), 356–7.
[121] Brown (1828), 98 (L. 16).
[122] Brown (1828), 99–100 (L. 16).   [123] Brown (1828), 100 (L. 16).

Table 1 *Thomas Brown's model of the human mind based on his 1820 Lectures*[124]

STATES, FEELINGS, OR AFFECTIONS OF THE MIND						
External Affections of the Mind				**Internal Affections of the Mind**		
SENSATIONS				INTELLECTUAL STATES or THOUGHTS		EMOTIONS
Smell Taste Hearing Touch Vision Muscle Sense				Simple Suggestion	Relative Suggestion	Retrospective Immediate Prospective

[124] See especially Brown (1828), 53–67, 97–109, 213–16, 338–40 (L. 9–11, 16–17, 33, 52).

The states of mind were first reduced by Brown to two classes, 'according as the causes, or immediate antecedents, of our feelings are themselves mental or material'.[125] The causes of external affections (sensations) were material objects acting on our sensory organs, the causes of the internal affections were mental feelings (either sensations or other internal affections). Brown introduced one of his 'new generalizations of the phenomena of each class' by dividing the internal affections into intellectual states of mind (or, in some places, 'thoughts') and emotions.[126] He was particularly at pains to justify the introduction of the term 'emotions' in the place of what Reid and others had called the 'active powers' of the mind. Morell was strongly opposed to this rejection of the language of powers and faculties and its replacement by the language of intellectual states and emotions:

The tendency of this exchange is most evidently of a sensational character; it diminishes the intensity of our notion of self, as an independent source of power, and contemplates the mind rather as a passive existence, moulded into its different states either by the force of circumstances on the one hand, or by its own inevitable and unalterable laws on the other.[127]

This criticism was essentially sound: treating only of mental states rather than of the mind and importing epistemological and ontological assumptions from the physical sciences did give rise to a passive and necessitarian psychology. Brown himself gave three main reasons for his change of terminology from 'active powers' to 'emotions': first, that he found the term 'active powers' awkward and ambiguous; secondly, that intellectual states were the really active states of mind; and thirdly that he wished to include in his category of emotions many states that were not active – such as grief or astonishment – and some also that had traditionally but wrongly been considered intellectual powers, such as the feelings of beauty and sublimity.[128]

The change of terminology from Reid's and Stewart's 'active powers' to Brown's 'emotions' was more than a mere verbal difference. Brown's category of 'emotions' was, by definition, a category of passive (rather than active), non-intellectual feelings or states (rather than actions of a power or faculty).[129] Consider, for example, his comments justifying the treatment of aesthetic feelings as emotions rather than intellectual states:

I speak, at present, it must be remembered, of the mere feelings produced by the contemplation of beautiful or sublime objects, – not of the judgment which we

---

[125] Brown (1828), 102 (L. 16). [126] Brown (1828), 102 (L. 16).
[127] Morell (1846), II, 27. For more on Morell's views on emotions, see chapter 6 in this volume.
[128] Brown (1828), 102 (L. 16). [129] Brown (1828), 103–4 (L. 17).

form of objects as more or less fit to excite these feelings; the judgment being truly intellectual, like all our other judgments; but being at the same time, as distinct from the feelings which it measures, as any other judgment from the external or internal objects which it compares.[130]

Emotions, then, were 'mere feelings' – passive states akin to Hume's 'secondary impressions' and Descartes' 'perceptions' – to be contrasted with active intellectual judgments.[131] Although disputing the division between intellectual and active powers and that between the understanding and the will, Brown seems to have done little more than produce his own modification of the dichotomy in his contrast between intellect and emotion. In one sense it was an inversion of the traditional dichotomy, in which movements of the will were active and the intellect was the passive recipient of sense impressions. On Brown's model intellectual states were now considered the more active states, and emotions were mere feelings.

In addition to the distinctly non-cognitive nature of Brownian emotions, two further features remain to be noted. First, Brown was a supporter of the Hobbesian–Humean 'agent' model rather than the Reidian 'advocate' model of human motivation; the springs of action were brute forces rather than reasoned judgments. We do what we do because of whichever appetite, passion, or emotion prevails (which might or might not be a benevolent or moral emotion) not because we judge it to be right.[132] The will was not a free and self-acting principle for Brown any more than it had been for Hume; for both it was merely the name for the prevailing passions or emotions, which were ontologically basic feelings brought about by precedent thoughts and feelings in law-like ways.[133]

Secondly, Brown failed to provide a clear definition of 'emotions'. He admitted at the outset something that virtually every emotion-theorist since has also acknowledged – that 'The exact meaning of the term *emotion*... is difficult to state in any form of words.' The best he could manage was an optimistic gesture in the direction of common understanding (an instance in which he revealed his debt to the common sense school): 'Every person understands what is meant by an emotion, at least as well as he understands what is meant by any intellectual power; or if he do not, it can be explained to him only, by stating the number of feelings to which we give the name, or the circumstances which induce them.' He went on to pick out 'peculiar vividness of feeling' (a phrase later parroted by Chalmers and Payne – see below) and the fact that they

---

[130] Brown (1828), 102 (L. 16).
[131] For another example of the contrast between emotion and judgment, see Brown (1828), 338–40 (L. 52).
[132] See Brown (1828), 397–8, 509–13 (L. 59, 76).   [133] See Hoeveler (1981), 102.

were not primary sensations such as taste or smell as two characteristics of emotions.[134] It was certainly true that the category of 'emotions' could be filled out ostensively by listing love, hate, joy, sorrow, fear, anger, surprise and so on (although not without controversy). The problem with such a practice was that in the absence of a definition of 'emotion' it was not at all clear what was being claimed about a certain mental state when it was included in the category of 'emotions'. The problem of the non-explanatory nature of the label 'emotion' has been a perennial problem ever since Brown.[135] It is no surprise that in 1884 William James was still asking the question 'What is an emotion?' (and failing to find an answer that persuaded most of his peers).

In fact Brown could have made explicit his tacit definition of emotions as (something like) 'non-cognitive feelings arising in a law-like way from precedent thoughts and sensations'. Another factor in the lack of definition by Brown must have been the fact that he was, by his own admission, including an 'innumerable' variety of different feelings under the umbrella term 'emotion'.[136] This has been one of the enduring weaknesses of the term – a term that sought to subsume not only the earlier categories of appetites, passions, desires, affections and sentiments, but also the multitude of individual movements or feelings that came under each of those heads. The lack of definition of the term 'emotions' has remained a central and problematic feature of the concept ever since Brown's lectures.

Brown's influence on later mental science and psychology was considerable. His introspective 'mental science' methodology and his new classification of mental states were both widely adopted. Brown had divided mental-scientific methodology into two tasks: first, analysing mental states into their components ('mental chemistry' – an idea picked up on by both the Mills), and, secondly, discovering the laws of succession of mental states ('mental physics').[137] These were what Brown called his 'laws of suggestion'. The division of mental phenomena into 'Sensations', 'Thoughts' and 'Emotions' was another characteristic feature of Brown's system that was adopted by several later psychologists; as was the classification of the emotions as 'Retrospective', 'Immediate' and 'Prospective'. Later writers also echoed Brown's statements that 'emotions' could not be given a precise definition but were distinguished by a peculiar vividness of feeling, and that they were not to be confused with 'sensations',

---

[134] Brown (1828), 102–3, 338 (L. 16, 52).
[135] See Campbell (1997), and chapter 8 below.
[136] Brown (1828), 338–40, 483 (L. 52, 72).
[137] J. Mill (1829); J. S. Mill (1843), II, 502–5.

which were feelings with external bodily causes rather than internal mental ones. Among the writers who showed their indebtedness to Brown by adopting some or all of these positions were James and John Stuart Mill, the Congregationalist divine George Payne, evangelicals such as Welsh, Chalmers and Thomas Upham, the Scottish philosophical writers John Abercrombie and George Ramsay, William Lyall, and later nineteenth-century psychologists including Herbert Spencer, G. H. Lewes, Bain and McCosh.[138]

Thomas Chalmers (1780–1847)

In February 1829, the Reverend Francis Henry, Earl of Bridgewater died. His will made provision for eight thousand pounds to be held at the disposal of the president of the Royal Society in London and used to finance the publication of one thousand copies of a work

On the power, wisdom and goodness of God, as manifested in the creation; illustrating such work by all reasonable arguments – as for instance the variety and formation of God's creatures in the animal, vegetable and mineral kingdoms; the effect of digestion and thereby of conversion; the construction of the hand of man, and an infinite variety of other arguments; as also by discoveries, ancient and modern, in arts, sciences, and the whole extent of literature.[139]

The first man approached to produce such a work was the evangelical Chalmers; he considered it an 'arduous and hitherto almost unattempted theme'.[140] He was to be joined by seven others, including William Whewell and Charles Bell (who wrote on astronomy and the hand respectively), in producing the 'Bridgewater Treatises', which have come to represent the high-tide of British natural theology in the 1830s.[141] Chalmers was the only theologian among the Bridgewater authors.[142]

---

[138] Payne (1828); Mill (1829); Chalmers (1833); Upham (1856); Mill (1843); Ramsay (1848, 1853, 1857); Lyall (1842, 1848, 1855); Spencer (1855, 1870–2); Bain (1859); McCosh (1880, 1886, 1887). On Lyall, see chapter 6 below, and McKillop (1979), 44–52; Page (1980); Dixon (2002b). On Ramsay, see chapter 6 below and Dixon (2002c). On Abercrombie see Dixon (2002a). On G. H. Lewes' adoption of the metaphor of mental chemistry, see Rylance (2000), 308.

[139] Quoted in an introductory notice to Chalmers (1853), xxxv.

[140] Chalmers (1853), xxxiii. For a summary of the evangelical worldview, see Hilton (1988), 7–8, and throughout. On Chalmers' life and theology, see Revd Dr Cumming's 'Biographical Preface' to Chalmers (1853); McCosh (1875), ch. 53; Oliphant (1893); Philip (1929); Rice (1971); Cheyne (ed.) (1985); Hilton (1988), 55–70, 361–4. For a philosophical exposition and critique of Chalmers' natural theology, see Addinall (1991), ch. 6. On Chalmers' Bridgewater Treatise, see Brown (1982), 218–20.

[141] On the Bridgewater treatises, see Gillispie (1959), esp. 209–16. For references to further secondary literature on the Bridgewater treatises, see Topham (1992).

[142] Addinall (1991), 107.

The treatise that Chalmers produced was *On the Power, Wisdom and Goodness of God as Manifested in the Adaptation of External Nature to the Moral and Intellectual Constitution of Man* (1833). It was prefaced by a letter of dedication to Charles James, Lord Bishop of London, in which Chalmers confessed that 'I have derived greater aid from the views and reasonings of Bishop Butler, than I have been able to find besides, in the whole range of our existent authorship.'[143] The influence of Butler was especially evident, as we shall see shortly, in Chalmers' treatment of physical and mental appetites alike as mechanisms rather than as movements or actions of an individual will.[144]

McCosh's partisanship was as evident as always in the high praise that he reserved for Chalmers. He observed that there had always been a certain separation bordering on hostility between Enlightenment Scottish philosophy and the Calvinist Scottish theology. The one magnified human nature, the other humbled man and exalted God; the one showed the existence and supremacy of the conscience, the other proclaimed that the conscience must pronounce man a sinner. But this separation, according to McCosh, was not to be permanent: 'The reconciliation between the philosophy and the religion was effected by Thomas Chalmers, who has had greater influence in moulding the religious belief and character of his countrymen than any one since the greatest Scotchman, John Knox.'[145] While it is true that Chalmers was an able exponent of mental and moral philosophy in the Scottish tradition and also a Calvinist preacher and theologian of the highest reputation, the fact that he was an exponent of both traditions is not the same as the claim that the two were ultimately reconciled in his work. Chalmers qua philosopher of the emotions and intellect was almost as unchristian as Brown, despite the dramatic divergence in actual religious conviction between them. As Daniel Rice has shown, Chalmers' work did not in fact live up to McCosh's description; the tensions between Calvinist anthropology on the one hand, and the rationalist and scientific mental philosophy of the Scottish school on the other, were never resolved.[146]

Chalmers himself, in his Preface to an 1846 reissue of the sections of Brown's *Lectures* relating to ethics, stated that the most important function of natural theology was 'guiding the way to our Revealed Theology'. He noted that Brown did 'not expressly treat of revelation'; later he would say that 'Brown had very low and inadequate views of the character of God'.[147] But Chalmers reassured his readers that many of Brown's views

---

[143] Chalmers (1853), xxxiii.
[144] On mechanism in Butler, see chapter 3 in this volume. On Butler's influence on Chalmers, see Hilton (1988), 173, 183–5.
[145] McCosh (1875), 393.   [146] Rice (1971).   [147] Quoted in Hilton (1988), 179.

'shed a pleasing and confirmatory light on what may be termed the moral dynamics of the gospel'.[148] What the Preface sought to show was that Brown's views could be used by Christians (to combat ethical utilitarianism, for instance) rather than that they were Christian views themselves. Brown's fundamental models and assumptions, as we have seen, were anything but Christian – especially his denial of efficient causation, his replacement of the treatment of reason, affection and passion of the Christian tradition with a stark division between thoughts and emotions, and his replacement of active principles such as understanding and will with quasi-autonomous affections of the mind connected in necessitarian chains of cause and effect.

Existing secondary literature has focussed on Thomas Chalmers' theology, social and political thought, and churchmanship – especially his views on poverty and the poor laws – but not on his contribution to psychological thought.[149] The influence of Brown's mental science upon Chalmers' thought about emotions and volition was considerable, although this influence too has not been noted until now. Such was the extent of Chalmers' admiration for Brown's work, that he tried to organise a subscription to fund the erection of a monument to Brown after his death.[150] This project was ultimately unsuccessful. However, Chalmers' work on mental philosophy was one of many intellectual monuments to Brown's influence. The very division of mental states into 'intellectual states of mind, and its states of emotion' was directly derived from Brown, and the definition of emotions given by Chalmers was nothing more than a paraphrase of Brown: 'They are distinguishable both from the appetites and the external affections, in that they are mental and not bodily – though in common with these, they are characterised by a peculiar vividness of feeling, which distinguishes them from the intellectual states of mind.'[151] Chalmers went on, exactly as Brown had, to note that the difference between intellectual states and emotions was not easily expressed in language but that in practice everyone knew to which of the two classes to refer acts of memory or judgment on the one hand or feelings of fear or shame on the other.[152] The Congregationalist divine George Payne, writing explicitly under the influence of Butler, Brown and Chalmers, in his *Elements of Mental and Moral Science* (1828), had

[148] Chalmers, 'Preface' to Brown (1846), xxii–xxiii.
[149] See e.g. Brown (1982); Cheyne (ed.) (1985); Hilton (1988); Dodds (1995); Gladstone (1995).
[150] On Chalmers' admiration for Brown, see Hanna (1878), I, 490–4, II, 4–5, 99, 104–5. Letters relating to the planned memorial are held in New College Library, Edinburgh, CHA 4.54.42; 4.64.3–7; 4.101.1–2; 4.240.83. See also National Library of Scotland, MS 3704, ff. 84–6.
[151] Chalmers (1853), 346, 348.   [152] See Brown (1828), 102–6 (L. 16–17).

also reproduced the Brownian definition: 'Our emotions differ, however, so manifestly from our intellectual states of mind, by that peculiar vividness of feeling which everyone understands though it may be impossible to embody it in any verbal definition.'[153]

The adoption of the strong rather than weak position on the applicability of the methods and concepts of the physics of matter to the science of mind also aligned Chalmers with Brown and Hume rather than with Reid in this instance. McCosh made the telling remark that Chalmers 'never wearied to dilate on the greatness of Sir Isaac Newton, and often introduced him somewhat inappropriately'. He also recorded (with some disapproval) that Chalmers used Jonathan Edwards' arguments for philosophical necessity to support the Scripture doctrine of predestination.[154] So in Chalmers we find an interesting combination of scientific and theological forms of determinism.[155]

Chalmers, in a preliminary terminological discussion at the start of his chapter on intellect and the emotions, noted that the intellectual states of mind belonged to the 'percipient' province of the mind and the emotions to 'what Sir James Mackintosh would term the *emotive* or *pathematic* part of our nature'. He further noted that Bentham had applied the word 'pathology' to refer to states of susceptibility of the mind but that this had been usurped by medical writers to refer only to distempers of the body. Nonetheless it was 'pathology' that Chalmers favoured as the general term for the emotional province of the mind. He defended this usage on the grounds that there were alternative translations into Latin of the Greek *pasco*: one was *patior* (to suffer), from which the medical sense of 'pathology' arose and the other was *afficior* (to be affected), from which the mental sense was derived. Chalmers appealed to the distinction between passions and affections in order to reinforce this distinction between the two kinds of pathology.

> The two differ as much the one from the other as passion does from affection, or the violence of a distempered does from the due and pacific effect of a natural influence... Medical pathology is the study of those diseases under which the body suffers. Mental pathology is the study of all those phenomena that arise from influences acting upon the mind viewed as passive, or as not putting forth

---

[153] Payne (1828), 318; Brown (1828), 102 (L. 16). For biographical details on Payne, see the *DNB*. Payne, along with Thomas Upham, was picked out by Porter as one of the psychological thinkers most influenced by Brown; Porter (1874), 413. Payne's work is particularly interesting as it draws on the two traditions of mental science and evangelical theology; Payne (1828), esp. xi–xii.

[154] McCosh (1875), 399–400. On the positive attitude to the sciences taken by Chalmers and by other evangelicals later in the nineteenth century, including McCosh, see Hilton (1988), 22–6, 361–72.

[155] See Hilton (1988), 14.

any choice or activity at the time. Now, when thus defined, it will embrace all that we understand by sensations and affections and passions.[156]

It is curious that, having displayed this familiarity with the language and etymological nuance of the terms 'passions' and 'affections', which he would have derived from his reading of Edwards amongst others, Chalmers effaced the distinction by adopting Brown's 'emotions'. Equally curiously, he claimed to favour the ambiguous 'pathology' as the umbrella term for these mental states. What this section of Chalmers' treatise does illustrate is that the 1820s–50s were decades when several terminological innovations were being contested by mental and moral philosophers, of which Brown's was only one (albeit the one that ultimately had most success).[157]

Chalmers was even more explicit than Brown in defining emotions as passive, non-cognitive and 'altogether unmodified by the will'. The states of feeling that were collected together under Chalmers' category of 'mental pathology' were defined as: 'the very states which result from the law of the external senses, or the laws of emotion operating upon us at the time, when the mind is either wholly powerless or wholly inactive'.[158] There was certainly nowhere other than Brown's *Lectures* from where Chalmers would in 1833 have derived the phrase 'laws of emotion'. The language of 'law' was indicative both of the importance of the analogy with physical science and of the necessitarian nature of the system and the lack of room for the will. Elsewhere Chalmers referred to the 'laws' that 'connect invariably' certain objects with certain emotions, such as the law that connected seeing another person in pain with feeling the emotion of compassion.[159] Chalmers' necessitarian, involuntary and non-intellectual view of the emotions could be described either as a clarification or as a caricature of Brown's theory. But certainly, alongside Brown's highly influential *Lectures*, Chalmers' popular Bridgewater Treatise was one of the most important vehicles for the dissemination of a necessitarian psychology of emotions. The Brownian theory supported by Chalmers was that emotions existed independently of an individual's will or understanding as items composed of mental elements in quasi-chemical combination, and connected by quasi-physical laws of cause and effect. Payne's book was a less influential work in the same vein, directly shaped by Brown's lectures and also informed by Chalmers' combination of evangelical theology and mental science.[160]

[156] Chalmers (1853), 346–7.
[157] On the contributions of Spencer, Rauch, Upham and Hickok to this terminological mêlée later in the century, and on Whewell's treatment of Mackintosh's suggested terminology, see chapters 5 and 6 in this volume.
[158] Chalmers (1853), 347–8.   [159] Chalmers (1853), 360.   [160] Payne (1828).

Chalmers used two analogies in particular that reinforced the involuntary nature of emotions. First, he drew an analogy between visual perception and emotion.

> If we look singly and steadfastly to an object of a particular colour, as red, there is an organic necessity for the peculiar sensation of redness, from which we cannot escape, but by shutting our eyes, or turning them away to objects that are differently coloured. If we think singly and steadfastly to an object of a particular character, as an injury, there seems an organic necessity also for the peculiar emotion of resentment, from which there appears to be no other way of escaping, than by stifling the thought, or turning the mind away to other objects of contemplation.[161]

Just as in the presence of a red object a certain sensation is impressed on my retina by organic necessity whether I will it or not, so in the presence of the thought of an injury to myself the emotion of resentment is impressed on my mind by organic necessity whether I will it or not. This was extraordinarily strong necessitarian language that contrasted sharply with the 'classical Christian' views discussed above, and the view still maintained by Reid, of passions and affections that were acts of the appetite and of the rational will, which could be moderated by reason.

The second analogy that Chalmers used that stressed the involuntary nature of emotions was again a bodily one; this time the analogy was derived from Butler – the analogy with the 'corporeal appetency' or hunger.

> The corporeal appetency seeks for food as its terminating object, without regard to its ulterior effect in the sustaining of life. The mental appetency seeks for knowledge, the food of the mind, as its terminating object, without regard to its ulterior benefits, both in the guidance of life, and the endless multiplication of its enjoyments. The prospective wisdom of man could be trusted with neither of these great interests; and so the urgent appetite of hunger had to be provided for the one, and the like urgent principle of curiosity had to be provided for the other. Each of them bears the same evidence of a special contrivance for a special object – and that by one who took a more comprehensive view of our welfare than we are capable of taking for ourselves; and made his own additions to the mechanism for the express purpose of supplementing the deficiency of human foresight. The resemblance between the two cases goes strikingly to demonstrate how a mental constitution might as effectually bespeak the hand of an intelligent Maker, as does a physical or material constitution.[162]

The result of combining the mechanistic design theology of Butler with the reductionist mental chemistry of Brown was a thoroughly noncognitive, involuntary and automatic view of emotions. The analogy implied that mental curiosity, and other emotions, were simply automatic

---

[161] Chalmers (1853), 361.
[162] Chalmers (1853), 349. For the source of this comparison, see Butler (1970), 21.

self-acting mechanisms provided by an intelligent Maker as contrivances to benefit the individual and the species – they were not acts, inclinations or movements of the will. In Butler's phrase, human beings were 'instruments in the hands of Providence', performing beneficial actions automatically – for Brown and Chalmers driven by automatic 'emotions' that arise in a law-like way – rather than voluntarily.

Where 'the emotions' really came from

In the century or so between the eras of David Hume and Alexander Bain a major conceptual transformation took place in the way that English-language psychological thinkers dealt with the phenomena of hope, fear, love, hate, joy, sorrow, anger and the like. As was noted in the Introduction, the wholesale change in psychological vocabulary (from talk of passions, affections and sentiments to talk of emotions), which took place relatively rapidly during this period is an arresting feature of the history of psychological categories. The huge popularity of Thomas Brown's *Lectures*, and the (unacknowledged) adoption of his views on emotions by Thomas Chalmers – described by one historian as the 'second most influential Scotsman of his generation' and by another as 'possibly the most influential Scot of the nineteenth century' – must together take a large measure of the credit for this terminological revolution.[163]

Where 'the emotions' really came from, then, was from within the increasingly de-Christianised texts and university lectures produced by moral and mental philosophers in Scotland from the 1730s onwards, reaching a decisive point in the *Lectures* of the physician-philosopher Thomas Brown. The Scottishness of 'emotions' is confirmed once more by the fact that what might be considered the first major psychological text on the emotions – psychological in the narrow sense of being produced by someone who might be recognisable today as a psychologist as a result of his emphasis on nerves, animals, infants, outward observation, physiology and so on – was produced by yet another Scot, Alexander Bain.[164]

This chapter has also established further evidence for the claim that non-cognitive and involuntary views of emotions were, contrary to what Robert Solomon and others have suggested, produced as a result of the neglect of traditional and Christian psychologies. It is suggested that the dichotomy between the intellect and the emotions was stronger and starker, in the mental science written under the influence of Brown, than the Christian division between reason and the passions had been. The

---

[163] Hilton (1988), 55; Devine (1999), 364. [164] See chapter 5 in this volume.

analysis of Chalmers in particular reveals how the combined influences of Butler and Brown – both proponents of methodologically atheological psychologies – produced an especially involuntary view of emotions as forces outside our control and acting either against or independently of our will. While passions and affections had been thought of by faculty psychologists as 'active powers', Brownian emotions were passive products of the operation of the laws of the physics and chemistry of the mind. In short, Solomon's and Rorty's view can be turned on its head. The stark divisions between intellect and emotions, and between will and emotions, are not to be ascribed to the influence of the Christian tradition but to the departure from traditional Christian faculty psychology by Brown, Chalmers and enthusiastic promulgators of their mental science, such as Payne. Individuals with deep Christian commitments as well as individuals with only thin or non-existent commitments to theism produced texts proposing secular psychologies in which involuntary and non-cognitive emotions – differentiated by their 'peculiar vividness of feeling' – were a central feature.

5 The physicalist appropriation of Brownian emotions: Alexander Bain, Herbert Spencer, Charles Darwin

> The influence of Brown's terminology and of his methods and conclusions has been potent in the formation and consolidation of the Associational Psychology – represented by J. Mill, J. S. Mill, Alexander Bain, and Herbert Spencer.
>
> Noah Porter, 'Philosophy in Great Britain and America', 410

> Emotion is the name here used to comprehend all that is understood by feelings, states of feeling, pleasures, pains, passions, sentiments, affections.
>
> Alexander Bain, *The Emotions and the Will*, 3

Physicalist theorists of emotion in Britain 1855–1875

In the intellectual world of the second half of the nineteenth century evolutionary theories were the subjects of endless public and professional disputes. The theory of evolution by natural selection was, however, just one part of a broader set of evolutionary hypotheses, including theories of inheritance of acquired characteristics and sexual selection. These, in turn, were just one part of a coalition of individuals and ideas, which predated the *Origin of Species* (1859), and which was broadly perceived in Victorian culture as connected not only with science and evolution, but also with 'materialism', 'atheism', 'positivism' and 'Comtism'. These terms were used loosely, largely inaccurately and almost always pejoratively by those who opposed the inroads being made by secular, evolutionary and physiological thinkers such as Bain, Spencer, Darwin, Huxley and Henry Maudsley into the preserves of the human mind, morality and religion.[1]

---

[1] See Jacyna (1981); Cashdollar (1989); Desmond (1989, 1994 and 1997). Desmond's studies of the political and ideological dimensions of Victorian science and medicine are immensely informative. Their main weakness, perhaps, is their tendency to reproduce uncritically inaccurate contemporary characterisations of thinkers including Huxley as 'materialists' and 'atheists'.

An entertaining piece of verse entitled *Our Modern Philosophers: Darwin, Bain and Spencer,* or *The Descent of Man, Mind and Body; A Rhyme with Reasons, Essays, Notes and Quotations,* published in 1884 under the pseudonym 'Psychosis' nicely illustrates the fact that these three were seen as leading spokesmen of scientific-evolutionary thought, which, in turn, was seen as comprising – as its two most dangerous components – evolutionary biology and physiological psychology. The author started in the preface by summarising the popular view in 'most of the Christian world' of these modern philosophers:

> Three men of genius and free-thought,
> An intellectual synod,
> In conclave sat to bring to naught
> The works and government of God.
> Says Darwin: 'God did not make man,
> To demonstration I'll prove this';
> Says Spencer: 'Since the world began,
> God's government has gone amiss';
> 'By my hypothesis,' says Bain,
> 'Man's immortality's a myth – his soul's his brain.'[2]

Although 'Psychosis' himself denied that there needed to be any link between psychological theories and religious beliefs, his caricature of the common view bore witness to the perceived antagonism between religion and the thought of Bain, Spencer and Darwin. There was some truth in the perception: these writers' endorsement of physiological and evolutionary approaches to the mind was, in some ways, motivated by hostility to Christianity and the churches.

The emotions – including especially those feelings and instincts that were still understood by many as moral, religious and aesthetic 'affections' or 'sentiments' – were, along with reason, hallmarks of what was especially dignified, superior and noble about the human mind. Physiological and evolutionary accounts of emotions were, therefore, particularly powerful weapons in wider science–religion debates. If man's very emotions could be reduced to mere physiological reflexes, or to inherited animal survival mechanisms, then he truly would have been removed from his unique position as the pinnacle of creation. Physiological and evolutionary psychologies were, like evolutionary biology and comparative anatomy, very important contributors to the debate about *Man's Place in Nature* (the title of Huxley's 1863 book). In chapter 4 we saw how design theology arguments could be applied to the mind as well as to the body; the same was true of the methodologies of natural history and evolutionary biology.

---

[2] 'Psychosis' (1884), vii.

The treatments that are considered in this section as the main examples of such accounts of the emotions were produced by three of the central figures of the new psychology: Bain, Spencer and Darwin.[3] Bain's widely used textbooks, *The Senses and the Intellect* (1855) and *The Emotions and the Will* (1859) (from here on *Emotions*), and Darwin's *The Expression of the Emotions* (1872) (from here on *Expression*) were particularly significant examples of physiological and evolutionary approaches to the emotions, as were the relevant sections of Spencer's *The Principles of Psychology* (1855) (from here on *Principles*), and his essays on Bain and on the physiology of laughter, both originally published in 1860.[4]

Darwin's treatment of the emotions has received much greater attention from historians of science and of psychology than have the treatments of Spencer and Bain, although it was these latter two whose influence was greatest on thought about the mind during the 1850s to 1870s in Britain and America. Bain and Spencer, along with Bain's friend and mentor John Stuart Mill (who introduced Bain to Comte's *Cours de Philosophie Positive* in 1842), formed a philosophical triumvirate associated in Britain and America with empiricism, naturalism, science and Positivism.[5] In 1870 the English Catholic, St George Mivart, wrote to Darwin that for a time he had felt himself a 'thoroughgoing disciple of the school of Mill, Bain and H. Spencer'.[6] Writing to Charles Revouvier in 1872, William James commented that 'With us it is the philosophy of Mill, Bain and Spencer which just now carries everything before it.'[7] And four years later it was James' judgment that 'The two philosophers of indubitably the widest influence in England and America since Mill's death are Messrs. Bain and Spencer, who have little in common except the tendency to explain things by physical reasons as much as possible and this abundance of illustrative fact.'[8] Finally, in 1888, Spencer had disappeared from James' recollection, which was now that 'Twenty-five years ago all of us whose education had any outlook and vitality were pupils of the Mills and Bain.'[9] In the English-speaking world in the second half of the nineteenth century, Bain's and Spencer's works were the authoritative texts of a new

---

[3] Brett (1921), III, 202–3, picks out Bain's physiological psychology along with the evolutionism of Spencer and that of Darwin as three of the four most important agencies shaping British psychology in the nineteenth century. The fourth is James Ward's article on 'Psychology' in the *Encyclopaedia Britannica*.
[4] Spencer (1863b and 1863c).
[5] From here on references to 'Mill' are to John Stuart Mill. His father will always be referred to as 'James Mill'. On Bain's association with Mill, which started in 1841, see Bain (1904), 112, 145–6, 153, 159, 229; Young (1970), 99n.; Cashdollar (1989), 21–3, 33–6.
[6] Quoted in Desmond (1994), 340.   [7] Quoted in Fisch (1954), 431.
[8] James (1876), 367. See also Lange (1881), III, 186–93.
[9] Quoted in Fisch (1954), 426.

scientific psychology.[10] Bain, who met Comte in Paris in 1851 and had been an admirer and critic for a decade previously, was considered by the American positivist John Fiske to be one of the 'English positivists'; and Porter, in 1872, picked out Comte, Mill, Bain and Spencer as the main representatives of dangerous sceptical and materialistic tendencies in philosophy and psychology.[11]

The physicalist appropriation of Brownian emotions

The influence of Scottish moral and mental science on the exact sciences, especially physics, in Britain in the eighteenth and nineteenth centuries has been well documented.[12] In this and subsequent chapters my focus is on the influence of Scottish mental science specifically on scientific psychology. Brown's influence on this generation of psychological thinkers was noted at the time. In 1874 Noah Porter, the President of Yale, wrote: '[T]he influence of Brown's terminology and of his methods and conclusions has been potent in the formation and consolidation of the Associational Psychology – represented by J. Mill, J. S. Mill, Alexander Bain, and Herbert Spencer.'[13] It is significant that Porter emphasised that it was Brown's terminology, in particular, that was adopted by the Mills, Bain and Spencer.[14] As we have seen, one of the most notable of Brown's terminological innovations was the newly systematic use of the term 'emotions' as a major psychological category alongside sensations and thoughts. The eminent physician, Sir Henry Holland, who had been studying in Edinburgh around the time that Brown first came to public attention through his involvement in the Leslie affair, later also judged that Brown's *Lectures* had contained 'much that has been appropriated, doubtless unconsciously, by later writers on Mental Philosophy'.[15]

Henry Holland was not the only writer acquainted with Brown's work later to be involved in the development of a new physiological psychology in England. Several of the new scientific psychologists of this period either were Scots themselves, or had studied in Scotland. Charles Darwin studied medicine for two years in Edinburgh (1825–7) before giving up the idea of becoming a physician and starting to study for the Anglican ministry in Cambridge. It was during his time in Edinburgh that he would

---

[10] Fisch (1954), 417.
[11] Bain (1904), 223–5. On Fiske, see Fisch (1954), 425; Porter (1872b), 58–64.
[12] Olson (1975). [13] Porter (1874), 410.
[14] Mill adopted the Brownian classification of mental states as sensations, thoughts and emotions, with the slight difference that he, unlike Brown, considered 'volitions' to be a category separate from 'emotions'. Mill (1843), II, 497.
[15] Holland (1872), 85; on Holland's own contributions to medical-psychological discourse, see Rylance (2000), 127–43.

have first become familiar with the work of the Scottish anatomist Charles Bell. Bell, in turn, had been a contemporary of Brown's while both were studying for the M.D. in Edinburgh at the turn of the century, and, like Brown, had studied with Dugald Stewart, and been on friendly terms with Francis Jeffrey and the other founders of the *Edinburgh Review*.[16] Darwin also studied works by several other Scottish writers including Henry Lord Brougham, John Abercrombie and Sir James Mackintosh, while thinking about expression and habit in the late 1830s (see below).[17] Alexander Bain was himself a Scot who had studied the philosophical writings of Brown and Chalmers; his mentor John Stuart Mill also came from a Scottish family. So there were many routes through which Scottish philosophy came to exercise an influence over mid-nineteenth-century physiological psychology in Britain and America.

While much new evidence and many new methodologies were imported into affective psychology during the middle decades of the nineteenth century (for example, by the introduction of evolutionary hypotheses, extensive observations of animal and infant behaviour, and the use of physiology), the categories of the new psychology were largely unchanged. Categories such as 'intellect', 'will' and the 'senses' that the new psychologists adopted were all ancient categories, and ones 'which have been established in popular thought and language', as Spencer put it.[18] One of the only exceptions to this was the case of 'emotions'. Although the term 'emotions' was no doubt in popular use among many by the 1850s and 1860s, it is the most striking instance of a major psychological category that was used differentially by scientific and non-scientific psychologists. The adoption of the category of 'emotions' by Bain, Spencer and Darwin was indicative of the fact that they were influenced more by their reading of Scottish mental scientists such as Brown, Chalmers and Mackintosh than by English theologians and moralists such as Butler, Paley and Whewell, who spoke the language of passions, affections and sentiments (see chapter 6). Physicalist scientific psychologists were not the only ones to use the word 'emotions', but they did so sooner and integrated the category into their psychology more readily than did more traditional, especially Christian, thinkers.

---

[16] Pichot (1860), 15–19, 28–32; Hartley (2001), 46. On Brown's links with the *Edinburgh Review*, see n.87 of chapter 4 in this volume.
[17] Campbell (1986) argues that Darwin was strongly influenced by the Scottish Common Sense tradition in his rhetoric of scientific methodology. Manier (1978) also discusses the influence on the young Darwin of Scottish philosophers including Stewart, Brown, Abercrombie and Mackintosh. Olson (1975), 252–70, examines the Scottish roots of Sir John Herschel's philosophy of science; Herschel was one of the philosophers of science who most influenced Darwin's own thinking. Darwin was also deeply influenced by the Scottish geologist Charles Lyell.
[18] Spencer (1863c), 138.

There are two points to be distinguished here. First, the term 'emotions' was anomalous. Unlike the terms 'sense', 'intellect', 'will', 'imagination', or 'memory', it was not an ancient category used by classical, medieval, Enlightenment and scientific psychologists alike. The term 'emotions', in comparison with its older psychological cousins – categories such as 'sense', 'intellect', 'will', 'affections' and 'passions' – was the merest infant, having been coined in the previous fifty years. Unlike these other categories, it had no resonance or significance within either traditional Christian psychology or neoclassical philosophical psychology. The language of the physicalist emotion theorists was full of 'brains', 'nerves', 'nerve currents', 'muscles', 'glands', 'viscera', 'organic processes'. These emotions theorists were also amongst the first generation of thinkers to produce textbooks and theories that described themselves as works of 'psychology' rather than 'mental science', 'philosophy of the mind', or 'metaphysics'.[19] Many Christian thinkers, especially in more conservative environments such as Oxford and Cambridge (and some American colleges), continued to use the terms 'will', 'passions', 'affections' and 'sentiments' much more than the term 'emotions'.

The second point, however, is that the term 'emotions' was, in a different respect, just like other terms in this period. Like 'will' and 'intellect', for example – and like the term 'psychology' itself – the term 'emotions' had different meanings depending on whether it was being used as part of a Christian, theistic, philosophical, or scientific psychology. McCosh, for example, used the term 'emotions' to refer to acts of the mind (see chapter 6); Bain, Spencer and James used it to refer to acts of the nerves and viscera. There were similar discrepancies in the use of the term 'will'. There was discontinuity of meaning of psychological terms across worldviews.

Throughout this book, I have tried to make connections between theories of will and theories of passions, affections and emotions. The way that the physicalist emotions theorists discussed in this chapter thought about will was in the non-realist tradition of Hobbes, Hume and Brown, all of whom had held that there was no substantial or immaterial 'will' that existed independently of the particular passions, appetites, desires

---

[19] Samuel Taylor Coleridge had been one of the first to suggest the introduction of the term 'psychology', which he had taken from Blumenbach's lectures on psychology at Göttingen. In his *Biographia Literaria* (1817), he wrote: 'We beg pardon for the use of this *insolens verbum*; but it is one of which our language stands in great need. We have no single term to express the philosophy of the Human Mind; and what is worse, the principles of that philosophy are often called "metaphysical", a word of very different meaning'; quoted in Hearnshaw (1987), 3.

and emotions. A 'volition' was conceived, in the new physiological psychology, not even primarily as a mental act, but as the nervous activity that preceded action – in other words, as a neurological version of Hobbes' 'final appetite'. As Boyd Hilton puts it: 'The will came to be regarded, no longer in terms of faculty psychology, but as a series of transient volitions, each one representing expenditure of acquired energy.'[20] It has already been noted above that a scientific approach to the mind, especially insofar as it sought to discover laws, was unlikely to provide a substantial role for a free will. This was further demonstrated by Bain's and Spencer's views of volition; they were responsible for reinvigorating the tradition of non-realist psychology using the resources of neurophysiology and positivism.

The physiological and evolutionary emotion theorists discussed in this chapter were also among the first to pioneer the belief that the science of the mind should, centrally, also be a science of matter – specifically a sort of physiology focussing on the nervous system (Bain) or a sort of natural history drawing principally on evolutionary hypotheses (Darwin) or both (Spencer), or, perhaps, a science of human behaviour (intimated by all three in various ways). So the transition was made in this period from the by-now very well-established tradition of applying methods connected with the physical sciences to the mind qua mind (observation, induction, analysis and classification of mental states), to the new practice of using the methods and results of the physical sciences per se (especially evolutionary biology and neurophysiology) as the basis of an understanding of the mind.

From the late eighteenth century onwards, medical men with interests in the relations of mind and body, such as William Falconer, Sayer Walker, Alexander Crichton, Thomas Cogan, Thomas Burgess and William Cooke, wrote on the passions and emotions in connection with the physiology of health and disease. (Thomas Brown too, of course, had trained and practised as a physician before turning to the philosophy of the mind.) The medical literature contributed to the currency of a physiological approach to affective psychology, which was to be philosophically and scientifically developed, systematised and popularised by Bain, Spencer and Darwin.[21] Cooke's natural theological and medical study of the emotions is considered further in chapter 6.

---

[20] Hilton (1988), 314.
[21] Falconer (1788); Cogan (1802, 1807 and 1812); Burgess (1839); Cooke (1838 and 1852). For Cogan's definitions of the terms 'passions', 'affections' and 'emotions', and an analysis thereof, see Cogan (1802), 1–16; Payne (1828), 320–32. For two very interesting accounts of medical treatises on the passions in the later eighteenth and early nineteenth centuries, see Grange (1961) and Luyendijk-Elshout (1990). See also Hunter and Macalpine (1963), 552–3, 559–64, and throughout.

Dual-aspect monism and man–animal continuism

A final important theme in this chapter is the newly accelerated development of an autonomous scientific worldview. The works of Bain, Spencer and Darwin shared a rejection of the design-theology account of the expressions of emotions that had been popularised by one of the Bridgewater authors, Sir Charles Bell. Bain and Spencer in particular, along with Thomas Huxley, were responsible for constructing an alternative metaphysics on which to build scientific psychology – namely agnostic monism. It was an atheological system derived from the influence of Scottish (Hume, Brown and Mill) and continental (Spinoza and Comte) teachings on the limitations of human knowledge. This alternative atheological and monist metaphysics of the unknown and unknowable nature of ultimate reality was given the title of 'agnosticism' by Huxley in 1869.[22] In short, the personal God who could be known through revelation and experience, albeit imperfectly, was replaced by a more radically unknown and unknowable 'something' that underlay the veil of mental and physical phenomena. Spencer called it 'The Unknowable'. This was the worldview which was in the process of crystallising, and within which Bain, Spencer and others developed their concepts of emotions in the 1850s to 1870s.[23]

I have called the new scientific emotion theorists 'physicalist' or 'physiological' because their psychology privileged physical facts and methods in a way that had never been done before. The physiological psychologists opposed mind–body dualism: Bain explicitly attacked the view (espoused by many Christians and theists – see chapter 6) that the mind used the body as its 'instrument'.[24] However, most of the physiological school equally denied that mind could be reduced to the operations of matter or was nothing more than matter. Instead they adopted an ontology of dual-aspect monism (also sometimes called Spinozism). This meant that there was an unknown reality that underlay both physical and mental phenomena. Each event was 'two-sided': it had both a physical or objective and a mental or subjective side.[25] In saying that every mental phenomenon was also a physical one, Bain and Spencer were not saying that mind was

---

[22] Desmond (1994), 374.
[23] For an account of the philosophical and theological debates about the limits of human knowledge surrounding the doctrines of Comtean positivism and agnosticism in the middle of the nineteenth century, see Cashdollar (1989). For a collection of articles on agnosticism published by its proponents and opponents between 1862 and 1899 with a useful introduction, see Pyle (1995). For further fuller studies of the nineteenth-century agnostic worldview, its development and its advocates, see Cockshut (1964); Budd (1977); Lightman (1987 and 1989).
[24] Bain (1873), 132–3.   [25] Bain (1873), 131–2.

nothing but nerve force, but that mental feelings and physical nervous processes were two sides of the same (unknowable) coin.[26] The event could be looked at from the mental point of view or the physical point of view.

Spencer's dual-aspect view of emotional feelings was that they were 'the subjective aspects of objective nervous changes'.[27] His hypothesis, he said, was that in any emotion, the feeling and the nervous action were 'the inner and outer faces of the same change'.[28] Note that he did not say that the feelings were the products or properties of nervous changes, nor that they *were* nervous changes – all of which might have been the claims of a materialist. His talk was of the different 'aspects' or 'faces' of the two-sided emotion, which was in itself described just as a 'change'. Bain also talked of giving an account of the physical 'side' as well as the mental 'side' of each emotion: the bodily symptoms of emotions were the physical side of the mental fact.[29]

So, dual-aspect monism was a symmetrical and non-reductionist philosophy; the dual-aspect monist did not reduce mental phenomena either to mere brain activity, in the manner of the materialist, or to the properties of an autonomous mind, in the manner of the idealist or spiritualist. Despite their theoretical profession of dual-aspect monism, however, Bain and Spencer often seemed in practice to teach a more physicalist and reductionist philosophy. Facts about bodies (especially about nerves, lower animals, infants, 'savages' and the insane) were given a privileged place in their psychologies – as they also were in Darwin's work.[30] Attention was constantly drawn to the 'dependence of all mental workings whatever on bodily organs', or to the fact that 'Every feeling, peripheral or central – sensational or emotional – is the concomitant of a nervous disturbance and resulting nervous discharge.'[31] Thomas Laycock, one of the pioneers of physiological psychology in Britain in the mid-nineteenth century, had made the same commitment in 1861: 'Medical psychology affirms the fundamental principle of physiology, that no change whatever arises in the consciousness without a corresponding change, or series of changes of some kind in the organism.'[32] Bain's and Spencer's asymmetric privileging of the body verged on becoming a tacit epiphenomenalism despite their professed dual-aspect monism. The doctrine of 'epiphenomenalism' – that conscious experience was a causally impotent by-product of

---

[26] On the combination of monist metaphysics with the conservation of energy and the correlation of forces by Spencer and Bain, see Hilton (1988), 311–14.
[27] Spencer (1870–2), I, 125.   [28] Spencer (1870–2), I, 128.
[29] Bain (1865), 3. See also Mischel (1966), 137.
[30] See e.g. Bain (1865), 57–65, 602; Spencer (1870–2), II, 518; Darwin (1998), 20–6.
[31] Bain (1865), 3; Spencer (1870–2), II, 540.   [32] Laycock (1861), 7.

neural activity; that mind is pure effect – was most famously put forward in this period by Huxley, who used the image of the conscious mind being like the steam whistle of a locomotive engine (the brain).[33]

The application of an epiphenomenalist view of mind to the emotions was implicit in the approaches of Bain, Spencer and Darwin, who all implied by their methodology and language that the real business of emotions went on at the physiological and neurological levels. The implication of their texts was that emotions were the mental 'side' of what was really and objectively an activity of the central nervous system. For example Bain, in *Body and Mind* (1873), described fear as follows: 'When a shock of fear paralyses the digestion, it is not the emotion of fear, in the abstract, or as a pure mental existence, that does the harm; it is the emotion in company with a peculiarly excited condition of the brain and nervous system; and it is this condition of the brain that deranges the stomach.'[34] While the 'emotion' was the mental feeling rather than the bodily conditions, which were the physical 'side' of the emotion, the tenor of the piece was physicalist and epiphenomenalist. The 'shock of fear', which disturbed the digestion, was in reality not an abstract mental emotion but the 'condition of the brain'. Elsewhere, Bain made even more explicit statements about the fundamental importance of the bodily in producing the mental: 'The transformations of the food and tissue are the *sine qua non*, the consciousness is the accidental part'; and, most succinctly of all, 'No currents, no mind.'[35] Bain made psychological explanations parasitic upon physiological ones; his professed dual-aspect monism was far from symmetrical.[36] William James' later theory of emotion was, in a sense, the reverse of this hypothesis: for James, the disturbance of the viscera caused the condition of the brain, not vice versa. In another sense, however, Bain's and James' theories were very similar – both attributed agency to the body and made the mind passive. James made explicit the tacit epiphenomenalism of earlier physiological theories of emotion.

Another feature, then, of this new approach to the body as part of the study of the mind was the view that the body was active, rather than the passive vehicle or instrument of an active soul. So in the case of emotions it was the spontaneous activity of the central nervous system that caused (passive) mental feelings of emotion. Bain, for example, in accounting for emotions, referred to the 'action of the viscera' and 'the action of the cerebrum upon involuntary muscles'.[37] If monism had been strictly

---

[33] Huxley (1894), 240, 243–4. [34] Bain (1873), 132.
[35] Bain (1859), 476. See also Rylance (2000), 172–82.
[36] Mischel (1966), 142–3. [37] Bain (1865), 10.

adhered to, the activity of the central nervous system would be assumed to have a mental side too, and so mind would be just as active as body. However, opposition to Christian dualism and its associated spiritualist psychology often overrode this strict monism, so that the claim in effect was that the body rather than the mind was active in emotions.[38]

As well as being committed to the ontological unity of mind and brain, physiological and evolutionary thinkers were committed to the unity of the animal kingdom. The division between man and the 'brute creation' had always been central to Christian psychology. This view was derived by many from the first chapter of the book of Genesis and was at the root of Christian thought about passions (shared to some degree with lower animals) and affections and sentiments (along with reason, hallmarks of human uniqueness, and shared in by the angels and God).[39] Its rejection was a prime example of how rejection of the ontology of the Christian worldview could shape secular psychologies.

The debate about 'man's place in nature', which became connected with evolutionism in the Victorian period, focussed both on physical and mental traits. There was a close analogy between the debate between Richard Owen and Huxley about the anatomy of ape and human brains and that between Bain, Spencer and, especially, Darwin and their critics about animal and human minds. The debate between Owen and Huxley in the 1850s and 1860s centred on the question of whether ape brains had a hippocampus minor. Owen claimed that possession of a hippocampus minor was one of the anatomical features that made human beings unique, and that no other species possessed a hippocampus minor, although some apes might possess a homologue; Huxley said they had the organ itself. Owen interpreted as a primitive, qualitatively different homologue what Huxley saw as an ape version of the same organ. Owen wished to keep the man–ape divide open, Huxley to close it.[40]

Darwin was extremely liberal in his ascription of emotions to animals – he described the expressions and attitudes of angry bees, proud, loving and humble dogs, impatient and sulky horses, irritated bulls, enraged deer and grieving, jealous, curious and depressed monkeys.[41] Darwin, as we saw above, seems to have been particularly carried away by the expressiveness of his dog: 'man himself cannot express love and humility by external signs so plainly as does a dog, when with drooping ears,

---

[38] E.g. Bain (1873), chs. 4 and 6; see Jacyna (1981).
[39] See e.g. Genesis 1.26; St Augustine (1961), XIII.32; St Augustine (1991), XII.13; O'Connell (1987), 249.
[40] For various accounts of the 'ape brain debate' between Huxley and Owen, see Huxley (1863), 96–118; Di Gregorio (1984), 134–43; Rupke (1994), 270–85; Cosans (1994).
[41] Darwin (1871), I, 39–43, 366; Darwin (1998), esp. 55–63, ch. 5.

hanging lips, flexuous body, and wagging tail, he meets his beloved master'.[42] It is rather ironic, in view of this tendency to anthropomorphism, that Darwin defended the amount of attention he paid to animals in his study of expression partly on the grounds that 'In observing animals, we are not likely to be biassed by our imagination.'[43]

By concentrating on the more basic emotions in humans (and by focussing on infants, 'savages' and the insane) he produced a picture in which humans and animals experienced and expressed a very similar range of emotions. Thomas Baynes (a man of letters, editor of the *Encyclopaedia Britannica* and advocate of Charles Bell's natural theological approach to the physiology of expression) produced a substantial critique of Darwin's *Expression* for the *Edinburgh Review*. In a letter to Bain, Darwin called the review 'magnificently contemptuous'.[44] It attacked Darwin's lax anthropomorphism, pointing out that not only was he exceedingly liberal with his ascription of emotions to animals, but also that his choice of examples was prejudicial – focussing, as he did, on simple and relatively organic emotions of fear, anger and the like rather than on more refined moral and aesthetic feelings, which it would be impossible to ascribe to any species but man. (Baynes' review is discussed further in chapter 6.)

Just as with the 'ape brain debate' between Huxley and Owen, the 'facts' of the matter were not at issue. Bain, Spencer, Darwin and Baynes could all agree about the animal, infant and adult human behaviour in question. What was at issue was interpretation, which was shaped by the worldview each inhabited and wished to promote. A secularist and anti-dualist desire to close the man–animal divide, mentally as well as physically, produced works of psychology that treated human and animal emotions virtually identically. The demise of the passions–affections distinction meant that to say that human emotions were like animal emotions (rather than that passions alone resembled animal states) was to reduce a much broader range of feelings to our animal nature.

Herbert Spencer (1820–1903)

It was only gradually that the two strands of science most useful to the scientific-positivist thinker (physiological psychology and evolutionary biology) came together.[45] Each was relevant to the big question of man–animal continuism and to debates about the existence of, and immortality of, the human soul. Spencer was one of the first to combine

---

[42] Darwin (1998), 18. [43] Darwin (1998), 24. [44] Bain (1904), 321.
[45] For a very interesting discussion of the long delay in bringing evolution and physiological psychology together, see Young (1973).

these two strands, and his was the earliest evolutionary treatment of 'emotions'.[46] He, like Darwin in his *Expression* (see below), originally relied on the mechanism of inheritance of acquired characteristics (or 'use inheritance') in his explanations of emotional behaviours. In the second edition of the *Principles*, however, Spencer began to introduce explanations in terms of evolution by natural selection. He imagined, for example, that certain of our ancestors may have frowned when experiencing disagreeable emotions of antagonism and anxiety when engaged in combat. His assumption was that doing so would improve the protagonist's vision for the duration of the bout:

> Hence, we may infer that during the evolution of those types from which Man more immediately inherits, it must have happened that individuals in whom the nervous discharge accompanying the excitement of combat caused an unusual contraction of these corrugating muscles of the forehead, would, other things being equal, be the more likely to conquer and to leave posterity – survival of the fittest tending in their posterity to establish and increase this peculiarity.[47]

This is an example of the sort of speculative account that evolutionary hypotheses about the origins of emotional expressions tended to generate, and with which both Bain and Baynes, amongst others, were unimpressed.[48]

An example that Spencer gave of how a simple scent could arouse complex emotions illustrated the way that he, like Bain, adopted the basic methods of the associationist psychology:

> If along with the running down of certain prey, a certain scent has been habitually experienced, then, the presentation of that scent will render nascent the motor changes and impression which accompany the running down of the prey. If the motor changes and impressions that precede and accompany the catching of prey, have been constantly followed by destructive actions, then, when they are rendered nascent, they will in their turn render nascent the psychical states implied by destructive actions. And if these have been followed by those connected with eating, then those connected with eating will also be made nascent. So that the simple olfactory sensation will make nascent those many and varied states of consciousness involved in the running down, catching, killing, and eating of prey: the sensations, visual, auditory, tactual, gustatory, muscular, that are bound up with the successive phases of these actions, will be present to consciousness as what we call ideas – will, in their aggregate, constitute the desires to catch, kill, and devour – and will, in conjunction with that olfactory sensation which

---

[46] Little has been written on Spencer's views on emotions; see Janet and Séailles (1902), II, 309–12; Gardiner *et al.* (1970), 282–90. On Spencer's psychology more generally, see Smith (1982); Richards (1987), ch. 6; Rylance (2000), ch. 6.

[47] Spencer (1870–2), II, 547.

[48] Nonetheless, Spencer did introduce the theory of evolution by natural selection into his psychological system, although Reed (1997), 202–4, asserts the contrary.

aroused them all, form the impulse which sets going the limbs in pursuit. The entire genesis of these emotions thus results from successive complications in the groups of psychical states that are co-ordinated; and is just as much determined by experience as is the union of any two simple sensations that constantly occur together.[49]

One of the major innovations of Spencer's evolutionary approach, however, was that it could depart from the basic associationist assumption that all the feelings and faculties of the mind in any given individual were the result only of the experiences of that single individual's life and their associations with pleasure or pain. The introduction of evolutionary hypotheses about the heritability of acquired mental powers and behavioural habits had the effect of transforming psychology from a study of individual histories to a study of the history of the species. Explanations could then be given in terms of the experiences of evolutionary ancestors, not just in terms of an individual's own limited experiences. Indeed, Spencer expressed astonishment that anyone had ever believed the central tenet of traditional associationism:

That the experience-hypothesis as ordinarily understood, is inadequate to account for emotional phenomena, will be sufficiently manifest. If possible, it is even more at fault in respect to the emotions than in respect to the cognitions. The doctrine that all the desires, all the sentiments, are generated by experiences of the individual, is so glaringly at variance with the facts, that I cannot but wonder how any one should ever have entertained it.[50]

Spencer thought it particularly obvious that the 'amatory passion', when first experienced, must at that stage be prior to the relevant experience of any given individual. The explanation must then lie, he thought, in the experience of the species. The guiding principle was that, 'The constant experiences of successive generations will gradually strengthen the tendency of all the component clusters of psychical states to make one another nascent', where the clusters of psychical states in question were the sensations and ideas that were associated together to form more complex states, namely emotions.[51]

Spencer was, like Hume and Brown before him, writing within a tradition that both appealed to science in psychology and denied the autonomous reality and/or the causal efficacy of the individual will. He defined will as the change of an imagined motor change into a real one. He then went on to explain that a psychology that was scientific could not also allow for the freedom of the will:

[49] Spencer (1870–2), I, 484–5.
[50] Spencer (1870–2), I, 493–4.   [51] Spencer (1870–2), I, 491.

To reduce the general question to its simplest form:– Psychical changes either conform to law or they do not. If they do not conform to law, this work, in common with all works on the subject, is sheer nonsense: no science of Psychology is possible. If they do conform to law, there cannot be any such thing as free will.[52]

Once Spencer had committed himself to the view that there could be a science of psychology and also to the view that all sciences must be in the business of discovering exceptionless laws, it followed that there could be no such thing as a freely and spontaneously acting will. He also had a second reason for denying agency to the will: in Spencer's evolutionary worldview, mental states and functions were the product of the collective experience of humanity over countless generations. It was the shaping of mental faculties and habits by the environment, and the inheritance of such faculties and habits, that accounted for the increasing perfection of the human mind. The 'inner relations' of the mind must be determined by the 'outer relations' of the environment for the perfection of the mind to be increased.[53] Just as Spencer endorsed laissez-faire economics on the grounds that competitive evolution must be allowed free play to perfect human society, without the intervention of government, so he denied agency to the will in his psychology on the grounds that evolution must be allowed exclusive agency in the perfection of the human mind, without the intervention of a governing will. The 'will', then, was nothing more than an inherited reflex, a simple mental state forming the link between feeling and action.[54] It was on the basis of doctrines such as these that one reviewer of the first edition of the *Principles*, writing for the *Spectator*, described the work as 'audaciously speculative, subversive of ordinary morality, and anti-Christian'.[55]

Following Brown, Spencer adopted the category of 'emotions' as the generality of feelings, from sexual lust to aesthetic sensibilities, which were neither cognitive nor merely sensational.[56] Unlike Brown, Bain, Darwin and James, however, Spencer – in a tacit acknowledgment of the over-inclusivity of the category – made relatively frequent use of the categories of 'passions' and 'sentiments' to refer to more organic and more abstract feelings respectively.[57] To complicate matters still further, however, he also introduced his own new system of classification of mental states, which divided them first into cognitions and feelings, and then further divided each of these into categories called 'presentative', 'representative', 'presentative-representative' and 're-representative'.[58] This system

---

[52] Spencer (1870–2), I, 485.   [53] Spencer (1870–2), I, 485.
[54] Rylance (2000), 216–18.   [55] Quoted in Rylance (2000), 213.
[56] Spencer (1863c), 139.   [57] E.g. Spencer (1870–2), I, 122, 487, 494; II, 578–9.
[58] Spencer (1870–2), II, 512–19.

of classification was adopted at least by Charles Mercier if no one else, but soon, needless to say, became just another example of a forgotten attempt to classify the feelings and emotions.[59]

Spencer's model of emotion was a rather crude 'aggregate' one. He saw emotions as additive products rather than as chemical compounds. Spencer suggested that emotions were more strongly felt if they were aggregates of a larger number of separate sensations: 'the power of an emotion thus compounded out of clusters of elementary feelings ideally revived, is proportionate to the number of elementary feelings united in it'.[60] He went on to expand on this by saying that 'Quantity of feeling is of two kinds – that which arises from intense excitation of few nerves, and that which arises from slight excitation of many nerves.'[61] Spencer also said that the further an emotion was evolved, the stronger it would be, since more evolution (on Spencer's progressivist view of evolution) meant more complexity, which meant that a larger number of sensations had been aggregated together.[62]

Alexander Bain (1818–1903)

Darwin's and Spencer's religious views have been examined extensively in the secondary literature.[63] Biographical information about Bain's relationship with Christianity and the churches is, however, much less well known (although Rick Rylance's recent study has helped, finally, to rectify that situation).[64] It will serve here as a useful example of how personal and social factors can be correlated with the adoption of a worldview, which in turn can determine the lexical and conceptual networks applied in an inquiry into the human mind.[65]

---

[59] For more on Mercier (1884a, 1884b and 1885), see chapter 7.
[60] Spencer (1870-2), I, 490.   [61] Spencer (1870-2), I, 486.
[62] Spencer (1870-2), I, 486-7.
[63] On Darwin's often ambiguous stance on theism, see Brooke (2003); see also Darwin (1958), 85–96; Herbert (1977), 201–3; Moore (1979), 346–8; Moore (1981 and 1989); Brooke (1985); Kohn (1989); Desmond and Moore (1992), esp. chs. 18 and 41; Browne (1995), esp. 394–9. On Spencer's dissenting background and agnostic beliefs: Spencer (1904); Lightman (1987 and 1989); Richards (1987), esp. 243–53; Hilton (1988), 311–14; Pyle (1995).
[64] See Rylance (2000), ch. 5.
[65] There is no separate study of Bain's views specifically on emotions, with the exception of a short section in Gardiner *et al.* (1970), 282–90, on Bain and Spencer on emotions. The closest thing to a study devoted to Bain's theory of emotions is Mischel (1966), which discusses the use of the concepts of 'emotion' and 'motivation' in Hartley, James Mill and Bain. Since neither Hartley nor James Mill used the concept of 'emotion', the article is a little misleading. It does provide, however, a very good account of the disappearance of the will in Associationist psychology. Aside from generally very brief mentions in general histories of psychology, the most useful secondary works on Bain

The making of an 'infidel'

Bain was born and raised in Aberdeenshire, in a strict Calvinistic family. From an early age, he recalled in his *Autobiography*, he would peruse his father's collection of books, almost all of which were tracts of popular Calvinist theology. One book that interested him was *The Hieroglyphic Bible*, which consisted of biblical narratives in which some of the words were replaced by pictures.

> Of these last, the most notable was a figure of God as a naked old man in sitting posture – I suppose suggested by some design of a pagan deity, or, more likely by the 'Ancient of Days' of Daniel. This figure has haunted me ever since when the name of God is pronounced, if I do not forcibly exclude it from consciousness.[66]

Bain also recounted his discomfort at being subjected, throughout his childhood, to sermons from his father at the Sunday breakfast table on the theme of hell and damnation.[67] During his adolescence he never experienced the conversion moment that was crucial to Calvinist Presbyterianism and so never joined church communion.[68] Once at Marischal college, Bain began, with a group of friends, to read Comte's *Cours de Philosophie Positive* (published in instalments between 1830 and 1842), which Mill had recommended to him as, despite certain errors, 'very nearly the grandest work of this age'.[69] He attributed the final demise of his precarious religious beliefs to these studies of Comte, and the acceptance of the threefold scheme of history in which theological modes of thought were displaced first by metaphysical and finally by scientific (or 'positive') knowledge.[70] Much later in his life, finally alienated from religion altogether, Bain expressed the wish that there should be no religious service at his funeral.[71]

Bain found himself, in the early 1840s, in an academic world in Scotland not entirely dissimilar from that encountered by Brown three decades previously. Bain, like Brown, was neither a minister of the church nor even religiously orthodox. As a result, there was often resistance to his applications for academic posts. Time and again he lost out to orthodox Christian rivals in competitions for academic positions because he was 'obnoxious to the Church party'.[72] In the 1840s and 1850s Bain applied unsuccessfully for the Chair of Natural Philosophy at Aberdeen, the

---

are Mill (1859); Spencer (1863c); Fisch (1954); Mischel (1966); Young (1970); Smith (1971 and 1973); and especially Rylance (2000), ch. 5. Less useful are Cardno (1955 and 1956) and Greenway (1973).
[66] Bain (1904), 9.   [67] Bain (1904), 9–10, 33–4.   [68] Bain (1904), 38–9.
[69] Quoted in Bain (1904), 112.
[70] Bain (1904), 153–9. For a summary of Comte's philosophy, see Cashdollar (1989), 9–12.
[71] Robertson (1929), 221.   [72] Letter from Craik quoted in Bain (1904), 231.

Chair of Moral Philosophy at Aberdeen and the Chair of Philosophy at Queen's College, Belfast.[73] This last post went to the Free Church minister, James McCosh (whose work on emotions is considered in chapter 6). McCosh was again Bain's rival when he applied for the Chair of Logic in Aberdeen in 1860. Bain recounted the incident in his *Autobiography*: 'No sooner was my application generally known, than a powerful agitation was commenced in favour of my chief rival, Professor McCosh of Belfast. He had the whole support of the Free Church of Scotland, and the sympathies of the greater number of the Established Church members as well.'[74] Those professors at Aberdeen University who opposed Bain's appointments urged their colleagues not to 'tamely sit and see an infidel appointed to a Chair'. It was only through the intervention of the Home Secretary (whose friend George Grote was also a friend of Bain's) that Bain was appointed.[75] It is hardly surprising to learn that, after these decades of struggling to gain academic posts in the face of church opposition, Bain was prone, in private conversation at least, to launch the occasional 'antiChristian onslaught', as his friend, the positivist writer G. H. Lewes described it.[76]

There are two important points to be made about this appointment. The first is a geographical point. It is notable that Bain was the 'London' candidate for the Aberdeen Chair. His allegiance with positivism and physiological psychology arose from his extended visits to London from 1841 onwards and a period living in London from 1856 to 1859 (his main occupation during which time was the composition of the first edition of the *Emotions*).[77] In the English-speaking world, it was London, rather than Scotland or Oxford or Cambridge, which was the location of the rise of physiological psychology and of positivism in the 1840s and 1850s.[78] The physicalist appropriation of the Brownian category of 'emotions' was an English development, specifically a development rooted in London. Bain's Scottish education (especially the influence of Brown via Chalmers), combined with his association with Mill, the positivists and the physiological psychologists of London, produced in Bain's work a theory of 'emotions' that was Scottish by birth but which owed much to the intellectual environment of London for its later development.[79]

---

[73] Bain (1904), 169, 179, 230–1.   [74] Bain (1904), 264.   [75] Bain (1904), 264–7.
[76] Rylance (2000), 164.   [77] Bain (1904), 242–52.
[78] On the radical artisans, atheists, medical men and budding scientists who constituted a politically and scientifically progressive coterie in London in this period, the perceived atheism of the new University of London and the contrast between London and Oxbridge, see Desmond (1989). See also Danziger (1982), esp. 139–41.
[79] On the developments in neuro-physiology and physiological psychology in England in the 1840s and 1850s, associated with figures such as Charles Bell, Marshall Hall, Thomas

The second significant point is that in two instances (Belfast in 1851 and Aberdeen in 1860) Bain's rival and opponent was James McCosh. This is particularly interesting since McCosh also wrote on the emotions. McCosh's approach to the emotions was a mixture of Calvinist theology, common sense philosophy and scientific psychology. (His insistence on an active and cognitive model of emotions will be examined below.) So, there was conflict between Bain and McCosh at the level of psychological theory, which was correlated with personal, social and professional oppositions between the two based around matters of religious belief.

Science, positivism and evolution

As Brown and other Scottish mental scientists had done before him, Bain turned to the physical sciences in his search for a preferable alternative to theological methodology. The debate as to whether psychology could be a science, and in what sense, continued throughout the nineteenth century.[80] Comte had excluded psychology from his classification of the sciences in his *Cours*. He felt that psychology was too bound up with old-school metaphysics to become a positive science. He endorsed only physiology and phrenology on the one hand, and sociology on the other, as authentic scientific approaches to human mental life. Mill, Bain and Spencer – the so-called 'English positivists' – took issue with this. They all believed that psychology could be a science in its own right.[81] Mill summarised the question as follows: 'But, after all has been said which can be said, it remains incontestable by M. Comte and by all others, that there do exist uniformities of succession among states of mind, and that these can be ascertained by observation and experiment.'[82] Indeed, it was Mill who, in his book on Comte, claimed that Bain and Spencer were responsible for having extended the positive philosophy to include psychology.[83] Theirs was a new way of applying science to the mind; they shared the belief of Hume, Brown and James Mill that mental scientists should be concerned with discovering regular cause-and-effect relationships between mental states. They did not, however, share the earlier associationists' belief that mental science should be based on introspection alone. The science that Bain and Spencer envisaged was based on positive facts about the mind, its relation to the body, its natural

Laycock, W. B. Carpenter and Benjamin Brodie, see Laycock (1861); Carmichael (1926); Brazier (1957); Hearnshaw (1964), 20–5; Smith (1971 and 1973); Jacyna (1981); Danziger (1982); G. Richards (1992), ch. 8.
[80] See Woodward and Ash (eds.) (1982).
[81] Mill (1843), II, chs. 3 and 4. Rylance (2000), 98–100.
[82] Mill (1843), II, 499.   [83] Cashdollar (1989), 157.

(evolutionary) history, its development in the individual and its objective manifestation in physiology and behaviour. Bain and Spencer went much further than Mill in giving an important role to physical facts in their scientific psychology.[84]

It is often supposed that Bain and Spencer were important figures in the history of psychology because they were responsible for making it a physiological science in its own right. It is important to remember, however, that they, along with Mill, by no means denied the reliability or value of introspection. Bain's and Spencer's books were full of substantial sections that resembled older non-physiological associationist psychology; these sections were simply introspective descriptions of feelings and how they arose based on personal experience, folk psychology and imagined examples.[85] They also both explicitly asserted the importance to psychology of introspected subjective experience, which then had to be correlated with physiology. Spencer even based his argument that psychology was a distinct science on the fact that mind is an irreducibly distinct phenomenon.[86] Warren is mistaken, then, in his claim that 'Bain's psychology is notable for its abandonment of introspection.'[87] Bain was, however, one of the first psychological thinkers to insist that introspection be wherever possible accompanied by (rather than replaced by) observation of physiological and behavioural correlates. For this reason he has been called 'the first psychologist' and 'the author of the first textbook of psychology written in the modern manner', and has been described as the man who 'did more than any other single figure to free psychology from its philosophic context and make it a natural science in its own right'.[88] However, writing in 1893, Bain could still state that introspection 'is the alpha and omega of psychological inquiry; it is alone supreme, everything else is subsidiary'.[89] For Wilhelm Wundt and his followers, too, introspection was still king.[90]

Bain also provided a particularly striking example of the new commitment to objectivity in the study of the human mind. Like his associationist predecessors, he believed that 'Each man has the full and perfect knowledge of his own consciousness' and that 'no living being can penetrate the consciousness of another'. He combined this view of the limits of

---

[84] For Mill's relative caution about physiology, see Mill (1843), II, 499, 507–10.
[85] In Bain, for example, emotions relating to self, intellect, aesthetics and morality are treated entirely from the mental side, relying on philosophy and associationist psychology to the complete exclusion of physiological or evolutionary facts or hypotheses.
[86] It is interesting to contrast this with the more reductionist approach taken by William James and others, which was to say that psychology was a science because it was just like the other sciences. See chapter 7.
[87] Warren (1921), 167.   [88] Flugel, quoted in Hearnshaw (1964), 1; Young (1970), 6.
[89] Quoted in Rylance (2000), 202.   [90] Fancher (1996).

our knowledge of other people's consciousness, however, with an observational methodology that made objective knowledge of outward signs paramount:

> But for our purposes, and for all purposes, two states of feeling must be held as identical when an identity exists between all the appearances, actions, and consequences that flow from, or accompany them. If there be any peculiar shade, tone, or colouring of emotion that has no outward sign or efficacy, such peculiarity is inscrutable to the inquirer. It is enough for us to lay hold of the outward manifestations, and to recognise all the distinctions that they bring to light.[91]

Bain's ideal psychological investigator would categorise emotions only by their objective observable outward signs. This was the sort of observational epistemological constraint that ended up shaping (at least tacitly) the ontology of the new emotion theorists.

While Bain was deeply indebted to the scientific tradition, he had no great enthusiasm for the new sciences of evolution. In the third edition of the *Emotions* (1875), Bain included a substantial new section on the evolution of the mind. He never fully integrated evolutionary hypotheses and explanations into his psychology, however. Bain used empirical material from Darwin's *Expression* as a source of descriptive examples of how certain emotions were expressed, independently of Darwin's hypotheses about the evolutionary origins of behaviours now associated with certain emotions.[92] Indeed, he thought that Darwin's hypothesis (that expressions such as frowns, smiles, grimaces and the like were the remnants of the once-useful behaviours of our ancestors) 'must be pronounced a total failure'.[93] Rylance is right, therefore, to draw a distinction between Bain, the associationist natural historian of the feelings, and Spencer, the evolutionary psychologist.[94] Even in 1881, in a review of the third edition of Spencer's *Principles*, Bain was still, as Rylance puts it, 'pointing, rather sniffily, to the fact that evolution was not yet a validated theory'.[95]

The embodiment of Brownian psychology

During 1837, Bain perused Brown's *Lectures*.[96] He would, however, have become familiar with Brown's extremely broad new category of the 'emotions' – and the definition of emotions as non-cognitive and involuntary – through his much more extensive reading of Chalmers' work,

---

[91] Bain (1865), 28–9.   [92] E.g. Bain (1875), ch. 9.
[93] Bain (1904), 318–19. Bain's full review of the *Expression* was appended to later print-runs of the third edition of *The Senses and the Intellect* (1868) and to the fourth edition (1894). See Bain (1894), 657–72.
[94] Rylance (2000), 211–12.   [95] Rylance (2000), 218.   [96] Bain (1904), 46.

especially his Bridgewater Treatise, which Bain had used as a textbook for some of his early teaching.[97] The beginning of the first chapter of the first edition of Bain's *Emotions* (1859) is as good an indication as any of the incredibly broad range of the category of 'emotions', which he had adopted from Brown and Chalmers: 'Emotion is the name here used to comprehend all that is understood by feelings, states of feeling, pleasures, pains, passions, sentiments, affections.'[98] In his 1860 review of Bain's *Emotions*, Spencer picked up on this definition, claiming that by 'feeling' Bain must include sensations, which should, however, be distinguished from emotions. Bain did not intend to include raw sensations (visual, aural, tactile etc.) under the heading of 'emotions'; the first volume of his psychology had dealt with these senses (along with the intellect). The point was clarified in agreement with Spencer from the second edition onwards, when Bain replaced the offending definition with the phrase: 'The Emotions, as compared with the Sensations, are secondary, derived, or compound feelings.'[99] In the third edition of *The Senses and the Intellect*, Bain explicitly acknowledged that Spencer's criticism had been the cause of his adoption, after 1860, of 'feeling' rather than 'emotion' as the generic term covering all those mental states to which a general stirring of the bodily members was attached. Feelings, Bain agreed, could then be divided into sensations and emotions.[100] In fact one of the things that Bain, Spencer and Darwin all agreed about (after 1860) was that emotions and sensations were distinct; this distinction had first been definitively made by Brown and was endorsed on all sides in later discussions. The innovation here was that the Brownian distinction between sensation and emotion, like the category of emotions itself, was now physicalised with reference to the nervous system by these mid-century scientific psychologists: emotions, they said, had a central nervous origin and were in some sense 'secondary' and sensations had a peripheral nervous origin and were primary.[101]

Along with the Brownian categorisation of mental states into thoughts, sensations and emotions, the evolutionary-physiological school inherited the problematic inclusivity of the category of 'emotions' that had been another feature of Brown's scheme. To take Bain as an example, a perusal even of the table of contents of the second edition of the *Emotions* gives an idea of the hodgepodge of feelings with which he was dealing.

[97] Bain (1904), 58.   [98] Bain (1859), 3.   [99] Bain (1865), 35.
[100] Bain (1868), 668; see also Rylance (2000), 171–2.
[101] Spencer (1863c), 138; Darwin (1998), 33n.; Bain (1875), 69. Baynes was scathing about the fact that Darwin, when proposing this distinction, cited Spencer as an authority – as far as Baynes was concerned this reveals Darwin's complete incompetence in mental science since the distinction was well known to everyone. [Baynes] (1873), 510.

After discussing feeling and emotion in general he considered thirteen topics: emotions of harmony and conflict, emotions of relativity, emotion of terror, tender emotions, emotions of self, emotion of power, irascible emotion, emotions of action/pursuit, emotions of intellect, emotions of sympathy and imitation, ideal emotion, the aesthetic emotions, the ethical emotions.

In Bain's, as in Spencer's definition of the concept of 'emotions', there was a failure to distinguish clearly between 'aggregate' and 'compound' models.[102] While endorsing the analogy of 'mental chemistry' introduced by Brown and the Mills, by which compound mental states were analysed into mental elements such as sensations and ideas, Bain and Spencer were both unclear in the way they used it. Mill had been clear that he opposed a reductionist sort of mental chemistry. He allowed that simple impressions or ideas might be associated together so many times as to 'generate' a new single idea, by a process similar to 'chemical combination' of elements into compounds. But he was cautious about what should be inferred from this analogy:

The generation of one class of mental phenomena from another, when it can be made out, is a highly interesting fact in psychological chemistry; but it no more supersedes the necessity of an experimental study of the generated phenomenon, than a knowledge of the properties of oxygen and sulphur enables us to deduce those of sulphuric acid without specific observation and experiment.[103]

Bain and Spencer were less clear and less cautious. They both called emotions sometimes 'compounds'[104] and sometimes 'aggregations'[105] or 'composites'.[106] The important difference is that a strictly chemical analogy – the 'compound' model – would imply that the emotion had qualitatively novel properties not possessed by any of its elements, in the same way that a chemical compound (e.g. sulphuric acid) had properties not possessed by its constituent elements (hydrogen, sulphur and oxygen). An 'aggregation' or 'assemblage' or 'composite' model, however, suggested a merely additive effect, so that an emotion was just a lot of sensations happening at the same time.[107] Like Spencer, Bain was, overall, more inclined towards the reductionist aggregate model. Bain said that emotions

---

[102] For a useful passage on the difference between emergent and additive properties, which corresponds to the difference between what are here called 'compound' and 'aggregate' properties, see Searle (1994), 111–12.
[103] Mill (1843), II, 505.   [104] Bain (1865), 35; Spencer (1870–2), I, 476–7, 485, 490–1.
[105] Bain (1865), 35–6; Bain (1875), 69–70; Spencer (1870–2), I, 477, 484–5, 490–1.
[106] Spencer (1870–2), I, 477; Bain (1875), 69.
[107] For more on Hartley, Priestley, Brown and the Mills on chemistry and the mind, see chapter 4. On contemporary uses of 'emotional chemistry' by basic emotions theorists, see Elster (1999), 242.

were certainly not sensations but that they 'resemble voluminous or massive sensation in all the senses'.[108] Elsewhere he described emotions as being 'worked up' from 'primordial and unborrowed sensibilities, intrinsic pleasures and pains', and said that they were formed by the association of a number of separate feelings into one 'aggregate whole'. All emotions were either 'aggregations' of feelings or transferred feelings that were originally aroused by one object but were now, by association, aroused by a third object (as in classical conditioning).[109] Bain, like Brown and Spencer, reduced 'emotions' to involuntary, non-cognitive feelings and their aggregations.

Theory of the will

Bain, but not Spencer or Darwin, adopted the increasingly popular threefold division of the mind into volition, cognition and emotion (various terms were used for the three categories – sometimes 'will' and 'intellect' were used instead of 'volition' and 'cognition', and 'conation' or 'feeling' were alternatives for 'emotion').[110] It was noted in chapter 3 that there were already in the eighteenth century some signs of a shift, away from the classical model in which the mind comprised the two faculties or principles of will and intellect, and towards a model in which there was a third faculty of feeling or affection. Classical Christian affective psychology had relied on the distinction between intellect and will, both of which were involved in the affections of the soul. The move to a tripartite model was a move away from that Christian psychology.[111]

Bain gave as physicalist a sense to 'will' as he had to 'emotion': 'The will, volition, or voluntary action is, on the outside, a physical fact; animal muscle under nervous stimulation is one of the mechanical prime movers; the motive power of muscle is as purely physical as the motive power of steam; food is to one what fuel is to the other.'[112] Volition, for Bain, was just another emotion. And emotions, as we have seen, were, in turn, defined as passive epiphenomenal feelings; the mental 'side' of 'purely physical' nervous activity. Mill was right that Bain had brought activity back into the associationist psychology; but it was activity of the nerves and muscles rather than of a self-acting will, in the traditional sense.[113]

---

[108] Bain (1875), 71. [109] Bain (1875), 61, 69–70. [110] Bain (1873), 43–4.
[111] On the other hand, the persistence of the bipartite division of psychology into the senses and the intellect on the one hand and the emotions and the will on the other in British and American textbooks in the later nineteenth century was indicative of the limited inroads made by the tripartite model – see chapter 7.
[112] Bain (1873), 76. See also Young (1970), 104–5.
[113] [Mill] (1859). See also Mischel (1966), 137.

Food had replaced God as the prime mover of the will. Christian readers of Bain such as John Grote, unsurprisingly, took exception to this new scientific psychology (see chapter 6).[114]

Charles Darwin (1809–1882)

If it was Spencer and Bain who were, at the time, the most widely read and influential contributors to physiological and evolutionary psychological theorising in Britain and America in the 1850s to 1870s, it is Charles Darwin who is, in retrospect, most frequently picked out as a leading contributor to that field. In contrast to the relative neglect of Bain and Spencer by historians, there is a wide array of excellent literature on Darwin's psychological thought in general and on the *Expression* in particular.[115] I will not try to replicate all the insights of this literature. Instead I will concentrate here on just a few specific questions of particular relevance to the current study, namely: what were the sources of Darwin's thinking about emotions and expression? What were the theoretical principles he developed to explain the expression of the emotions? Were any of his principles influenced by his attitude to theological accounts of human nature?

The *Expression* is a fascinating book. Part of the fascination derives from the fact that while it is, in one sense, a foundational text in evolutionary psychology, in other ways it is surprisingly different from more recent works of evolutionary psychology, as we shall see shortly.

---

[114] For more on Bain's theory of the will, and the significance of the will in the Victorian period, see Rylance (2000), 194–202.

[115] On Darwin's psychological thought generally: Swisher (1967); Gruber (1974); Herbert (1977); Richards (1982 and 1987); Burkhardt (1985); Hearnshaw (1987), ch. 8; Rochowiak (1988); Keegan (1989); Reed (1997), ch. 9. On Darwin's *Expression*: Bain (1868), 657–72; Barnett (1958); Swisher (1967), 37–42; Gardiner *et al.* (1970), 290–2; Browne (1985); Montgomery (1985); Richards (1987), 230–4; Desmond and Moore (1992), 592–8; Fridlund (1992); Oatley (1992), 138–43; Campbell (1997); Ekman (1998); Hartley (2001), ch. 5; Radick (2002). For Darwin's own brief account of the composition and publication of the *Expression*, see Darwin (1958), 131–2. There is no separate study of Bain's nor of Spencer's views specifically on emotions, with the exception of short sections in Janet and Séailles (1902), II, 309–12 on Spencer on emotions, and in Gardiner *et al.* (1970), 282–90 on Bain and Spencer on emotions. The closest thing to a study devoted to Bain's theory of emotions is Mischel (1966), which discusses the use of the concepts of 'emotion' and 'motivation' in Hartley, James Mill and Bain. Since neither Hartley nor James Mill used the concept of 'emotion', the article is a little misleading. It does provide, however, a very good account of the disappearance of the will in Associationist psychology. Aside from generally very brief mentions in general histories of psychology, the most useful secondary works on Bain are Mill (1859); Spencer (1863c); Fisch (1954); Mischel (1966); Young (1970); Smith (1971 and 1973); and especially Rylance (2000), ch. 5. Less useful are Cardno (1955 and 1956) and Greenway (1973). On Spencer's psychology, see Smith (1982); Richards (1987), ch. 6; Rylance (2000), ch. 6.

The genesis of the Expression

Darwin had started thinking about the expression of emotions as early as 1838, when he opened his 'M' and 'N' notebooks. Already he was considering the idea that our 'passions' (as he then called them) were signs of our animal ancestry. Referring to human descent from lower animals, he wrote 'Our descent, then, is the origin of our evil passions!! – The Devil under form of Baboon is our grandfather!'[116] From 1838 to 1840, in addition to making notes on metaphysical and psychological topics in his notebooks, Darwin was meticulously recording the facial expressions and behaviours of his infant son William, and also reading widely around the subject. Much later, in 1867, he circulated dozens of questionnaires around Britain and the Empire, asking missionaries, colonialists, zookeepers and asylum directors to observe the expressions of 'savages', animals and the insane. Darwin asked questions such as 'Does shame excite a blush? How far down does the blush extend? When a man is indignant or defiant does he frown, hold his body erect, clench his fists?'[117] Some of the questions concerned behaviours that we would not now necessarily think of as expressions of emotions – for example, nodding or shaking the head in agreement or disagreement; or frowning in concentration.

In addition to the answers gleaned from the thirty-six responses he received to his questionnaires, Darwin added the observations he had made of his son William (material which was eventually published in 1877 as a 'Biographical Sketch of an Infant' in Bain's recently founded journal *Mind*).[118] Together, these resources were supposed to constitute the basis of a single chapter in the *Descent* (1871). However, the amount of material got quite out of hand and expanded into a book of its own, *The Expression of the Emotions in Man and Animals* (1872), which came out a year later. The book was put together extremely quickly – in four months during 1871 between the reading of the proofs for the *Descent* and compiling the sixth edition of the *Origin*.[119]

Sources of Darwin's thinking on association and inheritance

Many of the books that Darwin had read when first thinking over these subjects in the late 1830s were works of moral philosophy and natural

---

[116] Barrett *et al.* (eds.) (1987a), 549–50.
[117] Darwin (1998), 22–3.   [118] Darwin (1877).   [119] Browne (1985).

theology.[120] In the former category were two works by Scottish moral philosophers: John Abercrombie's *Inquiries Concerning the Intellectual Powers and the Investigation of Truth* (1830) and the 1837 second edition of Sir James Mackintosh's *Dissertation on the Progress of Ethical Philosophy*. Abercrombie and Mackintosh were both admirers of Thomas Brown, and through their works Darwin would have become familiar with some of Brown's terminology and ideas.[121] Darwin's notes and marginalia reveal that he was particularly interested in how habits could be formed by the process of association, and whether explaining beliefs and actions in this way could leave any role for a free will.[122] Like Thomas Chalmers, Abercrombie was both an evangelical and an enthusiast for associationist mental science – a combination that favoured a deterministic picture of human mental life, in which the free will of an individual was reduced to the ability to direct attention more towards some feelings and desires than others, and thus to form wholesome rather than vicious habits.[123]

Darwin's extensive notes in the margins of Abercrombie's *Inquiries* and in his notebooks reveal that he found this a particularly intriguing work. These notes reveal that he was sympathetic to a materialistic understanding of the mind and thus opposed to Abercrombie's mind–body dualism. They also show that he wished Abercrombie had gone even further in his acknowledgment of the roles of habit and of the laws of association of ideas in determining action. It seemed to Darwin that the only conclusion to be drawn from the evidence was complete determinism – that all actions are determined either by habits, by hereditary character, by education or by chance. In the margins of Abercrombie's discussion of the will, Darwin wrote a note to himself about 'All this delusion of free will'.[124] Darwin's rejection of a freely acting will is also suggested by his marginal annotations of Mackintosh's discussion of the question. Next to a passage where Mackintosh had argued that conscience was in perpetual contact 'with all the dispositions and actions of *voluntary* agents' and that it had a direct action upon the will, Darwin wrote the one word 'trash'

[120] For an excellent discussion of Darwin's early thinking about instinct, reason, morality, free will and determinism, focussing on his responses to the works of moral philosophy and natural theology he was reading at this time, see Richards (1987), ch. 2.
[121] Darwin's marginal marks in his copy of Mackintosh (1837) suggest that he read at least some of Mackintosh's chapter on Thomas Brown.
[122] Darwin's own copies of these works are held in the Darwin Library in Cambridge University Library. Di Gregorio (ed.) (1990) provides a transcription of the marginalia and notes Darwin made in these books; for Darwin's notes on Abercrombie and Mackintosh in his notebooks, see the transcription provided by Barrett *et al.* (eds.) (1987a), esp. 606–8, 618–29.
[123] On Abercrombie, see Dixon (2002a).
[124] Darwin's copy of Abercrombie (1838), 202–3.

and added a hint of his own explanation of the same moral sentiments and actions as inherited and involuntary: 'because the primary instinctive feeling leads to action like an emotion. – Emotions having been formed of actions, will always lead to them.'[125]

Abercrombie's book also started Darwin speculating on how habits formed by individuals in the course of their lives (as in the classic Associationist picture) could then be inherited. This was a key development in the production of a new kind of psychology in the nineteenth century – an evolutionary psychology according to which mental faculties could be both innate and learned; innate to the individual, but initially learned and passed on to them by their evolutionary ancestors. The way Abercrombie wrote about the central place in human motivation held by the increasingly unconscious mental and behavioural habits developed in the course of an individual's life was parallel to the way that Darwin was thinking about the formation of instincts (inherited habits) in whole species in the course of natural history. Abercrombie had written: 'Attention is very much influenced by habit, and connected with this subject there are some facts of great interest. There is a remarkable law of the system by which actions, at first requiring much attention, are, after frequent repetition, performed with a much less degree of it, or without the mind being conscious of any effort.'[126] Darwin scored this section in his copy of the *Inquiries* and added a query in the margin wondering whether this would have been better expressed by saying that 'willing becomes unconscious'. Volition becoming unconscious (and hence no longer voluntary) would later be one of Darwin's leading explanatory devices for understanding expressions of emotions. This is a nice example of how Darwin (as well as Spencer) took insights from associationist theories of the development of mental powers in the individual and extended them to the history of the species, so that an action could become habitual and involuntary during the course of one individual's lifetime and subsequently inherited – or could do so more gradually through the course of many generations. This development created an interesting tension, in both Spencer's and Darwin's work, between associationist and evolutionary psychological methods, related to the age-old philosophical debate about innate ideas. The associationist psychologists, often labelled as thinkers in 'the school of Locke', sought to show how all an individual's ideas and mental faculties developed during their lifetime as a result of experience of the world, having started life with a mental tabula rasa. The opposing 'intuitionist' or a priori school held that certain ideas and faculties were innate.

---

[125] Darwin's copy of Mackintosh (1837), 380.   [126] Abercrombie (1838), 56.

But on which side of this well-established divide would the evolutionary psychologist such as Darwin or Spencer position himself? Both certainly had philosophical sympathies with Associationists and their prioritising of sensations and experience, as opposed to immaterial mental faculties, when it came to constructing psychological explanations. However, they were also squarely on the side of the a priori school in their belief that infants were born with innate ideas and mental faculties – namely those inherited from generations of evolving ancestors. As Rylance puts it, according to the new evolutionary psychology, 'what is *a priori* to the individual is *a posteriori* to the race'.[127] To put it another way, the true novelty of this evolutionary psychology lay in shifting the focus of the associationist tradition away from the experiences of the individual on to the experiences of that individual's ancestors, and thus away from ontogeny and on to phylogeny.[128] Darwin had been pondering this issue as early as 1840 when reading an anonymous article in the *Westminster Review* on the respective views of the schools of Locke and Kant on the sources of knowledge. In a notebook he entitled 'Old and Useless Notes', Darwin pondered: '[I]s this not almost a question whether we have any instincts, or rather the amount of our instincts – surely in animals according to the usual definition, there is much knowledge without experience, so there *may* be in men – which the reviewer seems to doubt.'[129] It was not surprising that the reviewer seemed to doubt this. The reviewer was John Stuart Mill, who was, of course, a stout defender of the 'school of Locke' – the school that would explain all mental faculties as the products of experience. In a footnote to his discussion of the moral sense, in the *Descent*, Darwin explicitly dissented from both Mill and Bain who, like Paley, had held that the moral sense, or conscience, was developed by learning during the course of each individual's lifetime. Darwin thought that since the social feelings were innate in lower animals it was reasonable to assume they were also innate in man.[130]

This realisation that associationist psychology needed to be supplemented with an account of innate, inherited capabilities was a transformative moment in the history of psychology. Spencer's and Darwin's psychologies combined the innatist and associationist insights from two opposed philosophical traditions with findings in physiological psychology, and situated them within a new, evolutionary paradigm. In some ways, this might be seen as a sort of psychology that was a little more in tune with traditional Christian psychology than Enlightenment mental

---

[127] Rylance (2000), 208–9, 235–6; quotation on 235.
[128] See also Richards (1987), esp. chs. 1–3.
[129] Barrett *et al.* (eds.) (1987a), 610.   [130] Darwin (1871), I, 71n.

science had been, in that it explained human traits by an appeal to the history of the race, rather than purely with reference to the experiences of the individual.

Four works employing design-theology arguments Darwin studied particularly closely in connection with psychological questions were William Kirby's Bridgewater Treatise, *On the Power, Wisdom, and Goodness of God as Manifested in the Creation of Animals and in Their History, Habits and Instincts* (1835), Thomas Burgess' *The Physiology or Mechanism of Blushing* (1839), Henry Lord Brougham's *Dissertations on Subjects of Science Connected with Natural Theology* (1839) and Sir Charles Bell's *The Anatomy and Philosophy of Expression, as Connected with the Fine Arts* (1844).[131] All of these books described instincts and expressions as boons bestowed on humanity (and other animals), and thus as evidence of the wisdom and intelligence of the Creator. These writers were not, incidentally, the first to describe expressions in this way. The most influential Scottish philosopher of the previous generation, Thomas Reid, had already described the 'involuntary signs of the passions and dispositions of the mind' as parts of the human constitution provided by 'the Author of our nature' to function as 'opening into the souls of our fellow-men, by which their sentiments become visible to the eye'.[132] Burgess, in one of the works on expression that Darwin studied, described blushing as a God-given 'check on the conscience' and a 'moral restraint' – a mechanism given to human beings that will 'in many cases... control the individual from violating the laws of morality', and which 'thus affords us a beautiful instance of the design, wisdom, and goodness of Providence'.[133] This was Paley's design argument extended from the anatomical realm to the moral, psychological and behavioural. The challenge Darwin set himself was to explain psychological adaptations, as well as anatomical ones, without reference to a designing God.

Given the familiar story of the way that Darwin replaced Paley's watchmaker-God with his own 'deity' (as he once light-heartedly called natural selection) in the case of anatomical features, one might expect that his strategy would have been the same when it came to instincts and behaviours – namely to explain them as adaptations produced by variation and natural selection rather than by the power, wisdom and goodness of

---

[131] Darwin read the first two editions of this work (1806, 1824) between 1838 and 1840; according to his own recollection when writing his autobiography, it was in the summer of 1840; see Barrett *et al.* (eds.) (1987a). The 1844 third edition was substantially expanded. It was to this third edition that Darwin referred in the *Expression*.
[132] Reid, *Essays on the Active Powers of Man* (1788), quoted in Gallie (1998), 174.
[133] Burgess (1839), 24–5.

God.[134] However, as we shall see, when his thoughts on expression were finally published in 1872, over thirty years after his earliest musings on the subject, this was not the line of argument that he took.

A final and significant influence on Darwin's thinking about expression was Spencer's essay on the physiology of laughter.[135] Darwin found in this essay three ideas, applied by Spencer just to the example of laughter, which would become important components of his own wider theoretical framework in the *Expression* about ten years later.[136] First of these was the idea that the excessive nervous excitement associated with emotions would, when it reached a certain threshold, have to find an outlet through some or other muscular motion; the channels taken by the excess nerve-force would be those that had most habitually been used in the past. Secondly, he found in Spencer's essay the view – one he already shared – that Charles Bell was wrong to suggest that man possessed special muscles bestowed upon him by the Deity to express peculiarly human emotions. Thirdly, and perhaps most significantly, Darwin was struck by the following sentence in Spencer's essay: 'Strong feeling, mental or physical, being, then, the general cause of laughter, we have to note that the muscular actions constituting it are distinguished from most others by this, that they are purposeless.'[137] In his copy of the essay Darwin underlined the word 'purposeless' and added the marginal note: 'so for frantic gestures of rage or intense grief'.[138] Darwin was, in the *Expression*, to lengthen still further the list of expressions that seemed to him to be purposeless. Taking these three ideas together – that expressions were the product of the involuntary action of the nervous system, that they were not the result of the action of any muscles or nerves specially bestowed upon man and that these actions were often purposeless – we can see in Spencer's essay on laughter a miniature version of the picture later painted in much broader and more ambitious terms by Darwin in the *Expression*.

Darwin's explanatory principles in the Expression

The first thing to note about Darwin's thinking about the expressions of emotions is that he did not think that they were 'expressions' at all.

---

[134] Darwin referred to natural selection as 'my deity' in a letter to Asa Gray in June 1861; Burkhardt *et al.* (1994), 162; I am grateful to John Brooke for this reference.
[135] Spencer (1863b).
[136] Darwin read the essay in his 1863 edition of Spencer's essays.
[137] Spencer (1863b), 111.
[138] Darwin's copy of Spencer's *Essays* is held by the Darwin Library in the Cambridge University Library; for a transcription of the marginalia, see Di Gregorio (ed.) (1990).

That is to say he did not think their primary or original function was to communicate a creature's inward mental state to its fellow creatures through outward signs. This communicative function, if and when it did exist, was a fortunate additional outcome of the development of facial and bodily movements that had originally had quite separate non-communicative purposes.[139] He explained the behaviours in question instead as inherited habits that were at some point in the past connected with the emotions of which they were now considered the 'expression'.

A second point to note about Darwin's theorising in the *Expression* is that he did not have any theory of emotions. He took the term 'emotions' to stand for a range of mental states such as fear, anger, pride, shame and the like, but never tried to explain the origins or functions of emotional feelings, nor did he try to define or classify the emotions per se. His primary interest was rather in the physiology and behaviour associated with them. Occasionally he seemed to go further and suggest (as William James later would more explicitly) that emotions were somehow constituted by their expression:

> Most of our emotions are so closely connected with their expression, that they hardly exist if the body remains passive... A man, for instance, may know that his life is in the extremest peril, and may strongly desire to save it, yet may exclaim as did Louis XVI, when surrounded by a fierce mob, 'Am I afraid? Feel my pulse.' So a man may intensely hate another, but until his bodily frame is affected he cannot be said to be enraged.[140]

Darwin had intimated a similar view in his 'N' notebook many years earlier: 'Emotions are the heredetary [sic] effects on the mind accompanying certain bodily actions... [W]ithout slight flush, acceleration of pulse, or rigidity of muscles – man cannot be said to be angry – he may have pain or pleasure but these are sensations [rather than emotions].'[141] During the same period, as we have already seen, Darwin noted on his copy of Mackintosh's *Dissertation*, 'Emotions, having been formed by actions, will always lead to them.'[142] All of this seems to imply that Darwin believed that emotions were constituted by bodily actions. However, Darwin's primary concern in the *Expression* was not to develop a theory of the emotions but rather to explain how particular emotions and the behaviours we have come to think of as their 'expressions' might initially

---

[139] Darwin only considers the communicative function of emotional expressions in the closing two pages of the *Expression*; Darwin (1998), 359–60. Radick (2002) gives an interesting account of how Darwin theorised about both the origins of articulate language and the origins of emotional expressions in both the *Descent* and the *Expression*.
[140] Darwin (1998), 234.   [141] Barrett *et al.* (eds.) (1987a), 581–2.
[142] Darwin's copy of Mackintosh (1837), 381; held by the Cambridge University Library. See Di Gregorio (ed.) (1990), 558–9.

have become connected. To do this Darwin proposed three different explanatory principles:

1. The principle of serviceable associated habits
Certain actions were useful to our ancestors when they found themselves in a certain state of mind – they relieved or gratified certain desires, or performed a useful physiological function (such as the screwing up of the eyes to protect them when screaming). These actions 'were at first voluntarily performed for a definite object', but over many generations were performed habitually and became innate and inherited.[143] Now when we experience the same state of mind, we involuntarily perform the same actions 'though they may not then be of the least use'.[144] For example, we now, when feeling a range of emotions, including disdain, contempt and disgust, carry out movements that would have been connected in the past with the rejection or avoidance of a noxious object. These actions include half-closing our eyes, turning away, or even retching or vomiting. We now perform these movements involuntarily when feeling disdain or contempt even if they are, in the present circumstances, not of the least use (because there is no harmful object physically present).[145]

2. The principle of antithesis
Certain actions become habitually associated with certain states of mind, as explained by the first principle. The principle of antithesis says that when a directly opposed state of mind is induced there is a strong involuntary tendency to perform movements of a directly opposite nature. Again Darwin added 'though these are of no use'.[146] He gave as examples of antithetically related expressions: nodding and shaking one's head; and the bodily postures associated with hostility and affection in dogs.[147]

3. The principle of the direct action of the nervous system
This was a rather more vague idea, borrowed from Spencer and from Bain.[148] The idea was simply that all mental feelings are accompanied by a diffuse exertion of the nervous system and that when nervous activity gets above a certain level it can cause the spontaneous movement of certain muscles. Darwin combined this third principle with his first by observing that excess nerve force will tend to follow the routes habitually associated with the relevant state of mind. So when in great pain, a

---

[143] Darwin (1998), 349. [144] Darwin (1998), 34. [145] Darwin (1998), 250–60.
[146] Darwin (1998), 34. [147] Darwin (1998), 57.
[148] Darwin (1998), 15–17. In a letter to Bain, Darwin later admitted that Bain had been right to criticise him for the vagueness of this principle; see Bain (1868), 657–72; Fridlund (1992), 122.

person's excess nerve force will follow the route that produces the action of shaking the affected limb in an apparent attempt to shake off the cause, as their ancestors were in the habit of doing, even when this is not of the slightest use.[149]

As this brief summary of Darwin's principles shows, the *Expression of the Emotions in Man and Animals* might have been more appropriately entitled *The Inheritance of Useless Habits in Man and Animals*. Why was there such an emphasis on the uselessness of expressions? And why was there such a lack of emphasis on natural selection? Part of an answer to these questions may lie in the natural theological context within which Darwin's thinking arose.

An anti-Darwinian because anti-theological book?

Bain, Spencer and Darwin were all alienated from the Christian religion for a complex mixture of personal, social, professional and intellectual reasons. According to Darwin's own recollections, written down in 1876 (and not necessarily entirely reliable, since they would have been written in the knowledge that among his readers would be his more religiously orthodox wife Emma), his religious views had gone through three stages – Christianity, theism and agnosticism. According to this account, his early biblical Christian faith faded in the two or three years after his return from the *Beagle* voyage (at the time that he was developing his ideas in the 'M' and 'N' notebooks). Darwin considered that he had still been a 'theist' around the time that he wrote the *Origin*, but that his belief even in an intelligent First Cause had gradually subsided. 'The mystery of the beginning of all things is insoluble by us', he concluded in 1876, 'and I for one must be content to remain an Agnostic.'[150]

When it came to their treatments of the emotions, Spencer, Bain and Darwin shared an opposition to the design theology approach to expression typified by the work of Sir Charles Bell. Bell had been responsible for the discovery of the distinction between afferent (sensory) and efferent (motor) nerves, and had produced a Bridgewater Treatise on the wonderful contrivance of the human hand.[151] Bell's book on expression was probably the most influential book on the physiological and expressive side of the passions and emotions prior to the 1850s.[152] Bain, Spencer

---

[149] Darwin (1998), 74–5.
[150] Darwin (1958), 94; for further references on Darwin's religious beliefs, see n.63.
[151] On Bell's life and works see Hartley (2001), ch. 2; Pichot (1860); Carmichael (1926); Gordon-Taylor and Walls (1958).
[152] On the successive editions of Bell's book and its popularity, see Hartley (2001), 79, 198 n.11.

and Darwin all read Bell's *Anatomy and Philosophy of Expression*, which contained detailed descriptions of the nerves and muscles involved in the expression of passions and emotions, with a particular focus on the respiratory system, in preparation for their own work on emotions.[153] Bain and Darwin both also incorporated examples from Bell's book in their own work. However, they, along with Spencer, placed these facts about the nervous system within a new psychological framework where physiological and evolutionary explanations were sought in preference to Bell's natural theological ones.

The thing that most commentators have found striking about Darwin's *Expression* is the almost complete absence of explanations in terms of natural selection (or sexual selection); this is in stark contrast with the *Descent*, for example.[154] The phrase 'natural selection' is used four times in the *Expression*, compared with over one hundred times in the *Descent*.[155] It has been pointed out by Alan Fridlund and others that the *Expression* is, in this sense, surprisingly 'anti-Darwinian'. The reason for this, it has been suggested, was Darwin's opposition to natural theology. Bell had argued that the communicative functions of our expressions were divinely contrived; God had made special arrangements of nerves and muscles to allow human beings to communicate their feelings to one another.[156] One of the principle ways in which Darwin attacked this natural theological theory was to deny that expressions had an expressive function, or indeed any useful function. Instead he largely sought to explain them as habits that were originally useful but which, in successive generations, as environmental conditions changed, had ceased to be useful. If the expressions of emotions did not have a useful function, then they could not survive preferentially as a result of natural selection. All that was left then was a use-inheritance account of the evolution of expressive behaviours. Thus opposition to design theology, it is claimed, shaped Darwin's theory-choice when it came to giving an evolutionary account of emotional expression.[157]

---

[153] Bain (1904), 229; Spencer (1870–2), II, 557; Darwin, (1872), 2–3, 9–11; Darwin (1958), 132.

[154] One of the handful of references to natural selection acknowledges that some instincts have developed through variation and natural selection; another sees it as a possible factor in strengthening the ability of various animals to cause their hair or feathers to stand on end – see Darwin (1998), 47, 107.

[155] The phrases 'survival of the fittest' and 'sexual selection' are used once each in the *Expression*; 'sexual selection' occurs over one hundred and fifty times in the *Descent*; see Barrett *et al*.(eds.) (1986, 1987b).

[156] Bell (1844), 98, 119–21, 131.

[157] For various versions of this standard account see Browne (1985); Burkhardt (1985); Montgomery (1985); Fridlund (1992); Campbell (1997), 454, 459–63; Ekman (1998); Hartley (2001), 146, 178; Richards (2003).

There is certainly some truth in this. We have already seen that the physiological and evolutionary schools shared an ontological commitment to the continuity of man with the rest of the animal kingdom. This commitment to sameness of ontology (humans and other animals are the same sort of being) was expressed also in the commitment to sameness of epistemology whether approaching man or animals, and the adoption of methodologies that emphasised the sameness of man and other animals. While Bell had sought to illuminate all that was distinctive about human physiology and physiognomy and all that elevated spiritual humans above the level of mere animal passion, Spencer and Darwin, to buttress their evolutionary hypotheses, sought evidence that pointed to the close relation of man to other animals. They both compared laughter in man and monkeys to argue for a common progenitor.[158] This was particularly significant since laughter had been one of the forms of expression, along with weeping, picked out by Bell as being 'peculiarly human, arising from sentiments not participated by the brutes'.[159] In the margin of his copy of Bell's book, next to the claim that humans have special muscles, lacked by other species, to express spiritual and moral feelings, Darwin had scribbled 'I suspect he never dissected [a] monkey.'[160] In 1867 he wrote to Alfred Russel Wallace of his planned book on expression: 'I want, anyhow, to upset Sir C. Bell's view... that certain muscles have been given to man solely that he may reveal to other men his feelings.'[161]

Bell was not the only author employing design-theology arguments with whom Darwin entered into debate in the *Expression*. His treatment of Burgess' arguments about the mechanism of blushing is also particularly interesting.[162] On the one hand, Darwin reproduced several of Burgess' ideas and examples – including quotations from the scriptures – more or less unchanged.[163] He also agreed with Burgess that a true blush was one produced by the emotion of shame (either about one's appearance or, by association, about others' views of one's conduct and character), and that blushing was a uniquely human expression. However, he rejected the suggestion made by both Bell and Burgess that blushing was a mechanism designed by the Creator for the purpose of expressing shame.[164] He gave

---

[158] Darwin (1998), 19; Spencer (1863b).   [159] Bell (1844), 145.
[160] Darwin's copy of Bell (1844) is held in the Darwin Library at Cambridge University Library; the comment in question is on p. 138. For a transcription of all Darwin's marginalia, see Di Gregorio (ed.) (1990).
[161] Quoted in Fridlund (1992), 117.   [162] Darwin (1998), ch. 13.
[163] For his notes and marginalia, showing Darwin's interest in the scriptural passages, amongst others, see Darwin's copy of Burgess (1839), held in the Darwin Library at Cambridge University Library. For a transcription of the marginalia, see Di Gregorio (ed.) (1990).
[164] Darwin (1998), 335–44.

two grounds for this. The first was the rather blunt assertion that the belief was simply 'opposed to the general theory of evolution, which is now so largely accepted'. The second reason he gave was the one that was central to Darwin's anti-creationist arguments in the *Expression*, namely that the expression in question – in this case blushing – far from being a boon to humanity and thus potential evidence of design, was quite useless: 'Those who believe in design, will find it difficult to account for shyness being the most frequent and efficient of all the causes of blushing, as it makes the blusher to suffer and the beholder uncomfortable, without being of the least service to either of them.'[165]

There were at least two different sets of facts that Bell and Burgess on the one hand and Spencer and Darwin on the other were trying to explain: physiological facts (the arrangement of nerves and muscles, especially in the face) and psychological ones (habitual behaviours associated with different emotions). Bell's argument was that we have the particular nerves and muscles we do in order to communicate our feelings to each other, and that both the physiology and the psychology are unique to humans. Darwin, in order to undercut the idea that the muscles and nerves were specially designed and endowed on humans by the Deity, argued that they were not for communicating our feelings. Despite the fact that his book was on 'the expression of the emotions', he thought the physiological facts could be explained entirely with reference to non-expressive functions. If the physiological features (nerves, muscles) used in so-called expressions were primarily there for some reason other than communicating feelings, and if they were also shared by other animals, then Bell's argument that our muscles and nerves were specially designed for us to communicate specially human feelings was doubly undermined.

If the connections between the emotions and their expression were not adaptive, then the explanation of the origins of these connections could not be in terms of natural selection. The importance for Darwin of the inheritance of acquired characteristics (rather than the selection of adaptive ones) is evident in a criticism he passed on the French anatomist Pierre Gratiolet in the introduction to the *Expression*: 'Gratiolet appears to overlook inherited habit, and even to some extent habit in the individual; and therefore he fails, as it seems to me, to give the right explanation, or any explanation at all, of many gestures and expressions.'[166] The model Darwin repeatedly appeals to was one in which useful voluntary actions (in both lower animals and humans) had been converted over time, by the repetition of the actions in similar circumstances over many generations, into involuntary movements that were often 'not of the least use' (a phrase

---

[165] Darwin (1998), 335.   [166] Darwin (1998), 14.

that Darwin used over and over again) in the circumstances in which they were now aroused. Darwin used as one example a story of his own unsuccessful attempt to prevent himself recoiling from the puff adder at the zoological gardens even though it was safely behind glass.[167]

The standard argument, then, is that the reason Darwin's *Expression* is so un-Darwinian – the reason that it relies almost exclusively on 'Lamarckian' explanations of expressions as inherited habits rather than 'selectionist' ones – is that Darwin was determined to deny Bell's claim that expressions were boons to the human race and evidence of divine design. If he could show that these expressions were basically useless, Bell's arguments would no longer stand. Darwin had used the strategy before of pointing out the existence of useless human features – usually rudimentary or vestigial organs such as male mammae – as a way to undermine the argument that each species was divinely designed. Why would God give men nipples? Why would he give us each an appendix and a vestigial tail? Why would an intelligent designer give us useless habits, such as jumping away from a snake even when we know we are safely protected from it by a layer of glass, or blushing on account of our shyness? Vestigial organs and vestigial behaviours alike could be better explained by evolutionary hypotheses. However, they could not, it seemed, be explained by natural selection, which should select only beneficial variations of form and behaviour. So Darwin had to look to other sorts of evolution – namely the inheritance of acquired characteristics – to explain these useless behaviours. Thus Darwin's anti-theological agenda required him to deny the utility of expression and so to miss the (to us) obvious fact that most expressions are very useful (because socially communicative).

Problems with the standard 'anti-theology' account

This standard account is an interesting one – and one that is in tune with my general argument that scientific emotion-theorists of this period were producing a psychology that was at least in some ways shaped by anti-theological commitments. Unfortunately, however, there are several facts that this account obscures, and several questions that it leaves unanswered. The main set of facts, already alluded to above, which the standard account tends to overlook, relate to the extent to which Darwin was positively influenced by the works of natural theological writers such as Thomas Burgess and Charles Bell. I have already noted that he adopted several of Burgess' examples and ideas about blushing and shame. A more

---

[167] Darwin (1998), 43.

significant point is that, although it is certainly true that Darwin contested Bell's suggestion that man had special muscles bestowed on him to express certain feelings, in other respects Darwin's account is rather similar to Bell's.

Bell, in his 1806 *Essays on the Anatomy of Expression in Painting*, had stated that only humans could properly be said to express their inner feelings through facial movements and other gestures. 'Other animals,' Bell continued, 'have no expression but that which arises by mere accident, the concomitant of the motions necessary to the accomplishment of the object of the passions.'[168] In the third edition this became the statement that with 'the lower creatures there is no expression but what may be referred, more or less plainly, to their acts of volition or necessary instincts'.[169] Darwin discussed this assertion in the introduction to the *Expression*.[170] The first striking thing about these passages in Bell is that they are essentially statements of the principle Darwin adopted and named 'the principle of serviceable associated habits'. What Bell was saying about animals – that we tend to mistake their functional actions (whether voluntary or instinctive) for communicative expressions of inward emotions – was exactly what Darwin himself was saying about many human and animal behaviours that we think of as 'expressions' (in Darwin's case the model was one in which once-voluntary actions had become instinctive). The second strange thing about Darwin's discussion of Bell at this point is that, even though Bell is here using the principle that Darwin himself adopted as his leading explanation in the *Expression*, Darwin castigated him for claiming that the animal movements in question were not actually expressing inward feelings:

But man himself cannot express love and humility by external signs so plainly as does a dog, when with drooping ears, hanging lips, flexuous body, and wagging tail, he meets his beloved master. Nor can these movements in the dog be explained by acts of volition or necessary instincts, any more than the beaming eyes and smiling cheeks of a man when he meets an old friend. If Sir C. Bell had been questioned about the expression of affection in the dog, he would no doubt have answered that this animal had been created with special instincts, adapting him for association with man, and that all further enquiry on the subject was superfluous.[171]

So while on the one hand Darwin seems simply to have taken over Bell's own account of animal expression and extended it to cover many human behaviours as well as animal ones, calling it the 'principle of serviceable associated habits', on the other hand he attacked Bell for failing to

---

[168] Bell (1806), 88.   [169] Bell (1844), 121.
[170] Darwin (1998), 17–18.   [171] Darwin (1998), 18.

acknowledge the genuinely expressive function of certain movements in both man and animals. The final sentence in the above quotation is particularly perplexing, since Darwin had just explained that Bell considered animal 'expressions' not to be genuine expressions of emotions but to be either voluntary or instinctive movements with other purposes; it is odd then for Darwin to have felt the need to invent an alternative imagined reply from Bell in terms of special creation.

The discussion of Bell in the introduction of the *Expression* seems to vindicate the standard account's ascription to Darwin of an anti-creationist animus that made him determined to refute Bell and to ridicule his creationism. The point that the standard account has missed, however, is that Darwin's determination to refute Bell was so great that, first, it led him to try to refute Bell even when he was proposing principles that Darwin himself had adopted and, secondly, it led him to endorse the view that certain movements in animals and humans functioned primarily to express inner feelings of love and humility – precisely the view that the standard account has Darwin at pains to deny. This whole confusing situation can be best understood as resulting from Darwin's overriding desire to close the man–animal divide that Bell and others wished to keep open. Applying the non-expressive explanation that Bell had applied only to lower animals also to humans, and applying the genuinely expressive explanation that Bell had applied only to humans also to lower animals were both ways of closing the gap between man and the 'brute creation'.

The standard account, in addition to overlooking some of these niceties in Darwin's relationship with Bell's work, leaves several further questions unanswered. If Darwin's anti-creationism was such a driving concern, then why did he make use of natural selection so widely in his explanations of many other anatomical and behavioural facts in the *Origin of Species* and in the *Descent of Man*? Why could he not argue, in the *Expression*, that just as natural selection could counterfeit design in anatomy, so it could counterfeit design in psychology? Why was he prepared to explain some instincts as the products of variation and natural selection (in the *Origin* and the *Descent*) but not those discussed in the *Expression*?[172] Why did Darwin believe that vestigial organs often wasted away into mere rudiments through disuse and by being selected against, but failed to apply this same thought to vestigial behaviours such as those discussed in

---

[172] In one passage of the *Origin*, for example, Darwin expressed the view that the effects of habit on the development of instincts 'are of quite subordinate importance to the effects of natural selection'; Darwin (1985), 236. In ch. 2 of the *Descent* Darwin also envisaged instincts developing though variation and selection; Darwin (1871), I, 35–8.

the *Expression*, which seem on his account to have persisted unchanged through many generations?[173]

There is a lot that could be said here, but I will confine myself to just a couple of observations.[174] I would suggest as one possibility, that it might have been a tacit criterion for inclusion in the *Expression* that the behaviours in question be apparently useless. The most obviously useful emotions and forms of expression (moral sentiments and language, respectively) were both dealt with in the *Descent*, the book in which the material in the *Expression* was initially intended to be included. It might have been that Darwin thought that the other habits we think of as expressions of emotion seemed to form a different (and less useful) set of behaviours. This judgment could have been made independently of his opposition to Bell's design theology. Any good answers to the puzzles highlighted here will need to take into account the fact that Darwin was prepared in some cases to acknowledge the useful function of both anatomical and behavioural variations (which would be favoured by natural selection) and in other cases denied this usefulness (and looked for explanations that did not appeal to natural selection). The latter cases (including vestigial organs and the behaviours discussed in the *Expression*), unlike the former, were useful ammunition in Darwin's anti-creationist campaign.

A naturalised fall narrative?

The development by evolutionists of a psychological system that appealed to the history of the race was in one way to return to the sort of models used more by Christian theologians than by Enlightenment mental scientists. The *Expression* provides us with a more specific illustration. One feature of Darwin's natural-historical psychology in the *Expression* that has not been noted in existing commentaries is the surprising similarity it bears to one part of traditional Christian anthropology, namely the story of the 'fall'. This similarity is surprising since the standard view would be that Darwinian anthropology was in most ways an inversion of the Christian picture. Christianity said that man was above the lower animals; Darwin said there was no real distinction between us and other animals. The Bible said that all species were created separately; Darwin said they were all descended from a common ancestor. Christianity said

---

[173] On rudimentary organs being produced through disuse and selection, see Darwin (1871), I, 17–32.

[174] For an interesting recent attempt to supplement the standard 'anti-creationism' explanation of Darwin's theorising in the *Expression*, which focusses on Darwin's doubts about the evidence for the existence of psychological and behavioural variations for natural selection to act upon, see Radick (2002).

we had fallen from a higher state of perfection to a lower, more bestial state; Darwin said that we had evolved from a lower animal state to a higher more civilised one. Or did he?

In fact, the natural-historical anthropology appealed to by Darwin in the *Expression* was much more like the Christian story than the progressive evolutionary one. The picture of the history of the human race that Darwin appealed to time and time again in the *Expression* was not simply a history of progression from a lower animal state to a higher, more rational and more civilised one. The picture Darwin painted was, rather, one in which our ancestors performed certain actions voluntarily, because they were of service to them in their particular environment, such as voluntarily vomiting to eject food which disagreed with them.[175] These actions then became habitual through repetition and were inherited – that is, they became involuntary and innate. We therefore behave in certain ways when in certain frames of mind or certain situations because we have inherited an involuntary tendency to behave in those ways; we may involuntarily retch or vomit in disgust when we come into contact with certain objects, even though we can no longer voluntarily do so, and even though, if we had voluntary control over our bodies, we would probably decide not to do so. In other words, most 'expressions' of emotions are vestigial behaviours that are now frequently not of the least use but which we cannot help performing; they are malfunctions, defects in the human machine. However, they are vestiges not of an earlier bestial stage in our evolution but of a time when human beings had much greater voluntary control over their bodies.

In short, the *Expression* offered a naturalised narrative of the fall of humanity from a state of extensive voluntary control over our bodies and behaviours – like that enjoyed by Adam and Eve before the fall, according to Augustine – to a state of enslavement to useless physical urges that are disobedient to our wills – like the state suffered by us all subsequent to the fall, according to Augustine. In both the Augustinian fall narrative and the Darwinian one, this disobedience of the flesh to the will was physically inherited. Augustine and Darwin both also drew their readers' attention to unusual cases of voluntary control over bodily organs in the present as evidence of the sort of voluntary control that was normal for our ancestors; Augustine used the examples of a man who could swallow and regurgitate a variety of objects at will and of individuals who could make musical notes 'issue from the rear of their anatomy'; Darwin also referred to people with the ability to regurgitate at will and, in the *Descent*,

---

[175] Darwin (1998), 257–8; (1871), I, 20–1.

to people with the vestigial ability to wiggle their ears voluntarily.[176] Finally, both the Augustinian account of human nature and the account offered in Darwin's *Expression* differed significantly from more optimistic views of human beings offered by natural theologians and evolutionists alike. Many design theologians tended to see human beings as perfectly designed machines, created by God with all the physical and mental functions necessary to live a good life. In a similar vein some evolutionary psychologists have seen every human attribute as an 'adaptation', while others have told the story of human evolution as an inevitably progressive one. Augustine and Darwin, in contrast to these rosy views, emphasised the imperfections of human beings – the flaws and malfunctions in the machine, the ways in which human beings had fallen or degenerated from a higher state.

There were, of course, many important differences between the Augustinian and Darwinian fall narratives. First, the cause of the fall for Augustine was the original sinful disobedience of Adam and Eve; for Darwin it was the tendency of habitual behaviours to become involuntary and inherited and to persist even in changed circumstances of life. Secondly, Darwin's notes in the M and N notebooks, and some of his marginalia, suggest that he did not believe that humans had free will – something that was, in contrast, central to the Augustinian story.[177] Volition for Darwin, as for Bain and Spencer, was a feeling and not a faculty that could spontaneously cause us to act independently of deterministic physical processes.

Emotions, the body and history

Darwin's ideas in the *Expression*, like other secular psychological theories of this period, could embody naturalised Christian ideas (such as the fall) as well as anti-Christian ones (such as opposition to design theology, to soul–body dualism, to belief in free will and to man–animal separatism). As in many other cases, any account that would describe this scientific psychology as either merely tacitly anti-theological or, for that matter, tacitly theological would be too simple a story. (This point is elaborated further in chapter 8.)

Of the three nineteenth-century psychological writers considered in this chapter, it was probably Darwin whose work had the most direct influence on later psychological theorising about emotions and expression. His work had its roots in the physiological and developmental turns

---

[176] *City of God*, XIV.24; also see chapter 2. Darwin (1998), 257n.
[177] On Darwin's views on determinism and free will, see Richards (1987), 122–4.

taken in psychology by writers such as Bain and Spencer, as well as in earlier works of moral philosophy and natural theology. The innovations in affective psychology that the work of these three writers made can be summarised under two heads: the body and history. All three of the figures discussed above gave a privileged role to information about the body (especially the bodies of animals, infants, 'savages' and the insane); Spencer and Darwin in particular were responsible for reintroducing history into psychological theorising – not just the history of individuals appealed to by associationist psychologists, but the deeper history of the human race that their evolutionary hypotheses invoked. The important agencies in these physiological and historical psychologies were brains, bodies and the evolutionary past.

Darwin's work had a particular impact on two of the most significant psychological thinkers working at the end of the nineteenth century, representatives of the new traditions of Anglo-American academic psychology and psychoanalysis respectively – namely William James and Sigmund Freud. Freud, in particular, was enthusiastic about Darwin's explanation of expressions as inherited habits – this idea worked well as part of his picture of the inheritance of primal (and sometimes animalistic) human emotions such as guilt, anger and lust. He shared Spencer's and Darwin's belief that, as one recent commentator puts it: 'Emotions are history-laden states of mind.'[178] Ironically, then, Freud's commitment to neo-Lamarckianism can be traced back to the influence upon him of Charles Darwin's un-Darwinian work on expression.[179] James and Freud both took theorising about emotions forward in the directions already taken by Bain, Spencer and Darwin, with their emphases on the body and on the history of the human race. Indeed, as I will suggest in chapter 7, James' famous theory of emotions was in one way merely a more explicit and more simple version of the theories suggested by writers such as Bain, Spencer and Darwin.

One of the arguments of this book is that the strong dichotomy between thinking, intellect or reason on the one hand and feeling and emotion on the other, which has been bemoaned by many contemporary writers, has been the result not primarily of the influence of the Christian tradition but, rather, of divergence from traditional Christian psychologies. Bain, Spencer and Darwin all produced non-cognitive 'feeling' theories of the emotions. Spencer adopted a model of the mind very similar to

---

[178] Baier (1990); this article draws on the theories of both Darwin and Freud in arguing for the importance of understanding the 'deep' objects of emotions in the evolutionary past. Wollheim (1999) and Evans (2001) also argue, in different ways, for an historical account of emotions.

[179] See Ritvo (1990), esp. ch. 12; Sulloway (1979).

Brown's, in which mental states were divided into cognitions on the one hand and non-cognitive 'feelings' on the other. The feelings were then divided into sensations and emotions.[180] Emotions for Spencer, as for Brown, Chalmers and Bain, were, simply by definition, non-cognitive feelings. For Spencer, Bain and Darwin these emotions were virtually constituted by the bodily agitations and nervous activities associated with them. These 'Three men of genius and free-thought' produced physiological and historical psychologies that both developed upon and reacted against the moral philosophies and natural theologies of an earlier generation, and which would inspire psychological writers of the next generation to look to inherited bodily processes in their attempts to understand emotions as non-cognitive feelings.[181]

Further conclusions arising from the material in this chapter will be elaborated at the end of the next chapter, in which we take a step back to consider the widespread resistance to these nineteenth-century physicalist and evolutionary treatments of emotions.

[180] Spencer (1863c), 139.   [181] 'Psychosis' (1884), vii; see above.

6 Christian and theistic responses to the new physicalist emotions paradigm

> Superficial sciolists in philosophy have need to learn as a first lesson, that the physiologist and pathologist, as such, can have nothing to do with what transcends the sphere of the mere corporeal organism. It is the proper province of the psychologist to investigate the soul and its mind.
>
> Thomas Gorman, *Christian Psychology: The Soul and the Body in their Correlation and Contrast*, 483

> Emotion is not what has often been presented by physiologists, a mere nervous reaction from a bodily stimulus, like a kick which the frog gives when it is pricked. It begins with a mental act, and throughout is essentially an operation of the mind.
>
> James McCosh, *The Emotions*, 4

Religion, materialism and the mind

There was no single Christian or theistic response to physiological and evolutionary psychological theories of emotions. Given the importance in the Christian tradition, from Genesis to Augustine and beyond, of the division between man and the lower animals, however, it is perhaps not surprising to find that attempts to equate human and animal emotions raised more opposition from some Christian conservatives even than the attempt to correlate emotions with physiological activity. Martyn Paine was quite typical of Christian writers in his rather generous and inaccurate use of the label 'materialist' for thinkers writing within positivist, physiological or evolutionary schools of thought. In his *Physiology of the Soul*, Paine listed Spencer, Huxley, Darwin's friend the botanist Joseph Hooker, the Irish physicist John Tyndall and the physiologists W. B. Carpenter and Henry Maudsley as 'materialistic Darwinists'.[1] There was of course no necessary connection between belief in evolution and philosophic materialism, as monists such as Spencer and Huxley repeatedly insisted. Huxley complained in 1886 of his treatment at the hands of W. S. Lilly,

[1] Paine (1872), 176.

a theological ally of Cardinal Newman. The truth is, Huxley said, that Mr Lilly is possessed by a 'zeal to paint "Materialism" in large letters on everything he dislikes'.[2] Paine, 'Psychosis' (see chapter 5) and Lilly were not the only Christian and theistic writers to suffer from this particular form of over-zealousness.

This chapter looks at the affective psychologies produced by those who were opposed to the perceived 'materialism' and reductionism of the school of Bain, Spencer and Darwin. Many of these thinkers were motivated, at least in part, by commitment to theistic or Christian beliefs. As already mentioned several times, the fact that 'emotions', unlike 'passions' and 'affections', was a psychological term unknown to traditional Christianity meant that some Christian writers even in the 1870s still felt more comfortable writing of the will, and the passions and affections of the soul, rather than adopting the category of 'emotions'. Many of those who did use the new term contested physicalist definitions of it and provided instead cognitive and 'component' or 'compound' theories.

The writers considered in this section represent a range of approaches taken by anti-physicalists to emotions in the same period that Spencer, Bain and Darwin were formulating their physiological-evolutionary theories. These writers, some of whom would have considered themselves writers of 'psychology' and others of whom would have thought of themselves more as metaphysicians or even as theologians, were all contributors to psychological understandings. Their theories have generally been neglected, however, by historians of psychology. Perhaps this neglect has been the result of restrictive twentieth-century assumptions about what counts as psychology (for instance that it is a secular, scientific, non-metaphysical or professional academic discourse). The neglect of writers such as J. D. Morell, Thomas Upham, William Lyall, George Ramsay, Martyn Paine and James McCosh resulted in a communal amnesia in the worlds of scientific and philosophical psychology with regard to nineteenth-century cognitive and compound views of emotions.

The authors of the works examined in this chapter shared, as well as their opposition to reductionist psychologies of emotion, some form of religious commitment. They fall into three categories – the more or less traditionally Christian, the natural theological and those whose works revealed only a metaphysical or philosophic theism. The Christian conservatives considered below – William Whewell, William Sewell, John Henry Newman, John Grote and Thomas Gorman – were all based in Oxford or Cambridge. They were advocates of a theological dualism in which the soul was superior to the body and created in the image of God.

---

[2] Huxley (1893), 139; see also Desmond (1997), 170–1.

They generally used the categories of the Christian tradition and showed no interest in physiology or evolution.

The 'natural theologians' or 'preacher psychologists', generally fall into Cashdollar's category of 'judicious conservatives'.[3] Looking at it from the other side, in view of the extent to which they were prepared to include physiological and (less often) evolutionary considerations in their accounts of passions and emotions, they could equally be called 'cautious liberals'. This group included, not only natural theologians in the classical Bridgewater mould, such as Charles Bell, Henry Brougham, Thomas Burgess and Henry Holland, who interpreted human mental faculties as signs and products of the wisdom and benevolence of the Creator, but also writers who went beyond this basic design-theology model in their dual commitments to Christianity and to the study of nature, especially of the human body.[4] Examples of the latter included Paine and McCosh. The last of these was a particularly interesting figure, since his book, *The Emotions* (1880) was one of the most substantial, as well as one of the last, books of psychology written in a way that was both significantly informed by Christian belief and also written as a contribution to the new academic psychology.[5]

The third category of texts in this chapter are examples of 'metaphysical theism'. Such texts displayed a commitment to belief in some form of Deity and, especially to the existence of spirit or mind and its priority over matter. They were only thinly theistic rather than Christian or natural theological, however, since they were more often informed by German Idealist philosophy or a very broad sort of 'spiritualism' than by theology of any sort. This group included Morell, Lyall and the American philosopher-theologians Laurens Hickok and Noah Porter.[6]

Mind-body dualism

All the treatments of passions, affections and emotions considered here were predicated on mind-body dualism. Their authors believed, in opposition to the physiological-evolutionary psychologists, that there could be such a thing as a mental act with no bodily correlate. For example, Charles Bell, in dealing with weeping and laughter, had described these expressions not only as arising from sentiments not shared by the brutes, but

---

[3] Cashdollar (1989), ch. 9.
[4] Bell (1806, 1844); Brougham (1835); Holland (1852).
[5] For a discussion of the account given by G. T. Ladd – another of the last generation of soul-psychologists – of emotions and sentiments, see chapter 7.
[6] On Hickok and Porter, see Roback (1964), 79–84, 103–6; Spilka (1987). On the broader issues surrounding the relationship of philosophic idealism to religious belief, see Willis (1988); Sell (1995).

also as arising from 'mental conditions, independent of physical causes'.[7] The mind or soul was conceived as a substance inhabiting or using a body. Paine taught that the soul was a self-acting substance, 'subserved' by the brain and the nervous system.[8] The body was often described as the 'tenement' or 'instrument' of the soul.[9] Lyall expressed this central commitment in a typical way: 'The most essential part of our nature is unquestionably the living soul within us – the spiritual substance of which we are possessed, or which is clothed in a material body, united to a material organization.'[10] Hickok taught that 'The psychology we attain must recognize through all its facts, the existence of a rational spirit, which dwells in a tabernacle of flesh and blood.'[11] As a result of this mind–body dualism it was clear for the Christian and theistic psychologists – while it was increasingly unclear in the works of monist scientific psychologists – that the 'emotion in the mind' and the 'exertion of the bodily frame' were different things, the former causing the latter.[12] As McCosh put it, in opposing the monist school associated with Spencer:

> There is no propriety in calling the nervous affection a correlate of the emotion, or representing the two, after the fashion of the school, as the sides of one thing. They are two things, each with its own properties, but acting and reacting on each other, and both should have a place in a full account of the phenomenon.[13]

It was important for McCosh, in order to avoid determinism, that the mind be an independent 'self-acting' substance with a free will: he achieved this, in the same way as Thomas Reid had before him, by insisting that matter itself was inert and could only be moved by an act of will (human or divine).[14]

In classical Christian psychology it had been the soul and not the body that was active. Even though 'passions', as the word suggests, were seen as passive phenomena, that was not, as has often been assumed from Descartes onwards, because the soul was the passive recipient of these feelings but because the body was passively moved by the actions of the animal soul (and also sometimes because the higher rational soul was acted on by the animal soul). Treatments of passions, affections and emotions that were authentic representatives of this Christian tradition insisted on the activity of the soul or mind rather than of the body. Lyall, although his methodology was that of a theistic metaphysician and not

---

[7] Bell (1844), 158.   [8] Paine (1872), 27.   [9] E.g. Cooke (1852), xi.
[10] Lyall (1855), 10. See also Lyall (1855), 14, where he states that the only true philosophy is one that allows a real existence to both mental and material substances.
[11] Hickok (1859), 27.
[12] Bell (1844), 176. See also Holland (1852), 13 and 213, where the 'passions and emotions' in the mind have an effect on bodily organs.
[13] McCosh (1880), 108.   [14] Hoeveler (1981), 102–3.

of a Christian theologian, was also committed to the active view of the mind, which he described as being 'possessed of a *spontaneous activity and inherent power*, by which our simple ideas are framed, products of the mind solely, and not indebted to sensation farther than as the prompter of a stimulant of mind'.[15] Lyall's view was that the emotions, as well as the movements of the intellect, were the products of the activity of the 'spiritual substance within'.[16]

Design-theology texts that made less use of Christian theological psychology than did McCosh's or Paine's – for instance, some of the works produced by Chalmers, Bell and the physicians William Cooke and Henry Holland – were less committed to the denial of spontaneous bodily activity. These authors, writing in the tradition of Butler, Paley and other design-theologians, were happy to ascribe agency not only to divinely created mental mechanisms such as appetites, passions, sentiments and instincts but also to divinely created bodily mechanisms. Secondary causes were often spoken of as if primary. Bell, for one, was happy to refer to the 'agency of the body' in certain passions, and to refer to 'the actions of and expressions of the body' that 'betray the emotions of the heart'.[17]

Man–animal separatism

The conventional Christian teaching that man was qualitatively distinct from the animals was defended in three ways in the context of opposition to physicalist theories of emotions in this period. First, even in the case of those emotions that might be common to man and animals (those still understood by some as passions), the difference was that man, unlike lower animals, could and should control his passions by the powers of reason and will. As Paine put it, instinct is common to man and animals, but man alone has the power of reason.[18] Frederick Rauch (a German Protestant Hegelian who moved to America and taught mental philosophy in Pennsylvania in the 1830s) in his *Psychology* (1841) made it clear how the traditional teaching on man–animal separatism applied to the emotions.[19] He defined emotions as disturbances of the otherwise peaceful motion of the mind, which in turn he defined (again in a conventional Christian way) as the union of reason and will. He then continued: 'From

---

[15] Lyall (1855), 106.   [16] Lyall (1855), 281–2.
[17] Bell (1844), 176–7, 199.   [18] Paine (1872), 28–9.
[19] On Rauch, see Eric Carlson's 'Introduction' to Rauch (1975); Roback (1964), 73–5. Rauch's *Psychology* was one of the first books published in English with the word 'psychology' in its title.

this definition it follows at once that the animal, having no mind [i.e. no reason or will], cannot have emotions.'[20]

Secondly, it was taught (as Butler and other eighteenth-century moralists had taught) that human beings, unlike animals, had a conscience and a moral duty to God and to their fellow men. The moral dimension was also at work in the methodology of Christian and theistic emotions theorists – they were not committed, as the physicalists were, to a morally disengaged and objectifying scientific epistemology that treated human beings as organic mechanisms rather than as personal agents. Newman in particular stressed the moral and personal dimension of the affections; he argued that 'Conscience has an intimate bearing on our affections and emotions, leading us to reverence and awe, hope and fear', and that such feelings were stirred by other people rather than by non-human objects – 'we are not affectionate towards a stone, nor do we feel shame before a horse or a dog'.[21]

Thirdly, human beings were seen as qualitatively different sorts of creature from the rest of the 'brute creation', and were therefore held to be able to feel and express a range of affections, sentiments or emotions not participated in by lower animals. For example, Bell held that because human beings differed from lower beings by having the power of imagination, they could experience a peculiar sort of fear:

I should apply the name of terror to that kind of fear in which there is a strong working of the imagination, and which is therefore peculiar to man. The eye is bewildered; the inner extremity of the eyebrows is elevated, and strongly knit by the action of the corrugator; thus producing an expression of distracting thought, anxiety, and alarm, and one which does not belong to animals.[22]

Belief in the independent existence of the soul went hand in hand with belief in man–animal separatism, as the work of Bell, amongst others, demonstrates. The belief was that man differed from the lower animals primarily by virtue of his soul, with its powers of reason, conscience and imagination. As Newman put it, 'Man is the highest of the animals, and more indeed than an animal, as having a mind.'[23] If it was at the level of physiology that the distinction was less clear-cut (although naturalists such as Richard Owen worked hard to maintain its reality), then it was at the level of the soul and its mind that the distinction was defended to the hilt by Christians and theists. Consequently it was also at the level of mind that the incentive was greatest for the physiological or evolutionary psychologist to efface the division (see chapter 5).

[20] Rauch (1975), 300.   [21] Newman (1870), 104, 107.
[22] Bell (1844), 168.   [23] Newman (1870), 341.

Varieties of anti-physicalist theories of emotion in Britain and America 1836–1884

The Christian conservatives

Traditionalists such as the Oxford theologian, Thomas Gorman, would have liked to exclude physiological considerations from the study of the soul altogether. He responded to the reductionism of physiological psychology by defending staunchly the autonomy and superiority of the spiritual part of the human being. Gorman, writing in 1876, characterised Henry Maudsley and other physiologists of mind as 'atheistic naturalists' who mistakenly treated mind as the activities of brute matter: 'Superficial sciolists in philosophy have need to learn as a first lesson, that the physiologist and pathologist, as such, can have nothing to do with what transcends the sphere of the mere corporeal organism. It is the proper province of the psychologist to investigate the soul and its mind.'[24] The absolute transcendence of the spiritual and supernatural was asserted as a reason for the incompetence of naturalists in the realm of psychology.[25] It is tempting to see an analogy here between the asserted supremacy of the supernatural and spiritual over the body, on the one hand, and the desired institutional dominance of Christian theology over natural science in the academic fields of psychology and ethics, on the other. Gorman and others ultimately failed to maintain this dominance.[26]

Two English texts – one produced by the Reverend William Whewell in Cambridge in 1836, the other by the Reverend William Sewell in Oxford in 1840 – serve as early examples of the fact that while Scottish mental scientists and their followers were increasingly using the category 'emotions', conservative English thinkers were still speaking more traditional and more Christian language. Whewell, like Chalmers and Bell a Bridgewater author, is well known as a polymath Anglican with an interest in the history and philosophy of the inductive sciences. In 1836 he composed a Preface to the Scottish moral philosopher Sir James Mackintosh's *Dissertation on the Progress of Ethical Philosophy*.[27] It was in his *Dissertation* that

---

[24] Gorman (1875), 483.
[25] For the reverse view, expressed by Havelock Ellis and others, that only physiological and experimental psychologists were competent in psychology, see chapter 7.
[26] On the ideological overtones of debates about mind and matter between theological dualists and naturalistic monists, see Jacyna (1981); Hilton (1988), 304–14.
[27] Mackintosh (1862). The dissertation was initially part of the introductory volume to the 8th edition of the *Encyclopaedia Britannica*. For an interesting biography of Mackintosh see McCosh (1875), ch. 46. McCosh scathingly concluded that Mackintosh had largely wasted his philosophical talents and had 'attained the highest eminence only as a *talker* in the best social circles of London' (359).

Mackintosh made the suggestions for a new affective terminology that Thomas Chalmers discussed in his Bridgewater Treatise (see chapter 4). The suggestions were made, as follows, in the context of a critique of Hartley:

> In the whole of his philosophical works, we find no trace of any desire produced by association, of any disinterested principle, or indeed any distinction between the percipient and what, perhaps, we may now venture to call the *emotive* or *pathematic* part of human nature until some more convenient name shall be hit on by some luckier or more skilful adventurer, in such new terms as seem to be absolutely necessary.[28]

This suggested innovation was not, as Whewell noted in his Preface, widely accepted. In a footnote Whewell added the following commentary on Mackintosh's use of 'emotion': '"The part of our nature" of which the author here speaks, has often been described by the compound phrase "the desires and affections". The proposal to call these "the Emotions" has not been generally accepted; but the adjective "emotional" is not unfrequently used.'[29] So according to Whewell, at least, Brown's terminology had not been adopted in England in 1836. In a footnote added to the Preface in the 1862 third edition Whewell added the following:

> These terms ['emotive' and 'pathematic'] have not had much 'luck' (to use Mackintosh's own phraseology in the passage). In common language, this part of our nature is often called the *heart*, as distinguished from the *head*. We may perhaps best describe it by the compound phrase used in the Dissertation itself; *the desires and affections*. Some recent writers have spoken of the *emotional* part of our nature.[30]

Throughout his 1836 Preface and in his 1862 notes Whewell spoke the language of Anglican moralism; engaging with Hobbes, drawing on Hutcheson, Butler and Paley. He used the phrase 'passions and affections' as well as 'desires and affections', thus locating himself firmly in the moralist tradition that seemed still, even in 1862, to have been kept relatively isolated from the Scottish mental scientists and their emotions.

William Sewell was, like Newman, one of the Tractarians. He was Professor of Moral Philosophy in Oxford from 1837 until 1841.[31] His *Christian Morals* was published in 1840. Sewell lectured on Butler's *Sermons* during the 1840s, and he, like Whewell, still spoke the language of British moralism.[32] He referred to 'moral duties and affections', 'devotional affections', 'moral sentiments', 'moral affections' and the regulation of sensual lusts by the intellect, but did not show any sign of familiarity with

---

[28] Mackintosh (1862), 202–3. [29] Footnote to Mackintosh (1862), 79.
[30] Footnote to Preface to Mackintosh (1862), xlv.
[31] Hilton (1988), 27, 47, 144, 172, 268–9. [32] See Hilton (1988), 172.

the Scottish Brownian psychology of sensations, thoughts and emotions, which was already common currency for writers such as Mackintosh and Chalmers in Scotland in the 1830s.[33] Newman himself, in his *Essay in Aid of a Grammar of Assent*, published in 1870, referred to the 'appetites', 'passions' and 'affections' as the motive causes of human action; his use of the specific formulation 'affections and passions' is especially indicative of the fact that Newman's thought about the mind was embedded in the Christian tradition.[34] Newman did use the term 'emotion', but only on a very small number of occasions and then only, it seems, as a variant for 'affections' or 'affections and passions'.[35]

The response of the Revd John Grote (a Cambridge rector, and the brother of George Grote, mentioned in chapter 5) in a letter to Bain on the subject of the first edition of his *The Emotions and the Will* (1859) is a particularly good example of a conservative Christian reaction. In his *Autobiography* Bain summarised the letter as follows: 'John Grote's criticism took exception to the thorough-going concomitance of mind and body, and gave certain indications of his own views, which had somewhat of the prevailing spiritualistic tendency.'[36] Grote's specific criticisms of Bain's *Emotions* draw attention to the fact that 'will' was radically physicalised by Bain. They also bear witness to the fact that the category of 'emotions' was alien to the Christian tradition and subsumed various categories that Christian thinkers had previously differentiated. On Bain's treatment of the will Grote commented:

We go up the stream of sensibility and then down the stream of will, and so far as I as yet understand, you will not let us have a watershed or pass between the two, a point of transition from one to the other, but show us will taking its independent rise in *irritability*, then it and sensibility running side by side and gradually getting linked one to the other till there results intelligent will, or the will with which we rationally act. Now, about this irritability as the source of all, what I doubt is, true as it doubtless in a measure is, and to me a novel and important view, whether it is sufficient to account for the *whole* of the primary or rudimentary fact of will – is there not something more than bodily or nervous irritability, even in the first seed of volition?

Next Grote went on to tackle Bain's approach to the emotions:

I have the same sort of doubt as to what you say about the emotions. The fact of the importance of the *bodily* change or modification (which is what some time ago in our language would have been known by the name of the *passion*, and which wants very much a special name for it now) corresponding to each sort of emotion, in respect of the analysis and classification of the emotions, is a thing which I have

---

[33] Sewell (1840), 308, 345, 346, 348–52.   [34] Newman (1870), 10, 27, 79, 80, 86, 117.
[35] Newman (1870), 104–7.   [36] Bain (1904), 252.

thought much about, but which rather wants one who, like you, knows more than I do of physiology to deal with it. But are you right in considering to the extent to which you apparently do the bodily phenomenon (wave of emotion, as you have, it seems to me, most happily described it) *the whole* of the emotion? What is the emotion, in its proper character, an affection of? Is it not of something, substance if we like to call it so, of which, perhaps, we may know nothing more than that it is so affectable and affected, but which there must be, and of which consciousness is a *sort* of knowledge to us? I cannot conceive that the utmost refinement of analysis of the corporeal phenomenon of emotion will carry us beyond the region of *organs* or instruments, and the *self* which *uses* them must be something which has its realities, over and above what belongs to *them*.[37]

This passage summarises very well the problems that some Christian believers faced in coming to terms with the new physicalist concept of 'emotions'. First, even man's most refined religious and moral feelings seemed to be being reduced to mere bodily disturbances. Secondly, the new category of 'emotions' unhelpfully effaced the distinction between passions shared with animals and intertwined with the body and the more rarefied affections. And finally, in the absence of belief in an autonomous soul or a will, it was unclear what emotions were movements *of*.

The natural theologians and 'preacher psychologists'

Unlike their more conservative colleagues, 'natural theologians', such as William Cooke, Sir Charles Bell and James McCosh, showed a positive interest in developments being made in medicine and in experimental neurophysiology and their use in gaining knowledge of the mind. Indeed, Bell was one of those who had made the most significant neurophysiological breakthroughs himself. Bell's book, which was explicitly about expression rather than about emotion per se, was devoted mostly to descriptions of nerves, muscles and internal organs.

William Cooke's *Mind and the Emotions Considered in Relation to Health and Disease* (1838) was one of the first books to be published in English with the term 'emotions' in its title. Its early use of the category of 'emotions' was testament to the fact that he drew both on Brown's *Lectures* and on Chalmers' Bridgewater Treatise.[38] Cooke's work is a fascinating example of a text that defies classification in terms with which we are today familiar. It was a work of 'medico-theology', or of 'Christian medicine', which jumped from Christian exhortations such as – 'What an influence the church of Christ would produce if every nominal believer were a real believer, exemplifying the true character of the Christian faith!' – on one page, to, on the very next page, a prosaic medico-physiological account

---

[37] Quoted in Bain (1904), 255–6.   [38] Cooke (1852), 3, chs. 4 and 8.

of the emotions aroused in the sensitive constitution by the perception of divine mercy:

> Under such circumstances there often is a sort of ecstasy, with accelerated pulse, and high excitement of the brain and nervous system. This sometimes goes on to hysterical mania, of longer or shorter duration, according to the degree of impression and tendencies of the constitution. Occasionally it will issue in actual inflammation of the brain, but more frequently in irritation or congestion.[39]

In an equally striking illustration of the mixed methods adopted by the theological physician, Cooke, in a subsequent passage, advocated Christian charity on the grounds that it awakened emotions that prolonged life by strengthening the brain and nervous system.[40] Cooke (who was later a president of the Hunterian Society) wrote very much in the same tradition as Chalmers and McCosh.[41] All three declared the subservience of natural theology to Christian revelation; all three also affirmed the great value of science, be it mental, physical, or medical; but all also would have added, as Cooke put it, that 'Christianity is undoubtedly the greatest of all sciences.'[42]

James McCosh (1811–1894)

McCosh, the historian of the Scottish philosophy, made his name as one of the evangelical party who seceded from the established church and set up the Free Church of Scotland in 1843 (a group led by Chalmers). His first book, *The Method of Divine Government, Physical and Moral* (1850) established him as a major theologian and philosopher, selling well in Britain and America to academic and non-academic readers alike, and as a result he was appointed to the Chair of Logic and Metaphysics at Queen's College, Belfast in preference to the infidel Bain (see chapter 5). In 1868 he travelled across the Atlantic to take up his position as the new President of the College of New Jersey in Princeton (now Princeton University). While at Princeton in the 1870s he was one of the only Christian ministers to speak in favour of the doctrine of evolution and its compatibility with belief in God.[43]

McCosh's interest was in the emotions rather than their expression, and he was also more cautious than the classical natural theologians in his use of physiological information. Despite including a substantial amount of

---

[39] Cooke (1852), 13–15.   [40] Cooke (1852), 19.
[41] On the Hunterian Society, see Fotherby (1869).   [42] Cooke (1852), 26–7.
[43] On the life and thought of McCosh, see Malone (ed.) (1933); Roback (1964), 109–13; Moore (1979), 245–50; Livingstone (1992), 408–28; Hoeveler (1981), 99–107, 180–211; Hilton (1988), 362–4; Brooke (1991), 310–17.

physiological material in *The Emotions*, and despite being a supporter of the doctrine of evolution (once divorced from materialist or positivist interpretations) McCosh was still fundamentally committed to a mentalistic rather than a physiological psychology. He stood in the same tradition of introspective faculty psychology as Thomas Reid and the other Scottish 'intuitionists' of the common sense school. As such he was seen, in his own time, as something of an anachronism. He opposed reductionist forms of physiological psychology, criticising 'the tendency on the part of the prevailing physiological psychology of the day to resolve all feeling, and our very emotions, into nervous action, and thus gain an important province of our nature to materialism'.[44]

But McCosh could not be fairly characterised as ignorant of, or in principle opposed to, the use of physiology in psychology. While he was more cautious about physiology than many classical natural theologians, he was, as Chalmers had been before him, more welcoming towards science than many other theologians. He did not simply retreat towards doctrinal conservatism in the face of the new physiological psychology.[45] One of the four elements of emotions that McCosh's theory delineated was, indeed, the 'organic affection' (or bodily disturbance). It was simply a question of priorities, and McCosh gave priority to the mental, or 'psychical', elements of emotion above the organic affections involved, specifically to the cognitive – 'Let a man stop himself at the time when passion is rolling like a river, he will find that the idea is the channel in which it flows.'[46]

Martyn Paine was a professor in the medical department of the University of New York, and an Episcopalian.[47] His *Physiology of the Soul and Instinct as Distinguished from Materialism* (1872) provided facts about the ways that nerves, viscera and muscles were involved in expressing passions and emotions, while demoting these organs to secondary status as the instruments upon which the immaterial soul acted.[48] The epistemological stance of natural theologians such as these was between that of conservatives such as Gorman on the one hand, and physiologically focussed thinkers such as Bain and Spencer on the other. Their view was that knowledge about the human mind could be gained by studying nerves, muscles and viscera, but that such knowledge was only secondary knowledge – knowledge of how the mind acted upon the external world; primary psychological knowledge was to be gained by introspection. Rather than adopting the reactionary position of insisting that only the theologian had anything useful to say about the soul, the natural theological psychologists

---

[44] McCosh (1880), iv. [45] Hilton (1988), 361. [46] McCosh (1880), 42.
[47] Roback (1964), 98–100. [48] Paine (1872), 33–43 and throughout.

transferred their ontological mind–body dualism into the realm of epistemology by proposing a methodological separatism between the scientist of the mind and the scientist of the body, while acknowledging the value of each:

> For the present, it is of importance that psychologists should pursue their observations with consciousness as agent, and that physiologists should conduct their experiments with all the appliances they can command, each part being under obligations not to speculate beyond his own province. As they do so, judicious men will rise up to combine the two in a consistent system, in which light will be thrown on both mind and body.[49]

These judicious comments of McCosh's could equally well have been made by Spencer, who also thought that the observations of consciousness and of the nervous system should be kept distinct, and should ultimately be combined in a science of psychology.[50] The difference was, above all, one of emphasis and priority. It was the apparent priority he gave to neurological facts and evolutionary hypotheses over the facts of subjective consciousness that earned Spencer labels such as 'materialist' and 'positivist'.

Thomas Baynes' attack on the 'Darwinian sect'

A considered – or alternatively 'contemptuous', as Darwin had called it – attack on the evolutionary approach to emotions came in Thomas Baynes' review of Darwin's *Expression,* published in the *Edinburgh Review* in April 1873. Baynes supported Bell's treatment of expression and criticised Darwin for artificially bringing animals and humans together by reading emotion into the slightest movement of an animal – 'the extent to which Mr Darwin persistently reads his own theory into the ambiguous muscular twitches and spasms of monkeys and other animals is often amusing in a high degree'. Baynes also noted that Darwin tended to concentrate only on man's lower passions and animal desires – 'The manner in which he continually degrades and vulgarises human emotion is equally striking.'[51] In short: 'There is an obvious effort from the first to bring vividly into view not what is most distinctive in the expression of human emotion, but what is common to men and animals.'[52] It was true that Darwin assumed, for example, that observations of animals were the 'safest basis for generalisations on the causes, or origin, of the various movements of expression'.[53] So he tended to present the generalisations that could be made about behaviours shared by human

---

[49] McCosh (1880), 89.   [50] Spencer (1870–2), I, 136–41.
[51] [Baynes] (1873), 512.   [52] [Baynes] (1873), 511–12.   [53] Darwin (1998), 24.

and non-human animals as the only generalisations of any kind that could be made about the expression of emotions in humans. This was all exacerbated by Darwin's reliance mainly on observations of lower animals, infants, 'savages' and the insane, rather than of civilised, sane European adults. Baynes put it like this: 'from the sources to which Mr Darwin exclusively refers for his facts, it is impossible to obtain illustrations of the higher and more characteristic human emotions'.[54]

Darwin had himself stated that he considered the most useful indication of a good mode of explanation to be that it could be 'applied with satisfactory results, both to man and to the lower animals'.[55] His deliberate neglect of explanations that could not equally be applied to human and to non-human animals rendered his conclusion – that the expression of the emotions is very similar in humans and in other animals – rather a foregone and circular one. In other words, Darwin's adoption of his particular scientific-evolutionary worldview involved commitment to the basic ontological sameness of human and non-human animals, and this commitment determined that the methodology of the evolutionary psychologist should be the same for humans and other animals, which methodology in turn determined the examples used and the results obtained, which results confirmed the original premise that, in Darwin's own words, 'there is no fundamental difference between man and the higher mammals in their mental faculties'.[56] A priori metaphysical commitments could play a role in shaping theory for the non-religious as much as for the religious psychologist.

Baynes also contrasted what he considered to be the sober, inductive and cautious tone of Darwin's *Origin* with the more strident approach of the *Descent* and the *Expression*. Indeed, his most serious criticism of Darwin was that his work was unscientific – his hypotheses were unverified, and causes were introduced for which there was not conclusive evidence (for instance the environments and behaviours of evolutionary ancestors).[57] Baynes implied that the selection of methods and examples that exaggerated the closeness of human and animal emotion was also an instance of the unscientific and a priorist favouring of a pet theory ahead of the evidence.

The accusation of a priorism was extended also to Bain, Huxley and Maudsley, who were all considered members of the 'Darwinian sect'.[58] Baynes saw these thinkers as sharing with other religious sects an element of 'strong but unenlightened' belief. The external evidence of the evolution of man from monkeys was notoriously deficient, he said, but,

---

[54] [Baynes] (1873), 513.   [55] [Baynes] (1873), 18.   [56] Darwin (1871), I, 35.
[57] [Baynes] (1873), 492–7.   [58] [Baynes] (1873), 502.

'The cavils of the sceptics are of no avail with the true evolutionist believer, because he has an unfaltering trust in his own sacred books and inspired writers... His [Huxley's] whole temper and spirit is essentially dogmatic of the Presbyterian or Independent type, and he might fairly be described as a Roundhead who had lost his faith.'[59] Baynes could see that the approach to psychology of the physiologists and evolutionists was not determined only by facts and evidence but also by their prior commitment to a particular scientific worldview, which determined what could be assumed to exist, what was a valid way to investigate it and how it could legitimately be explained. Such commitments were the results of personal, social and professional factors more than they were of empirical ones. Baynes' interpretation was that this scientific-evolutionary worldview was quasi-religious in its function.[60]

The problem of defining the 'emotions'

When it came to providing definitions of 'emotions', vagueness and confusion reigned among natural theological writers as much as among the new scientific psychologists. Bell, for example, expressed the situation as follows in 1844: 'Were we not to limit our inquiry to the agitations of the body, we should be embarrassed with the ambiguity of such words as passion, emotion, desire, inclination, appetite, the generous passions, the passion of pride or avarice; even the mere state of suffering is called passion.'[61] McCosh, in 1880, also complained of the 'vagueness' of the terms 'emotions' and 'feelings'.[62] He presumably had Spencer in mind when he criticised those thinkers who 'lose themselves and confuse their readers by speaking of *all* our mental states, even our intellectual exercises as feelings'.[63] There was, as has already been seen in the cases of Mackintosh, Chalmers and Spencer, with their suggested terms 'pathematic', 'pathological', 'emotive' and 'presentative-representative feelings', something of a terminological free-for-all in this period, which formed the background to the emergence of 'emotions' as the generally adopted category.

As an example of the over-inclusivity of 'emotions' among natural theological (as much as amongst physicalist) writers, McCosh devoted separate sections to each of the following emotions: self-satisfaction, regret, complacency, displacency, self-esteem, self-dissatisfaction,

---

[59] [Baynes] (1873), 504–6.
[60] For more on the quasi-theological roles of science, see Dixon (1999), esp. 320–5; on scientific atheism as a quasi-religious tradition, see Dixon (2002d).
[61] Bell (1844), 145n.   [62] McCosh (1880), iii–iv.   [63] McCosh (1880), iii.

self-congratulation, self-reproach, self-sufficiency, self-depreciation, self-adulation, self-accusation, mortification, bitterness, chagrin, pleasant memories, self-approbation, self-condemnation, self-gratulation, self-humiliation, repining, moral approbation, moral disapprobation, testimony of a good conscience, remorse, benignancy, thankfulness, anger, irritation, temper, indignation and many many more; over one hundred in total ranging from emotions of terror and surprise to emotions of intellectual beauty, the sublime and the fine arts. As with so many other important writers on emotions in the nineteenth century, McCosh was clearly indebted to Brown (and also to Chalmers' version of Brown's view of emotions) for his over-inclusive sense of 'emotions'; he also adopted the Brownian division of emotions into the retrospective, immediate and prospective.

The over-inclusivity of the category of 'emotions' also meant that any definition would have to be reductive. Any definition that was supposed to be applied to every member of the whole category of emotions was bound to be reductive either 'upwards' or 'downwards'. While physicalist definitions reduced everything downwards (to animal passion and physiology), anti-physicalist ones reduced upwards (to mind and cognition).[64] Each school adopted 'paradigm-determined' examples: reductionist evolutionists would concentrate on more organic instances of terror, anger, grief (i.e. what used to be called 'passions'); anti-reductionist writers (including believers in evolution such as McCosh) focussed more on moral, religious and aesthetic feelings (i.e. what used to be called 'affections' and 'sentiments'). The demise of the distinction between passions and affections had contributed to the emergence of this unsatisfactory situation.

Cognitive and compound approaches

There was a substantial coincidence between anti-physicalist writers suspicious of the new physiological psychology and writers who favoured active, mentalistic (or 'spiritual', or 'cognitive'), voluntary and compound approaches to the emotions. McCosh was an example of such a writer: he reduced all the emotions upwards. He insisted that all emotions were 'psychical acts', which produced only secondarily 'physiological concomitants and effects'.[65] This view made much more sense of complex and abstract feelings than it did of terror or sexual desire, for example. The

---

[64] Solomon (1993a) is one of the most striking recent examples of an emotions theorist reducing all the emotions 'upwards': Solomon's view is that emotions are 'self-involved and relatively *intense* evaluative judgments' (127).
[65] McCosh (1880), iv.

bodily element was, on McCosh's view, temporally last and also last in importance in the process of any emotional experience: 'Emotion is not what has often been presented by physiologists, a mere nervous reaction from a bodily stimulus, like a kick which the frog gives when it is pricked. It begins with a mental act, and throughout is essentially an operation of the mind.'[66] There was an evident continuity between McCosh's writing and the Calvinist teaching of Jonathan Edwards on the religious affections a century and a half before. Edwards had insisted, like McCosh, that:

> As 'tis the soul only that has ideas, so 'tis the soul only that is pleased or displeased with its ideas. As 'tis the soul only that thinks, so 'tis the soul only loves or hates, rejoices or is grieved at what it thinks of. Nor are these motions of the animal spirits, and fluids of the body, anything properly belonging to the nature of the affections; though they always accompany them, in the present state; but are only effects or concomitants of the affections, that are entirely distinct from the affections themselves, and no way essential to them; so that an unbodied spirit may be as capable of love and hatred, joy or sorrow, hope or fear, or other affections, as one that is united to a body.[67]

Paine – another writer influenced by eighteenth-century Christian thought – had shown the same tendency to give priority to the mental and cognitive:

> When speaking of the passions and mental emotions as elements of the mind, and as producing involuntary effects, I desire to be critically understood that it is not intended to be implied that they are not more or less associated with acts of intellection, and perhaps always, brought into operation by some act of the mind properly so called [i.e. reason].[68]

Paine, writing in 1872, spoke, primarily, the language of 'the Will' and its 'passions'.[69] He, like Newman, used the term 'emotion' relatively sparingly and secondarily.[70] It is particularly striking that Paine, in his *Physiology of the Soul*, revealed his indebtedness to eighteenth-century thought on the passions and affections by quoting from Isaac Watts and by using the analogy of watch and watchmaker – used by Hobbes, Butler and Paley amongst many others – in his discussion of the contrivance by the Creator of the mechanism of the human mind.[71] These authorities and images were not current among the new physiological and physicalist emotions theorists. Anti-physicalists' cognitive theories of emotion contrasted with the new physiological psychologists' views of emotions: for these writers passions, affections or emotions were seen as acts of the soul

---

[66] McCosh (1880), 4. [67] Edwards (1959), 98. [68] Paine (1872), 57.
[69] Paine (1872), 28, 30, 33, 40–1, 43, 55, 58, 60, 62.
[70] E.g. Paine (1872), 43, 54, 63. [71] Paine (1872), 60, 66, 83.

rather than passive products of the body. Secondly, these mental states were seen as intimately connected with the rational soul (products of intellectual activity) rather than feelings to be contrasted with intellectual states of mind.

It was also the anti-physicalists who favoured compound (as opposed to aggregate – see chapter 5) views of emotions, such as McCosh's, in which the emotion was an irreducibly qualitatively novel mental experience. To summarise McCosh's theory: emotions had four elements: the 'appetence' or basic inclination to avoid pains and seek pleasures, the idea or 'phantasm', the conscious feeling of excitement and finally the organic (bodily) affection. As we have seen, he was quite clear that the idea was essential and the bodily affection was not, it was only a secondary element. What was rather mysterious was how McCosh intended his two statements – that emotions were mental acts through and through, and that emotions had four elements – to be combined. It seemed that one or more of the elements were more important than the others, but also that the emotion was a single compound product of all the elements. McCosh equivocated between the claim that the emotions were really mental acts with bodily effects that were not part of the emotions themselves, and the claim that emotions were compounds with mental and bodily elements of which the former were somehow more important.[72] In short there was in this mentalistic and theistic psychology of emotions as much confusion when it came to definitions as there was in physiological psychologies of emotions.

An anonymous reviewer of McCosh's *The Emotions* (1880) writing for the *Journal of Mental Science* predicted that representatives of the Scottish school who sang the praises of introspection and common sense would 'very soon be as extinct as the schoolmen'.[73] The prediction was a good one. McCosh's theory vanished without trace. Apart from the one review just mentioned, which was short and dismissive, the psychological community seems very largely to have ignored the contribution. Gardiner *et al.*'s generally exhaustive history of theories of emotion does not even mention McCosh, and in Brett's equally thorough *History of Psychology* (1921) McCosh is granted a mere seven lines, suggesting that his many responsibilities at Princeton prevented him from making a significant contribution to psychology.[74] In many historical treatments there is a leap from Darwin (1872) to James (1884 and 1890), suggesting a smooth transition from one physicalist thinker to the next.[75] The breadth and depth of dissent from the physicalist paradigm is not reported.

[72] E.g. McCosh (1880), 2–4, 88, 101, 107, 113–14.
[73] Anonymous (1881), 582. [74] Brett (1921), III, 257.
[75] E.g. Fancher (1996); Elster (1999); Gardiner *et al.* (1970), ch. 10.

The metaphysical theists

While conservative Christians appealed to Scripture and tradition as well as to introspection as the most important authorities, and natural theologians extended the range of legitimate psychological methodologies to include, in addition to these, metaphysics and natural science, the metaphysical theists relied on philosophical analyses to the exclusion of the Christian tradition. These writers came to a view of the importance of adopting a spiritualistic or mentalistic account of emotions as a result of philosophical and religious opposition to materialism and/or as a result of commitment to (often German) Idealist philosophy.

Laurens Hickok, for example, was an American theologian whose methodology in his two volumes, *Rational Psychology* (1848) and *Empirical Psychology* (1854), owed almost nothing to the Christian tradition and much to Idealist philosophy. Hickok's psychological system has been described as the high-point of the German philosophical influence on American psychology.[76] Hickok was very cautious of the claim that psychology was a science. He aimed to produce primarily a description of the human mind, 'a psychography rather than a psychology', as he put it.[77] His view (one that was later attributed by William James to George Trumbull Ladd) was that psychology should be a descriptive and classificatory science rather than an exact, causal or physical one: 'It is a science, as Chemistry, Geology and Botany are sciences; the study of facts in their combinations as nature gives them to us, and thus teaching what is first learned by careful observation and experiment.'[78]

Reverend William Lyall was born near Glasgow in 1811. He was educated there and in Edinburgh, before being ordained into the Presbyterian ministry. In 1843 he, like Chalmers and McCosh, was one of the seceding evangelical party who formed the Free Church. He emigrated to Nova Scotia in 1848. There he held a succession of positions at colleges in Toronto and Halifax, before being appointed to the Chair of Metaphysics at Dalhousie College in 1863, where he stayed until his death in 1890.[79] His 1855 book, *Intellect, the Emotions, and the Moral Nature*, as was noted above (chapter 4), was one of the earliest American works with the word 'emotions' in its title. Lyall's indebtedness to Thomas Brown for his concept of and approach to the classification of emotions was evident throughout his book. Three features of Lyall's treatment of the emotions were especially revealing of Brown's influence: his recourse, in his attempt to find words to define 'emotions', to the

---

[76] Roback (1964), 79–84. [77] Hickok (1859), vi. [78] Hickok (1859), vi–vii.
[79] On Lyall, see McKillop (1979), 44–52; Page (1980); Dixon (2002b).

observation that 'all have a clear enough idea of the phenomenon who have once experienced it'; his division of mental states into the sensational, the intellectual and the emotional; and his adoption of the division of emotions into the three categories of retrospective, immediate and prospective.[80]

Lyall, like Chalmers, combined fervent personal Christian commitment with the adoption, when it came to writing philosophy, of the terminology and methodology of Thomas Brown's thinly theistic science of mind. His obituarist recorded that Lyall 'utterly scorned physiological psychology'.[81] His proposed science of mind (also called 'metaphysics') was one based on the belief that mind was as real an existence as matter and that its 'laws and phenomena' were as worthy of study as those of the 'external universe'.[82] The data of the science of mind for Lyall were the facts of consciousness: 'The mind is self-cognizant. Its own arcana are open to its own inspection. It can minutely observe its most intimate and secret workings: it can mark and record every thought, or feeling, or observation.'[83] This was the language of the Scottish mental science tradition (see chapter 4). Lyall, as a defender of this tradition, applied scientific methods to the mind qua mind, rather than trying to understand the mind as something physiological. He was concerned that 'the immense physical advantages resulting from the sciences may be purchased too dearly, if the science of our mental and moral constitution is neglected or uncultivated'.[84] Ramsay, another Brownian, defined 'psychology' as being synonymous with 'pure mental science' or 'metaphysics'.[85] Porter adopted a similar definition of psychology as the 'science of the human soul'; a science concerned with 'exact observation, precise definition, fixed terminology, classified arrangement, and rational explanation', but *not* a sort of chemistry or physiology *tout court*.[86] This all brings out the important point that being an anti-physicalist in psychology was not the same as being anti-scientific. It meant, rather, having a different set of beliefs from the physicalists about the nature of the scientific method and the way it should be applied to human mental life.

Of the metaphysical theists, it was Thomas Upham, Frederick Rauch and Laurens Hickok in particular who contributed to the terminological discussion. Rauch proposed his own unique set of definitions of 'desires', 'inclinations', 'passions' and 'emotions', while Hickok suggested that 'Susceptibility' be adopted as the name for 'the entire sentient or emotive capacity of the soul', which was distinct 'from both the intellect and the

---

[80] Lyall (1855), 281–9.   [81] Quoted in Page (1980), 59.   [82] Lyall (1855), 2.
[83] Lyall (1855), 6–7.   [84] Lyall (1855), 8.   [85] Ramsay (1857), vi–vii.
[86] Porter (1872a), 5–6; for Porter's hostility towards Bain and the 'cerebralists', see also Porter (1872b), 59.

will'. Within this category of 'Susceptibility' fell 'blind feeling', 'appetite', 'desire', 'inclination', 'emotion' and 'passion'.[87] Upham divided the mind into intellect, will and 'Sensibilities'; 'emotive susceptibility' was a subset of this last category.[88] Upham, Rauch and Hickok all provided novel ways of categorising these capacities of the soul, which drew partly on conventional Christian usage, and also on metaphysics.[89] This state of terminological and theoretical chaos in the middle of the nineteenth century might be seen as an example of the sort of 'crisis', which, according to Kuhn, precedes the emergence of a new paradigmatic theory – in this case the physicalist and scientific theories of emotions produced by Spencer and Bain under the influence of Brown, which eventually replaced the old will–passions–affections paradigm of earlier Christian theorists.[90]

J. D. Morell, another theist of the metaphysical and philosophical sort, endorsed a theory that reduced emotions 'upwards'. It was he who had coined the term 'sensationalist' to describe the sorts of reductionist psychology that he did not like. He used the distinction between emotions and sensations (the Brownian distinction used and endorsed in one sense or another on all sides of the discussion) as a way to express his support for a mentalistic, cognitive and voluntary view of the emotions:

> The one [sensation] arises immediately from the presence of an external object, the other, being an *emotion*, has nothing to do with such an object; the one comes from without, the other from within; the one follows upon an affection of the nerves, the other from a conception of the mind; the one is entirely uncontrollable so long as the bodily affection lasts, the other is, to a great extent, under the dominion of the will.[91]

The emotions, said Morell, arise 'from a purely intellectual idea involving good or evil to ourselves'.[92] Lyall was another example of a theistic psychologist reducing all the emotions upwards, seeing them all as spiritual phenomena. 'What is our higher spiritual being concerned with,' he asked, 'but the emotions?'[93] Emotion, for him, was a purely mental state, unlike sensation, 'which is partly bodily and partly mental'. Emotion was

---

[87] Rauch (1975), 293–310; Hickok (1859), 176–7.   [88] Upham (1856), 138–9.
[89] Upham (1856), in particular, like Chalmers and Payne, was an interesting case in which Brownian mental science and evangelical theology were combined. Upham, along with Payne, was picked out by Porter as one of the psychological thinkers most influenced by Brown; Porter (1874), 413. Upham's text also had many similarities with those of eighteenth-century revivalists such as Watts and Edwards, including a plea for balance between intellect and enthusiasm, the use of the term 'affections', and the emphasis on the nature–grace distinction.
[90] See chapter 8, Conclusions, in this volume, and Kuhn (1970), esp. chs. 7 and 8.
[91] Morell (1846), I, 320–1.
[92] Morell (1846), I, 472. See also Morell (1846), II, 268–9.   [93] Lyall (1855), 12.

differentiated not only by being different from sensation but also by being a 'higher state' even than 'pure intellect'. Emotion, he said, was 'the atmosphere or life of the soul'.[94]

'Emotions' in secular and religious worldviews

I hope that the sort of distinctions I have tried to make in this chapter will be a useful elaboration upon the rather more general (and sometimes rather vague) claims made by some historians about the secular human sciences being inherently 'theological' or 'anti-theological'. Edward Reed, for example, suggests that virtually all the varieties of nineteenth-century psychology were either inherently theological, or 'deistic' or compatible with religious belief.[95] It is important, however, to make more fine-grained distinctions than that. Commitments to biblical Christianity, natural theology or metaphysical theism all had different overtones and implications. As Robert Richards has argued, the spiritualistic monism of some of the more religiously inclined scientists of the later nineteenth century 'led to theism, not perhaps to religious orthodoxy, but certainly to a conception of God at work in the universe'.[96] Jacyna notes that the God of the monist scientists was certainly not 'the God of the churches'.[97] And as the analysis in this study of the differences between Christian, natural theological, thinly theistic, Idealist, agnostic and secular ways of approaching affective psychology should illustrate, it is not true that nineteenth-century psychologists, as Reed puts it, 'tended to align themselves along a fixed deistic axis'. Even if that *were* true, it would not be good evidence for the claim that nineteenth-century psychology was therefore inherently theological.[98]

Contrary to the impression given by almost all histories of psychology, the concept of emotions was not understood only in a physicalist, physiological and evolutionary sense in the era of the emergence of physiological and evolutionary psychology from the 1850s to the 1880s. The truth is that although, for the reasons given above, many conservative and religious thinkers were less quick to appropriate the concept of emotions, there were throughout the nineteenth century alternative, anti-physicalist theories of passions, affections and emotions being produced, which were characterised by compound and cognitive approaches.

This chapter, and the previous one, have shown how different terms, notably 'science', 'activity', 'will' and 'volition', and 'emotions' could mean different things within different worldviews. For example, Spencer's

[94] Lyall (1855), 284–5. [95] Reed (1997), 7. [96] Richards (1987), 405.
[97] Jacyna (1981), 119. [98] Reed (1997), 3.

'science' of psychology (combining neurological data with evolutionary theory) and Lyall's 'science' of mind (based on the commitment to the separate and real existence of mind) could hardly have been more different. Spontaneous mental activity for the Christian or theistic psychologist was activity of the soul, for Bain and Spencer it was reducible to the activity and irritability of the nerves. An 'emotion' for Bain was a sort of central nervous activity, for McCosh the act of an immaterial mind. One of the main arguments of this book is that 'passions' and 'emotions' are not and were not the same things. It is also true, from the mid-nineteenth century onwards, that more often than not 'emotions' and 'emotions' were not the same things (just as, for example, 'mass' and 'mass' are not the same thing in Newtonian and Einsteinian paradigms).[99]

In the psychology produced by inhabitants of a physicalist-agnostic worldview, the assumption at the root of natural theological treatises by Chalmers and Bell – that the external environment and the human body had been contrived by divine intelligence to subserve human mental and moral life – was inverted: it was instead assumed by some physiologists and evolutionists that the human mind was the product of the agency of the external environment and the human body. The new view of emotions, found in Bain, Spencer and Darwin that had not been found, for example, in Brown, was that they were nothing more than feelings produced by the involuntary workings of inherited habits and animal instincts. As Nietzsche put it in 1887, man had 'become an *animal*, literally and without reservation or qualification, he who was, according to his old faith, almost God'.[100]

Alongside this new physicalist concept of emotions there was still developing an alternative tradition of cognitive and compound theories of emotions, which have generally been forgotten by psychologists and historians of psychology. However, for most of the nineteenth (as well as, arguably, the eighteenth) century it was reductionist thinkers who were setting the agenda. Just as Butler had found himself tacitly adopting the Hobbesian agenda, Reid's psychology had been influenced by the questions asked by Hume, and Chalmers had bought into the mental science of Brown, so Morell, Lyall, McCosh, Paine and the others were most often producing a psychology that was responding to the dominant sect of their day, as represented by Bain, Spencer and Darwin.

It is appropriate that two of the main points focussed on in this chapter and the previous chapter have been, first, the tacit physicalism and epiphenomenalism of physiological-evolutionary theories of emotions and,

---

[99] Kuhn (1970), 102. For more on this point, see chapter 8 in this volume.
[100] Nietzsche (1967), 155.

secondly, the crisis of definition that plagued the category of 'emotions'. The final stage in this story of the creation of the 'emotions' in the nineteenth century is the attempt by William James in 1884 to answer the question that had produced a variety of vague and contradictory responses in the preceding decades – what *is* an emotion? And the answer he arrived at would make starkly explicit the epiphenomenalism of the 'feeling' theory of emotions adopted by Brown, Bain, Spencer and Darwin.

7 What was an emotion in 1884? William James and his critics

> Undoubtedly the stimulating and highly valuable influence of James' treatment – here as on many other points – has been due to a certain frankness and *naïve* clearness which has concealed in a measure the real complexity of the problem.
>
> James Mark Baldwin, 'The origin of emotional expression', 610

William James' theory of emotion

It should now be clear that Charles Darwin and William James were not the authors of 'the first studies of the emotions using scientific methodology'.[1] Nor was James the first nineteenth-century thinker to adopt a passive 'sensational' or 'feeling' theory of emotion; Brown, Spencer and Bain had all done so before him; they had all described emotions as aggregates or effects, whose constituents or causes were sensations. It is no coincidence that William James had spent his youth 'immersed in Dugald Stewart and Thomas Brown'; the latter's view of the emotions was at the root of James' own.[2] The 'feeling' theory of emotion was, nonetheless, given its most widely remembered formulation by William James: emotions for James were passive mental feelings of movements of the viscera. The most striking thing about James' theory of emotions, and the reason for its lasting fame, was its clarity and simplicity. What was most novel about it was the priority given to the viscera rather than the brain (or indeed the soul) in causing emotional feelings.

James agreed with Bain, Spencer and Darwin in making the real business of emotions bodily activity, but he inverted their assumption that emotions started in the nerves and secondarily acted upon the viscera. While Bain and Spencer had embodied the traditional model – in which the passions and affections of the soul acted on the body – so that the emotions of one part of the body (the brain or central nervous system) now acted on other parts of the body (the limbs, viscera, etc.), James took

---

[1] Elster (1999), 48. [2] James (1985), 2.

this embodied model and reversed the direction of causation. The result amounted to a complete contradiction of active, voluntary and cognitive views about the affections and emotions, such as those taught by Edwards and McCosh. Not only was the soul replaced by the brain in James' theory (as it had been in Bain's and in Spencer's), but the brain was itself not even active in emotions but was acted upon by the viscera.

James' psychological writings comprised an unusually heterogeneous collection of approaches. While in some cases (such as in his theory of emotion) espousing a psychology that seemed to be a reinforcement of Spencer's and Bain's associationism, in other pieces of work he attacked Spencer and the associationist school for their view that the mind was 'pure product', and advocated a much more phenomenological approach. He also vacillated between physical and spiritual interpretations of 'science', between criticisms of Bain's positivism and his own espousal of the positivist rejection of metaphysics and explanation, between monist and dualist interpretations of mind and matter, between introspective and physiological approaches to psychology and the self, and between support for and criticism of the new experimental psychology.[3] Indeed, a recent study of William James' philosophy makes the very irreconcilability of its different aspects its most important characteristic.[4]

The William James who forms the focus of this chapter, however, is the reductionist William James of the 1884 article 'What is an emotion?' The reductionist nature of the theory will be particularly surprising, perhaps, to those familiar with James' influential *Varieties of Religious Experience* (1902), a text much more sympathetic to the language of spirit; or with his speculations about unusual psychical phenomena, life after death and the supernatural.[5] This other William James even cited the eighteenth-century New England revivalist Jonathan Edwards in support of his own judgment, in the *Varieties*, that religious life should be understood by considering its (spiritual) fruits rather than its (possibly physical) roots.[6]

---

[3] On positivism see e.g. James (1876); and see below on James' positivist definition of psychology in the *Principles*. On James' vacillation on dualism see Skrupskelis (1995), 79–80. On his attitudes to the new psychology in America, Reed (1997), ch. 11.
[4] Gale (1999).
[5] In the *Varieties* James, significantly, talks a lot about 'feelings', which are understood mentalistically and less about 'emotions', which, in 1884, he had defined in a physicalist–behaviourist way. There are many striking differences between the reductionist James of 'What is an emotion?' and the more spiritualist James of the *Varieties*. Comparing the exposition in this chapter with Capek (1953); Richards (1987), ch. 9, esp. 441–3; Proudfoot (1989); Skrupskelis (1995); Reed (1997), ch. 11; Campbell (1997), 463–73; and Gale (1999) will give a good sense of these opposing poles in James' psychological thought, and of the debates about how to interpret the many apparent changes of direction in James' work.
[6] James (1985), 19–20; on Edwards see chapter 3 in this volume.

However, James employed, in his 1884 article on emotion, and in many parts of *The Principles of Psychology* (1890), materialistic rhetoric and reductionist explanations that seemed quite out of keeping with his well-known sympathies for religion.[7] This was partly a result of the great interest in physiology and anaesthesia that he had developed during visits to France and Germany; he was especially interested in the French psychiatrist Paul Sollier's work on generalised and hysterical anaesthesia, to which he would refer in both his 1884 and 1894 articles on the nature of emotion.[8] One reviewer of the *Principles*, writing in the year after its publication, found the most striking characteristic of the book to be 'the tendency everywhere to substitute a physiological for a mental explanation', and considered that, despite his professed religious instincts and hostility to materialism, James had, especially in the case of his theory of emotions, 'outdone the materialists themselves'.[9]

While the forays into the new discipline of 'psychology' (as distinct from the established branch of philosophy known as 'mental philosophy' or 'metaphysics') by scientists and philosophers such as Bain, Spencer and Darwin had been controversial, contested and, in a sense, 'amateur', James was one of the central figures through whom scientific psychology became mainstream and institutionalised. The Jamesian era saw shifts in the geography of academic psychology as well as its disciplinary boundaries. While Scottish philosophy, and English biology and neurophysiology, had led the way in the psychology of emotions earlier in the nineteenth century, the drive to experimentalism in psychology found the centre of gravity in psychology shifting first to Germany, during the 1880s, especially to Wilhelm Wundt's laboratory of 'psychophysics' in Leipzig – the first of its kind, founded in the late 1870s – and thence to America. In 1895 there were four psychological laboratories in Germany, and two in England in comparison with the sixteen or more that could be boasted by America.[10] Many of the professors of psychology in American universities at the end of the nineteenth century had spent time studying

---

[7] Feinstein (1970) discusses the particularly materialistic tendencies in James' treatment of emotions, and relates them to James' own experiences of psychological illness.

[8] See Gardiner (1894); James (1894b), 526–9. [9] Quoted in Feinstein (1970), 134.

[10] Although Havelock Ellis in 1895 reported that there were two psychological laboratories in England, according both to Hearnshaw's and to Misiak and Sexton's histories of psychology, W. H. Rivers' Cambridge laboratory and Sully's at University College London were established in 1897. It is possible that Ellis had Galton's laboratory of 'anthropometry' in mind or, more likely, that Rivers and Sully introduced experimental work prior to the official founding of university-endorsed laboratories, and it is to such work that Ellis is referring. In any case there is little doubt that the only two locations of experimental psychology in England at the end of the nineteenth century were Cambridge and London. Cattell (1928), 547; Murphy (1929), 187; Hearnshaw (1964), 171–5; Misiak and Sexton (1966), 225–6; Ellis (1895a), 157.

in German laboratories. This was true of James and of James Mark Baldwin, for example. They, along with John Dewey, George Trumbull Ladd, David Irons and James McCosh, ensured that the debate on the nature of emotions became not only a professional psychological one but also predominantly an American one. The William James era in the construction of the concept of emotion was dominated, if not by just one man, then at least by one country.

James' famous paper 'What is an emotion?' was published in Bain's journal *Mind* in 1884. It was this paper that was reproduced (with several changes but with the core intact) as the chapter on emotion in the *Principles of Psychology* in 1890.[11] James' theory stated simply that the bodily changes that people had been inclined to call the 'expression' of an emotion were in fact the primary constituent cause of the emotion. The following famous passage communicated the thrust of the theory:

Our natural way of thinking about these standard emotions is that the mental perception of some fact excites the mental affection called the emotion, and that this latter state of mind gives rise to the bodily expression. My thesis on the contrary is that *the bodily changes follow directly the* PERCEPTION *of the exciting fact, and that our feeling of the same changes as they occur* IS *the emotion*. Common sense says, we lose our fortune, are sorry and weep; we meet a bear, are frightened and run; we are insulted by a rival, are angry and strike. The hypothesis here to be defended says that this order of sequence is incorrect, that the one mental state is not immediately induced by the other, that the bodily manifestations must first be interposed between, and that the more rational statement is that we feel sorry because we tremble, and not that we cry, strike or tremble, because we are sorry, angry or fearful, as the case may be. Without the bodily states following on the perception, the latter would be purely cognitive in form, pale, colourless, destitute of emotional warmth. We might then see the bear, and judge it best to run, receive the insult and deem it right to strike, but we would not actually *feel* afraid or angry.[12]

The emotion, then, was not originally a psychic act that then affected the body, but was originally a bodily state that was subsequently felt as an emotion. The final sentence of this quotation makes it clear that James was simply assuming that emotions were feelings (rather than, for instance, judgments or voluntary acts).

At the outset of the original article James had issued a disclaimer: 'I should say first of all that the only emotions I propose expressly to consider here are those that have a distinct bodily expression.'[13] This implied that there were some emotions that had a distinct bodily 'expression' (a most unfortunate choice of word, given the intended import of James' theory that the bodily aspects were anything but 'expressions')

[11] James (1981), II, 1058–97.   [12] James (1884), 189–90.   [13] James (1884), 189.

and some emotions that did not. Indeed, James at this point specified certain aesthetic feelings as examples of emotions with no distinct bodily 'expression'. However, James rapidly shifted to the more extreme position that 'a purely disembodied human emotion is a nonentity' (a position that had been hinted at by Darwin and others earlier in the century – see chapter 5). He continued, a mere five pages after his original disclaimer:

> The more closely I scrutinise my states, the more persuaded I become, that *whatever* moods, affections and passions I have are in very truth constituted by, and made up of those bodily changes we ordinarily call their expression or consequence; and the more it seems to me that if I were to become corporeally anaesthetic, I should be excluded from the life of the affections, *harsh and tender alike*, and drag out an existence of merely cognitive or intellectual form.[14]

Whereas initially James had acknowledged that some emotions had bodily expressions and others did not, his position was now that all emotions, however harsh or tender, passionate or aesthetic, not only had bodily expression but furthermore were nothing but that bodily expression – that they were indeed 'constituted by' the bodily changes involved. James' most acute and persistent contemporary critic on emotions, David Irons, a philosophy professor at Cornell University, picked up on this shifting of the ground: 'from the description of the emotional process at the close of the whole argument, one must infer that the theory, at first applied to the coarser emotions alone, is supposed to have been successfully applied to the others without modification'.[15]

At the end of the paper James returned to the moral, aesthetic and intellectual feelings that he had initially indicated were emotions not covered by his theory. He characterised these as 'purely cerebral' emotions (as opposed to the 'standard' visceral cases he had focussed on in the rest of the paper). The line he took now, however, was that in fact these were not emotions at all:

> Unless in them there actually be coupled with the intellectual feeling a bodily reverberation of some kind, unless we actually laugh at the neatness of the mechanical device, thrill at the justice of the act, or tingle at the perfection of the musical form, our mental condition is more allied to a judgment of *right* than to anything else. And such a judgment is to be classed among awarenesses of truth: it is a *cognitive* act.[16]

---

[14] James (1884), 194 (emphasis added). It is notable that James used the terms 'passions' and 'affections' in his 1884 article; he gives them no conceptual role or clear definition, however, and they are subsumed along with 'moods' and 'sentiments' under the broad category of 'emotions'.

[15] Irons (1894), 89.

[16] James (1884), 201–2. Late twentieth-century cognitive theorists of emotion such as Solomon or Oatley would agree with James here that such feelings are constituted by

The original claim seemed to have been an empirical one: that a large proportion of those mental states that were habitually called emotions, on examination, revealed themselves to be primarily constituted by instinctive visceral and behavioural activities, and to be only secondarily felt subjectively as emotions. This in itself was controversial enough given the reductionist use of 'constituted by' rather than 'invariably involve', say. But the still more dogmatic a priori claim that prevailed a few pages later was that anything that was not primarily constituted by visceral or behavioural disturbance was by definition not an emotion but a cognition.

At the end of the article, having considered an inconclusive case study of a man suffering from an 'hysterical anaesthesia', James presented the question again as an ultimately empirical one:

Of course this case proves nothing, but it is to be hoped that asylum-physicians and nervous specialists may begin methodically to study the relation between anaesthesia and emotional apathy. If the hypothesis here suggested is ever to be definitively confirmed or disproved it seems as if it must be by them, for they alone have the data in their hands.[17]

There was, then, systematic confusion in the 1884 version of James' theory between at least three different claims: first there was the a priori claim that an emotion was by definition something that involved bodily disturbances, and secondly there was the more reductionist version that stated that an emotion was 'constituted' by those disturbances. But both these claims denied that a mental state without bodily disturbances could rightly be called an emotion. The third claim was the empirical one that those states that were habitually or conventionally called 'emotions' (and were distinguished from non-emotions perhaps by their subjective feel) were in fact constituted by bodily changes – this was a claim that could be tested by physicians and nervous specialists. It is interesting to note two other features of the final two sentences of the 1884 article. First, there was the rhetorical use of the language of science – James described his theory as an 'hypothesis' to be confirmed or disproved by 'data'. Secondly, there was the assertion that the psychology of the emotions was now the business of physicians and nerve specialists rather than, for example, philosophers or theologians. This prejudice in favour of the language and practitioners of science, especially physical science, was a central topic of debate during this period, and was part of the new psychology's project

---

cognitive judgments rather than by bodily reverberations. The only difference would be that Solomon and Oatley would not then deny that such feelings were emotions, but would happily accept that some emotions are primarily cognitive. Solomon even goes so far as to define emotions as a species of judgment. Solomon (1993a); Oatley (1992).

[17] James (1884), 204.

of wresting the professional and cultural authority to define the mind and its emotions away from theologians and metaphysicians.

In the modified version of the *Mind* article (1884) that appeared in the *Principles* (1890), James added an explicit denial of 'materialism' – a label that had understandably been attached to the theory in the intervening six years. The passage started as follows: 'Let not this view be called materialistic. It is neither more nor less materialistic than any other view which says that our emotions are conditioned by nervous processes.'[18] However, this followed the very paragraph, part of the original article, in which James had forcefully stated his conviction that all affections, passions and moods were 'in very truth *constituted*, and *made up of*, those bodily changes we ordinarily call their expression or consequence'.[19] Being 'conditioned by' nervous processes is really not the same as being 'constituted and made up of' bodily processes, the latter being an altogether more reductionist description. James, furthermore, conceded that his was a 'sensational' theory – i.e. a theory in which emotions were products of sensations caused by external objects. The ground on which he claimed to have avoided materialism was that he did not deny the subjective felt experience of emotions:

But our emotions must always be *inwardly* what they are, whatever be the physiological ground of their apparition. If they are deep worthy spiritual facts on any conceivable theory of their physiological source, they remain no less deep pure spiritual and worthy of regard on this present sensational theory. They carry their own inner measure of worth with them; and it is just as logical to use the present theory of the emotions for proving that sensational processes need not be vile and material, as to use their vileness and materiality as a proof that such a theory cannot be true.[20]

James' theory unambiguously reduced emotions to products, even epiphenomena, of physical processes. Nothing in his disavowal of materialism denied that. He saw the 'spiritual fact' of emotional experience as purely a product of bodily changes, and such a view might reasonably be called at least an epiphenomenalist if not a materialistic account of the spiritual aspect of human life. Consistent with this, he explicitly opposed 'platonizers in psychology' – a term that presumably referred to spiritualistic dualists – whom he criticised for believing sensational processes to be vile or base.[21]

Specific criticisms of James' original theory will be expanded upon below, as will the notable contrast between emotion and cognition drawn

---

[18] James (1981), II, 1068.
[19] James (1981), II, 1068; James (1884), 194 (emphasis added).
[20] James (1981), II, 1068–9.   [21] James (1981), II, 1068–9.

by James. For the moment it will suffice to say that James' original theory of emotion (along with the similar reductionist bodily theory independently published by the Danish psychologist Carl F. Lange early in 1885) was simplistic, reductionist and clearly philosophically and empirically flawed. Gardiner described the original (1884) version of the theory as being more like 'a good joke than a serious scientific hypothesis'.[22] The original theory was competently and repeatedly refuted in books and journals by many psychologists and philosophers in its early years. And yet it remained the single most cited theory and the starting point for virtually all academic discussion of emotion from the early 1890s onwards, and arguably up until the present day.[23]

Phoebe Ellsworth, in a recent article celebrating the centenary of the *Psychological Review*, whose first issue carried James' 1894 restatement of his theory, defends James and casts him in the role of misunderstood genius.[24] Ellsworth considers that the 1894 restatement, 'The physical basis of emotion', dealt with the critiques of the original reductionist version, and suitably adjusted the theory. It is true that this later article is little known and seldom cited by anti-Jamesians, who tend to focus on the original article and its equally reductionist restatement in the *Principles*. Ellsworth may, however, have been over-generous in her judgment that James was not to blame for the widespread association of his name with the original reductionist version. It could reasonably be suggested, furthermore, that James' 1894 restatement was so liberal and vague as to be almost vacuous – the reductionist assertiveness of a decade earlier was replaced in 1894 by a mild, unexciting and ultimately capitulatory formulation. Retractions and second thoughts, especially vague and non-committal ones, are never as striking nor as memorable as bold, original, easily refutable ideas.[25]

One of the themes of this chapter, then, is the counter-Popperian persistence of James' flawed and falsified theory. Perhaps the best explanation for that persistence was offered by Baldwin in 1894: 'Undoubtedly the stimulating and highly valuable influence of James' treatment – here as on many other points – has been due to a certain frankness and *naïve* clearness which has concealed in a measure the real complexity

---

[22] Gardiner (1896), 102.
[23] Some of the many discussions of emotions that took James' theory (only occasionally acknowledging Lange) as their starting point were: Worcester (1892–3); Irons (1894); Gardiner (1894 and 1896); Baldwin (1894); Dewey (1894); Wright (1895). On the disproportionate emphasis on James' theory in twentieth-century works, see the Conclusions in chapter 8 in this volume.
[24] Ellsworth (1994).
[25] Feinstein (1970), 137–8, also finds the 1894 restatement unpersuasive.

of the problem.'[26] The simplicity of James' theory made it easy to understand and debate, unlike the more complex cognitive and component approaches to emotion.[27] It was a theory that could be reduced to easy sound-bites. Secondly, it gained appeal by its 'scientific' appearance – James gave priority in his philosophy of emotion to 'nerve centres' and to physiology.[28] Thirdly, and following on from this, James' physicalist theory gained credibility by its contrast with 'bad old' spiritualistic views of emotions. These views were linked with the sort of dualistic theological anthropology (endorsed by many of the thinkers discussed in chapter 6) in which priority was given to the spirit over the body. Psychological theories that elevated the body at the expense of the spirit supervened upon the institutional and disciplinary elevation of natural science, and the new experimental scientific psychology, at the expense of theology. James' reductionist theory of emotion was a proud, if flawed, monument to the new psychological profession on whose behalf James successfully campaigned. It was a symbol of cultural and intellectual changes more than it was a good account of those mental states that people called emotions.

James' critics: cognitive and component approaches 1884–1903

The publication of James' writings on emotion coincided with the foundation of university departments and professional journals of psychology in America and Europe. He was thus guaranteed a professional audience and institutional identity that had not been vouchsafed to earlier 'amateur' psychological writers. James' theory of emotion was the foundational emotion theory of the new professional science of psychology, and thus the earliest contribution to the psychological tradition, in the narrow sense, that developed in the succeeding decades. As the James scholar Howard Feinstein puts it, James drew 'on the discoveries of Darwin,

---

[26] Baldwin (1894), 610.
[27] E.g. Mercier (1884–5) is particularly prolix and involved – partly as a result of being based on the frequently impenetrable Spencerian psychology – when compared with James' snappy theory. On the Spencerian scheme of classification of feelings see chapter 5.
[28] William Woodward and others have argued that psychology did not in fact become established as a scientific discipline until the twentieth century, and that prior to that time the use of scientific language and categories borrowed from biology and physiology was merely pseudo-scientific. There certainly was a significant and varied rhetorical dimension in the use of 'scientific' language by nineteenth-century psychologists from Brown and Mill to Bain, Spencer, Maudsley and Darwin, and finally to James. See William Woodward's 'Introduction' to Woodward and Ash (eds.) (1982).

Lotze, Bain, Montegazza, and others to provide the laboratories of the "new psychology" with a testable theory of the emotions'.[29]

Although James' theory of emotions is by far the best remembered emotion theory of this period, it was by no means the only approach on offer at the time. Other early professional psychologists took quite different lines. The British philosopher and psychologist G. F. Stout's approach, in his *Analytic Psychology* (1896), was particularly interesting. In a chapter entitled 'Feeling and Conation' he discussed terminological issues. He said that the terms 'feeling' and 'conation' were introduced by the Scottish philosopher William Hamilton, who had suggested them as equivalents for the German words *Gefühl* and *Streben*. Stout expressed his concern that the word 'feeling' had too broad a connotation in English, including sensations, pains, pleasures, desires and aversions. It is striking that he also almost entirely avoided the terms 'emotion' and 'emotional' and preferred instead to talk of 'volitional' mental functions, which he described as desires for or aversions to particular cognised objects.[30] However, in his 1903 *Groundwork of Psychology*, he returned to the language of 'emotion', adopting a non-reductive view of emotions, criticising James' theory and insisting that the psychologist, unlike the physiologist, was interested in the 'inner point of view'.[31]

Another alternative approach was taken by the Cambridge psychologist James Ward. Ward was a Gifford lecturer on two occasions, taking *Naturalism and Agnosticism* (1899) and *Pluralism and Theism* (1911) as his themes. Ward, a Fellow of Trinity College, Cambridge, and a religious sympathiser with a non-conformist background, was a defender of a non-reductive view of emotions. In his *Psychological Principles* (1918) he trenchantly criticised the James–Lange theory, insisting that 'a state of emotion is a complete state of mind' and that 'The higher forms of emotion and action belong to the intellective and self-conscious level.'[32]

In fact, examining the early responses to James' theory made by his contemporaries between 1884 and 1903, reveals a picture of comprehensive criticism and substantial alternative theoretical approaches, almost all of which have been neglected by psychology and its historians for the past hundred years.[33] The same 1884 volume of *Mind* that carried James' article contained a response from his friend Edmund Gurney, a writer on philosophical and religious subjects with a particular interest in psychical research. Subsequent to Gurney's initial critique, it was David

---

[29] Feinstein (1970), 142.   [30] Stout (1902), ch. 6.
[31] Stout (1903), ch. 15, esp. 192–5.   [32] Ward (1918), ch. 11, esp. 276, 285.
[33] Only a relatively small number of these alternative emotion theories are discussed here. For surveys of these theories, up to around 1900, see Janet and Séailles (1902), II, 249–313; Irons (1903), ch. 1; Baldwin (ed.) (1905); Gardiner *et al.* (1970).

Irons and the physician William L. Worcester who produced the most telling direct attacks on James' original theory, as was evident from the place given to their arguments by James in his 1894 restatement. And it was Charles Mercier (see below), Irons, Ladd and Dewey who produced the most substantial and interesting alternative theoretical approaches to emotion.[34]

The arguments against James' theory are well known to anyone with an academic interest in emotions. What is perhaps less well known is that they had all been rehearsed several times by the mid-1890s. I will produce here a brief summary of eleven principal arguments against James, most of which can be found in Gurney's 1884 response in *Mind*, Worcester's 1892 *Monist* article, and Irons' 1894 *Mind* article.

1. The theory fails to distinguish emotions from non-emotions. It is perfectly possible to have awarenesses of bodily disturbances that are not emotions – for example the awareness of a shiver of cold or of a sneeze. Equally one can have emotions that are not awarenesses of bodily disturbances or reflex actions. Such emotions might include mild amusement, aesthetic feelings or longer-lasting ones such as grief. James even admits the latter point. In other words, a list of emotions compiled using James' definition that an emotion is an awareness of bodily disturbances would include states not commonly considered to be emotions (such as indigestion) and omit many states commonly considered to be emotions (especially aesthetic and moral feelings).[35]

2. The theory fails to differentiate between different emotions. If the theory were true, and emotions were really nothing but awarenesses of bodily changes, then, at least in the same subject, one set of bodily changes should uniformly give rise to the same emotion, and, by the same token, any one emotion could be associated only with one set of bodily changes. However, different emotions arise in connection with the same bodily and behavioural symptoms. For example, extremes of the opposite emotions of joy and grief are both accompanied by weeping. Also, the same emotion can be 'expressed' in many different ways. Since there is not a one-to-one correlation between emotions and determinate bodily disturbances it cannot be true that particular emotions are nothing more than awarenesses of particular bodily changes.[36]

---

[34] Dewey's theory is not examined in detail here. For some discussion of his views on emotions, see Tiles (1988), 36–42.

[35] Gurney (1884), 423–4; Stanley (1886), 76; Read (1886), 80; Worcester (1892–3), 288–9; Irons (1894), 78, 81, 88; Ladd (1894a), 561–2; Bryant (1896), 52–4, 56–7; Irons (1897), 478–9, 490.

[36] Worcester (1892–3), 289–91; Irons (1894), 86; Ladd (1894a), 548–9; Irons (1895c), 282–3; Irons (1897), 482.

3. Even if it is conceded that all emotions involve felt bodily changes in some way, it does not follow that all emotions are nothing but the feeling of those bodily changes, or that they are exhaustively 'constituted' by those changes; bodily affections can be seen as just one element in the compound emotion.[37]
4. The theory unnecessarily denies the role played by 'cognitive', 'ideational', or 'intellectual' factors in generating emotions and consequently makes too stark a contrast between cognition and emotion. Emotions are not excited just by an object's immediate reflex impact on the body but also by the cognitive evaluation of an object by an individual – by the individual's ideas, judgments and beliefs.[38]
5. The behaviours precipitated by the perception of an emotion-arousing object are, on James' theory, mere instinctive reflexes rather than voluntary actions (or reactions). This is morally as well as psychologically unacceptable in that it removes the will entirely from the sphere of emotions and their expression. Experience teaches that emotions are prior to their expression and that the extent to which we give vent to an emotion is a matter of voluntary control.[39]
6. James' theory is either an unfalsifiable truism – emotions are by definition only those states that are perceptions of bodily changes, therefore potential counter-examples are dismissed as non-emotions – or is simply false, since James himself admits that there are aesthetic and moral emotions that have no bodily 'expression'.[40]
7. If, as James admits, reflex responses vary indefinitely between individuals, and, as his theory states, emotions are constituted by those reflex reactions, then there should be correspondingly an indefinite number of different emotions. However, we find that there is a determinate number of different emotions experienced by human beings. Therefore, assuming that James is right about the variability of reflex response, his theory of emotion must be false.[41]
8. The empirical evidence that James himself states to be crucial in confirming or disproving his theory is at best ambiguous. There are no clear-cut cases of complete somatic anaesthesia, and in the various cases of partial anaesthesia unearthed by James and his supporters (especially the French psychiatrist Paul Sollier) it is not clear that the subjects have no emotional life whatever, nor that their apparent

---

[37] Gurney (1884), 421; Worcester (1892–3), 288; Irons (1894), 77, 79, 81; Ladd (1894a), 535–7, 548; Gardiner (1894), 548; Dewey (1895), 15–18; Stratton (1895), 173; McLennan (1895), 465; Bryant (1896), 55.
[38] Gurney (1884), 425–6; Worcester (1892–3), 296–7; Ladd (1894a), 550–1; Baldwin (1894), 619; Dewey (1895), 15–18; McLennan (1895), 466; Irons (1895b), 298–9.
[39] Stanley (1886), 70–1, 76; Irons (1895c), 284; Irons (1897), 251.
[40] Irons (1894), 89; Gardiner (1896), 106–7. [41] Irons (1894), 82; Irons (1895a), 96.

emotional apathy might not be due to cognitive impairment rather than to a lack of visceral sensation.[42]

9. James' theory presupposes that the bodily and mental aspects of emotions must be related as cause and effect. He proceeds to advocate the view that the bodily aspects are the cause and the mental aspects the effect, and to criticise the apparent alternative that the mental aspects cause the bodily. However, the bodily and mental aspects need not be in a cause-and-effect relationship at all – they could be regarded as independent but concomitant, perhaps in terms of psychophysical parallelism or of association; or as two sides of a single event.[43]

10. James requires us to accept that the bodily changes follow directly the perception of the exciting object, without the intervention of any mental process. No mechanism is proposed for this chain of events (why one object rather than another sets off a particular reflex) and so the statement explains nothing. In the absence of such a mechanism or explanation, it seems more rational to suppose that cognitive and volitional factors, such as memories, beliefs or desires, must intervene between the perception of the object and the consequent bodily changes and movements.[44]

11. The notion of 'bodily changes' is too vague to perform such a central role in a theory of emotions.[45]

These were the most important arguments with which James' original theory of emotion was attacked. They were rehearsed many times in all the important psychological journals. One might consider that, almost however loose or strict a definition one cares to give to the word, James' theory had been 'refuted'. James' 1894 response, while presented as a plea that he had been misunderstood, amounted in reality to little more than an abject surrender. If relying on the standard histories of psychology, however, one could be forgiven for believing that most people – certainly most psychologists – assented to the James–Lange theory of emotion between 1884 and its refutation by Cannon's experimental work in the 1910s and 1920s.[46] In fact, by any reasonable logical and empirical criteria, the theory should have been dead by 1894.

The case of the persistence of the Jamesian view of emotion in psychology and its histories despite its refutation and its author's subsequent climb-down, is a good example of how the history of psychology, like

---

[42] Sollier (1894), 241–66; Gurney (1884), 421; Berkley (1891); Worcester (1892–3), 292–5; Irons (1894), 87; Gardiner (1894), 545; Irons (1895a), 96–7.
[43] Stanley (1886), 70; Irons (1895c), 283.
[44] Worcester (1892–3), 287–8; Irons (1894), 79; Irons (1895c), 280.
[45] Irons (1895c), 283.   [46] E.g. Lyons (1980), 16; see Cannon (1915 and 1927).

the history of other sciences, is not best characterised as a process of straightforward logical progress.[47] By most 'internalist' accounts, especially a Popperian one, refuted theories are discarded. But this did not happen in the case of James' theory. Indeed, the alternative theories, emphasising cognitive factors in the generation of emotion, and suggesting a component approach to emotions that acknowledged mental as well as bodily, evaluative as well as reflex, subjective as well as objective elements in emotion, seemed empirically superior whether one's data were introspective or clinical or both. So why did James' theory persist, and why is it remembered in the history of psychology at the expense of the theories of McCosh, Mercier, Irons, Ladd and Dewey? Before returning to attempt to answer that question, some of the alternative theories will be briefly outlined (see chapter 6 for an account of McCosh's theory).

Charles Mercier (1852–1919)

In the same 1884 volume of *Mind* as James' often-quoted article 'What is an emotion?' are to be found the first two of the English writer and physician Charles Mercier's three never-quoted articles: 'A classification of feelings I, II and III'.[48] Mercier's concern was, as the title of the articles revealed, the classification of 'feelings', rather than definition or causal explanation of 'emotions'. The writers to whom Mercier referred included Reid, Kant, Hamilton, Herbart and Wundt.[49] Mercier was especially dependent on Spencer's psychology and it is from Spencer that he adopted the practice of using the term 'feeling' to refer to all mental states.[50] Emotions were a subset of feelings, specifically feelings indirectly corresponding with an interaction between an organism and its environment. In other words, they were second-order feelings about feelings rather than primary sensations.[51] In fact Mercier's three articles, despite their title, were almost exclusively taken up with classifying second-order feelings – in other words, emotions.

Mercier's theory was a cognitive one. Like Irons (see below) he stated that the nature of an emotion depended on how the relation between the organism and its environment was 'cognised'. Mercier provided a

---

[47] Contrast the claim for 'cumulative' progress in emotion theories made by Mandler (1984), 15; on this, see the Introduction to this volume.
[48] Mercier (1884a, 1884b and 1885). Mercier also wrote on philosophy, criminology, insanity, lunatic asylums and spiritualism. He was opposed, on rationalist grounds, to Oliver Lodge's spiritualism; Bowler (2001), 100.
[49] Mercier (1884a), 330–1.
[50] For Spencer's own views, see chapter 5 in this volume.   [51] Mercier (1884a), 335.

complex and comprehensive classification of emotions in terms of the different cognitions that brought them about. His treatment of terror was representative of this approach:

> To take an example: the feeling of Terror which, I say, arises on the cognition of the accessibility of the organism to a noxious agent of overwhelming power, will not arise unless the accessibility is cognised, nor unless the noxiousness is cognised. But this is not all... [F]or this feeling to assume the gravity of Terror a further cognition must be added. The power of the agent must be cognised as overwhelming. The concurrence of these three cognitions is a necessary prerequisite of the feeling of Terror.[52]

The importance of bodily disturbances was not considered by Mercier at all. The conditions for the arousal of emotion were purely cognitive.

Secondly, Mercier's work provides a good example of the rhetorical use of the language of evolutionary science in psychology. He introduced his scheme as an evolutionary one: 'Those who admit the development of mind by evolution should... not need, any more than the botanist or the zoologist, a laboured demonstration that the states resulting from this process should be classified in accordance with it.'[53] Each emotion was considered to be a response of the organism to its environment; which emotion was experienced depended on how the environment was cognised. However no attempt was made to establish empirically the function of emotions in animals and humans in the course of evolution, nor to suggest in what order they emerged and why. In fact the use of the language of 'zoology' and 'evolution' was merely a rhetorical gloss on a philosophically conceived cognitive theory of emotion – a theory developed on the basis of introspection and analysis. The same was true of Mercier's use of 'class', 'sub-class', 'order' and 'genus' in his classification of the feelings – they were simply borrowed terms applied to mental states to give the impression of a scientific approach.[54] In a similar way, he consistently referred to the 'organism' rather than to the 'person', despite the fact that he was discussing only human emotions. In short, Mercier's 'science of psychology' – in some ways like the mental science of the Scottish empiricists before him – was scientific through methodological analogies and borrowed terms, but not through the application of outward experiment and observation, nor through the search for physical causes.[55] Where Brown, for example, had borrowed terms, methods and authority from chemistry – the most exciting scientific enterprise in turn-of-the-century Edinburgh – Mercier borrowed from the new science of the moment, evolutionary biology.

---

[52] Mercier (1884a), 341–2. [53] Mercier (1884a), 334.
[54] E.g. Mercier (1884b), 509. [55] Mercier (1884a), 325.

David Irons (1870–1907)

Irons is another notable absentee from the official history of psychology (he gets one footnote in Gardiner et al. (1970), but this is a reference to his comments on Descartes, rather than to his own thought on emotions and his place in the debates of the William James era).[56] Much of his contribution to the debate was a negative one, tirelessly attacking other people's theories, especially the James–Lange hypothesis. However he also made a positive contribution, especially in two articles for the *Philosophical Review* on 'The nature of emotion' in 1897, which formed the basis of his 1903 book *The Psychology of Ethics*.

Irons' distinctive understanding of emotions can be very briefly summarised: an emotion was an unanalysable fact of consciousness – 'an ultimate and primary aspect of mind' – not reducible to cognition, desire, pleasure–pain nor to bodily feeling, nor to any combination of these elements; an emotion was a 'phase or aspect' of the whole person, a 'feeling-attitude' towards a 'cognised' situation.[57] Finally, an emotion was not a passive feeling of an external object (i.e. not mere 'receptivity' as in James' theory) but a 'centrally initiated reaction'; emotions had a central rather than a peripheral origin; they were 'attitudes' that people adopt, not impressions made upon them from without.[58]

While Irons, unlike McCosh, Ladd and others, rejected a component or 'compound' approach to emotions, he did acknowledge that there were certain 'conditions' frequently associated with the occurrence of emotion, such as cognition, pleasure–pain or physical excitement. His view that emotions were irreducible, unanalysable aspects of mind, however, precluded the view that these conditions were elements, or constituents, that combined by some form of 'quasi-chemical combination' or 'chemical fusion' to produce the emotion.[59] Only one of these conditions of emotion was 'essential', and that was the 'intellectual condition'.[60] The object or situation towards which the emotion was directed must be 'cognised' as hateful or fearful, or in whatever other appropriate way, before an emotion was experienced. This cognition Irons referred to as the 'spiritual element' in his 1894 critique of James but by 1897 this had become the 'intellectual condition' or 'cognitive element'.[61]

Irons' non-Jamesian account of emotion was the result of a non-Jamesian psychological methodology. Irons privileged introspection. In considering the weaknesses of various alternative approaches to emotions he singled out reductionist methodology as the common deficiency:

---

[56] Gardiner et al. (1970), 162n.   [57] Irons (1894), 94–7; (1897).
[58] Irons (1897), 246–50.   [59] Irons (1897), 248, 489.
[60] Irons (1897), 493.   [61] Irons (1894), 83–4; (1897), 493, 496.

The root of the trouble seems to be that emotion is explained away before a serious effort is made to ascertain with accuracy its real nature. In attempting to rectify this omission, we must begin with an examination of the fact as it appears in consciousness. It is evident that direct observation alone affords absolutely reliable information with regard to the qualitative distinctions of psychical states.[62]

James would have agreed that 'direct observation' was the key to understanding the emotions, but the difference lay in the divergent views of what constituted proper psychological observation. Irons relied on introspective observation and hence produced a primarily descriptive, qualitative, mentalistic psychology. James, on the other hand, privileged a sense of observation derived from the physical sciences – quantitative observations of the body, especially its nerves and its outward behaviour – in addition to giving a necessary but limited role to introspection.

George Trumbull Ladd (1842–1921)

If the neglect of McCosh, Mercier and Irons by standard histories of psychology is surprising, then the extent to which the life and teachings of G. T. Ladd have been overlooked is really astonishing.[63] Ladd was one of the most important figures in the foundation of the new psychological profession in America in the 1880s and 1890s, despite being a trenchant critic of what he perceived to be the materialism and determinism of James' 'cerebral science'. He held the chair in philosophy at Yale from 1881 to 1905, founded the psychological laboratory there in 1892, was the second president of the American Psychological Association, and was described by the American experimental psychologist James McKeen Cattell as, along with G. Stanley Hall and William James, sharing 'the honor of leading in the development of psychology in America'.[64] Ladd's *Elements of Psychology* (1887) was a major textbook for two decades.[65] His treatment of emotions and sentiments in his second major text, *Psychology, Descriptive and Explanatory* (1894) was an original and thorough alternative to the Jamesian theory. Yet Ladd does not figure at all in Gardiner *et al.*'s history of theories of emotions, and is only mentioned once by Brett to record the simple fact that he published a textbook in 1887.

The historian of psychology A. A. Roback has characterised Ladd as 'the last of the Church Mohicans', and calls him a 'pre-scientific' 'preacher-psychologist'. It is true that Ladd had been a Christian minister and preacher for ten years before turning to academic philosophy and

[62] Irons (1897), 243.
[63] Ladd's biographer, perhaps unsurprisingly, agrees; Mills (1969), vii.
[64] Roback (1962), 174; Cattell (1928), 547.
[65] For a further summary of Ladd's achievements and importance, see Mills (1969), 1–10.

thence psychology. He published *The Doctrine of Sacred Scripture* (1883) and, later, *The Philosophy of Religion* (1905). Roback gives the following dismissive summary of Ladd's work: 'To Ladd, psychology was not a natural science. Ladd was still the soul psychologist, or if we wish to be gracious, we might say he was a personalist.'[66] Roback clearly intends the epithets 'preacher-psychologist' and 'soul psychologist' to be derogatory ones, hence the generous offer to save Ladd's honour by allowing him to be denominated a 'personalist'. Although few historians of psychology have been as explicitly anti-religious as Roback, it is interesting to wonder how widely (albeit tacitly) the assumption that religious thinkers do not belong in the authentic history of psychology has shaped the historiography of psychology.

Ladd's psychology was, like most psychology produced by Christian believers in the nineteenth century, predicated upon mind–body dualism. It is also interesting to note that his chapter on emotions in the *Psychology* (1894) was entitled 'The emotions and passions', the latter word being one that had resonance within the Christian tradition but which was virtually never used in psychological circles by the end of the nineteenth century. His theory of emotions concentrated on the intellectual elements in emotion – 'the dependence of the higher emotions and sentiments on the intellectual processes of memory, imagination and thinking is obvious and immediate' – and viewed emotions as compounds with various components or, as Ladd called them, 'variables'. Ladd's four variables were 'primitive feeling', 'bodily resonance', 'ideation and thought', and fourthly, in the more complex emotions, primary emotions.[67] Ladd's theory closely resembled, then, that of McCosh, whose era at Princeton overlapped considerably with Ladd's career at Yale.[68] Both included feeling, idea and bodily affection as three of the four elements in emotion.

The main difference between McCosh's and Ladd's theories was that the former's was more static, written in the tradition of Scottish faculty psychology and its meticulously 'botanical' categorisation of mental faculties, whereas Ladd's introduced a developmental element, albeit somewhat crudely. In the cases of anger, grief, joy, astonishment, curiosity and sympathy Ladd applied the same developmental model, tracing in each case the transition from basic 'animal' versions of the emotion in animals, infants and 'savages' to the cultured and intellectual 'sentiments' of civilised men. What we might generally term 'surprise' was described by Ladd as ranging from 'animal astonishment' to 'intellectual wonder'; jealousy was described as a spectrum between the jealousy of 'lower animals

---

[66] Roback (1962), 174.   [67] Ladd (1894a), 534–7.
[68] The period of overlap was c.1881–94.

and children' and that religious sentiment displayed by those souls who are 'jealous for God'.[69] So Ladd revealed his inheritance of a traditional Christian distinction between disorderly animal passions and spiritual, intellectual and Godly affections. The only difference was that Ladd tended to use 'emotions' where the traditional term would have been 'passions', and 'sentiments' where Edwards and others would have used 'affections':

> In general, great intensity and consequent strong 'bodily resonance' are characteristics of the emotions and passions. A much lower intensity, and a far larger admixture of influence from ideal considerations, are characteristic of the sentiments... In applying the word 'ideal' to the sentiments we should understand that these affective phenomena are the farthest possible distant from such relatively simple and content-less feelings as man has in common with the lower animals... But by calling the sentiments 'spiritual' forms of feeling, we mean to emphasise in a positive way the very thing which we emphasise negatively when we say that they *are not*, like the emotions, obviously built upon a basis of somatic reactions. They *are*, of all our affective phenomena, most obviously ascribed purely to a highly generalised and abstract conception of the *Ego*, considered as freed from all dependence on the bodily organism.[70]

It is interesting that Ladd appears not to have been familiar with the traditional distinction between passions and affections and seems, rather, to have reinvented it in his distinction between 'emotions and passions' and 'sentiments'.[71] His 'sentiments', like Augustine's, Edwards' and Wesley's 'affections', were full of ideas and reason and hence marked humanity out as superior to the lower animals, and as a 'spiritual' creature.

While Ladd clearly had one foot in the territory of traditional Christian psychology, his other foot was well inside the territory of the new Jamesian view of emotions. While he dissented from the reductionist theory as a whole, he shared with James and others the belief, *not* found in traditional Christian psychologies, that there was 'no form of sentiment – not even the most ideal, whether in the class of the ethical, or the aesthetical, or the religious feelings – which is not tinged with some discernible form of the same so-called bodily resonance which is so much more obvious in the coarser emotional states'.[72] Irons took the same view, describing the claim that all emotions were necessarily accompanied by bodily changes as 'the harmless statement of a matter of fact which nobody denies'.[73] Even if James' theory of emotion itself has generally only been remembered in order to be repeatedly refuted, his assumption that all emotions, harsh or tender, involved bodily disturbances of some kind – whether contingently

---

[69] Ladd (1894a), 538–42. [70] Ladd (1894a), 543, 561.
[71] For a discussion of other thinkers who reinvented the passions–affections distinction in new ways, see chapter 6 in this volume.
[72] Ladd (1894a), 543. [73] Irons (1894), 89.

or by definition – is a doctrine that gained consensus amongst psychologists of all kinds in the late nineteenth century, and which has persisted to the present day.

Science and religion in the William James era

The science of the mind

As has already been shown, in the eighteenth and earlier nineteenth centuries the 'science of the mind' was advocated not as a reductionist, physicalist or mathematical enterprise but primarily as an enterprise that applied induction and analysis to the mind qua mind. This science of the mind was a science because it discovered chains of cause and effect amongst mental states, as a physicist would discover physical causes and effects; because it analysed mental states into their elementary components, as a chemist would analyse compounds into elements; because it categorised mental states into orders and classes, as a naturalist would categorise plants and animals; and because it was based on (introspective) observations of mental states (or 'experimental' knowledge) and induction from these to general theories of mind, just as all science was supposed to be based on observations and induction. There was relatively little dissent from the goal of producing a 'science of mind', the question was which science to emulate – botany, natural history, chemistry, evolutionary biology, or even physics?

It was only now, in the heyday of the 'warfare between science and religion' (as popularised by Thomas Huxley, John Tyndall, Henry Maudsley, Leslie Stephen and others) that to be an advocate of a scientific psychology increasingly meant to be both an opponent of soul–body dualism and an advocate of an experimental and physicalist psychology. It was those who made the step from the 'halfway house' endorsement of a mentalistic science of mind to the demand that psychology become a physical science of mind who have generally been remembered as the founders of scientific psychology. James' view was in this, however, as in other matters, not entirely consistent.[74]

In a highly critical review of Ladd's *Psychology, Descriptive and Explanatory* (1894), James made it clear that he wished to see psychology move on from what one might call the botany of the soul (in which Ladd was characterised as being engaged) to a truly scientific stage in which causal explanations were given priority over introspective descriptions of mental states. James called introspectionist psychology 'a mere narrative of the

[74] Skrupskelis (1995).

spiritual being... developing according to its... unique laws'.⁷⁵ Psychology was crying out, James said, for a Galileo or a Lavoisier to transform it, or perhaps for a Darwin: 'And as the theories of inheritance have killed the taxonomic and biographic view of natural history by merely superseding it, and reduced the older books of classification to mere indexes, so will the descriptive psychologies be similarly superseded the moment some genuinely causal psycho-physic theory comes upon the stage.'⁷⁶ Elsewhere, in a review of Sully's *The Human Mind* (1892), James made the same criticism of introspection, calling for the causes of mental states to be investigated. Authors of introspectionist works of psychology might reasonably have replied that they did establish the causes of mental states, according to the laws of association; it just so happened that those causes were themselves mental. Irons, for example, held that the 'real cause' of emotional experience was the 'intellectual condition' of the subject.⁷⁷ It was implicit in James' criticisms of introspection and description, however, that real causes were necessarily physical causes, and it was his view in 1892 that, 'if psychology is ever to become scientific, as other sciences are scientific, it must mainly concern itself with causes'.⁷⁸ The rhetoric he used of causes, explanations, going beyond mere description of the spiritual and developing psycho-physical techniques (alluding to Wundt's Leipzig laboratory of 'psycho-physics') was indicative of his desire that psychology should free itself from religious 'soul' psychology and spiritual introspection and make the transition from being a science by analogy to being a natural science proper.⁷⁹ Two years earlier, in the *Principles*, as Skrupskelis has emphasised, James had been much more cautious. Then he had denied that psychology should be in the business of discovering causes at all; instead he had described psychology as a science concerned with establishing, in the absence of metaphysical explanations, merely the correlations of 'various sorts of thought and feeling with definite conditions of the brain'.⁸⁰ It is also ironic that later, in the *Varieties*, James' own method became classificatory and 'botanical' rather than physical and causal.⁸¹

Ladd was one of those who continued to fight against the reduction of psychology to a physical science. He was a defender of interactionist dualism and of the belief that, while the mind took its direction from the action of the physical element of the body, it also proceeded to unfold powers of its own that were bound by their own mental rather than physical laws. Ladd wrote two articles in the early 1890s on whether psychology could

---

[75] James (1894a), 292–3. [76] James (1894a), 292–3.
[77] Irons (1897), 484. [78] James (1892a), 286.
[79] On James' opposition to soul psychology, see Skrupskelis (1995), 80–1, 83.
[80] James (1981), 1, 6; Skrupskelis (1995), 74–7, 85.
[81] See n.5 above and Proudfoot (1989), esp. 159–67.

be considered a natural science.⁸² Both were directed specifically against James' assertion that it could. These were followed in 1895 by Ladd's *Philosophy of Mind: An Essay in the Metaphysics of Psychology* in which he set out again to defend the independent existence of mind, and the inappropriateness of the attempt to make psychology a natural science rather than a science of the mind qua mind.⁸³ Irons had also dismissed the idea that psychology could be a natural science as a 'delusion', and had ridiculed James for thinking that the principles of physics could be applied equally to mind as to matter.⁸⁴

Those who, like Ladd and Irons, continued to insist that mind (or psyche, soul or spirit) was not a physical thing and so could not be studied by physical methods, and especially those who wrote from a more or less explicitly religious point of view, gradually faded from view under the sort of rhetorical attacks mounted by influential figures such as Maudsley and James and have largely been forgotten. Spiritualistic botany and mentalistic chemistry of the mind were thus overtaken by the physical and experimental sciences of brain and behaviour. As one Christian critic of scientific psychology later put it, 'these writers...pretend to construct the science of the soul without a soul'.⁸⁵

In the case of theories of emotion, McCosh, Irons, Ladd and Mercier were only four of many (the majority) of writers on emotions in the 1880s and 1890s who dissented from the James–Lange theory, proposing theories that laid more stress on cognitive (or 'ideational') elements of emotion, or on the complex and multi-componential nature of emotions, or even on their moral, spiritual, religious and aesthetic dimensions. The only ways in which these writers could be said to have failed to be 'scientific' was in failing to give priority to physical processes – especially neurophysiology – and in failing to privilege observations of publicly observable behaviour, bodily arousal and emotional expression over observations of mental states.

This sort of exclusive privileging of scientific language and methods in psychology was also evident in a review of the debate between James and Irons on the nature of emotion written by the English physician and essayist Havelock Ellis. He dismissed Irons' critique of James in the following strident terms:

Unfortunately, however, for the writer of it, problems of modern psychology require something more than a merely logical equipment; they require a very considerable physiological and even pathological equipment of which Mr Irons is

---

⁸² Ladd (1892 and 1894b).
⁸³ On the debate between James and Ladd on the issue of whether psychology was a natural science, see Mills (1969), 119–30; Skrupskelis (1995), 78–85.
⁸⁴ Irons (1894), 92n.   ⁸⁵ Stalker (1914), 38.

obviously innocent. He takes for granted that 'coarse' physical disturbances cannot produce 'delicate' emotions, regardless of the fact that physical disturbances may be too delicate for the psychic apparatus to register. And he also assumes, without even question, that melancholia has no physical basis. *It is evident that a writer with such notions is not competent to discuss the nature of emotion. Something else is required than mere logical quibbling.*[86]

Independently of the question of the merit of each of Irons' arguments, it is striking to find his contribution being dismissed out of hand as incompetent because based on logic and philosophy rather than on physiology. Not only did Ellis imply that no psychologist was competent who believed that any aspect of mind could be treated independently of the body, he also implied that no one but a physiological psychologist was competent to discuss the nature of emotion at all. Such aggressive rhetorical separatism may have been a symptom of the insecurity of a young discipline seeking autonomy from philosophy and seeking its own scientific status – Irons was to be excluded from the psychological community because of his job (he was a philosopher) and because of his metaphysics (he was a non-reductionist). Ellis went on to recommend Paul Sollier's treatment of emotion which was, he said, 'of far greater value, because experimental in character'.[87]

Another example of such views was to be found in a paper discussing the nature of emotion in the journal *Brain* in 1895: 'It is the signal merit of Prof. James to have recognised that the physiological element is the predominant element in the emotions, and that the problem of the nature of the emotions is *essentially* a physiological problem... *Obviously* the easiest way to approach the study of the emotions is to proceed by the method of physiological experiment.'[88] It was a sign of the physicalist bias of the times that it could be considered obvious that physiology was the easiest way to gain knowledge about our emotions. It would not have been obvious to Edwards, Butler, Reid, Brown or James Mill, nor even to Bain or Spencer, that the passions, affections or emotions were best approached physiologically and experimentally rather than mentalistically and through introspection.

It was, then, a prejudice of several writers on emotion of the later nineteenth century to elevate science above philosophy and theology in matters of psychology and to equate science with 'physical science', just as James, at some points, identified 'cause' with 'physical cause'. It is suggested in this chapter that it was by their appeal to this prejudice that physicalist theories of emotion came to dominate in the new schools of

---

[86] Ellis (1895b), 160 (emphasis added).   [87] Ellis (1895b), 160.
[88] Wright (1895), 217 (emphasis added).

psychology and, ultimately, why James' theory of emotions and not that of McCosh, Irons or Ladd is studied by psychology students today. James' theory of emotions should be seen as part of a rhetorical and professional project to establish psychology as a physical science detached from its roots in various Christian, theistic and philosophical enterprises.

Reason and the emotions

The metaphors of the Jamesian theory – that emotions were constituted from 'below' and from the 'outside' by the involuntary activity of the viscera and the peripheral nervous system – bore a certain resemblance to those used in the Augustinian model of the person in which reason and truth were to be found by turning inwards and upwards, ultimately towards God, while the passions were movements of the 'outer man' who was bodily, sensual and 'below'.[89] The fact that James, furthermore, did not consider reason, or 'cognition', to be an instinct or a peripheral phenomenon like emotion, but a cerebral function, suggests that his model of emotions had something in common with traditional Christian ideas about the passions. James himself explicitly made the analogy between modern scientific and classical Christian psychologies: 'Cognition and emotion are parted even in this last retreat – who shall say that their antagonism may not be just one phase of the world-old struggle known as that between the spirit and the flesh? – a struggle in which it seems pretty certain that neither party will drive the other off the field.'[90] The traditional dichotomy between reason and the passions was embodied by James in the distinction between 'cerebral' cognition and 'visceral' emotion.[91] There were several important differences, however, between the Jamesian view and traditional Christian psychology. First, reason, affections and passions were all ultimately faculties of the soul in Christian psychology – even bodily passions were the result of a fallen and disordered will, quite the opposite of being 'constituted' by bodily activity.[92] Secondly, James' theory of emotions was expressed in language that was quite autonomous from traditional Christian teaching. It was constructed in the atheological language of science – the language of nerve centres, of musculature and viscera, of stimuli and responses, of hypothesis and data. Thirdly, James' theory was of the 'emotions' and

---

[89] See Augustine (1961), XIII and (1991), XII.
[90] James (1884), 203.   [91] James (1884), 201–2.
[92] It was the sinful soul that made the flesh corruptible, not the corruptible flesh that made the soul sinful. The fact that the devil harbours vicious passions of pride and envy also proves that disobedient flesh is not even a necessary part of sinful passions. For both of these points, see Augustine (1952), XIV.3.

not of the 'passions', and thus sought to involve bodily disorder in a much larger class of phenomena (including affections and sentiments) than had ever been done by Christian psychologists. Finally, the distinction between works of the spirit and works of the flesh functions in the Christian tradition to distinguish between two different states of the whole soul – grace/salvation and nature/sin – not between two faculties of the soul; it is not, therefore, the same as the distinction between reason and the passions.

While the new science of psychology had some success in moving away from mind–body dualism, there was little development in the deconstruction of the reason–emotion dichotomy. Indeed, as had been argued above, the adoption of the psychology of Thomas Brown, with its large category of 'emotions', all of which were contrasted with intellectual states, resulted in a starker dichotomy than had existed in the Christian tradition. In addition to being embodied in James' distinction between cerebral cognition and visceral emotion, the dichotomy was reinforced in several other ways during this period. Courmont, for example, in his *Le Cervelet et ses Fonctions* (1892) made a stark division between the cognitive functions of the cerebrum and the emotional functions of the cerebellum.[93] Many textbooks of psychology reinforced the division through the way the material was arranged. Bain, McCosh, Sully and Baldwin all produced two-volume textbooks of psychology that were amongst the most widely used. And all devoted volume one to the senses and the intellect, volume two to the emotions, feeling and will.[94] Not only was the division reinforced by dividing the two faculties into separate books, but the traditionally supposed priority of reason was implied by the first volume always being devoted to intellect and the second to emotion. Another example of the prevalence of belief in the separability of intellect and emotion was in the widely discussed psychiatric condition known as 'emotional insanity' or 'moral insanity', in which the subject's reasoning abilities were unimpaired but his or her emotional reactions were severely disordered and unpredictable.[95]

All these indications of the tendency towards intellect–emotion dualism in the emotions paradigm of the nineteenth century serve to

---

[93] See James (1892b).
[94] Bain (1855 and 1859); McCosh (1886 and 1887); Baldwin (1891); Sully (1892).
[95] For a report of the debate between Bucknill and Carpenter on emotional insanity, see Bucknill (1874). For an interesting discussion by Daniel Hack Tuke of various case studies drawn from his own experience in the York Retreat (founded by his great-grandfather, William Tuke) and in his practice as a consultant physician in London, see Tuke (1886). See also Skultans (1975), ch. 6; Skultans (1979), 65–8; Berrios (1996), 313–14, 426–7.

qualify Kurt Danziger's claim that one of the principal characteristics of the new concept of emotion in the nineteenth century was that it overcame the old reason–passion dichotomy.[96] If anything the emotions paradigm tended towards an even stronger contrast, given that the concept of affections, which had, in effect, been 'rational passions', had been discarded. This meant that in the Jamesian paradigm all the various affections and sentiments of more traditional psychologies were merged with the passions into the single non-cognitive bodily category of emotion.

We have seen above that some writers on emotion – frequently writers with religious commitments – took a much more positive view of the connection of cognition and emotion, specifically noting the role of ideas in arousing emotions. This might be best seen as a continuation of the tradition of teaching on the affections which, in the words of John Wesley, are 'full of the highest order and reason'.[97] Christian writers such as McCosh and Ladd perpetuated cognitive teaching on emotions, reducing them 'upwards', in the same tradition as Edwards and Wesley, by concentrating on what had been known as the 'affections'. The new scientific psychologists, however, notably Bain, James and Baldwin, reinforced the dichotomy between cognition and emotion by concentrating their attention on what previously been denominated 'passions'.

The new science of emotions

This chapter has told the story of the endorsement of an epiphenomenal and visceral emotions theory by the nascent academic psychological community. Along with chapter 6, it has also demonstrated how, in the second half of the nineteenth century, there were many anti-physicalist emotions theories that have been forgotten by historians of psychology, possibly in part as a result of their tendency to search for the 'precursors' of today's secular academic psychology. The neglect of anti-physicalist writers has resulted in cognitive and compound approaches such as those of Mercier, Irons and Ladd being forgotten.

It should now be clear that while a list of passions and affections of the soul from the start of the eighteenth century and a list of emotions from the end of the nineteenth century might contain many of the same items, such as anger, fear, joy, sorrow, hope, pride and so on, the underlying understanding of the person had been utterly transformed. 'Emotions' belonged (predominantly) to the psychology of a new sort of secular

[96] Danziger (1997), 39–42.   [97] Quoted in Clapper (1989), 59.

worldview, which was made up of new ontological and epistemological assumptions and new stories and metaphors derived from the sciences of matter. By the end of the nineteenth century, ideas that had started as 'halfway house' analogies between emotions and sensations, emotions and mechanisms, and between the sciences of mind and matter, had become tenets of the creed of physicalist psychologists.

8 Conclusions: how history can help us think about 'the emotions'

> Historically this term [emotion] has proven utterly refractory to definitional efforts; probably no other term in psychology shares its nondefinability with its frequency of use.
>
> A. S. Reber, *The Penguin Dictionary of Psychology*, 234

Recapitulation: an enriched history of emotion theories

Of all the theories of emotions produced in the nineteenth century, William James' theory was the only one that became famous and influential within academic psychology. James' theory is still the starting point for much contemporary theory and research into emotions.[1] Philosophers and psychologists of emotions of the last two decades, such as William Lyons, Rom Harré, Patricia Greenspan, Keith Oatley, Robert Solomon, Jon Elster and Peter Goldie, all relate their ideas to James' theory of emotions.[2] Many contemporary theorists also refer to Darwin's work on expression, but they generally refer to no nineteenth-century emotions theorists other than these two.[3] In the last three decades, those who have for various reasons appealed to the theories of passions and emotions of the past, have tended to refer to an increasingly stale canon of past theorists including Aristotle, Descartes, Hume, Spinoza, Darwin, James and Wundt.[4]

The neglect by philosophers, psychologists and historians of psychology and philosophy of other philosophical and, especially, religiously oriented writers on the passions, affections and emotions during the eighteenth and nineteenth centuries and, especially, during the

---

[1] Shultz (1975), 138, also makes this point.
[2] Lyons (1980), 12–16; Harré (1986), 3; Greenspan (1988), 180–1; Oatley (1992), 16–18; Solomon (1993a), ch. 4; Elster (1999), 48; Goldie (2000), 52–5.
[3] E.g. Harré (1986), 3; Greenspan (1988), 182; Oatley (1992), 138–43; Solomon (1993a), 175; Elster (1999), 48; Goldie (2000), 95–7.
[4] Klein (1970); Rapaport (1971), chs. 1 and 2; Murphy and Kovach (1972); Lyons (1980), chs. 1 and 2; Murray (1983); Solomon (1993b); Fancher (1996); Elster (1999), 50–1; Goodwin (1999).

professionalising William James era, seems to be a classic example of the phenomenon of 'victors' history'. McCosh's *The Emotions*, for example, was a considerable achievement, summarising evidence and arguments from the physiological and philosophical sides in a way that could be appreciated by academic psychologists as well as by members of the church and interested laypeople. Even A. A. Roback, an historian of psychology with no sympathy for Christian 'soul psychologists', felt that the 'oblivion' McCosh had fallen into by the middle of the twentieth century was undeserved. Roback, in fact, writing in 1964, went even further:

> It may sound out of tune or even an anachronism, on our part, even to suggest it, but possibly, McCosh's volume on the emotions, would, in its plenitude of insights, be more serviceable to present-day students, than the chapters on this topic in many contemporary textbooks with their citations of scores of experimental results, many of which are inconsequential, while the validity of others may be seriously questioned.[5]

Roback put the fact that McCosh's contributions had been forgotten down to his being associated with an old guard at Princeton who had usurped institutional power for too long.[6] It is also likely that McCosh's association with the church and with the traditional metaphysics of the Reidian school of mental philosophy (characterised by its realism, its introspective method and its faculty psychology classification) contributed to the exclusion of his contribution to the understanding of emotions, and others like it, from the 'official' history of psychology.

The foregoing chapters, then, have looked at some of the material on passions, affections, sentiments and emotions that has been lost as a result of the continual re-adoption by historians of psychology of the same old canon of affective theorists. Hopefully, my attempt to construe psychology's past more generously, paying particular attention to the psychological systems of philosophers, moralists and theologians, has produced a somewhat richer history than was previously available. I would pick out two aspects in particular that I hope will be useful new contributions to the historical understanding of the provenance of the category of 'emotions'. The first of these is the discussion of the Scottish tradition, including works by Hutcheson, Hume, Reid, Brown, Chalmers, Bain and McCosh, and the way that this Scottish mental and moral philosophy was successfully exported to England and America during the nineteenth century. The second aspect that might be particularly useful is the additional material on the history of the 'feeling' or 'sensational' theory of emotions. That history, until now, has generally contained only references to

---

[5] Roback (1964), 113. [6] Roback (1964), 109-10.

Descartes, Hume and James.[7] The espousal of non-cognitive 'sensational' or 'feeling' theories of emotions by Brown, Chalmers, Spencer and Bain were all important markers on the journey between Hume's and James' theories.

Theological, secular and scientific psychologies

Potential problems with secularisation narratives

One way that I have described the process being narrated is as a process of secularisation. At the Christian end of the spectrum were theories of appetites, passions and affections, which conceived of them as movements or acts of the will and intellect of a substantial soul. The passions were signs and symptoms of a disobedient fallen soul, and the affections were enlightened movements of the rational will. Gracious affections were the movements of a soul indwelt by the Holy Spirit. In the middle of the spectrum were fundamentally atheological 'Enlightenment' views; the halfway houses of moral and mental science in which passions and affections became autonomous components in the divinely designed human machine. Passions and affections were conceived as agents rather than advocates, as movers rather than movements, and as perceptions rather than actions. The introspective inductivist science of the mind was the preferred methodology. At the secular end of the spectrum were reductionist neurophysiological, evolutionary and proto-behaviorist accounts of emotions. The fact that the psychological category 'emotions' gained widespread currency in the way that it did during the nineteenth century was indicative of the fact that the most popular and influential psychological works of the time were those produced within the positivist and secular tradition represented by the psychologies of Brown and Bain (and, later, Darwin and James) as opposed to Christian and moralist theories of 'passions and affections' and 'moral sentiments', such as those of Hutcheson, Butler, Reid and Whewell.

Richard Olson has provided a summary of the broader version of this story of transitions in dominant worldviews.[8] As with all simple historical stories, this one is both enlightening and misleading. The main reason it is misleading is that it suggests that the theological era in psychology was, in a linear Comtean manner, irreversibly superseded by the metaphysical, which was in turn superseded by the positive and scientific. The truth of the matter, however, is that the Christian (theological) and thinly theistic (metaphysical) ways of thinking about human mental life

---

[7] E.g. Lyons (1980), 2–16.   [8] Olson (ed.) (1971), 1–2.

have persisted alongside the secular and scientific, albeit in a position of reduced academic influence. As noted at the outset, the persistence of theological and metaphysical psychologies throughout the nineteenth century has recently also been emphasised by Rick Rylance.[9] This persistence is evidenced by the fact that, as chapters 6 and 7 reveal, in the later nineteenth century there were still psychological thinkers adopting both Christian (Newman, Paine, McCosh, Ladd) and more metaphysically theistic (Morell, Lyall, Porter) approaches to the emotions. Often these writers were influenced by earlier Christian or theistic thinkers, especially Reid and Butler, respectively.

Certainly, in some cases, there was a clear correlation between personal and professional alienation from the Christian church and early endorsement of the category of 'emotions' (e.g. Brown and Bain). Other cases, however, were less straightforward. Chalmers, for example, combined personal commitment to evangelical Christianity with an endorsement of Brown's mental-scientific 'emotion' theory; a theory that owed almost nothing, methodologically or conceptually, to the Christian tradition. It was qua mental scientist that Chalmers endorsed the Brownian view of emotions. Butler was another example of a committed Christian who produced an affective psychology that seemed to appeal more to mechanical models of the mind than to anything distinctively Christian. Other Christians, such as Upham, Paine, McCosh and Ladd, achieved a more successful balance between the Christian and scientific psychological traditions to which they were committed.

Just as enthusiasm for scientific concepts and methods could be combined with Christian, non-Christian or anti-Christian commitments, so a lack of interest in new scientific psychologies was by no means always a symptom of a Christian commitment. Some conservative Oxbridge Christians such as Whewell, Sewell, Newman, Grote and Gorman *were* suspicious of physiological psychology as a result of the priority they gave to the Christian tradition in their approach to understanding the human mind. To some extent, each of these thinkers was anti-scientific when it came to the enterprise of understanding the soul and its mind. Others who neglected natural science in their attempt to understand the human mind, however, did so because of the priority they gave to metaphysics, often especially to certain forms of philosophic Idealism, rather than because of a traditional Christian commitment (e.g. Hickok, Rauch, Morell). Nineteenth-century proponents of Hegelian and post-Hegelian philosophical idealisms in Britain, for example, were sometimes religiously motivated, but sometimes were quite opposed to orthodoxy

---

[9] Rylance (2000).

and the church.[10] Alan Sell's study of idealism and religious belief particularly focusses on those thinkers who sought to combine traditional Christianity with philosophical idealism and the extent to which this was possible. All this makes it all the more important to distinguish between Christian, merely theistic, and Idealist versions of psychology and their relationships to science. Edward Reed's rather broad use of 'religious' and 'theological' to describe the assumptions behind nineteenth-century psychologies is an example of how these important distinctions are sometimes obscured.[11]

Similarly, it is important to be aware in thinking about the different connotations commitment to a 'scientific' study of the mind could carry. Those mental philosophers and psychologists considered in this study who were committed to 'science' fall into at least three groups: Newtonian-inductivist mental and moral scientists of the eighteenth century (e.g. Shaftesbury, Clarke, Hume and Hutcheson); those who endorsed a mentalistic science of the mind but opposed the view that this was a science of anything physical (e.g. Brown, the Mills, McCosh and Ladd); and those who proposed a more reductionist or physicalist scientific psychology (e.g. Bain, Spencer and James).

Commitment to science and commitment to Christianity were not mutually exclusive; there was no simple correlation between indifference or hostility to Christianity and promotion of a scientific approach to mental life. There was a complex interrelation of Christian and secular, scientific and non-scientific factors in the generation of different affective psychologies in the eighteenth and nineteenth centuries. The existence of Christian psychologists who were enthusiastically committed to science and of anti-scientific psychologists who were indifferent to Christianity makes it impossible to claim that there was a simple proportionality and correlation between the rise of scientific psychology and the neglect of Christian psychology. This evidence of complexity and of the persistence of theological and philosophical psychologies demands that we develop an historical account of the creation of the category of 'emotions' that is more subtle than a simplistic story of inexorable scientistic secularisation.

Potential problems with the metaphor of 'disguise'

Positivist 'triumph of science' stories are not the only sort of over-simple explanation that can be offered of historical relationships between theological and secular discourses. Another popular sort of explanation is that secular scientific discourses are theologies or anti-theologies 'in disguise'.

[10] Willis (1988), 110–11; Sell (1995). [11] Reed (1997).

I am of course sympathetic, in individual cases, with the idea that particular psychological theories bear the marks of their authors' theological and metaphysical assumptions about such things as mind, motivation and morality. However, it is necessary to be cautious in characterising a whole academic discipline or discourse as being theology or anti-theology in disguise.[12] John Milbank, for example, seems to be making too sweeping a judgment when, taking on the entire edifice of 'secular social theory', he claims to discover that 'all the most important governing assumptions of such theory are bound up with the modification or the rejection of orthodox Christian positions'.[13]

During the eighteenth and nineteenth centuries, certain fundamental assumptions were indeed made in psychology that seemed to be inversions of earlier Christian ones. Whereas in Christian psychologies 'affections' had been part of that higher soul that marked man out as superior to the brutes, in the new scientific psychology, 'emotions' of all kinds were to be understood the same way in human and non-human animals alike. Christian thinkers had made the spiritual and cognitive elements of affections and passions primary and bodily changes secondary; James' theory of emotions inverted this model. Edwards taught that true knowledge of another's soul cannot be had by observing mere outward appearances: '[T]he Scripture plainly intimates that this way of judging what is in men by outward appearances, is at best uncertain and liable to deceit; "The Lord seeth not as man seeth; for man looketh on the outward appearance, but the Lord looketh on the heart" (1 Samuel 16:7).'[14] In contrast, the scientific epistemology adopted by the new psychologists gave priority to external observable correlates of emotions and considered knowledge based on outward appearances much more reliable than that gained by introspection alone. We have also already seen that the denial by Spencer and Darwin of the expressive function of emotional expressions was in part motivated by opposition to Bell's design theology.

The demise of the Christian distinction between sensual passions and intellectual affections in the homogenous concept of 'emotions' might also be interpreted as an example of an inversion of Christian psychological assumptions. Christian theologians from Augustine to Edwards had taught the difference not only between grace and nature and between man and brute but also between affections and passions. This distinction was effaced in the seminal treatments of 'emotions' by Brown, Bain and James. These, then, are some of the ways in which the approach of

---

[12] For further discussion of this tendency in the works of John Milbank, Richard Webster and Edward Reed, see Dixon (1999), 312–20.
[13] Milbank (1990), 1.   [14] Edwards (1959), 181.

seeking out hidden anti-Christian assumptions in secular science might be successfully applied to the emergence of the psychology of 'emotions'.

Richard Webster, in his analysis of psychology and anthropology, adopts a methodology similar to Milbank's. In much the same way that Milbank tends to discover Nietzschean anti-Christianity hidden in secular human sciences, Webster in several cases discovers disguised versions of Judaeo-Christian anthropology itself. In his book *From Soul to Mind* (1997), Edward Reed similarly argues that the nineteenth-century birth of scientific psychology was inherently theological and that 'psychology succeeded in becoming a science in large part because of its defense of a theological conception of human nature typically associated with liberal Protestant theology'.[15] There are ways in which this analysis might also be applied to the emergence of the secular concept of 'emotions'. One example would be the suggestion made above, in the context of the discussion of the creation of 'emotions' as part of a science of mind by Brown, that certain Protestant commitments – especially to the priority of individual mental experience over church dogma – were imported into a systematic account of the human mind. Brown's psychology might therefore qualify as 'Protestantism in disguise' – this might be the sort of thesis that Reed would endorse.

Another example of an aspect of secular emotions theory that might be considered to be Christian teaching in disguise is Darwin's (evolutionary) version of the story of the fall of humanity from a state of perfect voluntary control to one in which the body no longer obeyed the mind (see chapter 5). Something similar might be claimed about James' rationalist distinction between cerebral cognition and visceral emotion (see chapter 7). We also saw in chapter 7 how the traditional dichotomy between reason and the passions was embodied in psychological textbooks of the later nineteenth century. Webster would, perhaps, find the Judaeo-Christian God hidden inside these embodiments of reason–emotion dualism.

There is a danger in taking this sort of 'theology in disguise' line, however. Often we can end up making it too easy for ourselves to find hidden theology in secular psychologies, especially if the features considered as tacitly theological, deistic, Judaeo-Christian, or whatever, are such general features of an author's work as a distinction between rational and irrational, mind and body, or human and animal. Webster and Reed both appeal to general tropes like these (especially the distinction between the conscious rational self and the unconscious irrational self) in making the ambitious claim that the Christian God is to be found at the roots

[15] Reed (1997), 7.

of certain secular psychologies and anthropologies.[16] If such common tropes are taken as evidence of a tacit theology, then almost any secular psychological text could be made to look tacitly theological. Without stricter criteria, it is also easy to find many different implicit theologies, anti-theologies or metaphysics within one single text – because many different theologies or worldviews will be compatible with (or 'implicit in') any given text.[17] This is why it is important to try to impose stricter criteria for the ascription of theological or anti-theological influences on secular texts.

Reed's judgment that psychology succeeded in becoming a science in large part because of its defence of a theological model of human nature needs to be qualified in two ways. Scientific psychology of the later nineteenth century was not inherently theological – at most it was combined, by some of its exponents, with deism, pantheism or spiritualist monism (as Reed himself really acknowledges). A 'spiritual view of reality' is not the same as a theological view of reality. 'Spiritualism' as used by later nineteenth-century psychological thinkers was closer in meaning to what we might call philosophic 'Idealism' than to any fundamentally religious conception. It was a term used to refer to a mentalistic rather than materialistic approach to the mind, not to a Christian rather than a secular methodology. Secondly, Reed is wrong to think that a discipline would succeed in becoming a science because it adhered to theological views about human nature. Wilhelm Wundt, William James, James Mark Baldwin and the other pioneering scientific psychologists were all quite uninterested, qua scientific psychologists, in traditional theological anthropology, and their reductionist observational epistemology was quite out of keeping with traditional introspectionist Christian psychology.[18] Psychology succeeded in becoming a science, at least in part, because it denied the primacy of the soul affirmed by Christian theological dualism and adopted instead an objectifying 'natural scientific' account of the human mind couched in quantifiable observations of brains, nerves, muscles, viscera and behaviour.

The secular psychological category of 'the emotions' was, then, neither a purely anti-Christian creation nor simply a covertly theological one. It was generated, rather, by the application of assumptions, methods, categories and concepts that were sometimes negatively, and sometimes positively derived from theological psychologies. The secular scientific

---

[16] E.g. Webster (1995), 470–5, 495; Reed (1997), 5–8.   [17] See Dixon (2001), 290–3.
[18] Further examples of Reed's failure to distinguish philosophical, spiritualistic monism and pantheism from Christian theology are his use of Baldwin's advocacy of spiritualism and James' pantheism as evidence that psychology succeeded because it was defending a Christian (Protestant) view of human nature. Reed (1997), 7–8, 214–20.

theories of emotions that arose in the nineteenth century contained – at least – both seemingly anti-Christian assumptions and models and seemingly Christian ones. Neurophysiological and evolutionary theories about emotions and their expression provide a good illustration. These theories were integrated both into Christian and natural theological frameworks by Bell, Cooke, McCosh, Paine and Ladd, and also into psychologies that were ambivalent or hostile to a Christian worldview by Spencer, Bain and Darwin. The secular emotions theories discussed above most often relied on a mixture of sources, some Christian, others anti-Christian, others thinly theistic, still others a very long distance (in time and cultural space) from any theological ideas. Many aspects of these texts possessed a degree of autonomy that is obscured by narratives appealing to the metaphor of disguised theologies or metaphysics.

Worldviews and psychological theories

How then, can we go beyond simple and reductionist explanations of the secularisation of the human sciences and provide a more cautious account? There are several different ways to do this – and I have tried to apply all of them, at least to some extent, to my analysis in the foregoing chapters. First, we can demand more substantial evidence of the religious convictions and intentions of the author of a text, before claiming to find theology or anti-theology in his or her ideas. We should not too quickly take the defence of certain philosophical or metaphysical positions to be evidence of an author's religious or anti-religious views, in the absence of further evidence. For example, nineteenth-century authors' metaphysical commitments to mind–body dualism on the one hand, or to a reductionist materialism about mind on the other, did not always have a religious or anti-religious flavour, although they often did. Secondly, we can acknowledge that a religious author might, despite his religious convictions, adopt secular language and methods; a religious author can compose an atheological text. Thirdly, we can look for rather more detailed and specific examples of parallels between psychological theories and religious or anti-religious ideas, rather than contenting ourselves with generalities such as a distinction between reason and emotion. Fourthly, we can ask whether a text, despite apparent affinities with some religious or anti-religious doctrine, might actually have very little connection with that doctrine. Finally, we must recognise the fact that one and the same secular psychological text or theory can be both positively and negatively shaped by theological ideas.

I think that another useful starting point, in thinking about how religious and metaphysical commitments can shape psychological theorising, is to think of an individual's a priori religious or non-religious metaphysical commitments as comprising their 'worldview'.[19] Three of the most important components of a worldview would be assumptions about the nature of reality (ontological commitments), assumptions about how best to acquire knowledge about reality (epistemological commitments) and commitments to particular textual and metaphorical resources as the best way to articulate knowledge of reality (narrative and explanatory commitments). To take some examples, a Christian worldview might assume that God is the ground and cause of all reality, that revelation and reason are the two most important sources of knowledge about that reality and that the Bible provides some of the best ways of explaining and narrating human reality. A secular-scientific worldview might assume matter or nature to be the ultimate reality, might privilege experimentation as the way to discover the nature of that reality and might look to natural history and mathematics for narrative and explanatory tools. I do not wish to suggest that there is just one Christian worldview, nor that there is just one scientific worldview; these examples are simply illustrative.

Further issues about evidence and explanation are raised by the appeal to worldviews. There is a danger that an appeal to a writer's worldview could be vacuous if 'worldview' simply meant whatever assumptions seemed to lie behind the theory in question. It is important that evidence external to the theory in question is adduced as evidence of its author's worldview. Even then the worldview itself stands in need of explanation – it is not an explanatory terminus (as, indeed, nothing is) although in some circumstances it might be as far as the historian can go down a particular line. It is at this stage that all the rich and complex psychological, social, cultural, political, economic and geographical facts investigated in any 'contextual' history need to be brought to bear. Reasons for inhabiting one worldview rather than another may often be complex and deep-seated.[20]

One of the ways that evidence of mere prima facie compatibility of prior worldview commitments with the content of psychological texts can be strengthened, even in the absence of further external evidence, is to seek broader trends rather than concentrating on isolated examples; to look for correlations between types of religious and anti-religious commitments and types of theory, rather than a clearly articulated chain of cause and effect in each individual case. This may be the best way to proceed when

---

[19] For further discussion of the 'worldview' produced by scientific writers in the nineteenth and twentieth centuries see Dixon (1999), esp. 314–25; on the worldview of scientific atheism in particular, see Dixon (2002d).

[20] For further reflections on this question of evidential standards, see Dixon (2001), 290–3.

one finds oneself lacking conclusive biographical or autobiographical evidence; it can also be used to supplement such evidence, and this is what I have tried to do above, looking for broader correlations between religious beliefs and psychological systems.

How far, then, can the evidence adduced in the foregoing narrative take us towards a good explanation of the creation of the concept of emotions in the nineteenth century that appeals broadly to secularisation and more specifically to particular psychological thinkers' worldview commitments? In many of the central cases, such as those of Brown, Bain, Darwin, McCosh and Ladd, the evidence marshalled certainly goes beyond mere prima facie compatibility between prior worldview commitments and psychological theories. The religious or anti-religious views that these authors actually held were established using evidence external to their psychological texts. Additional evidence was then found in statements made by the authors and their contemporaries about the links between their religious or anti-religious views and their psychological theories. Most of this evidence took the form of statements simply noting compatibilities between religious and psychological views, rather than suggesting causal connections. Finally, a small number of statements by psychologists and their contemporaries went further and suggested that religious views had played a causal role in shaping psychological theories. The claims made by some of Brown's and Bain's critics that their psychological systems were shaped by atheistic presuppositions is an example of weaker evidence of this sort, while the connection made by both Darwin and Spencer between their disbelief in a designing God and their choice of theoretical account of the emotions is an example of stronger evidence of this sort.

Having acknowledged that this evidence is partial and imperfect, certain general trends in theories of passions and emotions can still be discerned which seem to have been correlated with the religious, non-religious, or anti-religious views of their authors. In the psychology of emotions produced by inhabitants of secular worldviews, theological agents such as the will, the soul, God, the Holy Spirit and Satan were discarded as real agents, as were 'passions' and 'affections' of the soul. The ontology of the new psychology of emotions, as developed by Spencer, Bain, Darwin and, ultimately, James in the 1850s–80s, was one in which there were only two real psychical agencies – the evolutionary past and the body (especially the nerves and viscera). Introspection on one's own soul was replaced by observations of others' bodies and behaviours as the favoured epistemology. Moral–theological and salvation–historical stories about people as God's creatures who had sinned and fallen but could be saved, and who were moral agents in society were replaced with natural-historical ones about human organisms as evolved animals who were products of their environment.

For Christians and theists, in contrast, agency was still ascribed to God and the immaterial soul, especially the will, whose freedom and agency the 'infidel' psychologists denied; introspection was still favoured as an essential epistemological tool; and theories maintaining the distinction between soul and body and in which emotions were irreducible cognitive acts of the former were favoured over accounts that privileged evolutionary and physiological considerations. Thus rejections or endorsements of Christian beliefs seem to have been, to a significant extent, correlated with alternative approaches to theorising about the 'emotions' in the nineteenth century. However, we should remember that these correlations between worldview commitments and psychological theories can be interpreted in a number of different ways. It could be suggested that religious or anti-religious commitments directly shaped theory-construction; but alternatively it might be claimed that these commitments simply played the selective role of helping thinkers choose between existing theories; or that religious attitudes were only secondary by-products of, or glosses on psychological theorising; or even that they were largely independent from it. The causal explanatory story is not the only one that can be told about such correlations.

How history can help us think about 'the emotions'

Avoiding anachronism

As summarised in the recapitulation above, this book provides material that can serve as a supplement to existing historical and contemporary views of passions and emotions. It also reveals that our modern-day category of emotions is rather a blunt instrument when it comes to constructing histories of ideas about feelings, passions, affections and sentiments; its employment has led to several misconceptions and confusions.

Robert Solomon's work on the history and philosophy of passions and emotions, as already mentioned in the Introduction, was a particularly influential early contribution to the explosion of academic interest in emotions in the last three decades. For that reason Solomon's view is an interesting one to examine in the light of the suggestions about the history of the category 'emotions' being made here. Solomon's view, in his book *The Passions*, is that rationalist and Christian thinkers of the past were responsible for teaching physiological, non-cognitive and involuntary views of the passions. He suggests that the influence of classical, medieval and Enlightenment theories of passions as bodily feelings that overwhelmed people against their will is the reason that in the last century or so people have endorsed a physiological, non-cognitive and involuntary theory of emotions. He recommends an alternative theory: emotions are cognitive judgments that people actively and voluntarily make; they are things that people do to the world rather than things that their bodies do to them.

I would suggest, however, that Solomon has misrepresented the history somewhat by reading the Christian recommendation of the rational government of the passions as a warning against all that we now call 'emotion'. The object of Solomon's disapproval – the 'myth of the passions', which, it was suggested above was something of a straw man – is a view ascribed to 'Western rationalism' that he feels perniciously dominates our attitudes to emotions.[21] It is the belief that passions are unruly tyrants who bully us into wrong-doing, and that they must be repressed, policed and restrained by the powers of reason and will. Solomon's rogues' gallery of rationalist passions-bashers includes Plato, Aristotle, the 'Christian tradition' – from which Augustine and Aquinas are picked out for special mention – Shakespeare, Spinoza and Kant.[22] Subsequently Solomon presents a brief discussion of the use of 'passion' in English, French and German, noting correctly that the term has tended to have overtones of particularly troubling and violent commotions of the mind. 'It is because of this history of the word "passion", embodying within it everything I wish to argue *against*... that I have chosen it as the generic term to cover the entire range of those phenomena... that may be said to "move" us.'[23] Solomon is not being entirely true to the history of thought in this area in taking 'the passions' to 'cover the entire range of those phenomena that may be said to move us'. The passions, in the psychologies of Augustine and Aquinas, and of Hutcheson, Watts, Wesley, Edwards and Reid, formed only a subset of those phenomena that were movements of the appetite and will. The affections, i.e. the voluntary movements of the rational soul, were the crucial second half of the traditional picture.[24] It is because Solomon uses the twentieth-century term 'emotions' as a near-synonym for the medieval and Enlightenment word 'passions' (when in fact it covers many phenomena that used to be separated into sensual passions and appetites on the one hand and moral sentiments and rational affections on the other) that some misrepresentations of 'rationalist' and 'Christian' moral philosophies arise.[25]

By attending to the ways that 'emotions' is not a synonym for passions, affections or sentiments – how the extensions and intensions of these

---

[21] Solomon (1993a), xvii. [22] Solomon (1993a), 9–10. [23] Solomon (1993a), 68.
[24] See Augustine (1966), IX.4, XIV.6, 9; Aquinas (1981), Ia.82, 5 ad 1; Ia2ae.22–26.
[25] Rorty (1982) could be criticised along similar lines.

terms have diverged – this book has indicated that it was in fact those thinkers who departed from traditional (often morally and theologically engaged) categories, concepts, assumptions and methods in creating their affective psychologies who were responsible for producing theories of passions and emotions that were starkly physiological, non-cognitive and involuntary; thinkers such as Butler, Brown, Chalmers, Bain, Spencer and James. Similarly, many of the theorists who produced theories of affections and emotions as acts of the mind, which were cognitive and voluntary, were Christian psychologists including Watts, Edwards, Reid, McCosh, Lyall and Ladd. Ironically, then, Solomon might find theories of emotions that were closest to his own by turning to the very Christian tradition that he has impugned for teaching non-cognitive and involuntary affective psychologies.

The historical material described and analysed above may also be useful to contemporary emotions theorists, and might save them from reinventing alternative emotions theories in ignorance of their past incarnations, and of the strengths and weaknesses that criticisms of them revealed. For example, cognitive emotions theorists such as Solomon, Lyons, Thalberg, Marks and Searle might be interested to learn about the tradition of psychologists who, like them, reduced emotions 'upwards' to cognitive mental acts.[26] Equally, a contemporary philosopher such as David Pugmire, who argues against the prevailing cognitivism of recent philosophical emotion theories, might find that his thought is truer to the nineteenth-century heritage of the category of 'emotions', conceived as they were, by Brown and others, as feelings that were to be clearly distinguished from thoughts.[27]

The over-inclusivity of 'emotions'

Paul Griffiths, in *What Emotions Really Are: The Problem of Psychological Categories* (1997), has argued that 'emotions' is a perniciously over-inclusive category, which should be divided into two classes, the first class primitive and organic – the so-called 'affect programs' or pan-cultural basic emotions studied by Paul Ekman – the second class being the 'higher cognitive emotions', which are more culturally differentiated.[28] Jon Elster makes a related point – that there does not seem to be any single theory that satisfactorily accounts for all those states of mind – from primal fear to a thrill of joy induced by listening to music – we consider to be

---

[26] Lyons (1980); Marks (1982); Searle (1983), 32–6; Thalberg (1984).
[27] Pugmire (1998).
[28] Griffiths (1997), esp. 241–5. For a response arguing against this pessimism about the usefulness of emotion as a coherent category, suggesting in fact that emotion is a natural kind, see Charland (2002).

emotions.²⁹ A corollary of this is that we need more than one theory, and more than one category, to do justice to the phenomena we are seeking to include in the category 'emotions'. The present historical study could be applied to this contemporary question in the philosophy and psychology of emotions by providing examples of alternative psychological categorisations. I have shown above that those who have used the term 'emotions' have sought to comprehend under it a huge variety of different states and feelings, from sexual desire to jealousy, from terror to pity, from aesthetic feelings to pangs of conscience. An investigation of past affective psychologies reveals alternative, more differentiated systems that divide these mental states into appetites, passions, affections and sentiments. The central distinction between passions and affections in previous psychologies should be particularly interesting to contemporary theorists who share Griffiths' sense of the over-inclusivity of 'emotions'.³⁰ Some emotions may be more like sneezes (physiological, non-cognitive and involuntary) and others more like crimes (social, cognitive and voluntary): the former might best be called 'passions', the latter 'affections'. Even if the old-fashioned terminology of passions and affections does not find favour in future psychological theories, the old habit of distinguishing between affective states in some similar way may yet be revived. Looking even further back in the history of philosophy, the Stoics also made a distinction between involuntary 'pre-passions' or 'first movements' (*propatheia*) on the one hand and cognitive, voluntary passions (*pathē*) on the other.³¹

The demise of distinctions such as these resulted not only in the problem of the over-inclusivity of 'emotions' but also in the definitional problems that have plagued theorists from Brown onwards. James' theory, for example, was initially intended to deal only with the 'coarser emotions' – those 'that have a distinct bodily expression' – but this restriction was rapidly forgotten, and the physicalist theory was later applied to all emotions, so that emotion came to be synonymous with 'emotion with a distinct bodily expression'. And those who emphasised the intellectual, moral and spiritual nature of emotions obviously tended to choose examples of more refined emotional feelings – feelings of beauty and wonder, of sympathy for one's fellow man, of love for God and so on. The data of both camps were equally theory-laden; they were chosen because they were good examples for the particular theory being advanced; to use Kuhn's phrase, they were 'paradigm-determined'.³² The Christian psychologist would talk about fear of God, the physicalist about fear of a bear. If the distinction between passions and affections had been available,

---

²⁹ Elster (1999), ch. 4, esp. 239–41.
³⁰ Rapaport has also complained of the vague and over-inclusive sense of 'emotion': Rapaport (1971), 6.
³¹ Annas (1992), 110; Sorabji (2000).   ³² Kuhn (1970), 126.

it could have been acknowledged, perhaps, that the physicalist definition was more appropriate to appetites and passions such as fear of a bear, and that a cognitive definition was more fitting for affections such as the fear of God and for sentiments such as sympathy.

So, the over-inclusivity of 'emotion' has made it impossible for there to be any consensus about what an emotion is. The term 'emotions' has been described more recently as 'utterly refractory to definitional efforts', and as 'virtually impossible to define'.[33] Corsini says of 'emotion' that its 'exact nature has been elusive and difficult to specify', Reber that 'no other term in psychology shares its nondefinability with its frequency of use'.[34] Berrios has written of the 'terminological palimpsest' that has existed in affective psychology since the nineteenth century.[35] Reddy writes that the recent surge in experiments and studies on emotions 'has done little to clear up the vexed question of what, exactly, emotions are. Disagreements persist, uncertainties abound.'[36] Annette Baier also complains of the terminological problems surrounding the terms passions, emotions and sentiment as used in contemporary and historical philosophical discussions.[37] I have looked to the history of the term to discover some of the reasons for these problems. None of the significant early emotions theorists of the nineteenth century provided an adequate definition. James' famous 1884 theory was particularly problematic, but predecessors such as Brown and Bain did little better. This problem arose directly from the over-inclusivity of the category. Since the category 'emotions' seeks to include all sorts of very diverse mental states and feelings, it is therefore impossible to find a definition that covers all of them – theorists end up reducing, either 'upwards' or 'downwards'.

As well as making it almost impossible to define, the over-inclusivity of emotions has also made the concept less helpful than it might be in explanatory contexts. It is not a good explanation to say that a given state or feeling is an emotion, or that a given piece of behaviour was caused by an emotion. Some emotions are more like sneezes, others more like crimes. Explaining a piece of behaviour by appealing to the 'emotion' that caused it does not take the inquirer into motivation and responsibility much further forward, since it does not clarify whether the behaviour should be understood and treated like a sneeze or like a crime.[38]

---

[33] Reber (1985), 234; English and English (1958), 176.
[34] Corsini (1994), 478; Reber (1985), 234.   [35] Berrios (1996), 289.
[36] Reddy (2001), ix.   [37] Baier (1990), 1–2.
[38] For an excellent argument that 'emotion' was an unsuccessful explanatory principle for Darwin and James, see Campbell (1997). Campbell's argument is not based on the over-inclusivity of 'emotions' but on the fact that 'expressive' behaviours were really explained, by Darwin and James, by their initial survival value; additional references to 'emotions' were superfluous.

Finally, the over-inclusivity of the modern category of emotions means that claims about emotions being good things or bad things (frequently the former in recent years) are sweeping, unsubtle and unconvincing. Of course it is often useful to draw attention to the value of subjective, lively, warm, committed psychological states in various spheres, such as motivation, morality or meaning-making. However, to express across-the-board approval of 'emotions' is surely to go too far. Some of the worst acts of human violence and cruelty are the results of acting on emotions such as lust and anger. Some of the worst human misery is characterised by the emotions of anxiety and despair. On the other hand, without our emotions we would lack virtues such as sympathy and altruism. In short, it is necessary to distinguish between good emotions and bad emotions; virtuous ones and vicious ones; constructive ones and destructive ones. The all-encompassing amorality of the category 'emotions' has encouraged a psychological discourse that is blind to these distinctions. Perhaps a return to a more differentiated typology, again, would help us to think more clearly about this side of human mental life. A healthy sense of the potential destructiveness of human passions could be held in common with an appreciation of the importance of moral sentiments and more refined affections.

Some similarities between contemporary and older emotions theories

Amongst those who favour a view of emotions that makes them closer to crimes than to sneezes, social-constructivist philosophers such as James Averill and Rom Harré, moral philosophers including Rorty, Owen Flanagan and Justin Oakley, and social historians such as Peter and Carol Stearns, have all drawn attention to the constitutive role played by the language, moral norms and institutions of different cultures in creating emotions.[39] To take just one example, Peter Stearns has shown how evolving social norms of sexual fidelity, or the lack of it, have helped to construct the emotion of jealousy in new ways for successive generations in America.[40] The social-constructivist project, like the philosophical one of Solomon, is proposed in explicit opposition to the reductionist scientific approach of Darwin and James.[41] Harré proposes the view that socio-cultural phenomena are often 'more basic' than biology in the construction of emotions.[42] These morally and socially oriented emotions theories might be further enriched by comparing them with the debates

---

[39] Averill et al. (1990); Harré (ed.) (1986); For a critique of the social constructivist project, see Greenwood (1994); Flanagan and Rorty (eds.) (1990); Oakley (1992); Stearns (1989).
[40] Stearns (1989).   [41] Harré (ed.) (1986), 3.   [42] Harré (ed.) (1986), 4.

engaged in by Hutcheson, Butler, Reid and the other British moralists in the eighteenth century about the roles of reason, the passions and the benevolent sentiments in human motivation.

Mercier's (1884) theory of emotions also displayed striking similarities with twentieth-century developments. Mercier's approach shared many features with the cognitive theories of philosophers of emotion such as Anthony Kenny and especially the cognitive 'evaluation' or 'appraisal' theories of emotion that have been produced by psychologists such as George Mandler, Keith Oatley and Klaus Scherer in the 1980s and 1990s.[43] Mercier's cognitions of an object in the environment as noxious, overwhelmingly powerful and so on were nearly identical to the 'Stimulus Evaluation Checks' (SECs) posited by Scherer as the basic cognitive appraisals of an object in the environment that elicit an emotion. Scherer's SECs include 'intrinsic pleasantness', 'goal-conduciveness' and 'coping potential', all of which have striking parallels in Mercier's analysis.[44]

Irons' approach to emotion was also similar in important respects to certain later twentieth-century approaches. His methodological privileging of introspection and the subjective experience of the emotion was suggestive of later phenomenological approaches to emotions. Recently the philosopher Robert C. Roberts, for example, has put forward the theory that emotions are 'concern-based construals', specifically aiming to provide a definition that is consistent with the phenomenological experience of emotions as unified, irreducible states of mind.[45] Ironically, his theory of emotions as irreducible construals appeared in the same journal, albeit ninety-one years later, as Irons' defence of emotions as irreducible feeling-attitudes. Yet Roberts (like all other philosophers and psychologists of emotions of this century) seems quite unaware of the degree of commonality between his views and those of anti-Jamesians of the nineteenth century. Secondly, Irons' view that an emotion was a reaction of the whole person, an attitude rather than a passive feeling, an 'element of our own character',[46] resonates with the views of Solomon and of George Turski. Solomon thinks that emotions are not merely passive feelings but are judgments (or attitudes) that we make, integral aspects of our whole personality.[47] Similarly, Turski characterises an emotion as a 'modality of mind' or a 'personal posture'.[48] The final aspect of Irons' theory of emotions that has been particularly important in twentieth-century thought is that of 'intentionality' – the term used to describe mental states that are 'about' something, that have reference to objects outside of themselves.

---

[43] Kenny (1963), 193; Searle (1983), 34–6 and throughout; Mandler (1984); Oatley (1992); Scherer (1984).
[44] Scherer (1984), 310. [45] Roberts (1988), 209. [46] Irons (1897), 250.
[47] Solomon (1993a), xvii and throughout. [48] Turski (1994), 13–14.

Kenny, John Searle and Peter Goldie have all concentrated on the fact that emotions are intentional – that particular emotions have particular objects.[49] This acknowledgment of intentionality, absent from the Jamesian theory of emotions, was important for Irons, who defined emotions as 'feelings-in-reference-to-something', or feeling-attitudes to situations or objects 'cognised in a certain way'.[50] Goldie's argument that an irreducible 'feeling towards' an object is an essential part of all emotions is, again, interestingly similar to Irons' much earlier anti-Jamesian view.[51]

From passions and affections to emotions

James Moore has suggested that attention to language should be one of the main features of good historical treatments of 'science and religion'. He calls for 'textured analyses of contested terms', which will illustrate how '*language* maps cultural change', and how 'usage determines meaning'.[52] Offering a textured analysis of contested terms including 'nature', 'passions', 'emotions', 'will', 'soul', 'science' and 'psychology', I have suggested above that, in the case of affective psychologies of the eighteenth and nineteenth centuries, changes in language mapped deeper conceptual and cultural changes. By referring to the lexical and conceptual networks of which 'passions and affections' and 'emotions' were members, I have illustrated how, in these cases, context of usage determined meaning.

'Passions', for example, could have a resonance of sin and the fall in a traditional Christian context and of animal spirits and perception in a mechanical Cartesian one. 'Nature' might have been an antonym for 'grace' in a revivalist Christian context but an antonym for 'artifice' or for 'society' in the context of British moralism. 'Will' could mean a principle of a created soul, a succession of ungoverned appetites in a mechanical mind, or a feeling resulting from a certain kind of nervous activity. 'Science' could mean the systematic, inductive investigation of all aspects of reality, or could be limited to the discovery of physical causes. 'Experiment' could mean subjective introspection or quite the reverse – objective outward observation. 'Psychology' could, like 'metaphysics', mean the discovery of the mental causes and components of mental states, or, more like 'physiology', refer to the discovery of the neural and visceral side of mental states. 'Emotions' could mean cognitive acts of the soul for some, and epiphenomenal feelings of either cerebral or visceral activity

---

[49] Kenny (1963), 193; Searle (1983), 34–6 and throughout.
[50] Irons (1897), 471, 475.   [51] Goldie (2000), esp. ch. 3.   [52] Moore (1992), 314.

for others. This is in addition to the fact that 'passions and affections of the soul', a little like the 'phlogiston' of pre-chemical revolution natural philosophy, have been dropped from the scientific terminology altogether.

One of the most important fundamental shifts that was mapped by the terminological transition from 'passions and affections' to 'emotions' was the shift from a realist to a non-realist view of the will. The traditional Christian view was the realist one: the will was, with intellect, one of the two principle faculties of a substantial soul. It was a faculty with 'active powers', as writers such as Reid called them. 'Passions' and 'affections' were amongst the most important categories of active powers of the soul. Thomas Brown introduced the term 'emotions' as part of a very different psychology of the will, one that was within the Hobbesian–Humean non-realist tradition. There were two important elements to this tradition of thinking about the will. First, the non-realist taught that 'will' was a word used to described not a power or faculty, but a feeling. Secondly, the non-realist taught that, just as there was no faculty or power of 'will', so there were no other autonomous faculties, and certainly no autonomous self, 'having' sensory impressions, feelings and ideas. All that really existed for the non-realist was the stream of impressions, feelings and ideas themselves. For Brown these were categorised as 'sensations', 'emotions' and 'thoughts'. For James they became the 'stream of consciousness'.[53]

Uses of the terms 'passions', 'affections' or 'emotions' were, then, indicative of these differences in fundamental psychological assumptions. I have tried to draw attention to the fact that the use of particular pieces of terminology could indicate familiarity and sympathy with one particular tradition of psychological thought in preference to certain other traditions. Use of the term 'emotions' in the mid-nineteenth century indicated familiarity, and, more indirectly, suggested sympathy, with the Brownian psychology, its terminology and its positivist and non-realist philosophical basis. Use of the terms 'passions and affections' indicated familiarity and sympathy with an older, sometimes Christian psychological tradition, its terminology and its realist philosophical basis.

I have, therefore, argued that the difference between 'passions and affections' and 'emotions' in the history of psychological categories was 'more than a mere verbal difference'; it very speedily became a 'difference of doctrine', to use Thomas Brown's own words.[54] Although there have been those since Brown's day who have reduced emotions upwards as well as downwards – while seeking to escape the definitional mire that

---

[53] On James' use of this phrase, and its earlier coinage by G. H. Lewes, see Rylance (2000), 10–13.
[54] Brown (1828), 100 (L. 16).

the very creation of the category made inevitable – the doctrine with which this verbal change was from the outset more closely connected was the positivist and reductionist theory taught by Brown, Spencer and Bain. 'Emotions', from the outset, were involuntary: they were mini-agents in their own right, rather than movements or actions of a will or self. They were, furthermore, non-cognitive states: they were to be contrasted with intellectual judgments and thoughts. They were, finally, aggregates reducible to physical feelings: they were 'worked up from' bodily sensations. William James' infamous theory – that emotions were epiphenomenal products of the activities of the viscera – was to be the most widely remembered of the many 'differences in doctrine' in which Brown's 'mere verbal difference' resulted.[55]

[55] For an overview of the many different theories of emotions proposed by psychologists from the late-nineteenth to the late-twentieth century, see Salzen (2001), which identifies five basic sorts of theory. Misleadingly, I think, Salzen includes Bain and Spencer as 'cognitive appraisal' theorists of emotion on the grounds that they employed the methods of association psychology; however the elements associated in emotions for them were sensations rather than thoughts or appraisals and so they should rather be included in one of Salzen's other categories, such as 'response feedback', or 'neural systems'. Another misleading element of Salzen's analysis is his inclusion of Darwin's theory in the category of theories that makes emotions 'adaptive responses'; see chapter 5 in this volume. For other surveys of the immensely wide variety of nineteenth- and early twentieth-century emotions theories, see Janet and Séailles (1902), II, 249–313; Irons (1903), ch. 1; Baldwin (ed.) (1905); Ruckmick (1936); Dunbar (1954); Gardiner et al. (1970); Rapaport (1971).

Bibliography

Abercrombie, J. (1830), *Inquiries Concerning the Intellectual Powers and the Investigation of Truth* (Edinburgh: Waugh and Innes).
  (1833), *The Philosophy of the Moral Feelings* (London: Murray).
  (1838), *Inquiries Concerning the Intellectual Powers and the Investigation of Truth*, 8th edn (London: Murray).
Addinall, P. (1991), *Philosophy and Biblical Interpretation: A Study in Nineteenth-Century Conflict* (Cambridge: Cambridge University Press).
Albury, W. R. (1977), 'Experiment and explanation in the physiology of Bichat and Magendie', *Studies in History of Biology* 1: 47–131.
Alison, A. (1790), *Essays on the Nature and Principles of Taste* (London: Robinson).
Andrews, C. (1911), *Life, Emotion, Intellect* (London: Fisher Unwin).
Annas, J. (1992), *Hellenistic Philosophy of Mind* (Berkeley: University of California Press).
Anonymous (1881), 'The Emotions by James McCosh', *Journal of Mental Science* 26: 582–6.
Aquinas, St T. (1964–81), *Summa Theologiae*, trans. The Dominican Fathers (61 vols., London: Blackfriars).
  (1975), *Summa Contra Gentiles*, trans. C. O'Neill (Notre Dame: University of Notre Dame Press).
Arnold, M. (ed.) (1968), *The Nature of Emotion: Selected Readings* (Harmondsworth: Penguin).
Atkinson, H. G. and Martineau, H. (1851), *Letters on the Laws of Man's Nature and Development* (London: John Chapman).
Augustine, St (1952), *The City of God*, trans. G. Walsh and G. Monahan, in *The Fathers of the Church*, vols. XIII–XV (Washington: Catholic University of America Press).
  (1957), *Expositions on the Book of Psalms* (6 vols.), trans. Members of the English Church, in *A Library of Fathers of the Holy Catholic Church* (London: Rivington).
  (1961), *Confessions*, trans. R. Pine-Coffin (London: Penguin).
  (1966), *The City of God*, trans. Phillip Levine (7 vols., London: Heinemann).
  (1968), *The Free Choice of the Will*, trans. R. Russell, in *The Fathers of the Church*, vol. LIX (Washington: Catholic University of America Press).
  (1991), *The Trinity*, trans. E. Hill, in J. E. Rotell (ed.), *The Works of St Augustine: A Translation for the 21st Century*, Part I, vol. V (Brooklyn, NY: New City Press).

(1993), *Sermons on the Liturgical Seasons*, trans. E. Hill, in J. E. Rotelle (ed.), *The Works of St Augustine: A Translation for the 21st Century*, Part III, vol. VI (New Rochelle, NY: New City Press).
Averill, J. (1990), 'Inner feelings, works of the flesh, the beast within, diseases of the mind, driving force, and putting on a show: six metaphors of emotion and their theoretical extensions', in D. Leary (ed.), *Metaphors in the History of Psychology* (Cambridge: Cambridge University Press), 104–32.
Averill, J. et al. (1990), *Rules of Hope* (New York: Springer Verlag).
Baier, A. (1990), 'What emotions are about', *Philosophical Perspectives* 4: 1–29.
  (1991), *A Progress of Sentiments: Reflections on Hume's Treatise* (Cambridge, MA: Harvard University Press).
Bain, A. (1855), *The Senses and the Intellect* (London: Parker).
  (1859), *The Emotions and the Will* (London: Parker).
  (1861), *On the Study of Character, Including an Estimate of Phrenology* (London: Parker).
  (1865), *The Emotions and the Will*, 2nd edn (London: Longmans, Green, and Co.).
  (1868), *The Senses and the Intellect*, 3rd edn (London: Longmans, Green, and Co.).
  (1873), *Mind and Body: The Theories of their Relation* (London: King).
  (1875), *The Emotions and the Will*, 3rd edn (London: Longmans, Green, and Co.).
  (1894), *The Senses and the Intellect*, 4th edn (London: Longmans, Green, and Co.).
  (1899), *The Emotions and the Will*, 4th edn (London: Longmans, Green, and Co.).
  (1904), *Autobiography* (London: Longmans, Green, and Co.).
Baldwin, J. M. (1891), *Handbook of Psychology I: The Senses and the Intellect*; *II: Feeling and Will* (London: Macmillan).
  (1894), 'The origin of emotional expression', *Psychological Review* 1: 610–23.
Baldwin, J. M. (ed.) (1905), *Dictionary of Philosophy and Psychology* (3 vols. in 4), (London: Macmillan).
Ballantyne, J. (1828), *An Examination of the Human Mind* (Edinburgh: Blackwood).
Barker-Benfield, G. (1992), *The Culture of Sensibility: Sex and Society in Eighteenth-Century Britain* (Chicago: University of Chicago Press).
Barnett, S. (1958), 'The expression of the emotions', in S. Barnett (ed.), *A Century of Darwin* (London: Heinemann), 206–30.
Barrett, P. et al. (eds.) (1986), *A Concordance to Darwin's Expression of the Emotions in Man and Animals* (Ithaca: Cornell University Press).
  (1987a), *Charles Darwin's Notebooks, 1836–1844: Geology, Transmutation of Species, Metaphysical Enquiries* (Cambridge: Cambridge University Press).
  (1987b), *A Concordance to Darwin's The Descent of Man, and Selection in Relation to Sex* (Ithaca: Cornell University Press).
[Baynes, T.] (1873), '*The Expression of the Emotions in Man and Animals* by Charles Darwin', *Edinburgh Review* 137: 492–528.
Beattie, J. (1976), *Elements of Moral Science* (Delmar: Scholars' Facsimiles and Reprints) (first published 1790).

Beaumont, J. et al. (eds.) (1996), *The Blackwell Dictionary of Neuropsychology* (Oxford: Blackwell).

Beecher, E. (1855), *The Right Use of the Passions and Emotions in the Work of Intellectual Culture and Development* (Boston: Tickner and Fields).

Beiser, F. (1996), *The Sovereignty of Reason: the Defense of Rationalism in the Early English Enlightenment* (Princeton: Princeton University Press).

Bell, C. (1806), *Essays on the Anatomy of Expression in Painting* (London: Longman, Hurst, Rees, and Orme).

— (1844), *The Anatomy and Philosophy of Expression, as Connected with the Fine Arts*, 3rd edn (London: Murray).

Belsham, T. (1801), *Elements of the Philosophy of the Mind* (London: Johnson).

Berkley, H. J. (1891), 'Two cases of general cutaneous and sensory anaesthesia, without marked psychical implication', *Brain* 14: 441–64.

Berrios, G. (1996), *The History of Mental Symptoms: Descriptive Psychopathology Since the Nineteenth Century* (Cambridge: Cambridge University Press).

Bishop, J. (1996), 'Moral motivation and the development of Francis Hutcheson's philosophy', *Journal of the History of Ideas* 57.2: 277–95.

Blakey, R. (1848), *History of the Philosophy of Mind: Embracing the Opinions of all Writers on Mental Science from the Earliest Period to the Present Time* (4 vols.), (London: Trelawney W. Saunders).

Blandford, G. (1869), 'On the nature of emotion', *Fortnightly Review* 6: 103–15.

Boase, F. (1921), *Modern English Biography* (6 vols.), (Truro: Netherton and Worth).

Bowler, P. (2001), *Reconciling Science and Religion: The Debate in Early Twentieth-Century Britain* (London and Chicago: University of Chicago Press).

Bozeman, T. D. (1977), *Protestants in an Age of Science: The Baconian Ideal and Antebellum American Religious Thought* (Chapel Hill: University of North Carolina Press).

Brazier, M. (1957), 'The rise of neurophysiology in the nineteenth century', *Journal of Neurophysiology* 20: 212–26.

Brett, G. (1921), *A History of Psychology* (3 vols.), (London: George Allen).

Brinton, A. (1991), ' "Following nature" in Butler's sermons', *Philosophical Quarterly* 41: 325–32.

Brooke, J. H. (1985), 'The relations between Darwin's science and his religion', in J. Durant (ed.), *Darwinism and Divinity: Essays on Evolution and Religious Belief* (Oxford: Blackwell), 40–75.

— (1991), *Science and Religion: Some Historical Perspectives* (Cambridge: Cambridge University Press).

— (1996), 'Science and theology in the Enlightenment', in W. Richardson, and W. Wildman (eds.), *Religion and Science: History, Method, Dialogue* (London: Routledge), 7–27.

— (2003), 'Darwin and Victorian Christianity', in J. Hodge and G. Radick (eds.), *The Cambridge Companion to Darwin* (Cambridge: Cambridge University Press).

Brooke, J. H., and Cantor, G. (1998), *Reconstructing Nature: The Engagement of Science and Religion* (Edinburgh: T. and T. Clark).

Brooks, G. (1976), 'The faculty psychology of Thomas Reid', *Journal of the History of the Behavioral Sciences* 12: 65–77.

Brougham, H. (1835), *A Discourse of Natural Theology, Showing the Nature of the Evidence and the Advantages of the Study*, 3rd edn (London: Knight).
— (1839), *Dissertations on Subjects of Science Connected with Natural Theology* (2 vols.), (London: Knight).
Brown, S. (1982), *Thomas Chalmers and the Godly Commonwealth in Scotland* (Oxford: Oxford University Press).
Brown, T. (1818), *Inquiry into the Relation of Cause and Effect*, 3rd edn (Edinburgh: Constable); reprinted as vol. IV of Brown (2003).
— (1820a), *Lectures on the Philosophy of the Human Mind* (4 vols.), (Edinburgh: Tait).
— (1820b), *Sketch of a System of the Philosophy of the Human Mind* (Edinburgh: Bell and Bradfute); reprinted as vol. V of Brown (2003).
— (1828), *Lectures on the Philosophy of the Human Mind* (Edinburgh: Tait); reprinted as vol. VI of Brown (2003).
— (1846), *Lectures on Ethics, with a Preface by Thomas Chalmers* (Edinburgh: Tait).
— (1860), *Lectures on the Philosophy of the Human Mind*, 20th edn (London: William Tegg and Co.).
— (2003), *Collected Life and Works of Thomas Brown*, ed. T. Dixon (8 vols.), (Bristol: Thoemmes Press).
Brown, W., Murphy, N. and Malony, H. N. (eds.) (1998), *Whatever Happened to the Soul? Scientific and Theological Portraits of Human Nature* (Minneapolis: Fortress Press).
Browne, J. (1985), 'Darwin and the expression of emotions', in D. Kohn (ed.), *The Darwinian Heritage* (Princeton: Princeton University Press), 307–26.
— (1995), *Charles Darwin: Voyaging; Volume 1 of a Biography* (London: Jonathan Cape).
— (1998), 'I could have retched all night: Charles Darwin and his body', in C. Lawrence and S. Shapin (eds.), *Science Incarnate: Historical Embodiments of Natural Knowledge* (Chicago: University of Chicago Press), 240–87.
Bruno, F. (1986), *Dictionary of Key Words in Psychology* (London: Routledge and Kegan Paul).
Bryant, S. (1896), 'Professor James on the emotions', *Proceedings of the Aristotelian Society* 3.2: 52–64.
Buckley, M. (1987), *At the Origins of Modern Atheism* (New Haven: Yale University Press).
Bucknill, J. C. (1874), 'Correspondence; on the theory of emotional insanity', *Journal of Mental Science* 20: 484–6.
Budd, S. (1977), *Varieties of Unbelief: Atheists and Agnostics in English Society 1850–1960* (London: Heinemann).
Burgess, T. (1839), *The Physiology or Mechanism of Blushing; Illustrative of the Influence of Mental Emotion on the Capillary Circulation* (London: Churchill).
Burkhardt, F. *et al.* (eds.) (1994), *The Correspondence of Charles Darwin: Volume IX, 1861* (Cambridge: Cambridge University Press).
Burkhardt, R. (1985), 'Darwin on animal behaviour and evolution', in D. Kohn (ed.), *The Darwinian Heritage* (Princeton: Princeton University Press), 327–65.
Burnaby, J. (1991), *Amor Dei: A Study of the Religion of St Augustine* (Norwich: Canterbury Press) (first published 1938).

Bushnan, J. S. (1851), *Miss Martineau and Her Master* (London: Churchill).
Butler, J. (1970), *Fifteen Sermons Preached at the Rolls Chapel and a Dissertation on the Nature of Virtue*, ed. T. A. Roberts (London: SPCK) (first published 1726).
Calhoun, C. (1984), 'Cognitive emotions?', in C. Calhoun and R. Solomon (eds.), *What is an Emotion? Classic Readings in Philosophical Psychology* (Oxford: Oxford University Press), 327–42.
Calhoun, C., and Solomon, R. (eds.) (1984), *What is an Emotion? Classic Readings in Philosophical Psychology* (Oxford: Oxford University Press).
Campbell, J. A. (1986), 'Scientific revolution and the grammar of culture: the case of Darwin's *Origin*', *Quarterly Journal of Speech* 72: 351–76.
Campbell, S. (1997), 'Emotion as an explanatory principle in early evolutionary theory', *Studies in History and Philosophy of Science* 28: 453–73.
Cannon, W. B. (1915), *Bodily Changes in Pain, Hunger, Fear and Rage* (New York: Appleton).
—— (1927), 'The James–Lange theory of emotions: a critical examination and an alternative theory', *American Journal of Psychology* 29: 106–214.
Cantor, G. (1975), 'The Academy of Physics at Edinburgh 1797–1800', *Social Studies of Science* 5: 109–34.
Capek, M. (1953), 'The reappearance of the self in the last philosophy of William James', *Philosophical Review* 62: 526–44.
Cardno, J. (1955), 'Bain and physiological psychology', *Australian Journal of Psychology* 7: 108–20.
—— (1956), 'Bain as a social psychologist', *Australian Journal of Psychology* 8: 66–76.
Carmichael, L. (1926), 'Sir Charles Bell: a contribution to the history of physiological psychology', *Psychological Review* 33: 188–217.
Cashdollar, C. D. (1989), *The Transformation of Theology, 1830–1890: Positivism and Protestant Thought in Britain and America* (Princeton: Princeton University Press).
Castiglio, D. (1986), 'Considering things minutely: reflections on Mandeville and the eighteenth-century science of man', *History of Political Thought* 7: 463–88.
Cattell, J. M. (1928), 'Early psychological laboratories', *Science* 67: 543–8.
Chalmers, T. (1833), *On the Power, Wisdom and Goodness of God as Manifested in the Adaptation of External Nature to the Moral and Intellectual Constitution of Man* (2 vols.), (London: Pickering).
—— (1853), *On the Power, Wisdom and Goodness of God as Manifested in the Adaptation of External Nature to the Moral and Intellectual Constitution of Man* (London: Bohn) (first published 1833).
Charland, L. (2002), 'The natural kind status of emotion', *British Journal for the Philosophy of Science* 53.4: 1–27.
Cherry, C. (1966), *The Theology of Jonathan Edwards: A Reappraisal* (Garden City: Doubleday).
Cheyne, A. (ed.) (1985), *The Practical and the Pious: Essays on Thomas Chalmers (1780–1847)* (Edinburgh: The Saint Andrew Press).
Chitnis, A. (1986), *The Scottish Enlightenment and Early Victorian English Society* (London: Croom Helm).

Clapper, G. (1989), *John Wesley on Religious Affections: His Views on Experience and Emotion and their Role in the Christian Life and Theology* (Metuchen: The Scarecrow Press).
Clarke, S. (1706), *A Discourse Concerning the Unchangeable Obligations of Natural Religion, and the Truth and Certainty of the Christian Revelation* (London: James Knapton).
Clodd, E. (1885), 'Science and the emotions. A discourse delivered at South Place Chapel, Finsbury, E.C. on Sunday December 27th 1885' (London: E. W. Allen).
(1902), *Thomas Henry Huxley* (Edinburgh: Blackwood).
Cockburn, H. (1909), *Memorials of His Time*, new edn (Edinburgh: Foulis).
Cockshut, A. (1964), *The Unbelievers: English Agnostic Thought 1840–1890* (London: Collins).
Cogan, T. (1802), *A Philosophical Treatise on the Passions* (Bath: S. Hazard).
(1807), *An Ethical Treatise on the Passions* (Bath: Hazard and Binns).
(1812), *Theological Disquisitions; or An Enquiry into those Principles of Religion, which are most influential in directing and regulating the Passions and Affections of the Mind* (Bath: Hazard and Binns).
Condillac, E. de (1930), *Treatise on the Sensations*, trans. G. Carr (London: Favil Press) (first published 1754).
Cooke, W. (1838), *Mind and the Emotions Considered in Relation to Health and Disease* (London: Longman).
(1852), *A Commentary on Medical and Moral Life; or Mind and the Emotions Considered in Relation to Health, Disease and Religion* (London: Longman Brown).
Cooper, S. (1776), *The Power of Christianity Over the Malignant Passions, A Sermon Preached before the University of Cambridge, on Sunday November 3rd, 1776* (Cambridge: Woodyer and Merrill).
Cooter, R. (1984), *The Cultural Meaning of Popular Science: Phrenology and the Organization of Consent in Nineteenth-Century Britain* (Cambridge: Cambridge University Press).
Corrigan, J. (1993), '"Habits from the heart": the American Enlightenment and religious ideas about emotion and habit', *Journal of Religion* 73: 183–99.
Corsini, R. (ed.) (1994), *Encyclopedia of Psychology*, 2nd edn (New York: Wiley).
Cosans, C. (1994), 'Anatomy, metaphysics and values: the ape brain debate reconsidered', *Biology and Philosophy* 9: 129–65.
Coslett, T. (ed.) (1984), *Science and Religion in the Nineteenth Century* (Cambridge: Cambridge University Press).
Cottingham, J. (1998), *Philosophy and the Good Life* (Cambridge: Cambridge University Press).
Cousin, V. (1852), *Course of the History of Modern Philosophy*, trans. O. Wight (2 vols.), (Edinburgh: T. and T. Clark).
Craig, E. (2000), 'Hume on causality: realist *and* projectivist?' in R. Read and K. Richman (eds.), *The New Hume Debate* (London: Routledge), 113–21.
Craig, R. C. (1980), 'The continuity of the associationist aesthetic: from Archibald Alison to T. S. Eliot (and beyond)', *Dalhousie Review* 60: 20–37.

Crosland, M. (1962), *Historical Studies in the Language of Chemistry* (London: Heinemann).
(1980), 'Chemistry and the chemical revolution', in G. Rousseau and R. Porter (eds.), *The Ferment of Knowledge: Studies in the Historiography of Eighteenth-Century Science* (Cambridge: Cambridge University Press), 389–416.
Cross, R. (1998), 'Aquinas on psychology', *Journal of Psychology and Christianity* 17: 306–20.
Cunliffe, C. (ed.) (1992), *Joseph Butler's Moral and Religious Thought* (Oxford: Clarendon Press).
Damasio, A. (1994), *Descartes' Error: Emotion, Reason and the Human Brain* (New York: Avon Books).
Danziger, K. (1982), 'Mid-nineteenth century British psycho-physiology: a neglected chapter in the history of psychology', in W. Woodward and M. Ash (eds.), *The Problematic Science: Psychology in Nineteenth-Century Thought* (New York: Praeger), 119–46.
(1990), 'Generative metaphor and the history of psychological discourse', in D. Leary (ed.), *Metaphors in the History of Psychology* (Cambridge: Cambridge University Press), 331–56.
(1997), *Naming the Mind: How Psychology Found its Language* (London: Sage Publications).
Darwall, S. (1995), *The British Moralists and the Internal 'Ought', 1640–1740* (Cambridge: Cambridge University Press).
Darwin, C. (1871), *The Descent of Man, and Selection in Relation to Sex* (2 vols.), (London: Murray).
(1872), *The Expression of the Emotions in Man and Animals* (London: Murray).
(1877), 'A biographical sketch of an infant', *Mind* 2: 285–94.
(1882), *The Descent of Man, and Selection in Relation to Sex*, 2nd edn (London: Murray).
(1958), *The Autobiography of Charles Darwin*, ed. N. Barlow (London: Collins).
(1985), *On the Origin of Species by Means of Natural Selection*, ed. J. Burrow (London: Penguin) (first published 1859).
(1998), *The Expression of the Emotions in Man and Animals*, 3rd edn (London: Harper Collins).
Darwin, E. (1794), *Zoonomia* (London: Johnson).
Daston, L. (1982), 'The theory of will versus the science of mind', in W. Woodward and M. Ash (eds.), *The Problematic Science: Psychology in Nineteenth-Century Thought* (New York: Praeger), 88–115.
Davie, G. (1991), *The Scottish Enlightenment and Other Essays* (Edinburgh: Polygon).
(1994), *A Passion for Ideas: Essays on the Scottish Enlightenment II* (Edinburgh: Polygon).
Davies, W. (1880), 'The border-land between physiology and psychology', *Journal of Mental Science* 26: 201–15.
Davis, A. (1948), *Isaac Watts: His Life and Works* (London: Independent Press).
Dawkins, R. (1976), *The Selfish Gene* (Oxford: Oxford University Press).
De Sousa, R. (1987), *The Rationality of Emotion* (Cambridge, MA: MIT Press).
Denby, D. (1994), *Sentimental Narrative and the Social Order in France, 1760–1820* (Cambridge: Cambridge University Press).

Descartes, R. (1984), *The Passions of the Soul*, in J. Cottingham, R. Stoothoff and D. Murdoch (eds.), *The Philosophical Writings of Descartes* (Cambridge: Cambridge University Press).
(1988), *Selected Philosophical Writings*, trans. J. Cottingham *et al.* (Cambridge: Cambridge University Press).
Desmond, A. (1989), *The Politics of Evolution* (Chicago: University of Chicago Press).
(1994), *Huxley: The Devil's Disciple* (London: Michael Joseph).
(1997), *Huxley: Evolution's High Priest* (London: Michael Joseph).
Desmond, A., and Moore, J. (1992), *Darwin* (London: Penguin).
Devine, T. (1999) *The Scottish Nation 1700–2000* (London: Allen Lane).
Dewey, J. (1894), 'The theory of emotion. I. Emotional attitudes', *Psychological Review* 1: 553–69.
(1895), 'The theory of emotion. II. The significance of emotions', *Psychological Review* 2: 13–32.
Di Gregorio, M. (1984), *T. H. Huxley's Place in Natural Science* (New Haven: Yale University Press).
Di Gregorio, M. (ed.) (1990), *Charles Darwin's Marginalia, Vol. 1* (New York: Garland).
Dixon, T. (1999), 'Theology, anti-theology and atheology: from Christian passions to secular emotions', *Modern Theology* 15: 297–330.
(2001), 'The psychology of the emotions in Britain and America in the nineteenth century: the role of religious and antireligious commitments', *Osiris*, 16: 288–320.
(2002a), 'John Abercrombie', in W. J. Mander and A. P. F. Sell (eds.), *Dictionary of Nineteenth-Century British Philosophers* (2 vols.), (Bristol: Thoemmes Press).
(2002b), 'William Lyall', in W. J. Mander and A. P. F. Sell (eds.), *Dictionary of Nineteenth-Century British Philosophers* (2 vols.), (Bristol: Thoemmes Press).
(2002c), 'George Ramsay', in W. J. Mander and A. P. F. Sell (eds.), *Dictionary of Nineteenth-Century British Philosophers* (2 vols.), (Bristol: Thoemmes Press).
(2002d), 'Scientific atheism as a faith tradition', *Studies in History and Philosophy of Biological and Biomedical Sciences* 33: 337–59.
Dockrill, D. W. (1971), 'T. H. Huxley and the meaning of "agnosticism"', *Theology* 74: 461–77.
Dodds, J. (1995), *Thomas Chalmers: A Biographical Study* (London: Routledge/Thoemmes Press) (first published 1870).
Douglas, J. (1839), *On the Philosophy of the Mind* (Edinburgh: Black).
Dunbar, F. (1954), *Emotions and Bodily Changes: A Survey of Literature on Psychosomatic Interrelationships 1910–1953*, 4th edn (New York: Columbia University Press).
Dunlop, A. (1846), 'Memoir of David Welsh', in D. Welsh (ed.), *Sermons* (Edinburgh: Kennedy).
Durant, J. (1989), 'Evolution, ideology and world view: Darwinian religion in the twentieth century', in J. Moore (ed.), *History, Humanity and Evolution: Essays for John C. Greene* (Cambridge: Cambridge University Press), 355–73.
Dwyer, J. (1998), *The Age of the Passions: An Interpretation of Adam Smith and Scottish Enlightenment Culture* (East Linton: Tuckwell Press).

Edwards, J. (1957), *Freedom of the Will*, ed. P. Ramsey (New Haven: Yale University Press) (first published 1754).
 (1959), *A Treatise Concerning Religious Affections*, ed. J. Smith (New Haven: Yale University Press) (first published 1746).
Ekman, P. (1998), Preface and commentary, C. Darwin, *The Expression of the Emotions in Man and Animals*, 3rd edn (London: Harper Collins).
Ellis, H. (1895a), 'German psychological laboratories', *Journal of Mental Science* 41: 157–9.
 (1895b), 'The psychology of emotion', *Journal of Mental Science* 41: 159–62.
Ellison, J. (1999), *Cato's Tears and the Making of Anglo-American Emotion* (Chicago: University of Chicago Press).
Ellsworth, P. (1994), 'William James and emotion: is a century of fame worth a century of misunderstanding?', *Psychological Review* 101: 222–9.
Elster, J. (1999), *Alchemies of the Mind: Rationality and the Emotions* (Cambridge: Cambridge University Press).
Emerson, R. (1990), 'Science and moral philosophy in the Scottish Enlightenment', in M. Stewart (ed.), *Studies in the Philosophy of the Scottish Enlightenment* (Oxford: Clarendon Press), 11–36.
English, H., and English, A. (1958), *A Comprehensive Dictionary of Psychological and Psychoanalytic Terms* (New York: Longmans, Green, and Co.).
Escott, H. (1876), *Papers on Emotion in Religion, and Preaching to the Uneducated* (London: Elliot Stock).
Evans, D. (2001), *Emotion: The Science of Sentiment* (Oxford: Oxford University Press).
Eysenck, M. (ed.) (1990), *The Blackwell Dictionary of Cognitive Psychology* (Oxford: Blackwell).
Falconer, W. (1788), *A Dissertation on the Influence of the Passions upon Disorders of the Body* (London: C. Dilly).
Fancher, E. (1996), *Pioneers of Psychology*, 3rd edn (New York: Norton).
Feinstein, H. (1970), 'William James on the emotions', *Journal of the History of Ideas* 31: 133–42.
Fisch, M. (1954), 'Alexander Bain and the genealogy of Pragmatism', *Journal of the History of Ideas* 15: 413–44.
Fitzer, J. (ed.) (1989), *Romance and the Rock: Nineteenth-Century Catholics on Faith and Reason* (Minneapolis: Fortress Press).
Fitzpatrick, M. (1993), 'Latitudinarianism at the parting of the ways: a suggestion', in J. Walsh *et al.* (eds.), *The Church of England, c.1689–c.1833: From Toleration to Tractarianism* (Cambridge: Cambridge University Press), 209–27.
Flanagan, O., and Rorty, A. O. (eds.) (1990), *Identity, Character and Morality: Essays in Moral Psychology* (Cambridge, MA: MIT Press).
Flynn, P. (1980), 'Scottish aesthetics and the search for a standard of taste', *Dalhousie Review* 60: 5–19.
 (1988), 'Scottish philosophers, Scotch reviewers, and the science of mind', *Dalhousie Review* 68: 259–83.
Fotherby, H. (1869), *Scientific Associations, Their Rise, Progress, and Influence, with A History of the Hunterian Society* (London: Bell and Daldy).

Frey, R. (1992), 'Butler on self-love and benevolence', in C. Cunliffe (ed.), *Joseph Butler's Moral and Religious Thought* (Oxford: Clarendon Press), 244–66.
Fridlund, A. (1992), 'Darwin's anti-Darwinism in the *Expression of the Emotions in Man and Animals*', in K. Strongman (ed.), *International Review of Studies on Emotion* (2 vols.), (Chichester: Wiley), II, 117–37.
Fulcher, J. R. (1973), 'Puritans and the passions: the faculty psychology in American Puritanism', *Journal of the History of the Behavioral Sciences* 9: 123–39.
Gale, R. (1999), *The Divided Self of William James* (Cambridge: Cambridge University Press).
Gallie, R. (1998), *Thomas Reid: Ethics, Aesthetics and the Anatomy of the Self* (Dordrecht: Kluwer).
Gardiner, H. N. (1894), '"Recherches sur les rapports de la sensibilité et de l'émotion" by P. Sollier, and "Professor James' Theory of Emotion" by D. Irons', *Psychological Review* 1: 544–51.
  (1896), 'Recent discussion of emotion', *Philosophical Review* 5: 102–12.
Gardiner, H. N. et al. (1970), *Feeling and Emotion: A History of Theories* (Westport: Greenwood Press) (first published 1937).
Gaskin, J. (1988), *Hume's Philosophy of Religion* (London: Macmillan).
Gaustad, E. (1957), *The Great Awakening in New England* (New York: Harper).
Gellner, E. (1992), *Reason and Culture* (Oxford: Blackwell).
Gergen, K. (1995), 'Metaphor and monophony in the twentieth-century psychology of emotions', *History of the Human Sciences* 8: 1–23.
Giancotti, E. (1999), 'The theory of the affects in the strategy of Spinoza's *Ethics*', in Y. Yovel (ed.), *Desire and Affect: Spinoza as Psychologist. Papers Presented at the Third Jerusalem Conference (Ethica III)* (New York: Little Room Press), 129–38.
Gibbons, T. (1780), *Memoirs of the Rev. Isaac Watts D.D.* (London: Buckland).
Gillispie, C. (1959), *Genesis and Geology: A Study in the Relations of Scientific Thought, Natural Theology, and Social Opinion in Great Britain, 1790–1850* (New York: Harper and Row).
Gilman, J. (1994), 'Reenfranchising the heart: narrative emotions and contemporary theology', *Journal of Religion* 74: 218–39.
Gladstone, D. (1995), 'Thomas Chalmers on poverty, pauperism and political economy', introduction to J. Dodds, *Thomas Chalmers: A Biographical Study* (London: Routledge/Thoemmes Press), v–xcvi.
Goldie, P. (2000), *The Emotions: A Philosophical Exploration* (Oxford: Clarendon Press).
Goleman, D. (1995), *Emotional Intelligence* (New York: Bantam Books).
  (1996), *Emotional Intelligence: Why It Can Matter More Than IQ* (London: Bloomsbury).
Goodwin, C. J. (1999), *A History of Modern Psychology* (New York: Wiley).
Goodwin, H. (1880), 'God and nature', *Nineteenth Century* 7: 503–15.
Gordon-Taylor, G., and Walls, E. W. (1958), *Sir Charles Bell: His Life and Times* (Edinburgh: E. & S. Livingstone).
Gorman, T. (1875), *Christian Psychology: The Soul and the Body in their Correlation and Contrast, being a new translation of Swedenborg's* Tractate de Commercio

Animae et Corporis, etc. *with preface and illustrative notes* (London: Longman's, Green, Reader and Dyer).

Graham, G. (2001), 'Morality and feeling in the Scottish Enlightenment', *Philosophy* 76: 271–82.

Grange, K. (1961), 'Pinel and eighteenth-century psychiatry', *Bulletin of the History of Medicine* 35: 422–53.

—— (1962), 'The ship symbol as a key to former theories of the emotions', *Bulletin of the History of Medicine* 36: 512–23.

Grave, S. (1960), *The Scottish Philosophy of Common Sense* (Oxford: Clarendon Press).

Greenblatt, S. (1991), 'The development of modern neurological thinking in the 1860s', *Perspectives in Biology and Medicine* 35: 129–39.

Greene, J. C. (1981), *Science, Ideology and World View: Essays in the History of Evolutionary Ideas* (Berkeley: University of California Press).

Greenspan, P. (1988), *Emotions and Reasons: An Inquiry into Emotional Justification* (London and New York: Routledge).

Greenway, A. (1973), 'The incorporation of action into Associationism: the psychology of Alexander Bain', *Journal of the History of the Behavioral Sciences* 9: 42–52.

Greenwood, J. (1994), *Realism, Identity and Emotion: Reclaiming Social Psychology* (London: Sage).

Gregory, R. (ed.) (1987), *The Oxford Companion to the Mind* (Oxford: Oxford University Press).

Griffin, N. (1990), 'Possible theological perspectives in Thomas Reid's common sense philosophy', *Journal of Ecclesiastical History* 41: 425–42.

Griffiths, P. (1997), *What Emotions Really Are: The Problem of Psychological Categories* (Chicago: University of Chicago Press).

Griswold, C. (1999), *Adam Smith and the Virtues of Enlightenment* (Cambridge: Cambridge University Press).

Gruber, H. (1974), *Darwin on Man* (New York: Dutton).

Gurney, E. (1884), 'What is an emotion?', *Mind* 9: 421–6.

Haakonssen, K. (1999), 'Thomas Reid', in J. Yolton *et al*. (eds.), *Dictionary of Eighteenth-Century British Philosophers* (2 vols.), (Bristol: Thoemmes).

Hacking, I. (1998), 'By what link are the organs excited?', *Times Literary Supplement*, July 17: 11–12.

Hallam, G. (1955), 'Source of the word "agnostic"', *Modern Language Notes* 70: 265–9.

Hamlyn, D. (1987), *A History of Western Philosophy* (Harmondsworth: Viking).

Hanna, W. (1878), *Memoirs of Thomas Chalmers*, new edn (2 vols.), (Edinburgh: David Douglas).

Harré, R. (ed.) (1986), *The Social Construction of Emotions* (Oxford: Blackwell).

Harré, R., and Parrot, G. (eds.) (1996), *The Emotions: Social, Cultural and Biological Dimensions* (London: Sage Publications).

Harris, J. (2002), 'Thomas Brown', in W. J. Mander and A. P. F. Sell (eds.), *Dictionary of Nineteenth-Century British Philosophers* (2 vols.), (Bristol: Thoemmes Press).

Hartley, L. (2001), *Physiognomy and the Meaning of Expression in Nineteenth-Century Culture* (Cambridge: Cambridge University Press).

[Haywood, E.] (1748), *Life's Progress Through the Passions: or, The Adventures of Natura* (London: T. Gardner).

Hearnshaw, L. (1964), *A Short History of British Psychology 1840–1940* (London: Methuen).

—— (1987), *The Shaping of Modern Psychology* (London: Routledge and Kegan Paul).

Herbert, S. (1977), 'The place of man in the development of Darwin's theory of transmutation. Part II', *Journal of the History of Biology* 10: 155–227.

Hickok, L. (1859), *Empirical Psychology; or The Human Mind as Given in Consciousness*, 2nd edn (New York: Ivison and Phinney).

Hilton, B. (1988), *The Age of Atonement: The Influence of Evangelicalism on Social and Economic Thought, 1795–1865* (Oxford: Clarendon Press).

Hirschman, A. (1997), *The Passions and the Interests: Political Arguments for Capitalism before its Triumph*, Twentieth Anniversary Edition (Princeton: Princeton University Press) (first published 1977).

Hobbes, T. (1994), *Human Nature and De Corpore Politico* (Bristol: Thoemmes Press) (first published 1650).

—— (1997), *Leviathan*, ed. R. E. Flathman and D. Johnston (New York and London: Norton) (first published 1651).

Hodgson, S. (1870), *The Theory of Practice: An Ethical Enquiry* (2 vols.), (London: Longmans, Green, Reader and Dyer).

Hoeveler, D. J. (1981), *James McCosh and the Scottish Intellectual Tradition: From Glasgow to Princeton* (Princeton: Princeton University Press).

Holland, H. (1852), *Chapters on Mental Physiology* (London: Longman, Brown, Green and Longmans).

—— (1872), *Recollections of Past Life* (London: Longmans, Green and Co.).

Hoy, D. (1986), 'Nietzsche, Hume, and the genealogical method', in Y. Yovel (ed.), *Nietzsche as Affirmative Thinker* (Dordrecht: Martinus Nijhoff), 20–38.

Hoyles, J. (1971), *The Waning of the Renaissance 1640–1740: Studies in the Thought and Poetry of Henry More, John Norris, and Isaac Watts* (The Hague: Martinus Nijhoff).

Hume, D. (1978), *A Treatise of Human Nature*, ed. L. Selby-Bigge and P. Nidditch (Oxford: Clarendon Press) (first published 1739–40).

—— (1998), *An Enquiry Concerning the Principles of Morals*, ed. T. Beauchamp (Oxford: Oxford University Press), (first published 1777).

Hunt, J. (1896), *Religious Thought in England in the Nineteenth Century* (London: Gibbings and Co.).

Hunter, R., and Macalpine, I. (1963), *Three Hundred Years of Psychiatry, 1535–1860* (Oxford: Oxford University Press).

Hunterian Society (1869), *Transactions of the Hunterian Society Session 1868–9* (London: Brown).

Hutcheson, F. (1742), *An Essay on the Nature and Conduct of the Passions and Affections. With Illustrations on the Moral Sense*, 3rd edn (London: Ward et al.).

Huxley, L. (ed.) (1903), *Life and Letters of Thomas Henry Huxley*, 2nd edn (3 vols.), (London: Macmillan).
Huxley, T. (1863), *Evidence as to Man's Place in Nature* (London: Williams and Norgate).
  (1893), 'Science and morals', in *The Collected Essays of T. H. Huxley* (9 vols.), (London: Macmillan), IX, 117–46.
  (1894), 'On the hypothesis that animals are automata and its history', in *The Collected Essays of T. H. Huxley* (9 vols.), (London: Macmillan), I, 199–250.
Innes, R. (1997), 'Integrating the self through the desire of God', *Augustinian Studies* 28: 67–109.
Irons, D. (1894), 'Professor James' theory of emotion', *Mind* NS 3: 77–97.
  (1895a), 'The physical basis of emotion: a reply', *Mind* NS 4: 92–9.
  (1895b), 'Descartes and modern theories of emotion', *Philosophical Review* 4: 291–302.
  (1895c), 'Recent developments in theory of emotion', *Psychological Review* 2: 279–84.
  (1897), 'The nature of emotion I, and II', *Philosophical Review* 6: 242–56, 471–96.
  (1903), *The Psychology of Ethics* (Edinburgh: Blackwood).
Jacobson, D. (1987), 'Jonathan Edwards and the "American difference": Pragmatic reflections on the "sense of the heart"', *Journal of American Studies* 21: 377–85.
Jacyna, L. (1981), 'The physiology of mind, the unity of nature, and the moral order in Victorian thought', *British Journal for the History of Science* 14: 109–32.
James, S. (1997), *Passion and Action: The Emotions in Seventeenth-Century Philosophy* (Oxford: Clarendon Press).
James, W. (1876), '*The Emotions and the Will* by Alexander Bain and *Essais de Critique Générale* by Charles Renouvier', *Nation* 22: 367–9.
  (1884), 'What is an emotion?', *Mind* 9: 188–205.
  (1885), 'The function of cognition', *Mind* 10: 27–44.
  (1892a), 'Sully's human mind', *Nation* 55: 285–6.
  (1892b), '*Le Cervelet et ses Fonctions* by F. Courmont', *Philosophical Review* 1: 319–22.
  (1894a), '*Psychology: Descriptive and Explanatory*, by George T. Ladd', *Psychological Review* 1: 286–93.
  (1894b), 'The physical basis of emotion', *Psychological Review* 1: 516–29.
  (1981), *The Principles of Psychology* (2 vols.), (Cambridge, MA: Harvard University Press) (first published 1890).
  (1985), *The Varieties of Religious Experience* (London: Penguin) (first published 1902).
Janet, P., and Séailles, G. (1902), *A History of the Problems of Philosophy*, trans. A. Monahan (2 vols.), (London: Macmillan).
Jeeves, M. (1997), *Human Nature at the Millennium: Reflections on the Integration of Psychology and Christianity* (Leicester: Apollos).
[Jeffrey, F.] (1811), 'Archibald Alison, *Essays on the Nature and Principles of Taste*', *Edinburgh Review* 18: 1–46.

Jenson, R. (1988), *America's Theologian: A Recommendation of Jonathan Edwards* (Oxford: Oxford University Press).
Johnson, S. (1785), *The Life of the Rev. Isaac Watts D.D.* (London: Rivington).
— (1967), *A Dictionary of the English Language* (New York: AMS Press) (first published 1755).
Johnson, W. (1850), *The Morbid Emotions of Women: Their Origin, Tendencies and Treatment* (London: Simpkin, Marshall and Co.).
Jones, P. (ed.) (1988), *Philosophy and Science in the Scottish Enlightenment* (Edinburgh: John Donald).
Kallich, M. (1999), 'Archibald Alison', in J. Yolton *et al.* (eds.), *Dictionary of Eighteenth-Century British Philosophers* (2 vols.), (Bristol: Thoemmes).
Kames, H. (1765), *Elements of Criticism*, 3rd edn (2 vols.), (Edinburgh: Kincaid and Bell).
Keegan, R. (1989), 'How Charles Darwin became a psychologist', in D. Wallace and H. Gruber (eds.), *Creative People at Work: Twelve Cognitive Case Studies* (Oxford: Oxford University Press), 107–26.
Kenny, A. (1963), *Action, Emotion and Will* (London: Routledge and Kegan Paul).
— (1993), *Aquinas on Mind* (London: Routledge).
Kirby, W. (1835), *On the Power, Wisdom, and Goodness of God as Manifested in the Creation of Animals and in Their History, Habits and Instincts* (London: William Pickering).
Klein, D. (1970), *A History of Scientific Psychology: Its Origins and Philosophical Backgrounds* (London: Routledge and Kegan Paul).
Knight, D. (1986), *The Age of Science: The Scientific World-view in the Nineteenth Century* (Oxford: Blackwell).
Koch, S., and Leary, D. (eds.) (1985), *A Century of Psychology as Science* (New York: McGraw-Hill).
Kohn, D. (1989), 'Darwin's ambiguity: the secularization of biological meaning', *British Journal for the History of Science* 22: 215–39.
Kuhn, T. (1970), *The Structure of Scientific Revolutions*, 2nd edn (Chicago: University of Chicago Press).
Ladd, G. T. (1892), 'Psychology as so-called "natural science"', *Philosophical Review* 1: 24–53.
— (1894a), *Psychology, Descriptive and Explanatory: A Treatise of the Phenomena, Laws, and Development of Human Mental Life* (London: Longmans, Green, and Co.).
— (1894b), 'Is psychology a science?', *Psychological Review* 1: 392–5.
Lange, F. A. (1879–81), *History of Materialism and Criticism of its Present Importance*, trans. E. C. Thomas, 2nd edn (3 vols.), (London: Trübner).
Laurie, H. (1902), *Scottish Philosophy in its National Development* (Glasgow: Maclehose).
Laycock, T. (1861), *The Scientific Place and Principles of Medical Psychology: An Introductory Address* (Edinburgh: Murray and Gibb).
Lazarus, R. (1991), *Emotion and Adaptation* (Oxford: Oxford University Press).
Leary, D. (1987), 'Telling likely stories: the rhetoric of the new psychology, 1880–1920', *Journal of the History of the Behavioral Sciences* 23: 315–31.
Leary, D. (ed.) (1990), *Metaphors in the History of Psychology* (Cambridge: Cambridge University Press).

LeDoux, J. (1996), *The Emotional Brain: The Mysterious Underpinnings of Emotional Life* (New York: Simon and Schuster).
Letwin, O. (1987), *Ethics, Emotion and the Unity of Self* (London: Croom Helm).
Leventhal, H., and Scherer, K. (1987), 'The relationship of emotion to cognition: a functional approach to a semantic controversy', *Cognition and Emotion* 1: 3–28.
Levi, A. (1964), *French Moralists: The Theory of the Passions 1585–1649* (Oxford: Clarendon Press).
Lewes, G. H. (1879), *The Study of Psychology: Its Object, Scope and Method* (London: Trübner).
——— (1880), *The History of Philosophy from Thales to Comte*, 5th edn (2 vols.), (London: Longmans, Green, and Co.).
Lewis, A. (1951), 'The twenty-fifth Maudsley lecture – Henry Maudsley: his work and influence', *Journal of Mental Science* 97: 259–77.
Lewis, M., and Haviland, J. (eds.) (1993), *Handbook of Emotions* (London: Guildford Press).
Lightman, B. (1987), *The Origins of Agnosticism: Victorian Unbelief and the Limits of Knowledge* (Baltimore: Johns Hopkins University Press).
——— (1989), 'Ideology, evolution and late-Victorian agnostic popularizers', in J. Moore (ed.), *History, Humanity and Evolution: Essays for John C. Greene* (Cambridge: Cambridge University Press), 285–309.
Lind, M. (1990), 'Hume and moral emotions', in O. Flanagan and A. O. Rorty (eds.), *Identity, Character and Morality: Essays in Moral Psychology* (Cambridge, MA: MIT Press), 133–47.
Lindberg, D. (1992), *The Beginnings of Western Science* (Chicago: University of Chicago Press).
Livingstone, D. (1992), 'Darwinism and Calvinism: the Belfast–Princeton connection', *Isis* 83: 408–28.
Locke, J. (1975), *An Essay Concerning Human Understanding*, ed. P. Nidditch (Oxford: Clarendon Press) (first published 1690).
Luyendijk-Elshout, A. (1990), 'Of masks and mills: the enlightened doctor and his frightened patient', in G. Rousseau (ed.), *The Languages of Psyche: Mind and Body in Enlightenment Thought* (Berkeley: University of California Press), 186–230.
[Lyall, W.] (1842), *Strictures on the Idea of Power; With Special Reference to the Views of Dr Brown in his 'Inquiry into the Relation of Cause and Effect'* (Edinburgh: Johnstone).
Lyall, W. (1848), *Sermons* (Edinburgh: Johnstone).
——— (1855), *Intellect, the Emotions, and the Moral Nature* (Edinburgh: Thomas Constable and Co.).
Lyons, W. (1980), *Emotion* (Cambridge: Cambridge University Press).
Mackintosh, J. (1836), *Dissertation on the Progress of Ethical Philosophy* (Edinburgh: Black).
——— (1837), *Dissertation on the Progress of Ethical Philosophy*, 2nd edn (Edinburgh: Black).
——— (1862), *Dissertation on the Progress of Ethical Philosophy*, 3rd edn (Edinburgh: Black).

Malone, D. (ed.) (1933), *The Dictionary of American Biography* (New York: Scribner).
Mandelbaum, M. (1984), *History, Man and Reason: A Study in Nineteenth-Century Thought* (Baltimore: Johns Hopkins University Press).
Mandeville, B. (1970), *The Fable of the Bees*, ed. P. Harth (Harmondsworth: Penguin) (first published 1714).
Mandler, G. (1984), *Mind and Body: Psychology of Emotion and Stress* (New York: Norton).
Manier, E. (1978), *The Young Darwin and his Cultural Circle: A Study of Influences which Helped Shape the Language and Logic of the First Drafts of the Theory of Natural Selection* (Dordrecht: Reidel).
Marcil-Lacoste, L. (1980), 'Hume's scepticism and Reid's challenge', *Dalhousie Review* 60: 67–86.
Marks, J. (1982), 'A theory of emotion', *Philosophical Studies* 42: 227–42.
Martin, T. (1961), *The Instructed Vision: Scottish Common Sense Philosophy and the Origins of American Fiction* (Bloomington: Indiana University Press).
Maudsley, H. (1870), *Body and Mind: An Inquiry into their Connection and Mutual Influence, Especially in Reference to Mental Disorders, being the Gulstonian Lectures for 1870, delivered before the Royal College of Physicians* (London: Macmillan).
(1876), *The Physiology of Mind* (London: Macmillan).
McAleer, G. (1999), 'The politics of the flesh: Rahner and Aquinas on *concupiscentia*', *Modern Theology* 15: 355–65.
McCosh, J. (1857), 'Scottish metaphysicians', *North British Review* 27: 404–9.
(1861), *The Association of Ideas and its Influence on the Training of the Mind: A Lecture* (Dublin: Hodges, Smith, and Co.).
(1875), *The Scottish Philosophy from Hutcheson to Hamilton* (London: Macmillan).
(1877), 'Elements involved in emotions', *Mind* 2: 413–15.
(1880), *The Emotions* (London: Macmillan).
(1886), *Psychology: The Cognitive Powers* (London: Macmillan).
(1887), *Psychology: The Motive Powers; Emotions, Conscience, Will* (London: Macmillan).
McKillop, A. (1979), *A Disciplined Intelligence: Critical Inquiry and Canadian Thought in the Victorian Era* (Montreal: McGill-Queen's University Press).
McLennan, S. F. (1895), 'Emotion, desire and interest: descriptive', *Psychological Review* 2: 462–74.
Melhado, E. (1985), 'Chemistry, physics and the chemical revolution', *Isis* 76: 195–211.
Mercier, C. (1884a), 'A classification of feelings I', *Mind* 9: 325–48.
(1884b), 'A classification of feelings II', *Mind* 9: 509–30.
(1885), 'A classification of feelings III', *Mind* 10: 1–26.
Midgley, M. (1985), *Evolution as a Religion: Strange Hopes and Stranger Fears* (London: Methuen).
(1991), *Science as Salvation: A Modern Myth and its Meaning* (London: Routledge).

Milbank, J. (1990), *Theology and Social Theory: Beyond Secular Reason* (Oxford: Blackwell).
Miles, M. (1992), *Desire and Delight: A New Reading of Augustine's Confessions* (New York: Crossroad).
Mill, J. (1829), *Analysis of the Phenomena of the Human Mind* (London: Baldwin and Craddock).
Mill, J. S. (1843), *A System of Logic, Ratiocinative and Inductive, Being a Connected View of the Principles of Evidence, and the Methods of Scientific Investigation* (2 vols.), (London: Parker).
[Mill, J. S.] (1859), 'Bain's psychology', *Edinburgh Review* 110: 287–321.
Mill, J. S. (1996), *Essays on Ethics, Religion and Society*, ed. J. Robson (London: Routledge).
Millar, A. (1988), 'Following nature', *Philosophical Quarterly* 38: 165–85.
Miller, P. (1952), 'Jonathan Edwards and the Great Awakening', in D. Aaron (ed.), *America in Crisis* (New York: Knopf), 3–19.
  (1959), *Jonathan Edwards* (New York: Meridian).
Millingen, J. G. (1847), *Mind and Matter, Illustrated by Considerations on Heredity, Insanity, and the Influence of Temperament in the Development of the Passions* (London: Hurst).
Mills, E. S. (1969), *George Trumbull Ladd: Pioneer American Psychologist* (Cleveland and London: The Press of Case Western Reserve University).
Milner, T. (1834), *The Life, Times, and Correspondence of the Rev. Isaac Watts* (London: Simpkin and Marshall).
Mischel, T. (1966), '"Emotion" and "motivation" in the development of English psychology: D. Hartley, James Mill, A. Bain', *Journal for the History of the Behavioral Sciences* 3: 123–44.
Misiak, H., and Sexton, V. S. (1966), *History of Psychology: An Overview* (New York and London: Grune and Stratton).
Montgomery, W. (1985), 'Charles Darwin's thought on expressive mechanisms in evolution', in G. Zivin (ed.), *The Development of Expressive Behavior* (Orlando, FL: Academic Press), 27–50.
Moore, J. R. (1979), *The Post-Darwinian Controversies: A Study of the Protestant Struggle to Come to Terms with Darwin in Great Britain and America 1870–1900* (Cambridge: Cambridge University Press).
  (1981), 'Creation and the problem of Charles Darwin', *British Journal for the History of Science* 14: 189–99.
  (1992), 'Speaking of "science and religion" – then and now' (review of J. H. Brooke, *Science and Religion: Some Historical Perspectives*), *History of Science* 30: 311–23.
Moore, J. R. (ed.) (1989), *History, Humanity and Evolution: Essays for John C. Greene* (Cambridge: Cambridge University Press).
Moore, J. W. (1990), 'The two systems of Francis Hutcheson: on the origins of the Scottish Enlightenment', in M. Stewart (ed.), *Studies in the Philosophy of the Scottish Enlightenment* (Oxford: Clarendon Press), 37–59.
More, J. (1872), 'The emotions and the psychology of Darwin', *Lancet*: 112–14.
Morell, J. D. (1846), *An Historical and Critical View of the Speculative Philosophy of Europe in the Nineteenth Century* (2 vols.), (London: William Pickering).

Morgan, C. L. (1923), *Emergent Evolution: The Gifford Lectures, 1922* (London: Williams and Norgate).
Morrell, J. (1975), 'The Leslie affair: careers, kirk and politics in Edinburgh in 1805', *Scottish Historical Review* 54: 63–82.
Müller, J. (1837), *The Elements of Physiology*, trans. W. Baly (London: Taylor and Walton).
Murphy, G. (1929), *Historical Introduction to Modern Psychology* (London: Kegan Paul, Trench and Trubner).
Murphy, G., and Kovach, J. (1972), *Historical Introduction to Modern Psychology*, 3rd edn (New York: Harcourt Brace Jovanovich).
Murphy, N. (1990), *Theology in the Age of Probable Reasoning* (Ithaca: Cornell University Press).
Murray, D. (1911), *Christian Faith and the New Psychology* (London and Edinburgh: Fleming and H. Revell).
  (1983), *A History of Western Psychology* (Englewood Cliffs, NJ: Prentice-Hall).
Myers, G. (1969), 'William James' theory of emotion', *Transactions of the Charles S. Peirce Society* 5: 67–89.
Newman, J. H. (1870), *An Essay in Aid of a Grammar of Assent* (London: Burns, Oates and Co.).
  (1974), *The Letters and Diaries of John Henry Newman*, vol. XXVI, ed. C. Dessain (Oxford: Clarendon Press).
Newton-Smith, W. (1981), *The Rationality of Science* (London: Routledge).
Nietzsche, F. (1967), *On the Genealogy of Morals*, trans. W. Kaufmann and R. Hollingdale (New York: Vintage Books, Random House) (first published 1887).
Oakley, J. (1992), *Morality and the Emotions* (London: Routledge).
Oatley, K. (1992), *Best Laid Schemes: The Psychology of Emotions* (Cambridge: Cambridge University Press).
Oatley, K., and Jenkins, J. (1996), *Understanding Emotions* (Oxford: Blackwell).
O'Connell, R. (1987), *The Origin of the Soul in St Augustine's Later Works* (New York: Fordham University Press).
O'Connor, H. (1837), *Connected Essays and Tracts* (Dublin: Hodges and Smith).
O'Daly, G. (1987), *Augustine's Philosophy of Mind* (Berkeley and Los Angeles: University of California Press).
Oden, T. (1984), *Care of Souls in the Classic Tradition* (Philadelphia: Fortress Press).
Oldroyd, D. and Langham, I. (eds.) (1983), *The Wider Domain of Evolutionary Thought* (Dordrecht: Reidel).
Oliphant, Mrs (1893), *Thomas Chalmers: Preacher, Philosopher and Statesman* (London: Methuen).
Olson, R. (1975), *Scottish Philosophy and British Physics 1750–1880: A Study in the Foundations of the Victorian Scientific Style* (Princeton, NJ: Princeton University Press).
Olson, R. (ed.) (1971), *Science as Metaphor: The Historical Role of Scientific Theories in Forming Western Culture* (Belmont, CA: Wadsworth).
Owen, D. (1999), *Hume's Reason* (Oxford: Oxford University Press).
Page, F. H. (1980), 'William Lyall in his setting', *Dalhousie Review* 60: 49–66.

Paine, M. (1849), *A Discourse on the Soul and Instinct, Physiologically Distinguished from Materialism*, enlarged edn (New York: Fletcher).
 (1872), *Physiology of the Soul and Instinct as Distinguished from Materialism, with Supplementary Demonstrations of the Divine Communication of the Narratives of Creation and the Flood* (New York: Harper).
Paley, W. (1785), *The Principles of Moral and Political Philosophy* (London: Faulder).
Payne, G. (1828), *Elements of Mental and Moral Science* (London: Holdsworth).
Philip, A. (1929), *Thomas Chalmers: Apostle of Union* (London: Clarke).
Pichot, A. (1860), *The Life and Labours of Sir Charles Bell* (London: Richard Bentley).
Pinch, A. (1995), 'Emotion and history: a review article', *Comparative Studies in Society and History* 37: 100–9.
 (1996), *Strange Fits of Passion: Epistemologies of Emotion, Hume to Austen* (Stanford: Stanford University Press).
Pinker, S. (1997), *How the Mind Works* (London: Allen Lane).
Plato (1974), *The Republic*, trans. H. D. P. Lee, 2nd edn, revised (Harmondsworth: Penguin).
Pope, A. (1993), *An Essay on Man*, ed. M. Mack (London: Routledge) (first published 1733).
Pope, S. (1997), 'Neither enemy nor friend: nature as creation in the theology of Thomas Aquinas', *Zygon* 32: 219–30.
Porter, N. (1872a), *The Human Intellect with an Introduction upon Psychology and the Soul* (London: Strahan).
 (1872b), *Science and Humanity; or A Plea for the Superiority of Spirit over Matter* (London: Hodder and Stoughton).
 (1874), 'Philosophy in Great Britain and America: a supplementary sketch', in F. Ueberweg, *History of Philosophy from Thales to the Present Time. Vol. II: History of Modern Philosophy*, trans. G. Morris (London: Hodder and Stoughton), 349–460.
Porter, R. (1997), *The Greatest Benefit to Mankind: A Medical History of Humanity from Antiquity to the Present* (London: Harper Collins).
Priestley, J. (1774a), *An Examination of Dr Reid's Inquiry into the Human Mind on the Principles of Common Sense, Dr Beattie's Essay on the Nature and Immutability of Truth, and Dr Oswald's Appeal to Common Sense in Behalf of Religion* (London: Johnson).
 (1774b), *Experiments and Observations on Different Kinds of Air* (London: Johnson).
 (1775), *Hartley's Theory of the Human Mind, on the Principle of the Association of Ideas; with Essays Relating to the Subject of it* (London: Johnson).
Proudfoot, W. (1989), 'From theology to a science of religions: Jonathan Edwards and William James on religious affections', *Harvard Theological Review* 82: 149–68.
Psychosis (1884), *Our Modern Philosophers: Darwin, Bain and Spencer, or The Descent of Man, Mind and Body; A Rhyme with Reasons, Essays, Notes and Quotations* (London: Fisher and Unwin).
Pugmire, D. (1998), *Rediscovering Emotion* (Edinburgh: Edinburgh University Press).

Pyle, A. (ed.) (1995), *Agnosticism: Contemporary Responses to Spencer and Huxley* (Bristol: Thoemmes Press).
Radick, G. (2002), 'Darwin on language and selection', in D. Hull (ed.), *Language Change as a Selection Process*, special issue of *Selection* 3: 7–16.
Ramsay, G. (1848), *Analysis and Theory of the Emotions* (London: Longman, Brown, Green and Longmans).
 (1853), *An Introduction to Mental Philosophy* (Edinburgh: Black).
 (1857), *Principles of Psychology* (London: Walton and Maberly).
Rapaport, D. (1971), *Emotions and Memory*, 5th edn (New York: International Universities Press).
 (1974), *The History of the Concept of Association of Ideas* (New York: International Universities Press).
Raphael, D. D. (ed.) (1969), *British Moralists 1650–1800* (2 vols.), (Oxford: Clarendon Press).
Ratcliffe, S. (1955), *The Story of South Place* (London: Watts and Co.).
Rather, L. (1965), 'Old and new views of the emotions and bodily changes: Wright and Harvey versus Descartes, James and Cannon', *Clio Medica* 1: 1–25.
Rauch, F. (1975), *Psychology or A View of the Human Soul, Including Anthropology*, 2nd edn (Delmar: Scholars' Facsimiles and Reprints) (first published 1841).
Read, C. (1886), 'Mr Mercier's classification of feelings', *Mind* 11: 76–82.
Reber, A. (1985), *The Penguin Dictionary of Psychology* (Harmondsworth: Penguin).
Reddy, W. (2001), *The Navigation of Feeling: A Framework for the History of Emotions* (Cambridge: Cambridge University Press).
Reed, E. (1997), *From Soul to Mind: The Emergence of Psychology from Erasmus Darwin to William James* (New Haven: Yale University Press).
Reid, T. (1785), *Essays on the Intellectual Powers of Man* (Edinburgh: Bell).
 (1788), *Essays on the Active Powers of Man* (Edinburgh: Bell).
Réthoré, F. (1863), *Critique de la Philosophie de Thomas Brown* (Paris: Auguste Durand).
Rice, D. (1971), 'Natural theology and the Scottish philosophy in the thought of Thomas Chalmers', *Scottish Journal of Theology* 24: 23–46.
Richards, G. (1992), *Mental Machinery: The Origins and Consequences of Psychological Ideas. Part 1: 1600–1850* (London: Athlone Press).
Richards, R. (1979), 'Influence of the sensationalist tradition on early theories of the evolution of behavior', *Journal of the History of Ideas* 40: 85–105.
 (1982), 'Darwin and the biologizing of moral behaviour', in W. Woodward and M. Ash (eds.), *The Problematic Science: Psychology in Nineteenth-Century Thought* (New York: Praeger), 43–64.
 (1987), *Darwin and the Emergence of Evolutionary Theories of Mind and Behavior* (Chicago: University of Chicago Press).
 (2003), 'Darwin on mind, morals and emotions', in J. Hodge and G. Radick (eds.), *The Cambridge Companion to Darwin* (Cambridge: Cambridge University Press).
Richardson, W., and Wildman, W. (eds.) (1996), *Religion and Science: History, Method, Dialogue* (London: Routledge).

Ritvo, L. (1990), *Darwin's Influence on Freud: A Tale of Two Sciences* (New Haven: Yale University Press).
Rivers, I. (1993), 'Shaftesburian enthusiasm and the evangelical revival', in J. Garnett and C. Matthew (eds.), *Revival and Religion Since 1700: Essays for John Walsh* (London: Hambledon Press), 21–39.
  (2000), *Reason, Grace, and Sentiment: A Study of the Language of Religion and Ethics in England 1660–1780*, vol. II: *Shaftesbury to Hume* (Cambridge: Cambridge University Press).
Roback, A. (1962), *History of Psychology and Psychiatry* (London: Vision Press).
  (1964), *History of American Psychology*, revised edn (London: Collier Macmillan).
Roberts, R. C. (1988), 'What an emotion is: a sketch', *Philosophical Review* 97: 183–209.
  (1992), 'Emotions among the virtues of the Christian life', *Journal of Religious Ethics* 20: 37–68.
Robertson, J. (1886), 'Emotion in history: A glance into the springs of progress. A discourse delivered in South Place Chapel, Finsbury, E.C., on Sunday March 14th 1886' (London: E. W. Allen).
  (1929), *A History of Free Thought in the Nineteenth Century* (London: Watts).
Robertson, J. C. (1976) 'A Bacon-facing generation: Scottish philosophy in the early nineteenth century', *Journal of the History of Philosophy* 14: 37–49.
Robinson, D. (1981), *An Intellectual History of Psychology*, revised edn (London: Collier Macmillan).
Rochowiak, D. (1988), 'Darwin's psychological theorizing: triangulating on habit', *Studies in the History and Philosophy of Science* 19: 215–41.
Romanes, G. (1888), *Mental Evolution in Man* (London: Kegan Paul).
Rorty, A. O. (1982), 'From passions to emotions and sentiments', *Philosophy* 57: 157–72.
Rothschild, E. (2001), *Economic Sentiments: Adam Smith, Condorcet, and the Enlightenment* (Cambridge, MA: Harvard University Press).
Rousseau, G. (1980), 'Psychology', in G. Rousseau and R. Porter (eds.), *The Ferment of Knowledge: Studies in the Historiography of Eighteenth-Century Science* (Cambridge: Cambridge University Press), 143–210.
Rousseau, G. (ed.) (1990), *The Languages of Psyche: Mind and Body in Enlightenment Thought* (Berkeley: University of California Press).
Ruckmick, C. (1929), 'Why we have emotions', *Scientific Monthly* 28: 252–62.
  (1936), *The Psychology of Feeling and Emotion* (New York: McGraw-Hill).
Rupke, N. (1994), *Richard Owen: Victorian Naturalist* (New Haven: Yale University Press).
Russell, B. (1991), *History of Western Philosophy* (London: Routledge) (first published 1946).
Rylance, R. (2000), *Victorian Psychology and British Culture 1850–1880* (Oxford: Oxford University Press).
Salzen, E. (2001), 'A century of emotion theories – proliferation without progress?', *History and Philosophy of Psychology* 3: 56–75.
Schenk, H. G. (1966), *The Mind of the European Romantics: An Essay in Cultural History* (London: Constable).

Scherer, K. (1984), 'On the nature and function of emotion: a component process approach', in K. Scherer and P. Ekman (eds.), *Approaches to Emotion* (Hillsdale: Erlbaum), 293–318.

Schleiermacher, F. (1988), *On Religion: Speeches to its Cultured Despisers*, trans. R. Crouter (Cambridge: Cambridge University Press) (first published 1799).

Searle, J. (1983), *Intentionality: An Essay in the Philosophy of Mind* (Cambridge: Cambridge University Press).

(1994), *The Rediscovery of the Mind* (Cambridge, MA: MIT Press).

Sell, A. (1995), *Philosophical Idealism and Christian Belief* (Cardiff: University of Wales Press).

Sewell, W. (1831), *Sermons on the Application of Christianity to the Human Heart* (London: Rivington, Bohn, and Bohn).

(1840), *Christian Morals* (London: James Burns).

Shaftesbury, Anthony Ashley Cooper, Third Earl of (1999), *Characteristics of Men, Manners, Opinions, Times*, 2nd edn, ed. L. E. Klein (Cambridge: Cambridge University Press) (first published 1714).

[Shepherd, M.] (1824), *An Essay Upon the Relation of Cause and Effect, Controverting the Doctrine of Mr Hume Concerning the Nature of That Relation; With Observations upon the Opinions of Dr Brown and Mr Lawrence Connected with the Same Subject* (London: Hookham).

Sherman, N. (1990), 'The place of emotions in Kantian morality', in O. Flanagan and A. O. Rorty (eds.), *Identity, Character and Morality: Essays in Moral Psychology* (Cambridge, MA: MIT Press), 149–70.

Sherrington, C. S. (1900), 'Experimentation on emotion', *Nature* 62: 328–31.

Shultz, D. (1975), *A History of Modern Psychology*, 2nd edn (New York: Academic Press).

Shuttleworth, S. (1996), *Charlotte Brontë and Victorian Psychology* (Cambridge: Cambridge University Press).

Sidgwick, H. (1880), 'On historical psychology', *Nineteenth Century* 7: 353–60.

Sihvola, J., and Engberg-Pedersen, T. (eds.) (1998), *The Emotions in Hellenistic Philosophy* (Dordrecht: Kluwer).

Simonson, H. (1987), 'Jonathan Edwards and his Scottish connections', *Journal of American Studies* 21: 353–76.

Skrupskelis, I. (1995), 'James's conception of psychology as a natural science', *History of the Human Sciences* 8: 73–89.

Skultans, V. (1975), *Madness and Morals: Ideas on Insanity in the Nineteenth Century* (London: Routledge and Kegan Paul).

(1979), *English Madness: Ideas on Insanity 1580–1890* (London: Routledge and Kegan Paul).

Smart, J. J. C., and Haldane, J. J. (1996), *Atheism and Theism* (Oxford: Blackwell).

Smith, A. (1976), *The Theory of Moral Sentiments*, ed. D. D. Raphael and A. L. Macfie (Oxford: Clarendon Press), (first published 1759).

Smith, C. (1982), 'Evolution and the problem of mind; Part 1. Herbert Spencer', *Journal of the History of Biology* 15: 55–88.

Smith, R. (1971), 'Physiological psychology and the philosophy of nature in mid-nineteenth-century Britain', unpublished Ph.D. thesis, Cambridge University Library, thesis no. 7588.

(1973), 'The background of physiological psychology in natural philosophy', *History of Science* 11: 75–123.

(1997), *The Fontana History of the Human Sciences* (London: Fontana Press).

Sollier, P. (1894), 'Recherches sur les rapports de la sensibilité et de l'émotion', *Revue Philosophique* 37: 241–66.

Solomon, R. (1993a), *The Passions: Emotions and the Meaning of Life* (Indianapolis: Hackett) (first published 1976).

(1993b), 'The philosophy of emotions', in M. Lewis and J. Haviland (eds.), *Handbook of Emotions* (London: Guildford Press), 3–15.

Sorabji, R. (2000), *Emotion and Peace of Mind: From Stoic Agitation to Christian Temptation* (Oxford: Oxford University Press).

Spencer, H. (1855), *Principles of Psychology* (2 vols.), (London: Longman, Brown, Green and Longmans).

(1863a), *Essays: Scientific, Political, and Speculative*, 2nd series (London: Williams and Norgate).

(1863b), 'The physiology of laughter', in H. Spencer, *Essays: Scientific, Political, and Speculative*, 2nd series (London: Williams and Norgate), 105–19.

(1863c), 'Bain on the emotions and the will', in H. Spencer, *Essays: Scientific, Political, and Speculative*, 2nd series (London: Williams and Norgate), 120–42.

(1870–2), *The Principles of Psychology*, 2nd edn (2 vols.), (London: Williams and Norgate).

(1904), *An Autobiography* (2 vols.), (London: Williams and Norgate).

Spilka, B. (1987), 'Religion and science in early American psychology', *Journal of Psychology and Theology* 15: 3–9.

Spiller, G. (1904), 'The problem of the emotions', *American Journal of Psychology* 15: 569–80.

Spinoza, B. (1996), *Ethics*, trans. E. Curley (London: Penguin) (first published 1677).

(2000), *Ethics*, trans. G. H. R. Parkinson (Oxford: Oxford University Press) (first published 1677).

Stalker, J. (1914), *Christian Psychology* (London: Hodder and Stoughton).

Stanley, H. M. (1886), 'Feeling and emotion', *Mind* 11: 66–76.

Staum, M. (1978), 'Medical components in Cabanis' science of man', *Studies in History of Biology* 2: 1–31.

Stearns, C., and Stearns, P. (1986), *Anger: The Struggle for Emotional Control in America's History* (Chicago: University of Chicago Press).

Stearns, P. (1989), *Jealousy: The Evolution of an Emotion in American History* (New York: New York University Press).

(1993), 'History of emotions: the issue of change', in M. Lewis and J. Haviland (eds.), *Handbook of Emotions* (London: Guildford Press), 17–28.

Stearns, P., and Haggerty, T. (1991), 'The role of fear: transitions in American emotional standards for children 1850–1950', *American Historical Review* 96: 63–94.

Stephen, L. (1886), 'What is materialism? A discourse delivered in South Place Chapel, Finsbury E.C., on Sunday March 21st 1886' (London: E. W. Allen).

(1900), *The English Utilitarians, vol. II: James Mill* (London: Duckworth and Co.).

Stephens, J. (1999), 'Isaac Watts', in J. Yolton *et al.* (eds.), *Dictionary of Eighteenth-Century British Philosophers* (2 vols.), (Bristol: Thoemmes).
Stewart, D. (1828), *The Philosophy of the Active and Moral Powers of Man* (2 vols.), (Edinburgh: Black).
Stewart, M. (ed.) (1990), *Studies in the Philosophy of the Scottish Enlightenment* (Oxford: Clarendon Press).
Stocker, M., with Hegeman, E. (1996), *Valuing Emotions* (Cambridge: Cambridge University Press).
Stout, G. F. (1902), *Analytic Psychology*, 2nd edn (2 vols.), (London: Swann Sonnenschein).
——(1903), *The Groundwork of Psychology* (London: W. B. Clive).
Stratton, G. M. (1895), 'The sensations are not the emotion', *Psychological Review* 2: 173–4.
Stratton, P., and Hayes, N. (1992), *A Student's Dictionary of Psychology*, 2nd edn (London: Edward Arnold).
Sturgeon, N. (1976), 'Nature and conscience in Butler's ethics', *Philosophical Review* 85: 316–56.
Sulloway, F. (1979), *Freud, Biologist of the Mind: Beyond the Psychoanalytic Legend* (London: Burnett Books).
Sully, J. (1892), *The Human Mind: A Textbook of Psychology* (2 vols.), (London: Longmans, Green, and Co.).
Sutton, J. (1998), *Philosophy and Memory Traces: Descartes to Connectionism* (Cambridge: Cambridge University Press).
Swisher, C. (1967), 'Charles Darwin on the origins of behavior', *Bulletin of the History of Medicine* 41: 24–43.
Tannoch-Bland, J. (1997), 'Dugald Stewart on intellectual character', *British Journal for the History of Science* 30: 307–20.
Taylor, J. B., and Shuttleworth, S. (eds.) (1990), *Embodied Selves: An Anthology of Psychological Texts 1830–1890* (Oxford: Clarendon Press).
Taylor, M. C. (1984), *Erring: A Postmodern A/theology* (Chicago: University of Chicago Press).
Teichgraeber, R. (1986), *'Free Trade' and Moral Philososphy: Rethinking the Sources of Adam Smith's* Wealth of Nations (Durham, NC: Duke University Press).
Thalberg, I. (1984), 'From *Emotion and Thought*', in C. Calhoun and R. Solomon (eds.), *What is an Emotion? Classic Readings in Philosophical Psychology* (Oxford: Oxford University Press), 291–305.
Tiles, J. E. (1988), *Dewey* (London: Routledge).
Topham, J. (1992), 'Science and popular education in the 1830s – the role of the Bridgewater Treatises', *British Journal for the History of Science* 25: 307–430.
Tottie, J. (1738), *A View of Reason and Passion, as in Their Original and Present State: A Sermon Preached before the Rt. Hon. Lord-Mayor, Aldermen and Sheriffs of the City of London, at the Cathedral-Church of St Paul on Sunday, December 21st, 1735*, 2nd edn (London: C. Rivington).
Trotter, A. (1901), *East Galloway Sketches: or Biographical, Historical, and Descriptive Notices of Kirkcudbrightshire, Chiefly in the Nineteenth Century* (Castle-Douglas: Adam Rae).

Tuke, D. H. (1886), 'Moral or emotional insanity', *Journal of Mental Science* 31: 174–90.
Turner, F. (1978) 'The Victorian conflict between science and religion: a professional dimension', *Isis* 69: 356–76.
Turski, W. G. (1994), *Toward a Rationality of Emotions* (Athens: Ohio University Press).
Tyndall, J. (1871), *Fragments of Science* (London: Longman).
Ueberweg, F. (1872), *History of Philosophy from Thales to the Present Time. Vol. I: History of the Ancient and Mediaeval Philosophy*, trans. G. Morris (London: Hodder and Stoughton).
(1874), *History of Philosophy from Thales to the Present Time. Vol. II: History of Modern Philosophy*, trans. G. Morris (London: Hodder and Stoughton).
Upham, T. (1856), *Principles of the Interior or Hidden Life; Designed Particularly for the Consideration of those who are Seeking Assurance of Faith and Perfect Love*, new edn (London: Sampson Low, Son, and Co.).
Wainwright, W. (1990), 'Jonathan Edwards and the sense of the heart', *Faith and Philosophy* 7: 43–62.
(1995), *Reason and the Heart: A Prolegomenon to a Critique of Passional Reason* (Ithaca: Cornell University Press).
Waldstein, C., (1878), *The Balance of Emotion and Intellect: An Essay Introductory to the Study of Philosophy* (London: C. Kegan Paul and Co.).
Ward, G. (ed.) (1997), *The Postmodern God: A Theological Reader* (Oxford: Blackwell).
Ward, J. (1918), *Psychological Principles* (Cambridge: Cambridge University Press).
Ward, L. (1884), 'Mind as a social factor', *Mind* 9: 563–73.
Ward, W. (1913), *The Life of John Henry Cardinal Newman, Based on his Private Journals and Correspondence*, 3rd edn (2 vols.), (London: Longmans, Green, and Co.).
Warren, H. C. (1921), *A History of the Association Psychology* (London: Constable).
Watts, F. (1997), 'Psychological and religious perspectives on emotion', *Zygon* 32: 243–60.
(1998), 'Brain, mind and soul', in F. Watts (ed.), *Science Meets Faith* (London: SPCK), 59–72.
(2002), *Theology and Psychology* (Aldershot: Ashgate).
Watts, I. (1746), *Discourses of the Love of God, and its Influence on all the Passions; With A Discovery of the Right Use and Abuse of Them in Matters of Religion*, 3rd edn (London: Oswald and Buckland) (first published 1729).
(n.d.), *The Doctrine of the Passions Explained and Improved: or, A Brief and Comprehensive Scheme of the Natural Affections of Mankind* (Coventry: Luckman) (first published 1729).
Webster, R. (1995), *Why Freud Was Wrong: Sin, Science and Psychoanalysis* (London: Harper Collins).
Weiner, D. (1990), 'Mind and body in the clinic: Philippe Pinel, Alexander Crichton, Dominique Esquirol, and the birth of psychiatry', in G. Rousseau (ed.), *The Languages of Psyche: Mind and Body in Enlightenment Thought* (Berkeley: University of California Press), 331–402.

Welsh, D. (1825), *Account of the Life and Writings of Thomas Brown M.D.* (Edinburgh: Tait); reprinted as vol. 1 of Brown (2003).
  (1851), 'Memoir of Dr, Brown', in T. Brown, *Lectures on the Philosophy of the Human Mind*, 19th edn (4 vols.), (Edinburgh: Black), 1, 1–84.
White, E. (1878), *Life in Christ: A Study of the Scripture, Doctrine on the Nature of Man, the Object of the Divine Incarnation, and the Conditions of Human Immortality* (London: Elliot Stock).
Wildsmith, W. (1828), *An Inquiry Concerning the Relative Connexion which Subsists between the Mind and the Brain, with Remarks on Phrenology and Materialism* (London: Effingham Wilson).
Willis, K. (1988), 'The introduction and critical reception of Hegelian thought in Britain 1830–1900', *Victorian Studies* 32: 85–111.
Wilson, F. (1998), 'Mill on psychology and the moral sciences', in J. Skorupski (ed.), *The Cambridge Companion to Mill* (Cambridge: Cambridge University Press), 203–54.
Windelband, W. (1958), *A History of Philosophy, Volume II: Renaissance, Enlightenment, and Modern*, trans. J. Tufts, revised edn (1901), repr. (New York: Harper and Row).
Wollheim, R. (1999), *On the Emotions* (New Haven and London: Yale University Press).
Wood, J. (2001), *Passion and Pathology in Victorian Fiction* (Oxford: Oxford University Press).
Wood, P. B. (1989), 'The natural history of man in the Scottish Enlightenment', *History of Science* 27: 89–123.
  (1990), 'Science and the pursuit of virtue in the Aberdeen Enlightenment', in M. Stewart (ed.), *Studies in the Philosophy of the Scottish Enlightenment* (Oxford: Clarendon Press), 127–49.
Woodward, W., and Ash, M. (eds.) (1982), *The Problematic Science: Psychology in Nineteenth-Century Thought* (New York: Praeger).
Worcester, W. L. (1892–3), 'Observations on some points in James' psychology. II. Emotion', *Monist* 3: 285–98.
Wright, A. E. (1895), 'On the nature of the physiological element in emotion', *Brain* 18: 217–26.
Wright, J. P. (1990), 'Metaphysics and physiology: mind, body, and the animal economy in eighteenth-century Scotland', in M. Stewart (ed.), *Studies in the Philosophy of the Scottish Enlightenment* (Oxford: Clarendon Press), 251–301.
Yolton, J. (1983), *Thinking Matter: Materialism in Eighteenth-Century Britain* (Minneapolis: University of Minnesota Press).
Young, E. (1728), *A Vindication of Providence: or A True Estimate of Human Life, in which the Passions are Considered in a New Light*, 2nd edn (London: Worrall).
Young, R. M. (1970), *Mind, Brain and Adaptation in the Nineteenth Century: Cerebral Localisation and its Biological Context from Gall to Ferrier* (Oxford: Clarendon Press).
  (1973), 'The role of psychology in the nineteenth-century evolutionary debate', in M. Henle *et al.* (eds.), *Historical Conceptions of Psychology* (New York: Springer), 180–204.

Yovel, Y. (ed.) (1999), *Desire and Affect: Spinoza as Psychologist. Papers Presented at the Third Jerusalem Conference (Ethica III)* (New York: Little Room Press).

Zeldin, T. (1982), 'Personal history and the history of emotions', *Journal of Social History* 15: 339–47.

(1993), *A History of French Passions* (Oxford: Clarendon Press).

Index

Abercrombie, John   127, 139, 161, 162; *see also* Darwin
Aberdeen: Marischal College   151; University of   151, 152, 153
Adamson, Robert   111
affects   18, 29, 40, 53, 72, 112; *see also* affections
affectiones   19, 40, 45, 48, 54, 56, 59
affections   3, 4, 5–6, 11, 18; Christian views of   17, 18, 21–2, 29, 39, 40–1, 45–8, 53, 54–6, 58, 60–1, 66–7, 70, 72, 75–6, 77–8, 87, 236–7; in eighteenth century   62–7, 69–70, 71; and the life to come   29, 59–60; models of: as mechanisms   22, as movements of the soul   45–8, 53, 54, as perceptions   22, 77, 80, 93, as voluntary and rational   39, 55–6, 229; Puritan views on   75; and sin   48, 56; varieties of: general and particular   84, public and private   81, 87, religious   75–6; *see also* Butler; Edwards; emotions; Johnson; moralists; passions; Reid; Smith; will
affectus   19, 40, 41, 45, 46, 47, 48, 49, 72
agnosticism   142, 168
Alison, Archibald   101
apathy, *apatheia*   40–1, 50, 59–60, 63
appetite(s)   18; higher (rational, intellective; *appetitus intellectivus*)   54, 58–9, 61, 83; lower (sensitive; *appetitus sensitivus*)   54, 58–9, 83, 87; as mechanisms   128; public and private   68; traditional Christian views of   21, 22, 35; *see also* Aquinas; Augustine; Chalmers; Johnson
Aquinas, St Thomas   7, 18, 21, 22, 26, 103, 112; on affections   29, 46, 55–6; on appetite, higher (rational, intellective; *appetitus intellectivus*)   43, 46, 47, 53, 70; on appetite, lower (sensitive; *appetitus sensitivus*)   35–6, 43, 46, 47, 53, 56, 70; on appetites (concupiscible and irascible)   36, 41–2, 43; and Aristotle   28, 35, 36, 38–9, 41–2, 43–5, 46; and Augustine   28, 35, 42–3, 45; on Cicero   52; on intellect/understanding   35, 36, 38–9, 46, 52, 53; on love   45, 46; on matter and form   36, 38–9; on the passions   58, distinguished from affections   46, different classifications of   29, 36, 41–3, as movements   41–2, 43–5, 46, 52, and reason   41–2, 52, terminology (*passiones, affectus, actus voluntatis*)   45, 46; passivity and activity   36, 41–2, 58; on the soul: model of   35–9, 53, and the body   38–9, 'subsistence' of   38–9; on Stoics   46; *Summa Theologiae*   26, 28, 40, 45; on the will   35–6, 45, 46, 53, 70; *see also* Hutcheson

Aristotle   7, 10, 28, 35, 36, 46, 99, 243; *De Anima*   28, 42–3; Aristotelians   38; on matter and form   38; on motion   43–5; on the nutritive, sensitive and intellectual soul   30, 35, 46; on passivity and activity   36, 41–2
associationism: *see* psychology, theoretical paradigms
atheism   116, 135, 186, 241
'atheology'   9; *see also* psychology, theoretical paradigms
Atkinson, Henry   116
Augustine of Hippo, St   7, 18, 21, 26, 96, 103, 227; on affections   29, 40–1, 46–7, 54–5, 222; on appetites   30, 35; on the body   57–8; *City of God*   27, 33, 40, 45, 46, 47, 48; on concupiscence   32, 55; *Confessions*   27, 31, 32, 49, 51, 52, 57; conflict and peace in the theology of   59; dualism in   29–30, 33; on the fall   49, 51, 57–8, 176–7; on flesh and spirit   33, 50, 57, 78–9; on grief as sin   49, 55; on *imago Dei*   31–2;

279

Augustine of Hippo, St (*cont.*):
on the intellect 29, 31–2, 33, 35; on the life to come 30; on love as basis of passions and affections 40, 55; and Manichees 33; and Neoplatonism 30–1; on the passions 29, 40, 41, 57–8: distinguished from affections 46–7, classification and terminology 40, 45, 48, as diseases of the soul 41, 49–50, 55, as movements 50, and reason 48–52, Stoic ideas about 40–1, 47, 50–1, 59; on reason differentiating man from lower animals 30, 31–2; on sex 51–2, 57; model of the soul 29–35; *The Trinity* 27, 31, 32; on the will 33, 35, 40, 47, 57–8; on woman's subordination to man 32, 59; *see also* Aquinas; Darwin

Bacon, Francis 11, 63, 94–5, 103–4, 118
Baier, Annette 18, 105, 107, 246
Bain, Alexander 5, 23, 72, 127, 133, 135–6, 139, 145, 146, 149, 150–2, 188–9, 207, 233; as associationist 100, 135, 138, 147, 155, 158, 163; and Bell 120, 142, 168–9; and Chalmers 156; and Comte 151, 152, 153–4; on emotions 94, 96, 133, 135, 139, 140, 141, 155–9, 178–9, 188–9, 202, 204, 229: as aggregates 96, 120, 157–8, 204, and feelings 156, 158, distinguished from sensations 156; *The Emotions and the Will* 137, 152, 155, 156–7, 188, 228; and epiphenomenalism 143–4; on evolution 147, 155; influence of 137–8, 159; on introspection 153–5; and McCosh 152, 153, 190, 202; and Mill 151, 152, 153–4, 157, 158; and monism 142, 143; religious views of 150–3, 168, 241; *The Senses and the Intellect* 137, 156, 228; on the will 107, 141, 158–9, 176–7, 188; *see also* Darwin; James; Spencer
Baldwin, James Mark 1, 17, 207, 211–12, 228, 229, 238
Ballantyne, John 116
Baynes, Thomas 147; *see also* Darwin
Beattie, James 112
Belfast, Queen's College 152, 153, 190
Bell, Charles 10, 139, 170, 171, 172, 182, 184, 185, 189, 192, 194; *The Anatomy and Philosophy of Expression, as Connected with the Fine Arts* 164, 169; Bridgewater Treatise 168, 186; design theology of 23, 127, 142, 146, 168–9, 170, 171, 172, 173–4, 175, 184, 202, 236; *Essays on the Anatomy of Expression in Painting* 173;

on imagination 185; on laughter and weeping 170, 182–3; *see also* Bain; Darwin; Spencer
Bentham, Jeremy 120, 130
Berkeley, George 100
Bible, the 5, 28, 35, 104, 151, 170, 175, 190, 198; *Colossians* 76; *1 Corinthians* 60; *Galatians* 31, 33, 57; *Genesis* 31, 52; New Testament terms for passions and desires (*pathē*, *epithumiai*) 39; *Revelation* 60
Blakey, Robert 115, 116
blushing: *see* Burgess; Darwin
Brett, George Sidney: *History of Psychology* 8, 197, 220
Bridgewater, Francis Henry, Earl of 127
Bridgewater Treatises 127, 128, 142, 156, 164, 182, 186, 189
Brooke, John Hedley 16
Brougham, Henry 102, 116, 139, 164, 182
Brown, Thomas 7, 10, 11, 17, 23, 72, 98, 142, 151; and the Academy of Physics 116–17, 118–19, 121; as associationist 100, 110, 120; on cause and effect 114, 115–16, 120; classification of mental states 122–5, 126–7, 156, 179, 188, 250; and common sense philosophy 110–11, 120–2, 125; and Condillac 115; and emotions: replaces 'active powers' 113, 124–6, as aggregates 96, 120, 204, definition of 23, 125–6, 129, 130, 149, 156, 179, 195, as inventor of 'emotions' 101, 109–13, 122, 124–6, 133–4, 152, 187, 250–1, as feelings 124–5, 126, 204, distinguished from intellect 97, 124–5, 126, 228, distinguished from sensations 105, 124, 126, 156; opposition to faculty psychology 23, 107, 115, 120–1, 122; and Hume 109, 110, 111, 114, 115–16, 120, 125; influence of 125, 126–7, 128, 129–33, 135, 138, 139, 149, 156, 161, 189, 195, 198–9, 204; *Lectures on the Philosophy of the Human Mind* 23, 101, 109–13, 138, 189; and 'Leslie affair' 114, 138; and 'mental chemistry' 115, 118–20, 126, 157; and phrenologists 115; as physician 109, 114, 133, 141; as 'positivist' 116, 121, 233; and Reid 110–11, 115, 120–1, 122, 124; religious views of 113–16, 117, 128–9, 237, 241; and Scholasticism 117; and science of mind 113, 115, 116–20, 122, 126–7, 153; and Stewart 110–11, 124; on the will 107, 122, 125, 140, 148, 250; *see also* Chalmers; James; McCosh

Index

Burgess, Thomas: on blushing 141, 164, 170–1, 172, 182
Butler, Joseph 7, 9, 10, 11, 22, 68, 69, 70, 81, 82, 83, 100, 102, 112, 114, 129, 139, 187; on affections 84, 85, 86–8; *Analogy of Religion* 82; departures from traditional Christian psychology 82, 84–5, 87, 90–2, 93, 134, 234; on conscience, moral sense 85, 87, 90, 92, 93, 185; and Deism 82–3; design theology applied to human mind 82, 83, 88, 90–2, 95, 102, 113, 132–3; on Hobbes 86–8, 90–2; mechanical model of mind 90–2, 94, 95, 128, 132–3, 184, 234; on the passions: and reason 84–5, and self-interest 86–8, and the will 87; on self-love 84–5, 87, 90, 93; *Sermons* 67, 82, 85, 86–8, 187

Calvin, John 27; Calvinism 82, 128, 151, 153, 196
Cannon, Walter B. 216
Cantor, Geoffrey 16
Carpenter, William B. 180
Cashdollar, Charles 101, 182
Cattell, James McKeen 220
Chalmers, Thomas 7, 17, 23, 102, 103, 113, 127–33, 139, 188, 190; Bridgewater Treatise 127–8, 131, 156, 186, 187, 189; and Brown 125, 127, 128–33, 134, 152, 234; influenced by Butler 128, 132–3, 134; and Calvinist theology 128; and Edwards 130, 131; on emotions as non-cognitive and involuntary 129, 131–3, 134, 156, 179, 234; influence of 133, 139, 152, 156, 189, 195; mechanical model of mind 128, 132–3, 184; and natural theology 102, 127–8, 190, 202; passions distinguished from affections 130–1; and science of mind 129–33, 161, 234; *see also* Bain; McCosh
Charland, Louis 2
chemistry: chemical revolution 103, 118–20; 'mental chemistry' 103, 109, 115, 117, 118–20, 126, 132, 157–8, 223, 225; *see also* Brown
Chrysippus 50, 54
Cicero: on passions as perturbations of the soul 40, 43, 45; on passions as diseases 52
Clarke, Samuel 95; *Discourse of Natural Religion* 73
Cockburn, Henry 111
Coleridge, Samuel T. 63
Combe, George 115

common sense philosophy: *see* philosophy, common sense
Comte, Auguste 99, 116, 135, 137–8, 142, 151, 153–4, 233; *see also* Bain; Mill
concupiscence, *concupiscentia* 32, 41, 55, 57
Condillac, Étienne Bonnot de 94, 99; *see also* Brown
conscience 64, 68, 74, 163; distinguishes man from lower animals 185; *see also* Butler; sense, moral
Cogan, Thomas 141
Cooke, William 141, 184, 189–90
Cooper, Samuel 92
Courmont, Frédéric 228
Crichton, Alexander 141
cupidity, *cupiditas* 41

Damasio, Antonio 2
Danziger, Kurt 14–15, 17, 229
Darwall, Stephen 84, 92
Darwin, Charles 5, 7, 11, 12, 18, 23, 135–6, 137, 143, 145, 149, 150, 158, 159–79, 193, 233; on Abercrombie 161, 162; and associationist psychology 162–4; and Augustine 175–7; and Bain 155, 163, 167; on Bell 23, 142, 164, 165, 168–9, 170, 171, 172, 173–4, 175, 236, 241; and Burgess on blushing 170–1; *The Descent of Man, and Selection in Relation to Sex* 160, 163, 169, 174, 175, 176–7, 193; *The Expression of the Emotions in Man and Animals* 10, 137, 146, 147, 155, 159, 160, 165, 166–8, 171, 172, 173, 174–7, 193: anthropomorphism of 145–6, 192, reviewed by Baynes 146, 192–4, emotions and their expressions 137, 139, 141, 144, 145–6, 156, 159–79, 204, 231, 236, lack of a developed theory of emotions 167, expressions as inherited habits 166, 167, 168, 169, 171–2, 173, expressions as purposeless actions 165, 168, 171–2, 175, inheritance of acquired characteristics 171–2; on laughter 165, 170; on Mackintosh 161–2, 166; on moral sentiments 162, 163, 175; on natural selection 164, 168, 169, 171, 172, 174, 175; *On the Origin of Species* 135, 160, 168, 174, 193; and Paley 164–5; religious views of 168; and Scottish philosophy 138, 139, 161–2; and Spencer 165, 167, 171; on the will 107, 161–2, 171, 176–7
Darwin, Emma 168
Dawkins, Richard 91

Defoe, Daniel 63
de la Mettrie, Julien Offray 89–90, 94
Descartes, René 7, 13, 17, 18, 20, 59, 80, 82, 117, 219; on animal automatism 89–90; on animal spirits 27, 76; uses of *émotions* 76, 108–9; on the passions 76–9, 104–5, 125, 183; on soul and body 76–9, 80, 92; *Traité des Passions de l'Ame* 13, 20, 76, 108–9; *see also* Edwards; Hume; Watts
design theology: *see* natural theology
desires 18, 29, 32, 39, 41, 51–2, 60; *see also* concupiscence; *libido*
de Sousa, Ronald 2
Devil, the: passions of 58
Dewey, John 207, 214, 217
Doddridge, Philip 74
dualism, mind–body 142–5, 161, 181, 182–4, 210, 212, 221, 223, 228, 238, 239, 242; *see also* mind; soul
Dwyer, John 65

Edinburgh Review 116, 139
Edwards, Jonathan 7, 11, 17, 22, 27, 58, 69, 71, 78, 93, 114, 130, 131, 196, 222, 236; on affections 45, 67, 75–6, 79–81, 85, 95; affections divided into the natural and the gracious 79–81, 85; and Descartes 77–8, 92; *Freedom of the Will* 69; middle way between reason and passions 96; on self-love 85; *Treatise Concerning Religious Affections* 45, 67, 75–6, 79–81, 95; *see also* James
Ellis, Havelock 225
Ellison, Julie 16
Ellsworth, Phoebe 211
Elster, Jon 10–11, 231, 244–5
Emerson, Roger 82
emotions: anachronistic uses of 14–15, 18–19, 39–40, 47, 53–4, 64–5, 66, 242–4; and Christian discourse 4–6, 23, 39, 59, 133–4, 139–40, 181, 227, 234; corresponding terminology: in French 20, 76, 108, 109, in German 20, 70–1, 213; definitional problems 25, 125–6, 129, 130, 194–5, 203, 231, 245–6: explanatory ambiguities 246, moral ambiguities 25, 247, over-inclusivity of category 1–2, 23, 25, 61, 126, 149, 156, 194–5, 244–7; early uses of: non-psychological meanings 45, 63, first scientific treatments 10–11, 23, 139–40, 141, 142–6, 156, 204, first uses of as psychological category 4, 14, 17, 22–3, 65, 101, 104–13, 122, 124–6, 133–4, 189; histories of theories of 7, 13–15, 19, 231–3; intentionality of 248–9; and medicine 141; as a natural kind 2, 25; number of distinct 18, 42–3; and other psychological categories: affections 140, 146, intellect/reason 3–4, 17, 22, 54, 56, 97, 124–5, 126, 129, 131–4, 149, 156, 178, 227–9, passions 2–4, 13–14, 18–19, 20, 59, 140, 146, 202, 228, 229, 243–4, sensations 105, 124, 126, 149, 156, will 3–4, 97, 131–4, 140, 156, 158–9, 161–2, 189, 200, 250, 251; social histories of 15, 247; theoretical approaches: aggregate 96, 150, 157–8, 197, 204, anti-physicalist 181–203, 212–13, 225, 229, cognitive 5, 25, 96, 140, 181, 195–7, 200, 217–18, 225, 229, 243, 244, 248, component/compound 25, 96, 157–8, 181, 197, 219, 225, 229, epiphenomenal 24, 143–4, 158, 202–3, 210, 229, evolutionary 23, 24, 141, 146–50, 178–9, 202, 239, 241–2, feeling 23, 124–5, 126, 131–3, 149, 158, 178–9, 202, 203, 204, 217, 232, phenomenological 248, physiological 23, 24, 139–40, 141, 142–50, 177–9, 202, 226, 239, 241–2; *see also* Bain; Brown; Chalmers; Darwin; Hume; Irons; James; Ladd; McCosh; Smith; Solomon; Spencer
empiricism 11, 22, 81, 103, 110
Enlightenment, the 64, 68, 163, 233; Scottish 103, 109, 128
epithumiai 39
eupatheiai 60
Evans, Dylan 2, 66
evolution 135–7; as quasi-religion for 'Darwinian sect' 193–4; *see also* Darwin; emotions; Lamarckianism; natural selection; psychology
expression of emotions: *see* Bell; Darwin; emotions; James

Falconer, William 141
fall, the 29, 30, 56, 82, 83, 87, 93, 103, 175–7, 237, 249; *see also* Augustine
feeling(s) 149, 156, 158, 194, 213, 217; *see also* emotions; Johnson
Fiske, John 138
Flynn, Philip 117
Fordyce, David 74
free will: *see* will, freedom of
Freud, Sigmund 178
Frey, R. G. 85

Index

Fridlund, Alan 169
Fulcher, Rodney 75

Gardiner, H. N. 211; *Feeling and Emotion: A History of Theories* 7, 15, 26, 110, 197, 219, 220
Gilman, James 53
God: as pure activity in Aquinas 36; affections of 55–6, 60, 61; affections as movements towards 54, 55; and the life to come 59; and love 55
Goldie, Peter 2, 231, 249
Gorman, Thomas 181, 186
Grange, Kathleen 63
Greenspan, Patricia 231
Griffiths, Paul 244, 245
Grote, George 152, 188
Grote, John 159, 181, 188–9
Gurney, Edmund 213, 214

Hall, G. Stanley 220
Hamilton, William 101, 112, 213, 217
Harré, Rom 231, 247
Hartley, David 11, 94, 99, 100, 101, 110, 117, 119, 120, 187
Haywood, Eliza 64
Herbart, Johann Friedrich 217
Hickok, Laurens 182, 183, 198, 199
Hilton, Boyd 16, 102, 141
Hirschman, Albert 65–6, 84
Hobbes, Thomas 18, 62, 68, 70, 81, 82, 89, 90, 94, 97, 99, 106, 109, 187; *Leviathan* 89; on the will 85, 107, 125, 140–1; *see also* Butler
Holland, Henry 138, 182, 184
Hooker, Joseph 180
Hooker, Thomas 75
Horner, Francis 116, 118
Hume, David 7, 11, 13, 17, 18, 72, 81, 99, 110, 130, 133, 142; on cause and effect 114; and Descartes 104–5, 108–9; uses of 'emotions' 101, 104–9; *Enquiry Concerning the Principles of Morals* 105; on the passions 104–9, 125; on reason and the passions 86, 106; religious scepticism of 107, 109; and science of mind 107, 117, 118, 122, 153; *Treatise of Human Nature* 17, 22, 104, 105, 106, 107; on the will 106–7, 125, 140, 148; *see also* Brown; McCosh; Reid
Hutcheson, Francis 28, 69, 70, 81, 88, 100, 118, 187; influenced by Aquinas 83, 112; *Essay on the Nature and Conduct of the Passions and Affections* 45, 67, 83–4
Huxley, Thomas Henry 94, 135, 136, 142, 144, 145, 146, 180, 193, 223

Idealism: *see* philosophy, Idealist
ideas, innate 80, 99, 101, 162–4
intellect 139, 140, 158; *see also* Aquinas; Augustine; emotions; reason; will
Irons, David 207, 208, 214, 217, 225; on emotions 219–20, 222, 225–6, 229, 248–9

Jacyna, L. S. 201
James, Susan 13, 27, 40
James, William 7, 11, 17, 21, 24, 59, 137, 149, 178, 233; and associationist psychology 205; and Bain 205; and Brown 204; and Edwards 205; on emotions 140, 144, 166, 203, 204–13, 225, 226, 229, 231, 236, 245, 249, 251: confused definitions of 207–9; early criticisms of his theory 210–11, 212–3, as epiphenomenal 24, 144, 210, and their 'expressions' 207–8, 210, distinguished from intellect and reason 97, 227–8, 237, and Lange 211; and materialism 206, 210; 'The Physical Basis of Emotion' 211; *Principles of Psychology* 206, 207, 210, 224; on psychology as a science 223–4, 238; religious views 205, 206; and 'stream of consciousness' 250; *Varieties of Religious Experience* 205, 224; 'What is an emotion?' 10, 24, 126, 205, 207
Jeffrey, Francis 116, 139
Johnson, Samuel: *Dictionary* entries for affection, appetite, emotion, feeling, passion, sensibility, sentiment 62–3, 108

Kames, Lord (Henry Home) 101
Kant, Immanuel 8, 18, 71, 99, 163, 217, 243
Kenny, Anthony 38, 248, 249
Kirby, William 164

Ladd, George Trumbull 7–17, 207, 214, 217, 220–3; on the emotions and passions 221–2, 229; on psychology as a science 224–5
Lamarckianism 172, 178
Lange, Carl F. 211
Laplace, Pierre 90
laughter: *see* Bell; Darwin; Spencer

Index

Lavater, Johann Caspar 27
Lavoisier, Antoine 12
Laycock, Thomas 119, 143
Lazarus, Robert 2
Le Brun, Charles 27
Leslie, John: 'Leslie affair' 114, 138
Lewes, G. H. 99, 119, 127, 152; as associationist 100
libido 41, 49, 51, 57
Lilly, W. S. 180
Locke, John 80, 82, 99, 103–4, 105, 115, 117; and associationist psychology 99–100, 102–3, 162, 163; *Essay Concerning Human Understanding* 99, 112
love: as basis of all passions and affections 18, 40, 45, 55, 67; and God 55; and knowledge 35; as motion 43–5; self-love 84–5, 87, 90; *see also* Aquinas; Augustine; will
Luther, Martin 27
Lyall, William 7, 10, 23, 113, 127, 181, 182, 183–4, 198, 202
Lyons, William 96, 231, 244

Mackintosh, James 110, 130, 139, 161, 186–7, 188
Mandeville, Bernard 68, 70, 81
Mandler, George 7–8, 10, 248
Marks, Joel 96, 244
Martineau, Harriet 116
materialism 135, 138, 180–1, 191, 192, 198, 206, 210, 239
Maudsley, Henry 135, 180, 186, 193, 223, 225
McCosh, James 7, 23, 82, 101, 107, 127, 181, 183, 184, 189, 190, 192, 228, 232; on Brown 111, 113, 115; on Chalmers 128, 130; on the emotions 18, 182, 190–1, 194–6, 197, 202, 207, 217, 221, 229, 232: component approach to 96, as mental acts 140; on Hume 108; *see also* Bain
medicine 8, 9, 109, 114, 133, 138, 139, 141, 189–90
Mendelssohn, Moses 70
Mercier, Charles 150, 214, 217–18, 229, 248
Milbank, John 59, 236, 237
Miles, Margaret 51, 55
Mill, James 11, 94, 99, 119, 120, 126, 127, 137, 157; as associationist 100, 117, 135, 138, 153
Mill, John Stuart 99, 116, 119, 127, 137–8, 139, 142, 154; as associationist 100, 135, 138, 163; on mental chemistry 119–20, 126, 157; *see also* Bain
mind: active powers of 23, 101, 113, 122, 124–6, 134, 250; and body 141, 142–5; as machine 89–92, 94, 95, 128, 196; tripartite models of 70–1, 72, 97, 158; *see also* philosophy; psychology; soul
Mivart, St George 137
Moerbeke, William of
monism, dual-aspect 142–5
Moore, James 249
moral philosophy: *see* moralists; philosophy, moral
moral sense: *see* conscience; sense, moral
moralists, British 67–9, 70, 81–92, 139, 233, 249; departures from traditional Christian psychology 93; natural theology of 93; on passions and affections 83–6, 93, 97, 139, 187, 248
Morell, J. D. 10, 29, 99, 112, 115, 124, 181, 182, 200
motives 18
motus (animae) 39, 40, 43, 45, 47, 48

natural selection 135, 147, 164, 168, 169, 171, 174, 175
natural theology 23, 127, 128, 168, 172; applied to human mind 101–2, 103, 113, 132–3, 142, 164–5, 168–9, 172, 181, 182, 189–97, 202; *see also* Bridgewater Treatises; Butler; Chalmers; moralists
nature, concept of: central to eighteenth-century theories of passions and affections 69–70, 93
Neoplatonism 28; *see also* Augustine
Newman, John Henry 181, 185, 188
Newton, Isaac 12, 90, 103–4, 130; Newtonianism applied to the mind 11, 94, 103–4, 107, 116, 118, 235; *Opticks* 11, 104, 107, 118

Oatley, Keith 2, 231, 248
O'Connor, Henry 116
Olson, Richard 110, 233
original sin 21, 29, 87, 103
Owen, Richard 145, 146, 185

Paine, Martyn 180–1, 182, 183, 184, 191, 196–7
Paley, William 139, 163, 184, 187
passiones (animae) 19, 28, 39, 40, 41–2, 43, 45, 46, 47, 48, 50, 52, 56, 58
passions 3, 4, 5–6, 11; and the body 56–9; Christian views of 14, 17, 18, 21–2, 29, 40–1, 45–52, 53–4, 56–9,

Index

60–1, 66–7, 70, 72, 75–6, 87, 183, 236–7, 243, 249; in the eighteenth century 62–7, 69–70, 71; and literature 15; and medicine 141; models of: as diseases/sicknesses 52, 56, as judgments 50, as mechanisms 22, as movements of the soul 27, 43, 50, 52, 60, as perceptions 22, 76, 77, as unruly forces 29, 50, 54, 73, 243; number of 18, 41–3; and other psychological faculties: affections 29, 40–1, 45–8, 53, 54–6, 58, 60–1, 75–6, 83–6, 87, 130–1, 146, 189, 222, 229, 236–7, interests 65–6, 84, 'pre-passions' 28, 245, reason 17, 22, 29, 48–54, 66, 72–6, 83–6, 106, 237, 242–3, will 29, 33, 48, 59, 60, 61, 64, 242–3; Protestant views of 27; seventeenth-century theories of 27, 40; and sin 48, 52, 56, 59, 60, 61, 249; Stoic views of 3, 28, 40–1, 50–1, 54, 59, 60, 61, 245; *see also* Aquinas; Augustine; Butler; Cicero; Descartes; emotions; Johnson; moralists; Reid; Smith; Solomon

pathē 19, 28, 39, 40, 45, 50, 54, 61
Paul, St 31, 33, 78, 79, 103; *I Corinthians* 60; *Galatians* 31, 33, 57, 80
Payne, George 119, 125, 127, 129, 131
perturbationes (animae) 40, 45, 50, 52
philosophy: common sense 11, 100–1, 110–11, 120–2, 125, 153, 191, 197; Idealist 112, 182, 198, 234–5, 238; moral 11, 23; *see also* empiricism; moralists; psychology; Scotland; Stoicism
phrenology 115, 153
physiognomy 27
Plato 31, 39, 99, 243; and Platonic views on immorality of the soul 38
Plotinus 30
Pope, Alexander 63–4
Porphry 30
Porter, Noah 10, 135, 138, 182, 199
positivism 116, 121, 135, 137–8, 141, 151, 152, 153–4, 180, 192, 205, 233, 235
Priestley, Joseph 19, 101, 119
Primaudaye, Pierre de la 75
psychology: historiographical issues: broadening the canon 8–9, 12, 16, 24, 181, 182–4, 231–3, presentism 6–12, 14–15, 18–19, 24, 181, 182–4, religious and theological factors 4–10, 21, 23, 24–5, 181, 182–4, 201–3, 220–1, 227, 231–3, 239–42, secularisation 4–6, 17, 21, 24, 145, 146, 201–3, 229–30, 233–42, theology or anti-theology 'in disguise' 24, 235–9; role of introspection in 153–5, 191, 197, 219–20, 223–4, 226, 232, 233, 241, 242; professionalisation of 16, 21, 24–5, 206–7, 209, 212–13, 229, 232; as a science 10–12, 16, 21, 24–5, 149, 153–4, 198, 199, 202, 209, 223–7, 234–5, 238, 249; theoretical paradigms: associationist 11, 94, 100, 101, 102–3, 110, 117, 120, 147, 148, 153, 154, 155, 158, 161, 162–4, 178, 'atheological' 9, 117, 134, 142, 227, 233, Christian 23, 26–9, 56, 58–9, 70, 75, 79, 106, 132, 145, 158–9, 175–7, 181–2, 183, 185, 186–9, 221, 227–8, 233, 234, 236–7, 238, 242, evolutionary 23, 135–7, 141, 146–50, 154, 155, 159, 162–4, 170, 175–7, 178–9, 180, 185, 218, experimental 205, 206–7, 212, 213, 223, 225, 226, faculty 23, 107, 115, 120–1, 134, 141, 191, 221, 232, natural theological 101–2, 181, 182, 189–97, physiological 23, 135–7, 138–9, 141, 143, 146–50, 152, 156, 170, 177–9, 180, 185, 189, 191–2, sensationalist 94, 99, 100, 115, theistic 23, 181, 182, 183, 185, 198–201, 234; *see also* mind; natural theology; philosophy
psychopathology and psychiatry 15
Pugmire, David 244

Ramsay, George 119, 127, 181, 199
Rapaport, David 10
Rauch, Frederick 184–5, 199
reason: 'Age of Reason' as term for eighteenth century 64, 66; distinguishes man from lower animals 30, 31–2, 52–4, 145, 184–5, 222; *see also* emotions; passions; sentiments
Reber, Arthur S. 231, 246
Reddy, William 13, 246
Reed, Edward 9, 201, 235, 237, 238
Reid, Thomas 7, 11, 22, 71, 81, 82, 89, 94, 99, 105, 109, 112, 117, 124, 164, 183, 217, 232; on the active powers of the mind 67, 96, 122, 124, 250; and common sense philosophy 100–1, 110–11, 120–1, 191; cognitive and component views of passions and affections 95–6; and faculty psychology 115, 120–1; on Hume 85–6, 94, 95–6; on reason and the passions 84, 85–6, 132; on science of mind 94–5, 117, 118, 130; *see also* Brown

Renouvier, Charles 137
revivalists, Christian: in eighteenth century 67, 68, 69, 70, 72–81, 249
Rice, Daniel 128
Richards, Graham 8
Richards, Robert 201
Rivers, Isabel 67
Roback, Abraham A. 220–1, 232
Roberts, Robert C. 248
Rorty, Amélie Oksenberg 17, 53, 134
Rylance, Rick 8–9, 21, 150, 155, 163, 234

sapientia (wisdom) 32, 35
Scherer, Klaus 248
Schopenhauer, Arthur 71
science and religion: historiography 16, 249; in nineteenth-century psychological debates 223–7, 234–5; 'warfare' between 223
science of mind: see mind; psychology
scientia (knowledge, understanding) 32, 35
Scotland: church in 82, 114, 116, 151–2: disruption and creation of Free Church 103, 190, 198; as birthplace of 'emotions' 103, 133–4, 152, 187, 188; Enlightenment in 103, 109, 128; connections with France 108; philosophy of 11, 13, 22, 81, 82, 94, 100–1, 103, 104, 110–11, 127, 128, 133, 138–9, 142, 153, 161–2, 232; and physiological psychology 138–9; theology of 128, 151; universities in 82, 103, 114, 117, 133, 151–2
Searle, John 96, 244, 249
secularisation: see psychology, historiographical issues
Sell, Alan 235
Seneca 50
sensationalism: see psychology, theoretical paradigms
sense, moral 64, 66, 85, 163; see also conscience
sensibility 64–5; see also Johnson
sentimentalism, see sentiments
sentiments 3, 4, 5, 11, 18, 66; Christian views of 17; moral sentiments 3, 22, 64, 66, 247; and reason 22; sentimentalism in eighteenth-century culture 64–5, 66; see also Darwin; Johnson; Smith
Sewell, William 181, 186, 187–8
Shaftesbury, Anthony Ashley Cooper, Third Earl of 67–8, 70, 89, 91, 94, 118
Shepard, Thomas 75

Shepherd, Lady Mary 116
Skrupskelis, Ignas K. 224
Smith, Adam: on affections 65; on moral sentiments 64, 65–6, 106; on the passions 65
Smith, Roger 14, 71
Sollier, Paul 206, 226
Solomon, Robert 13, 53–4, 96, 133, 134, 231, 244; on emotions 243, 244, 247, 248; and the 'myth of the passions' 2–4, 13–14, 53–4, 242–3
Sorabji, Richard 13, 28, 51
soul: activity of 183–4; and body 29–30, 33, 38–9, 52, 56–9, 76–9, 80, 142–5, 181; higher (intellective, rational) 21, 22, 33, 36, 38–9, 52–4, 58–9; lower (animal) 21, 22, 29, 30, 58–9; nineteenth-century Christian views of 181, 182–4; nutritive 30; sensitive 27, 30, 36, 53; traditional Christian views of 26–9, 52, 56, 142–5; vegetative 30, 33, 53; see also Aquinas; Augustine; dualism; mind; psychology
Spencer, Herbert 5, 8, 23, 94, 127, 135–6, 139, 145, 146–50, 153–4, 158, 168, 180, 201, 241; as associationist 100, 135, 138, 147, 148, 162–4; on Bain 156; on Bell 142, 168–9, 170; on emotions 94, 139, 140, 141, 143, 146–50, 156, 165, 178–9, 204, 236–7: as aggregates 96, 150, 157–8, 204, as epiphenomena 143–4, and feelings 194; as evolutionary psychologist 146–50, 155, 162–4, 192; influence of 137–8, 159, 217; on introspection 153–5, 192; on laughter 137, 165, 170; and monism 143, 180, 183; *Principles of Psychology* 137, 147, 149, 155; and the unknowable 142; on the will 107, 141, 148–9, 177; see also Darwin
Spinoza, Benedict de 7, 18, 72, 142, 243; *Ethica* 72; Spinozism 142
spirit: and flesh 33, 50, 57, 77, 78, 79–81, 228; see also soul
Stearns, Carol 15
Stearns, Peter 15, 247
Stephen, Leslie 110, 116, 118, 223
Stewart, Dugald 11, 110–11, 112, 117, 120, 124, 139
Stocker, Michael 2
Stoicism 63; see also Aquinas; Augustine; passions
Stout, George F. 17, 213
Sully, James 224, 228

Index

Taylor, Mark C. 9
Tempier, Etienne 38
Tetens, Johann 70
Thalberg, Irving 96, 244
theology, natural: *see* natural theology
Tottie, John 73, 92, 93, 95
Turnbull, George 81, 103, 107
Turski, George 248
Tyndall, John 180, 223

understanding: *see* intellect
Upham, Thomas 127, 181, 200

volition: *see* will

Walker, Sayer 141
Wallace, Alfred Russel 170
Ward, James 213
Warren, Howard C. 154
Watts, Isaac 11, 62, 69, 72, 76, 93, 114, 196; and Descartes 78, 92; *Discourses of the Love of God, and its Influence on all the Passions* 67, 73; *Doctrine of the Passions Explained and Improved* 67; middle way between reason and passions 74–5, 96
Webster, Richard 237

Welsh, David (biographer of Thomas Brown) 114, 127
Wesley, John 75, 114, 222, 229
Whewell, William 139, 181, 186–7
will, the 3–4, 5–6, 139, 140, 249; and affections 48, 60–1; importance in Christian thought 22, 60–1, 70–1, 87, 122, 158–9; disappearance of 22, 70–1, 77, 93, 106–7, 122, 131–3; freedom of 59, 125, 148–9, 161–2, 177, 183; and intellect 35, 61, 87, 122, 158; and love 35, 40, 55; and physiological psychology 140–1; realist and anti-realist views of 250; *see also* Aquinas; Augustine; Bain; Brown; Darwin; emotions; Hobbes; Hume; passions; Spencer
Wolff, Christian 70, 71
Wood, P. B. 103
Woodward, William 8
Worcester, William 214
worldviews 24–5, 146, 150, 233, 238, 239–42; scientific 142, 146, 149
Wundt, Wilhelm 7, 154, 206, 217, 224, 238

Young, Edward 75

For EU product safety concerns, contact us at Calle de José Abascal, 56–1º, 28003 Madrid, Spain or eugpsr@cambridge.org.

www.ingramcontent.com/pod-product-compliance
Ingram Content Group UK Ltd.
Pitfield, Milton Keynes, MK11 3LW, UK
UKHW040159230326
469255UK00012B/183